LAW IN NORTHERN IRELAND

This is the latest edition of a book which is the standard introductory text for newcomers to the legal system of Northern Ireland. After explaining how law-making has evolved in Northern Ireland, particularly since the partition of Ireland in 1921, the book devotes separate chapters to the current constitutional position of Northern Ireland, to the making of legislation and case law for that jurisdiction, and to the influence of EU and European Convention law. It examines the principles of public law applying in Northern Ireland and outlines the role of some of the public authorities there. It then moves to chapters on criminal law and criminal procedure, followed by chapters on private law and civil procedure. It ends by examining the legal professions, legal education, the legal aid regimes and legal costs. There are also appendices with sample sources of law. Throughout the book, the focus is on conveying in comprehensible terms the essential features of this small, but historically very controversial, legal jurisdiction.

Law in Northern Ireland

Brice Dickson

6+9

·H A R T·
PUBLISHING
OXFORD AND PORTLAND, OREGON
2013

Published in the United Kingdom by Hart Publishing Ltd
16C Worcester Place, Oxford, OX1 2JW
Telephone: +44 (0)1865 517530
Fax: +44 (0)1865 510710
E-mail: mail@hartpub.co.uk
Website: http://www.hartpub.co.uk

Published in North America (US and Canada) by
Hart Publishing
c/o International Specialized Book Services
920 NE 58th Avenue, Suite 300
Portland, OR 97213-3786
USA
Tel: +1 503 287 3093 or toll-free: (1) 800 944 6190
Fax: +1 503 280 8832
E-mail: orders@isbs.com
Website: http://www.isbs.com

© Brice Dickson 2013

First edition published by SLS Legal Publications (NI), 2011

Brice Dickson has asserted his right under the Copyright, Designs and Patents Act 1988, to be
identified as the author of this work.

British Library Cataloguing in Publication Data
Data Available

ISBN: 978-1-84946-459-8

Typeset by Criteria International
Printed and bound in Great Britain by
TJ International, Padstow

Preface

The first edition of this book grew out of a previous book, *The Legal System of Northern Ireland*, which SLS Legal Publications (NI) Ltd first published in Belfast 1984 and which appeared in new editions in 1989, 1993, 2001 and 2005. Although that book was gratifyingly popular, I felt that it needed to be considerably revamped to take account of the needs of today's law students and of others who have an interest in the law of Northern Ireland. Hence this book focuses less on the way law is practised in Northern Ireland and more on the actual content of the law. The order in which the material is presented has also been altered, in a way which I hope makes it more approachable for both students and non-students. I have tried to provide the relevant information in a readable, but not elementary, fashion, although I am very conscious that a great deal more could be said about virtually everything that is mentioned. Readers are encouraged to search other sources, some of which are referred to in the footnotes, for additional information. They should also not rely solely on this abbreviated text when seeking detailed advice on a particular legal problem. For that they need to go to a legal advice centre or a solicitor.

For this second edition I have reviewed every section of the book in an attempt to keep it as accurate and topical as possible. Many paragraphs have been completely re-written and several new ones have been added. I have tried to ensure that the information provided is correct as of 1 March 2013, but occasionally I have been able to insert references to more recent developments.

Numerous people read sections of this book when they were at a draft stage and I have benefited enormously from their expert comments. What remains is entirely my own responsibility and no-one but myself should be held to account for the final version of the text. Those to whom I am particularly indebted include Les Allamby, Jack Anderson, Gordon Anthony, David Capper, Dimitrios Doukas, Mark Finegan, Sharon Geary, Lisa Glennon, Drusilla Hawthorne, Terence McGleave, Ronagh McQuigg, Tom Obokata, Marny Requa and Sally Wheeler. As ever I must reserve my greatest thanks to my wife, Patricia Mallon, who was always ready with a *bon mot* when I was flagging.

Brice Dickson
Queen's University Belfast
22 May 2013

Table of Contents

Table of Cases

Table of Acts
(including Acts of the Northern
Ireland Parliament and Assembly)

Table of Legislation other than Acts (including Orders in Council made for Northern Ireland)

List of Abbreviations

AC	Appeal Cases
All ER	All England Law Reports
BCLC	British Company Law Cases
BNIL	Bulletin of Northern Ireland Law
Cm / Cmd / Cmnd	Command Paper
DETI	Department of Enterprise, Trade and Investment
DUP	Democratic Unionist Party
EHRR	European Human Rights Reports
EPL	European Public Law
EWCA Civ	Civil Division of the Court of Appeal of England and Wales
EWHC Admin	Administrative Court of the High Court of England and Wales
IACHR	Inter-American Court of Human Rights
Ibid	Ibidem (ie the note just cited)
Ir	Ireland
IRA	Irish Republican Army
IRLR	Industrial Relations Law Reports
J	Mr / Ms / Mrs Justice (mode of address to a High Court judge)
LCJ	Lord Chief Justice
LJ	Law Journal or Lord / Lady Justice
LR / L Rev	Law Review
MLR	Modern Law Review
NI	Northern Ireland or Northern Ireland Reports
NICA	Court of Appeal of Northern Ireland
NICC	Crown Court of Northern Ireland
NICty	County court of Northern Ireland
NIJB	Northern Ireland Judgments Bulletin
NILQ	Northern Ireland Legal Quarterly
NILSC	Northern Ireland Legal Services Commission
NIMags	Magistrates' court of Northern Ireland
OFMDFM	Office of the First Minister and Deputy First Minister
OJLS	Oxford Journal of Legal Studies
PACE	Police and Criminal Evidence
PL	Public Law
QB	Queen's Bench Division or Queen's Bench Reports
QC	Queen's Counsel
UDA	Ulster Defence Association
UKHL	The House of Lords of the United Kingdom
UKSC	The Supreme Court of the United Kingdom
UVF	Ulster Volunteer Force
WLR	Weekly Law Reports
Ybk	Yearbook

1

The Evolution of Law-Making in Northern Ireland

INTRODUCTION

1.1 This opening chapter explains how Northern Ireland, and its law-making arrangements, have evolved to be as they are. As in most fields of study, a good historical perspective can help shed light on why things operate as they do today. Of necessity, political more than purely legal developments need to be considered. The chapter begins with an explanation of the origins of 'the common law' in Ireland, continues with an account of the creation of Northern Ireland and the arrangements for governing it between 1921 and 1998, and concludes with a summary of the Belfast (Good Friday) Agreement of 1998 and of the impact of the St Andrews Agreement of 2006 and the Hillsborough Castle Agreement of 2010. Subsequent chapters look in more detail at specific aspects of the current law of Northern Ireland, starting in Chapter 2 with an account of the constitutional law.

BREHON LAW[1]

1.2 Before the arrival of the Normans in 1169, the island of Ireland was largely governed by Brehon law. This was a legal system based on traditional custom, with laws being formulated and applied by respected native jurists called Brehons. Brehon law continued to apply after 1169 in areas outside the Normans' control and even in areas within their control it continued to govern the native Irish. The Normans themselves were subject to the English 'common law' system, which at that time was unifying the various local legal systems throughout England following William I's invasion and conquest in 1066: it was creating a system which was common to the whole country.

---

[1] For more details see F Kelly, *A Guide to Early Irish Law* (Dublin Institute for Advanced Studies, 1988) and L Ginnell, *The Brehon Laws: A Legal Handbook* (Littleton, Colorado, Fred B Rothman & Co, 1993).

1.3   As the Normans extended their influence in Ireland, English law slowly became more important.[2] By 1300 English law applied in most of Ireland, and some 30 years later the policy of leaving the native Irish to be governed by Brehon law was reversed. By this time, however, the Irish were beginning to regroup, with the object of repelling the Norman invaders. Consequently, the influence of English law went into gradual decline. By 1500 English law extended only to the area around Dublin known as the Pale and the rest of Ireland had returned to Brehon law.

1.4   All this changed again with the Tudor re-conquest of Ireland in the sixteenth century, which culminated in the Flight of the Earls in 1607 and the Plantation of Ulster in the ensuing decades.[3] The whole of Ireland was then under English control and Brehon law completely ceased to apply. In a famous piece of litigation known as *The Case of Tanistry* in 1607,[4] Brehon law was declared to be incompatible with the common law of England and therefore incapable of remaining any part of the law in Ireland.

COMMON LAW

1.5   The system of law which has existed throughout Ireland since the seventeenth century is called the common law system, although it is important to note that this is only one sense in which the expression 'common law' can be used. The most fundamental feature of the common law system is that judges as well as legislatures can make the law. Moreover judges in lower courts are required to apply the law that has been laid down in previous decisions by higher courts: this is known as the doctrine of binding precedent. Today, many more laws are created by legislatures than was the case a century or so ago (such laws are called 'legislation'), so there are not many matters which are regulated only by judge-made law. But part of a judge's function is to interpret the legislation applicable to an issue, and the doctrine of precedent operates just as much in the context of those interpretative decisions as it does to decisions on purely common law issues. The doctrine of precedent does not operate in so rigid a fashion in the countries of continental Europe, where a so-called 'civil law' system exists that is largely derived from concepts developed as part of the law of ancient Rome. In such countries the law is contained almost exclusively in codes and even when judges interpret these codes their decisions are not binding on judges in later cases. The *Code civil* in France, which dates from Napoleonic times, actually prohibits judges from making law.[5]

---

[2] See F Newark, 'The Bringing of English Law to Ireland' (1972) 23 *NILQ* 3.

[3] See J Bardon, *The History of Ulster* (Belfast, Blackstaff Press, 1992), chs 4 and 5.

[4] See F Newark, 'The Case of Tanistry' (1952) 9 *NILQ* 215. Tanistry was the native Irish system for passing on land to an heir; the Irish word Tánaiste is still used to refer to the Deputy Prime Minister of Ireland.

[5] Article 5.

1.6 After the seventeenth century the law in Ireland and England developed along much the same lines in both places. The territories were administered differently, but the actual content of the law was almost identical. Precedents from both islands were cited in all the courts. Even since the partition of Ireland in 1921 the law throughout the two islands has been based on the same fundamental common law concepts (with the exception of Scotland, where the legal system is more of a mixture of common law and civil law[6]). The legal system in Wales is virtually identical to that in England, although the creation of the Welsh Assembly in 1999 has allowed greater scope for differences to emerge.

PARLIAMENTS

1.7 In England the Parliament in London developed out of the King's Council (the 'Curia Regis'), and in Ireland the Parliament in Dublin likewise evolved, during the thirteenth century, out of the jurisdiction of the Justiciar, the King's official representative in Ireland. For two centuries there were Parliaments in both England and Ireland, each claiming the power to make laws for Ireland, and it was not until 1495 that a gathering at Drogheda declared that only legislation approved by the English Council could be passed by the Parliament in Ireland. This was the so-called Poynings' Law, named after Sir Edward Poynings, who was the Secretary for Ireland at the time. The Irish Parliament continued to exist until 1800 and it did make some unapproved laws. Between 1782 and 1800, when it was known as Grattan's Parliament, it even regained some of its former pre-eminence. Yelverton's Act, passed by the Irish Parliament in 1781, was accepted by the government in England as a measure which increased the devolution of powers to Ireland.[7]

1.8 In 1800 the Parliament in London passed the Act of Union, which abolished the Irish Parliament as from 1 January 1801 and joined Ireland to what was then the United Kingdom of Great Britain (ie England, Wales and Scotland). From 1801 until 1921 the only legislative body with powers to make laws for Ireland was therefore the Parliament of the new United Kingdom (UK), sitting at Westminster in London. But, while a lot of the legislation enacted for all or part of Great Britain also extended to Ireland,[8] not all of it did so. Some Acts were applied to Ireland only at a later date or

---

[6] See A Wylie and S Crossan, *Introductory Scots Law: Theory and Practice* (London, Hodder Gibson, 2nd edn, 2010).

[7] Barry Yelverton, later Lord Avonmore, was an Irish patriot (though he voted in favour of the Act of Union in 1800).

[8] Eg Offences Against the Person Act 1861, sections of which are still in force today in the Republic of Ireland as well as in Northern Ireland and England: see para 7.18.

in an amended version,[9] some were not extended to Ireland at all[10] and some were specifically enacted for Ireland and never applied in England, Wales or Scotland.[11] Some significant differences between the legislation applying in Ireland and Great Britain emerged during the nineteenth century, when attempts were made to solve the intractable land problem in Ireland, and the two islands got out of step with regard to some issues in family law. Generally speaking though, their laws remained very similar.

THE CREATION OF NORTHERN IRELAND

1.9   In the nineteenth century extensive efforts were made in some quarters to break the union between Ireland and Britain so that Ireland could become an independent country. The government in London did propose some Home Rule Bills, which would have gone a long way towards granting autonomy to Ireland, but these were rejected by Unionist politicians in the northern part of Ireland and also by Parliament in London. Parliament did eventually pass such a measure – the Government of Ireland Act 1914 – but the outbreak of the First World War prevented its implementation. There followed the so-called Easter Rising in Dublin in 1916 and bitter fighting between British soldiers and Irish 'rebels' broke out in 1919 in the aftermath of World War One. Eventually negotiations for a transfer of power were successfully concluded and were adopted by Parliament at Westminster in the form of the Government of Ireland Act 1920. Under this settlement the island of Ireland was partitioned, with both the Northern part (comprising six counties) and the Southern part (comprising 26 counties) acquiring its own Parliament and government, each with extensive devolved powers. In the future there was also to be a Council of Ireland, which would allow for some all-Ireland policies to be adopted.

1.10   The 1920 Act took effect in the northern part of Ireland, but in the southern part fighting between British forces and Irish rebels continued, being brought to an end only when the Anglo-Irish Treaty was signed on 6 December 1921. This treaty provided that the southern part of Ireland would become the Irish Free State and have the same kind of independence from the British Crown as had already been acquired by countries such as Canada and Australia, with King George V as Head of State. The provisional Parliament in Dublin, created by the 1920 Act, approved a constitution for the new State, as did the Parliament at Westminster, and it came into existence exactly one year after the Anglo-Irish Treaty had been signed.

---

[9] Eg Supreme Court of Judicature Act (Ir) 1877, based on the Supreme Court of Judicature Act 1873.

[10] Eg Matrimonial Causes Act 1857, which gave courts the power to authorise divorces.

[11] Eg Landlord and Tenant Law Amendment (Ir) Act 1860 ('Deasy's Act'). See para 9.10.

However there was still significant opposition to the settlement in Southern Ireland and a civil war cost many hundreds of lives in the months between June 1922 and May 1923 before the pro-Treaty faction won the upper hand. In 1937 the Irish Free State adopted a new Constitution[12] and a year later appointed its first President as Head of State, Douglas Hyde. Ireland became a full Republic in 1949, thereby severing all remaining constitutional links with the UK, and in 1955 it joined the United Nations.[13]

1.11   In accordance with the Government of Ireland Act 1920, Northern Ireland officially came into existence as a separate legal entity on 3 May 1921, when the union with Britain was re-named 'the United Kingdom of Great Britain and Northern Ireland'. In time Northern Ireland became known as a 'province' of the UK, but that is not a legally recognized term. Its use is based on the fact that in ancient times the island of Ireland was divided into four provinces – Ulster, Leinster, Munster and Connacht. Most of what is now Northern Ireland lies within the ancient province of Ulster, but some parts of Ulster are today located within the Republic of Ireland, where they form the counties of Cavan, Monaghan and Donegal. Northern Ireland's six counties are Fermanagh, Tyrone, Londonderry, Antrim, Down and Armagh.

THE STORMONT PARLIAMENT[14]

1.12   The arrangements for governing Northern Ireland after the partition of the island were set out in the Government of Ireland Act 1920. This document is often referred to as 'the Constitution of Northern Ireland', although it was never officially given that title. The Act created the first ever regional Parliament within the new UK – the Parliament of Northern Ireland. In its early days this Parliament sat in a building owned by the Presbyterian Church in Ireland near Queen's University in South Belfast,[15] but in 1932 it moved to a grandiose building specially constructed for the purpose on a hill at Stormont in East Belfast. Hence the institution became known as the Stormont Parliament.

1.13   The 1920 Act conferred extensive powers on the Parliament of Northern Ireland, namely the right to enact legislation 'for the peace, order

---

[12] The most authoritative work is G Hogan and G Whyte, *Kelly's The Irish Constitution* (Dublin, Butterworth Ireland, 4th edn, 2003).

[13] The best introduction to Ireland's legal system is *Byrne and McCutcheon on the Irish Legal System* (Dublin, Bloomsbury Professional, 5th edn, 2009).

[14] For details see T Hennessey, *A History of Northern Ireland 1920–1996* (Dublin, Gill and Macmillan, 1997), P Buckland, *A History of Northern Ireland* (Dublin, Gill and Macmillan, 1981), M Farrell, *Northern Ireland: The Orange State* (London, Pluto Press, 2nd edn, 1980), J Oliver, *Working at Stormont* (Dublin, Institute of Public Administration, 1978).

[15] It is now called the Union Theological College.

and good government' of the province.[16] This was the same phrase as had been used when Britain had previously transferred powers to Parliaments in Canada, Australia and South Africa as part of the decolonisation process. In practice it meant that the Parliament of Northern Ireland had very considerable scope to make laws on matters such as criminal justice and policing, local government, health and social services, education, planning, internal trade, industrial development and agriculture. However it was still a subordinate Parliament, and the Acts it produced were therefore not 'primary' but 'secondary' legislation. The 1920 Act made it clear that certain matters could still be dealt with only by Parliament at Westminster. These matters fell into two categories. First, 'excepted matters', which were those of imperial or national concern, for which it was felt to be undesirable to enact local variations. They included the armed forces, external trade, weights and measures and copyright law. Secondly, 'reserved matters', which were those which it was hoped would be eventually given to the proposed Council of Ireland (a body that was never in fact created). They included the postal services, the registration of deeds, some taxes (but not road tax or stamp duty) and the judicial system.

1.14 The Northern Ireland Parliament consisted of two chambers – the House of Commons and the Senate – but there continued to be elections for representatives to sit at Westminster on behalf of Northern Ireland constituencies. A person could sit in both Parliaments if elected or appointed to both. There were 52 seats in Northern Ireland's House of Commons and 26 in the Senate; the number of Northern Ireland Members of Parliament at Westminster was initially set at 13 (a reduction from the 30 seats that existed prior to partition), but was reduced to 12 in the 1940s. The government of Northern Ireland was composed of people drawn from the party which won the largest number of seats in the Northern Ireland House of Commons, with the leader of that party taking the title of Prime Minister of Northern Ireland.[17] The King or Queen was represented in Northern Ireland by a Governor, whose official residence was at Hillsborough Castle in County Down.[18]

The Special Powers Acts

1.15 The general policy of the government of Northern Ireland after 1921 was to keep in step with the policies and laws devised by the government and

---

[16] Government of Ireland Act 1920, s 4(1).

[17] The successive Prime Ministers of Northern Ireland were Sir James Craig (1921–40), John Andrews (1940–43), Sir Basil Brooke (1943–63), Terence O'Neill (1963–69), James Chichester-Clark (1969–71) and Brian Faulkner (1971–72).

[18] The successive Governors of Northern Ireland were the Duke of Abercorn (1922–45), Earl Granville (1945–52), Lord Wakehurst (1952–64), Lord Erskine (1964–68) and Lord Grey (1968–72).

Parliament in London. On some issues Acts were passed by the Parliament of Northern Ireland a year or two after the equivalent Acts had been passed at Westminster. But the Parliament of Northern Ireland did deviate from Westminster in some respects.[19] Most importantly, it put in place draconian measures to enable the police to combat attempts to undermine the security of the state. The most notorious of these measures was the Civil Authorities (Special Powers) Act (NI) 1922. This was initially enacted for just one year, but at the end of that year, and in each of the next five years, it was re-enacted. In 1928 it was again re-enacted, this time for a further five years, and then it was made permanent. In 1944 it was amended by a further Act of the same name, so the Acts became known as the Civil Authorities (Special Powers) Acts (NI) 1922–44 or, more colloquially, as the Special Powers Acts. They remained in force until 1973 and were not mirrored by similar Acts passed at Westminster for Great Britain. Nor did Northern Ireland adopt the liberal reforms which occurred in Great Britain in the 1960s: when Westminster passed Acts de-criminalising abortion and homosexuality, the Parliament of Northern Ireland did not follow suit.[20] Even divorce was not made generally available in Northern Ireland until 1939.[21]

DIRECT RULE[22]

1.16 Devolution of powers in the North continued until March 1972, when, despite its best efforts to achieve positive change,[23] the Stormont Parliament had to be suspended by Westminster because of its inability to cope with serious civil unrest that had developed in the province since 1968. The unrest was prompted by allegations that the Unionist Government of Northern Ireland was presiding over a system which discriminated against Catholics in the way that electoral boundaries were drawn, in the way public housing and public sector jobs were distributed, and in the manner in which the police force – the Royal Ulster Constabulary – went about maintaining law and order. The unrest was made the subject of a tribunal of inquiry chaired by an English High Court judge, Mr Justice Scarman,[24] while a commission chaired by an English Law Lord, Lord Diplock, was tasked with bringing forward

[19] For an interesting survey see C Brett, 'The Lessons of Devolution in Northern Ireland' (1970) 41 *Political Quarterly* 261.
[20] Abortion law in Northern Ireland is still largely governed by the Offences Against the Person Act 1861: see para 9.139. The law on homosexuality was mostly brought into line with that in Great Britain by the Homosexual Offences (NI) Order 1982.
[21] By the Matrimonial Causes Act (NI) 1939.
[22] An almost day-by-day chronology of events in Northern Ireland since 1968 is available on www.cain.ulst.ac.uk.
[23] See *A Record of Constructive Change*, Cmd 558 (NI) 1971.
[24] Later Lord Scarman. See *Violence and Civil Disturbances in Northern Ireland in 1969*, Cmd 566 (NI) 1972.

proposals for how the law could better deal with the problem of terrorism.[25] Internment (ie detention without trial) had been introduced by the Northern Ireland Government in August 1971[26] and allegations of security force brutality in that context led to a further inquiry.[27]

1.17 'Direct rule' is the name given to the form of government used for Northern Ireland after March 1972. Most matters which would have been legislated for by the Parliament of Northern Ireland were instead dealt with by the Privy Council in London, in the form of Orders in Council. The Privy Council is effectively a body comprising senior members of the UK Government. Executive powers were exercised by a team of ministers headed by the Secretary of State for Northern Ireland, a member of the British Cabinet, rather than by a government formed from the MPs elected to the Stormont Parliament. The first such Secretary of State was William Whitelaw. The detailed arrangements for direct rule were set out in the Northern Ireland (Temporary Provisions) Act 1972. They were renewed by the UK Parliament in one form or another on an almost annual basis until 1999.

THE TROUBLES

1.18 The civil unrest which broke out in a serious way in Northern Ireland in 1968 was a further manifestation of the communal difficulties which had existed there ever since the partition of the island in 1921. Opinions differ over what event marked the beginning of the euphemistically named 'troubles'. It could be the killing of three people on different days in June 1966 by the Ulster Volunteer Force, a loyalist group which adopted the same name as the citizens' army which had helped push for the retention of Northern Ireland as part of the UK in 1921.[28] It could be the occupation of a vacant house in Caledon, County Tyrone, in June 1968 by people protesting about its allocation by the local council to a young childless Protestant woman rather than to an older Catholic family with children. Or it could be the breaking-up by the Royal Ulster Constabulary in October 1968 of a march organised in Derry by the Northern Ireland Civil Rights Association.[29]

---

[25] See *Report of the Commission to consider legal procedures to deal with terrorist activities in Northern Ireland* (the Diplock Report), Cmnd 5185, 1972. See too T Hadden and P Hillyard, *Justice in Northern Ireland: A Study in Social Confidence* (1973).

[26] As it had been on earlier occasions in both Northern Ireland and the Republic of Ireland.

[27] See *Report of the enquiry into allegations against the security forces of physical brutality in Northern Ireland arising out of events on the 9th August 1971* (the Compton Report), Cmnd 4823, 1971.

[28] For a death-by-death account of the victims of the troubles in Northern Ireland see D McKittrick, S Kelters, B Feeney, C Thornton and D McVea, *Lost Lives* (Edinburgh, Mainstream Publishing, rev edn, 2007). After these 1966 killings, which led to the UVF being outlawed, there were no further troubles-related deaths until July 1969.

[29] This is the start date chosen by T Hennessey in his *The Evolution of the Troubles 1970–72* (Dublin, Irish Academic Press, 2007).

There is no doubt, however, that once the violence started it very quickly escalated. In 1969, 14 people died, including the first RUC officer.

1.19 The British army was called in to assist the police in August 1969 and the death toll was contained to 25 in 1970. But in 1971 it shot up to 174, with no fewer than 48 soldiers being killed. The use of internment, begun in August 1971, continued until December 1975. It was used mainly against people suspected of violent republican sympathies, not violent loyalists. On 30 January 1972, on what became known as 'Bloody Sunday',[30] British soldiers shot dead 14 unarmed civilians when trying to disperse a crowd participating in an illegal march in Derry. The total number of people killed during 1972 was 470. In the next four years the deaths averaged 254 per year, and the violence spread to the Republic of Ireland and England. In May 1974, 33 people were killed by car bombs in Dublin and Monaghan, in October 1974 five people died in an explosion in a pub in Guildford, and in November 1974 21 were killed in a pub explosion in Birmingham. The Government in London took steps to try to counter the violence by persuading Parliament to enact the Northern Ireland (Emergency Provisions) Act 1973, which applied only in Northern Ireland, and the Prevention of Terrorism (Temporary Provisions) Act 1974, which applied throughout the UK. These gave the police and army wider powers of arrest, stop, search and seizure. The 1973 Act also created a special juryless court in which to try people accused of troubles-related offences, the so-called Diplock courts; there were fears that if jurors were used for such trials not all of them could be relied upon to be impartial, and they might be subject to intimidation if not outright attack by associates of some of the accused.

Victims of the troubles

1.20 Despite concerted efforts to suppress the violence, it continued at a fairly high rate for many years. The Irish Republican Army (IRA) became ever more efficient and daring in its exploits and neither the British army nor the political system was able to effectively contain the resulting terror.[31] Between 1977 and the IRA ceasefire announced in 1994 an average of 83 people died each year. Several dozen more people were to die before the Belfast (Good Friday) Agreement was reached in 1998. Most estimates suggest that, throughout the troubles, 60 per cent of the deaths were attributable to republican paramilitaries, 30 per cent to loyalist paramilitaries and 10 per cent to actions of the security forces (not all of which actions were lawful).

---

[30] This was actually the second Bloody Sunday. The first had occurred in Dublin on 21 November 1920. 'Bloody Friday' designates 21 July 1972, when the IRA exploded 19 bombs in Belfast, killing 9 people.
[31] See, generally, R English, *Armed Struggle: The History of the IRA* (London, Macmillan, 2003).

In addition, more than 40,000 people were injured during the troubles, some very seriously indeed. Between 1969 and 2009 there were more than 37,000 shooting incidents and almost 19,000 real or hoax explosive devices were planted (see para 7.41).[32]

1.21   The impact of the troubles was very severe, not just as regards the achievement of political progress but also as regards the development of the legal institutions and the substantive law in Northern Ireland. With attention focused on combating terrorism, less regard was had for how improvements could be made to the 'ordinary' criminal and civil justice systems.[33] Modernisation of the legal system of Northern Ireland has really only taken place in earnest since the peace settlement of 1998.

EFFORTS TO RESTORE DEVOLUTION

1.22   In September 1972 the seven political parties which had previously had representatives in the Parliament of Northern Ireland were invited by the UK Government to take part in a conference in Darlington, England, but only three of them attended.[34] The following month the Government published a consultative document stating the criteria which firm proposals for the future of Northern Ireland would have to meet.[35] On 8 March 1973, a referendum was held on whether the border between Northern Ireland and the Republic of Ireland should be retained;[36] out of an electorate of just over one million, some 600,000 voted (many nationalists did not vote) and, of these, 591,820 voted to stay within the UK. Later that same month the Government published a White Paper containing further proposals for the way forward.[37] These suggested that there should be a new legislature in Northern Ireland elected by proportional representation, with the executive and other legislative committees containing representatives from both communities. The proposals were then given legislative form through the Northern Ireland Assembly Act 1973 and the Northern Ireland Constitution Act 1973. Two-thirds of the 78 people who were then elected to the Assembly, which met for the first time in July 1973, were in favour of the Government's proposals.

1.23   After further talks, and a conference in Sunningdale in Berkshire in December 1973, agreement was reached on creating a Northern Ireland

---

[32] Detailed statistics are available on the website of the Police Service of Northern Ireland: www.psni.police.uk.
[33] For an assessment see B Dickson, 'Northern Ireland's Legal System – An Evaluation' (1992) 43 *NILQ* 315.
[34] The Ulster Unionist Party, the Alliance Party and the Northern Ireland Labour Party.
[35] *The Future of Northern Ireland: A Paper for Discussion.*
[36] Under the Northern Ireland (Border Poll) Act 1972.
[37] *Northern Ireland Constitutional Proposals* (Cmnd 5259).

Executive and Assembly, and also on setting up a Council of Ireland comprising seven members of the Executive and seven ministers from the Irish Government, a consultative Assembly and a secretariat. The Northern Ireland Executive was sworn in on 1 January 1974, with the Chief Executive (effectively the Prime Minister) being Brian Faulkner, leader of the Official Unionist Party. Powers to make laws (called 'Measures') were vested in the unicameral elected Assembly.

The 1974 Assembly

1.24 However, due to further civil unrest linked to a strike called by the Protestant-dominated Ulster Workers' Council, this experiment in devolution collapsed in May 1974, when the Assembly was suspended and responsibility for governing Northern Ireland was again returned to the Secretary of State.[38] More proposals were put forward in a government White Paper issued in July 1974[39] and these were given effect in law by the Northern Ireland Act 1974. They provided for a Constitutional Convention to be elected, again with 78 members, with the job of considering over a six-month period 'what provision for the government of Northern Ireland is likely to command the most widespread acceptance among the community there'. Elections were held for the Convention in May 1975 and it began work almost immediately, under the chairmanship of the then Lord Chief Justice of Northern Ireland, Sir Robert Lowry. It reported, as planned, in November 1975,[40] but as its proposals were based very largely on unionist ideas the British Government rejected them[41] and the Convention was formally dissolved in March 1976.

1.25 In 1982 another 78-member Northern Ireland Assembly, again with only one chamber and sitting at Stormont, was elected under the Northern Ireland Act 1982.[42] In the same year the number of MPs that could be elected to Westminster from Northern Ireland was increased from 12 to 17, partly to compensate for the lack of a fully operational devolved Parliament in Belfast. The new Assembly did not have any law-making powers (only scrutiny, consultative and deliberative powers) but the UK Government hoped that in due course some such powers could be transferred to it under

[38] See D Anderson, *14 May Days* (Dublin, Gill and Macmillan, 1994). Only four Measures were made in the less than five months of the Assembly's existence.
[39] *The Northern Ireland Constitution* (Cmnd 5675).
[40] *Report of the Northern Ireland Constitutional Convention*, HC 1 (1975–76).
[41] It made one last effort to allow the Convention to reach agreement, but this too failed: see *The Northern Ireland Constitutional Convention: Text of a letter from the Secretary of State for Northern Ireland to the Chairman of the Convention* (Cmnd 6387; 1976).
[42] This followed three government discussion papers: *The Government of Northern Ireland: A Working Paper for a Conference* (Cmnd 7763; 1979), *The Government of Northern Ireland: Proposals for Further Discussion* (Cmnd 7950; 1980) and *Northern Ireland: A Framework for Devolution* (Cmnd 8541; 1982).

the principle of 'rolling' devolution. Once again the experiment proved unsuccessful and the Assembly was dissolved in 1986.[43]

1.26   The signing of the Anglo-Irish Agreement at Hillsborough Castle, County Down, in November 1985[44] led to the establishment of the Anglo-Irish Inter-Governmental Conference, which convened periodically to allow representatives from the Government of the Irish Republic to put forward their views on the governance of Northern Ireland. It also created an Anglo-Irish Parliamentary Council, which allowed 25 members from each of the British and Irish Parliaments to meet from time to time to discuss matters of mutual interest. The 1985 Agreement, however, was a treaty between two sovereign states and did not have the force of internal domestic law in either country. It was bitterly opposed by unionists.

THE BELFAST (GOOD FRIDAY) AGREEMENT 1998

1.27   Following various additional inter-governmental initiatives, including a Downing Street Declaration in 1993, a Framework Document in 1995[45] and the publication of ground rules for substantive all-party negotiations in 1996,[46] the political parties within Northern Ireland and the British and Irish Governments eventually reached a new agreement on the way forward in Northern Ireland on Good Friday (10 April) 1998.[47] A path facilitating the agreement had been cleared by ceasefires that had been declared by both loyalist paramilitaries in October 1994 and republican paramilitaries in July 1997 (an earlier IRA ceasefire in August 1994 was breached in February 1996). The underlying principle of the settlement was power-sharing, in what political scientists call a 'consociational' framework, one which required a coalition of parties to form the government of Northern Ireland and provided for no official opposition.

1.28   The Belfast (Good Friday) Agreement[48] was put to the electorates in both Northern Ireland and the Republic of Ireland on the same day in May

---

[43] C O'Leary, S Elliott and R Wilford, *The Northern Ireland Assembly 1982–1986: A Constitutional Experiment* (London, St Martin's Press, 1988).

[44] See A Kenny, *The Road to Hillsborough: The Shaping of the Anglo-Irish Agreement* (University of Michigan, Pergamon Press, 1986); T Hadden and K Boyle, *The Anglo-Irish Agreement: Commentary, Text and Official Review* (London, Sweet & Maxwell, 1989).

[45] Cm 2964.

[46] Cm 3232. See also E Mallie and D McKittrick, *The Fight for Peace: The Secret Story of the Irish Peace Process* (London, Heinemann, 1996).

[47] Cm 3883. Available online at, eg, ofmdfmni.gov.uk/publications/ba.htm. For the story of the genesis of the Agreement, see M Mansergh, 'The Background to the Irish Peace Process' in M Cox, A Guelke and F Stephen (eds), *A Farewell to Arms? From 'long war' to long peace in Northern Ireland* (Manchester, Manchester UP, 2nd edn, 2005) ch 1.

[48] See generally A Morgan, *The Belfast Agreement: A practical legal analysis* (Belfast Press, 2000) and T Hennessey, *The Northern Ireland Peace Process: Ending the Troubles?* (Dublin, Gill and Macmillan, 2000).

1998 and was approved by substantial majorities in both jurisdictions – 71 per cent in Northern Ireland and 95 per cent in the Republic of Ireland. Dissident republicans, however, were still active: in August 1998 they planted a car bomb in Omagh, County Tyrone, which killed 29 people as well as unborn twins.

1.29 In June 1998 an election was held in Northern Ireland to choose six representatives from each of the 18 Westminster constituencies to sit as Members of a new Northern Ireland Assembly (the number of constituencies had been raised from 17 to 18 in 1995). The powers of this Assembly, and other aspects of the Belfast (Good Friday) Agreement, were then enshrined in law by a Westminster Act, the Northern Ireland Act 1998. By section 1 of that Act Northern Ireland is to remain a part of the UK unless and until a majority of the electorate in Northern Ireland vote to join a united Ireland.[49] The Assembly's powers were to become live whenever the Secretary of State determined that an Executive Committee (ie a Cabinet) could be formed, and seats on this Executive Committee were to be allocated in accordance with the 'd'Hondt' system, thereby giving proportional ministerial representation to the four largest parties in the Assembly. The First Minister designate was to be David Trimble MP, the leader of the Ulster Unionist Party, and the Deputy First Minister designate was to be Seamus Mallon MP, the deputy leader of the Social Democratic and Labour Party (SDLP).[50]

IMPLEMENTING THE GOOD FRIDAY AGREEMENT

1.30 Considerable difficulties were encountered in securing agreement for the formation of the full Executive Committee. The largest unionist party, the Ulster Unionist Party, would not agree to share power with the second largest nationalist party, Sinn Féin, unless there were greater guarantees concerning the decommissioning of weapons held by the IRA. Eventually, in November 1999, a deal was hammered out and on 2 December 1999 powers were finally devolved to the new administration in Belfast. This was a few months after slightly different forms of devolution had already commenced in Scotland and Wales,[51] for it was a policy of the UK Government at the time to support devolution throughout the UK.

---

[49] See generally B O'Leary, 'The Nature of the Agreement' (1999) 22 *Fordham International LJ* 1628; C Harvey, 'The New Beginning: Reconstructing Constitutional Law and Democracy in Northern Ireland' in C Harvey (ed), *Human Rights, Equality and Democratic Renewal in Northern Ireland* (Oxford, Hart Publishing, 2001); G Anthony, 'Public Law Litigation and the Belfast Agreement' (2002) *EPL* 401; C Campbell, F Ní Aoláin and C Harvey, 'The Frontiers of Legal Analysis: Reframing the Transition in Northern Ireland' (2003) 66 *MLR* 317.

[50] For their part in producing the Agreement, David Trimble and John Hume, the leader of the SDLP, were jointly awarded the Nobel Peace Prize in 1998.

[51] Under, respectively, the Scotland Act 1998 and the Government of Wales Act 1998.

1.31   On 11 February 2000 the Secretary of State for Northern Ireland suspended the Assembly[52] because the Ulster Unionist Party was on the verge of withdrawing from it due to the fact that no republican weaponry had yet been decommissioned. After a few more weeks of negotiations a deal was again struck and the Assembly was reinstated on 30 May 2000.[53] When there was further stalling on decommissioning, however, David Trimble resigned as First Minister on 30 June 2001 and the Assembly was dissolved for single days in both August and September 2001 to allow further six-week periods to elapse so that new elections for a First and Deputy First Minister could take place. Meanwhile the British and Irish Governments agreed at Weston Park in Shropshire on how best to proceed on a range of issues if the Assembly were restored.[54] An act of decommissioning by republicans took place on 23 October 2001[55] and David Trimble and Mark Durkan (the new leader of the SDLP) were finally elected on 6 November 2001[56] but on 14 October 2002 the Secretary of State again suspended the Assembly[57] because of allegations of 'spying' by republicans.

1.32   The 2002 suspension was to continue for well over four years, despite a Declaration by the British and Irish Governments in April 2003[58] and new elections to the Assembly in November 2003. An agreement between the two parties which performed best in those elections, the Democratic Unionist Party (DUP) and Sinn Féin,[59] was almost reached in December 2004 (after preliminary talks at Leeds Castle in Kent in September 2004), but negotiations broke down at the last minute, supposedly over the unwillingness of Sinn Féin to allow the decommissioning of weapons to be photographed. The British and Irish Governments published their own proposals for the basis for an agreement but it soon became clear[60] that there was no prospect of a further settlement being reached until well after

---

[52] By the Northern Ireland Act 2000 (Commencement) Order 2000 (SI 396).

[53] By the Northern Ireland Act 2000 (Restoration of Devolved Government) Order 2000 (SI 1445).

[54] www.nio.gov.uk/proposals0108.pdf.

[55] Two further such acts took place on 8 April 2002 and 21 October 2003, but on none of these occasions were details made public of exactly what arms were destroyed.

[56] Their election was challenged by Peter Robinson MP as being unauthorised under the Northern Ireland Act 1998 (see para 2.5). He eventually lost in the House of Lords (by 3 to 2): [2002] NI 390. See M Lynch, '*Robinson v Secretary of State for Northern Ireland*: Interpreting Constitutional Legislation' [2003] *PL* 640.

[57] By the Northern Ireland Act 2000 (Suspension of Devolved Government) Order 2002 (SI 2574). During suspension, for a period of 6 months, para 1 of the Schedule to the Northern Ireland Act 2000 allowed legislation to be made by Order in Council for any matter for which the Assembly might have legislated; the 6 month period could be extended.

[58] See www.nio.gov.uk.

[59] The DUP won 30 seats in the Assembly, the Ulster Unionist Party 27, Sinn Féin 24, the SDLP 18, the Alliance Party 6 and three smaller parties 1 each.

[60] Especially after a massive bank robbery in Belfast on 20 December 2004, attributed to the IRA, and the murder of Robert McCartney in Belfast on 30 January 2005, again allegedly committed by members of the IRA.

the UK general election due in May 2005. In that election the DUP and Sinn Féin increased their mandates even further.[61]

The St Andrews and Hillsborough Castle Agreements

1.33   In September 2005 the Independent International Commission on Decommissioning reported that the IRA had decommissioned all its weapons, and this paved the way for further talks between political parties. In October 2006 an agreement was reached at St Andrews, in Scotland.[62] This committed Sinn Féin to fully support the Police Service of Northern Ireland and the DUP to share executive power with republicans and nationalists. Responsibility for policing and criminal justice was to be devolved within two years of the restoration of the Executive. Fresh elections to the Northern Ireland Assembly took place in March 2007[63] and the Executive was restored on 7 May 2007, the day when Rev Ian Paisley of the DUP was filmed sitting at a table side by side with Gerry Adams of Sinn Féin. However it was not until 5 February 2010 that final agreement on the devolution of policing and criminal justice was reached after lengthy discussions at Hillsborough Castle.[64] Devolution of those issues took effect on 12 April 2010, with the election of David Ford, the leader of the Alliance Party, as the Minister of Justice in Northern Ireland.[65] From then on the Northern Ireland Assembly and Executive had just as much power to govern Northern Ireland as the old parliament and government of Northern Ireland had between 1921 and 1972.

1.34   In May 2010 electoral support for the DUP and Sinn Féin held up reasonably well in the UK general election.[66] In the elections for the Northern Ireland Assembly in May 2011, the 108 seats were distributed as follows: the DUP (38), Sinn Féin (29), the Ulster Unionist Party (16), the SDLP (14), the Alliance Party (8) and others (3). In 2012 one of the Ulster Unionist Party MLAs resigned from that party and now represents the UK Independent Party; two others resigned in early 2013, to set up another unionist party. In 2011 Peter Robinson of the DUP was elected by the Assembly as First

---

[61] In those elections the DUP won 9 of the 18 seats at Westminster, Sinn Féin 5, the SDLP 3 and the UUP 1. In 2001 the seats won, respectively, had been 6, 4, 3 and 5. Sinn Féin MPs do not actually take their seats at Westminster, nor (because of their refusal to declare allegiance to the state) do they qualify for certain grants available to political parties: see *In re Sinn Féin's Application* [2004] NICA 4.

[62] The full text of the St Andrews Agreement is available on the NIO's website: www.nio. gov.uk.

[63] The DUP won 36 seats, Sinn Féin 28, the UUP 18, the SDLP 16, Alliance 7, and others 3.

[64] The full text of the Hillsborough Castle Agreement is available on the website of the NIO: www.nio.gov.uk.

[65] His election occurred as a result of a cross-community vote in the Northern Ireland Assembly, not by applying the d'Hondt process (see para 1.29).

[66] The DUP won 8 of the 18 seats, Sinn Féin 5, the SDLP 3, Alliance 1, and an independent 1. The UUP won no seats.

Minister and Martin McGuinness of Sinn Féin as Deputy First Minister. As of February 2013 they were still in office. The next Assembly elections are not due until May 2015.

Statistics

1.35   In 2012 the results of the 2011 census were made public. They revealed that the total population of Northern Ireland was 1.81 million, a rise of more than 7 per cent since 2001. Of this total, 48 per cent identified themselves as Protestants (down from 53 per cent in 2001) and 45 per cent identified themselves as Catholics (up from 44 per cent in 2001). Already the majority of people under the age of 35 in Northern Ireland are Catholics. As regards 'national identity', the first time this question had been asked in the census, in 2011 40 per cent designated themselves as British only, 25 per cent as Irish only, and 21 per cent as Northern Irish only.[67] Significant reports published by the Community Relations Council in 2012 and 2013 provide a further plethora of fascinating facts, figures and analysis detailing the extent to which Northern Ireland has moved towards 'peace' since the Belfast (Good Friday) Agreement of 1998.[68]

Imminent reforms

1.36   Early in 2013 the Northern Ireland Office proposed a set of further amendments to the constitutional arrangements for Northern Ireland, in the form of a draft Northern Ireland (Miscellaneous Provisions) Bill. It hopes to have this enacted at Westminster before the end of 2013.[69] The Bill follows a consultation process conducted by the Northern Ireland Office in 2012 on measures to improve the operation of the Northern Ireland Assembly. The main changes which will be made by the Bill, if it is enacted in its current form, are the extension of the current Assembly term by one year to 2016 (and the introduction of five-year terms thereafter), the ending of dual mandates between the Northern Ireland Assembly and the House of Commons (so that a person can no longer be both an MLA and an MP at the same time),[70] the provision of greater transparency in political party funding (at present the names of generous donors to parties do not need

[67] For more details on the census results, see the website of the Northern Ireland Statistics and Research Agency: www.nisra.gov.uk/Census.html.
[68] Paul Nolan, *The Northern Ireland Peace Monitoring Report*, Numbers 1 and 2 available at www.three-creative.com/nipmr.pdf.
[69] Cm 8653. A copy is also on the website of the Northern Ireland Office: www.nio.gov.uk.
[70] At present there is no such prohibition with regard to members of the Assembly in Wales or of the Parliament in Scotland, but none of the current members of those regional legislatures is also a Member of the UK Parliament.

to be disclosed), the provision of greater security of tenure for the Minister of Justice (who at present can be replaced if there is a cross-community vote to that effect in the Assembly), improvements to the way elections are administered in Northern Ireland, and enabling UK-wide public authorities to be designated for the purposes of equality of opportunity and good relations duties under section 75 of the Northern Ireland Act 1998 (see para 6.58).[71] Amongst the changes mooted in 2012 but not provided for in the draft Bill are a reduction in the number of seats in the Northern Ireland Assembly (at present there are 108), an extension in the length of the current and/or future Assembly terms (from four to five years), an extension of the dual mandate prohibition (eg to prevent MLAs from being district councillors at the same time), and the authorisation of an official 'opposition' within the Assembly.

---

[71] This last point follows a report on the 2011 Assembly elections in Northern Ireland by the Electoral Commission (2011). The chief change will be that a person will be entitled to register to vote even if he or she has not been resident in Northern Ireland for three months.

2

Constitutional Law in Northern Ireland

THE UNITED KINGDOM'S CONSTITUTION

2.1 Every country in the world has a 'Constitution', which is the name given to the collection of rules and principles according to which the country is organised and governed. But the UK is one of only three countries in the world (the others are Israel and New Zealand) which has not written down its Constitution in a single document. Instead the Constitution of the UK has emerged over the centuries and is now contained in a number of documents. These are Acts of Parliament, decisions by courts, or textbook descriptions of long-standing custom and practice (called 'constitutional conventions'), but there is no prior or 'higher' document which lays down what the status of these Acts, decisions and conventions is to be. Instead they have acquired their constitutional status by dint of having been accepted and applied for such a long period. From time to time a campaign is mounted for a single written Constitution to be adopted in the UK,[1] and even the former Prime Minister, Gordon Brown, was in favour of such a reform.[2] For the foreseeable future, though, the country will have to make do with an 'unwritten' Constitution. Many commentators believe that it provides much-needed flexibility and avoids unproductive hair-splitting over the meaning of provisions in one single document.[3]

2.2 It is generally accepted that there are three fundamental principles in the UK's Constitution. The first is the principle of the rule of law, according to which no-one is above the law, not even the Head of State or those who make the law (ie Parliamentarians and judges). The second is the principle of parliamentary sovereignty, according to which Parliament has complete

---

[1] For recent examples see Robert Gordon, *Repairing British Politics: A Blueprint for Constitutional Change* (Oxford, Hart Publishing, 2010) and the Report of the Constitutional Working Group (Justice, 2010).

[2] Gordon Brown, 'What I Believe', *Prospect*, October 2009.

[3] Justices of the US Supreme Court are notoriously divided on how to interpret the wording of the US Constitution.

freedom to make whatever laws it likes. The third is the principle of the separation of powers, which holds that the power to make laws, the power to administer laws, and the power to judge disputes about laws, should all be exercised by separate bodies. This chapter begins with some explanation of what those three principles mean in practice, and whether they may be potentially contradictory.

THE RULE OF LAW

2.3   The rule of law is the idea that every person and every action is uniformly governed by a set of laws that are easily accessible and understandable. No-one is above the law and no-one can claim immunity from the law's reach. It is an ancient idea, one that can be traced back to classical Greece, but in the modern era it is most often associated in the English-speaking world with the writings of Albert Venn Dicey, a professor of law at the University of Oxford, who in 1885 published a famous book entitled *An Introduction to the Study of the Law of the Constitution*. In Dicey's view the rule of law had three components:

(i)   everyone is equal before the law
(ii) no-one should be punished for breaking the law unless he or she is in clear breach of it
(iii) the rights of individuals are to be protected by the courts.

Debate has raged ever since about the exact scope of the rule of law in the UK.[4] The concept is often invoked in argument and debate, but no authoritative definition of it has been provided by either Parliament or the courts. The paramount importance of the concept, however, is reflected in the fact that the very first section of the Constitutional Reform Act 2005, one of the most recent examples of Parliament intervening to provide precise rules on constitutional matters (including the function of the official called the Lord Chancellor), states that the Act does not adversely affect either the existing constitutional principle of the rule of law – however defined – or the Lord Chancellor's existing constitutional role in relation to that principle.

The rule of law in practice

2.4   A good example of the rule of law in operation is the decision of the Divisional Court of Northern Ireland in the case of *R (Hume) v*

---

[4] For an important recent contribution see Tom Bingham, *The Rule of Law* (London, Allen Lane, 2010). Lord Bingham was the Senior Law Lord from 2000–2008 and prior to that had served as the Lord Chief Justice of England and Wales and as Master of the Rolls (ie head of the criminal and civil justice systems in England and Wales respectively).

Londonderry Justices.[5] A member of the Social Democratic and Labour Party (SDLP), John Hume, had been arrested, along with others, for not dispersing when ordered to do so by British soldiers when they were policing a civil rights march in 1971. The lawyers representing the defendants argued that, in law, the British soldiers had no legal right to order the marchers to disperse because the only authority they could rely upon for giving that order were regulations issued by the Minister of Home Affairs in the Government of Northern Ireland. Those regulations, said the lawyers, were not legally valid because the Stormont Parliament, when it purported to give the Minister the power to issue the regulations, had operated outside the powers conferred on it by the Government of Ireland Act 1920, an Act passed by the UK Parliament in London. As mentioned in Chapter 1, that Act allowed the Northern Ireland Parliament to enact legislation 'for the peace, order and good government' of Northern Ireland, but one of the expressly 'excepted matters' was the army. The judges in the Divisional Court accepted the lawyers' argument that a Stormont minster had no power to issue regulations affecting the army and that therefore the arrests of John Hume and the others were unlawful. Another way of describing this decision is to say that it is an example of 'the *ultra vires* doctrine'. *Ultra vires* is Latin for 'beyond the powers', so the doctrine means that an action is unlawful if it is beyond the powers of the body in question to take.

2.5 The Attorney General for Northern Ireland, whose functions are set out in more detail later in this chapter (paras 11.2–11.5), also claims to be the guardian of the rule of law in Northern Ireland.[6] In practice, however, the exact way in which the rule of law should be applied is likely to give the Attorney General some difficulties. Does the rule of law mean, for example, that when an Act of Parliament lays down a time limit for certain actions to be taken, actions taken outside of that time limit will be unlawful? That was the issue which arose in the case of *Robinson v Secretary of State for Northern Ireland,*[7] where Peter Robinson, who later became the First Minister of Northern Ireland, challenged the election of David Trimble and Mark Durkan as First and Deputy First Ministers in the Northern Ireland Executive in 2001, on the basis that their election had occurred two days after the deadline imposed by the Northern Ireland Act 1998. That Act specifies that 'where the offices of the First Minister and the Deputy First Minister become vacant at any time an election shall be held under this section to fill the vacancies within

---

[5] [1972] NI 91.

[6] See www.attorneygeneralni.gov.uk/index/about-us.htm.

[7] [2002] NI 390. Counsel for Peter Robinson was John Larkin QC, who is now the Attorney General for Northern Ireland.

a period of six weeks beginning with that time'[8] and it goes on to say that if the six-week period ends without the ministers having been elected, 'the Secretary of State shall propose a date for the poll for the election of the next Assembly'.[9] In other words, a date for fresh elections to the whole Assembly must be proposed if the six-week deadline for election of the First and Deputy First Ministers is missed. The question whether David Trimble and Mark Durkan had been lawfully elected even though the six-week deadline had been missed went all the way to the highest court in the UK at the time (the Appellate Committee of the House of Lords) and by three votes to two the judges in that court decided that, despite the wording of the 1998 Act, the election two days after the deadline was *not* unlawful. The majority's view was not that missing the deadline by two days was trivial, but that:

> [w]here constitutional arrangements retain scope for the exercise of political judgment they permit a flexible response to differing and unpredictable events in a way which the application of strict rules would preclude.[10]

The two judges in the minority, on the other hand, held that the words in the Northern Ireland Act 1998 were clear on their face and could not be side-stepped.

2.6   The *Robinson* case shows that there is room for disagreement, even amongst the most senior judges, as to what the rule of law precisely demands. The biggest challenge to the rule of law, however, is that presented by the doctrine of parliamentary sovereignty.

PARLIAMENTARY SOVEREIGNTY

2.7   Mainly as a result of there being no single written Constitution for the UK, and because senior judges, including the current President of the UK Supreme Court, have repeatedly asserted the point,[11] a very definite feature of the unwritten UK Constitution is that Parliament is supreme, or 'sovereign'. Whatever Parliament decides to do, it does not need to worry about violating some other higher norm. This contrasts sharply with the position in many other countries, such as Ireland, France and the United States of America, where the national Parliaments (the Oireachtas, the *Assemblée nationale*, and Congress, respectively) must always have regard to the constraints imposed upon them by the national Constitution. It also makes it extremely difficult

---

[8] s 16(8).
[9] s 32(3).
[10] [2002] NI 390, [12], per Lord Bingham.
[11] See the Lord Alexander of Weedon lecture, *Who are the masters now?*, delivered by Lord Neuberger on 6 April 2011 and available at www.judiciary.gov.uk/Resources/JCO/Documents/Speeches/mr-speech-weedon-lecture-110406.pdf.

to argue that a law approved by Parliament is in some way invalid because those who voted for it in Parliament were in some way misled.[12]

2.8 The UK Parliament can pass any law it likes. In 1701 the English Parliament determined who should succeed to the throne of England,[13] and in 1707 and 1800 it passed Acts uniting England and Wales first with Scotland and then with Ireland.[14] In 1920 the UK Parliament voted to create separate, subordinate, Parliaments in Belfast and Dublin. In 1974 it voted to abolish the Parliament of Northern Ireland. In 1998 it voted to set up a subordinate Parliament (or Assembly) not just in Northern Ireland, but also in Scotland and Wales. On several occasions the UK Parliament has passed legislation changing the number of seats available in Parliament, and setting out rules for who is qualified to stand for election to those seats. It has even changed the way in which legislation is approved within Parliament, laying down rules for when the House of Commons can pass legislation without having to get the approval of the second parliamentary chamber, the House of Lords.[15] At the end of the last century Parliament voted to abolish the right of all but 92 hereditary peers to sit in the House of Lords[16] and in 2011 it passed the Fixed-term Parliaments Act, which requires the current and all future Parliaments to last for a set period of five years.

Constraints on Parliament

2.9 In practice, however, there are some constraints on what Parliament can do. Some of these are political in nature (there is likely to be great upheaval in society if, for example, Parliament were to vote to abolish the National Health Service), but others are self-imposed. When it enacted the European Communities Act in 1972 Parliament volunteered to give up some of its sovereignty by conferring powers on institutions of the European Union to make laws that were directly applicable in the UK. Likewise, when it passed the Human Rights Act in 1998 Parliament required all previous and future legislation to be interpreted, so far as possible, in a way that is compatible with the human rights set out in that Act.[17] Of course Parliament could remove these self-imposed constraints by amending or repealing the European Communities Act and the Human Rights Act but then again the political

---

[12] See *In re Carter's Application* [2011] NIQB 15, [2011] 4 BNIL 68, where the applicant challenged the validity of the Smoking (NI) Order 2006 (also arguing that it violated human rights).

[13] Act of Settlement 1701. In 2013 Parliament recently altered the rules of succession through the Succession to the Crown Act 2013, which makes succession no longer dependent on a person's gender.

[14] Act of Union 1707 and Act of Union 1800.

[15] Parliament Acts 1911 and 1949.

[16] House of Lords Act 1999.

[17] s 3(1).

consequences of doing so might be so serious that the Government of the day (which largely controls Parliament) would lose all credibility and be likely to be voted out of office at the next election.

2.10   A moment's thought presents the question whether the doctrine of parliamentary sovereignty is itself consistent with the idea of the rule of law. If Parliament can do whatever it wants, does that not allow it to pass laws which remove equality before the law from some people, or which make some people punishable for breaking the law even though they are not in clear breach of it, or which deny courts the power to protect the rights of individuals? The answer to this question is in theory yes, but in practice no. Politically (especially given the power of the media), a blatant breach of the rule of law by Parliament would make it very difficult for the political party which dominates Parliament to continue in that position. And the judges would speak out too. An example of this occurred in 2004 when the Labour Government proposed to include a provision in an Act of Parliament which would have denied immigrants the right to go to court to challenge a minister's ruling that they had entered the UK illegally. The Lord Chief Justice of England at the time, Lord Woolf, gave a speech at the University of Cambridge in which he made it clear that he thought such a provision would be contrary to the rule of law.[18] A few weeks later the Government dropped the proposal.

2.11   There has not yet been a court case in which judges in the UK have ruled that a provision in an Act of Parliament is contrary to the rule of law and therefore unconstitutional and invalid. The idea that courts can declare Acts to be unconstitutional is alien to the UK. But it is not an unthinkable possibility, as several senior judges have recently admitted. This occurred in *R (Jackson) v Attorney General*,[19] a case in which a challenge was raised by the Countryside Alliance against the Hunting Act 2004, which banned the hunting of live animals with dogs in England and Wales. The Act had been passed, in accordance with the Parliament Act 1949, by the House of Commons alone, as the House of Lords would not agree to it. Although all nine of the Law Lords who dealt with the case in the highest court (itself, at the time, a committee of the House of Lords!) ruled that the challenge must fail, because the 1949 Act had specifically authorized the House of Commons to make legislation on its own account, three of the Law Lords appeared to suggest that, on the right facts, they would consider declaring an Act, or a provision within an Act, to be invalid.[20] If and when that were to occur, we would then truly be able to say that the paramount principle in the constitutional law of the UK (and therefore Northern Ireland) is the rule of law, not parliamentary sovereignty.

---

[18]   http://news.bbc.co.uk/1/hi/uk_politics/3531439.stm. In the same speech Lord Woolf criticised the proposal to create a UK Supreme Court, but that reform went ahead in 2009.
[19]   [2005] UKHL 56, [2006] 1 AC 262.
[20]   Lord Steyn, at [102]; Lord Hope, at [104]–[107]; Lady Hale, at [159].

SEPARATION OF POWERS

2.12   The separation of powers principle was famously championed by Baron de Montesquieu in France, whose book published in 1748, *De l'esprit des lois*, argued that legislative, executive and judicial powers should not be exercised by the same people. Constitutional law throughout the UK usually seeks to adhere to this idea, but in practice it is often inconsistent with it. The most obvious respect in which the principle is ignored is in the way the government of the day effectively controls the actions of Parliament because it commands a majority of the Members of Parliament (MPs): the whipping system ensures that those MPs will almost always vote in accordance with the wishes of the party leader. The principle was also breached when the top court in the UK was the Appellate Committee of the House of Lords: senior judges were given peerages precisely to allow them to serve as 'Law Lords' and they were only discouraged, not disqualified, from contributing to debates in the House of Lords when it was acting in a legislative capacity. Since 2009 this anomaly has been removed because the top court is now the Supreme Court of the UK and those of them who are still peers are disqualified from taking their seats in the House of Lords until after they have reached retirement age. Prior to the Constitutional Reform Act 2005 the Lord Chancellor was a living contradiction of the separation of powers principle, for he or she was a member of the Government, the Speaker of the House of Lords and the country's most senior judge. The 2005 Act stripped the Lord Chancellor of the last two roles.

2.13   The separation of powers principle is perhaps most visible in the realm of administrative law, which contains a number of rules designed to ensure that when people challenge the decisions of administrative bodies they obtain a hearing before an adjudicating body that is completely independent of the State's administrative arm (see paras 6.5–6.11). Article 6 of the European Convention on Human Rights, which is part of the law of the whole of the UK as a result of the Human Rights Act 1998, guarantees that all determinations of a person's 'civil rights or obligations', as well as of any criminal charges against him or her, must be made 'by an independent and impartial tribunal established by law'. Government ministers therefore need to be extremely careful not to do or say anything which might be perceived as an attempt to influence the determination of such an issue by the 'tribunal' (a term which includes courts).

CONSTITUTIONAL ACTS

2.14   Whether or not courts will ever declare an Act of Parliament to be unconstitutional, some judges, and others,[21] are already of the view that particular Acts have a constitutional status. Lord Justice Laws, a senior judge in England and Wales, has tried to develop the concept of 'constitutional Acts',[22] and in practice it does appear to be the case that certain Acts are treated as more important than others. Their importance lies in the fact that they take priority over Acts that are passed later if there is a clash between them. Normal Acts are considered to be impliedly repealed by later inconsistent Acts, so constitutional Acts are exceptions to this doctrine of implied repeal. The Acts which are commonly cited as falling into this category are the Bill of Rights 1689 (which, amongst other things, protects MPs against having to face legal proceedings based on what they say during parliamentary debates), the European Communities Act 1972, the Human Rights Act 1998, and the devolution Acts (the Northern Ireland Act 1998, the Scotland Act 1998, and the Government of Wales Acts 1998 and 2006). The devolution Acts are so treated because they represent, to some extent, mini-constitutions for the devolved regions in question. The Northern Ireland Act 1998 is particularly 'constitutional' because it puts into law most of the terms of the Belfast (Good Friday) Agreement: no judge will lightly decide that the Northern Ireland Act 1998 has been impliedly repealed by some future Act, because it is just too important to be so treated.

2.15   In 2011 the Supreme Court gave some guidance as to the status of legislation passed by the devolved legislatures in the United Kingdom. This was in *Axa General Insurance Ltd v Lord Advocate*,[23] where the appellant insurance companies argued that the Scottish Parliament, by enacting the Damages (Asbestos-related Conditions) (Scotland) Act 2009, had deprived the companies of their property rights in a way which was unreasonable, irrational or arbitrary. The Supreme Court rejected this argument, saying that legislation enacted by the Scottish Parliament could not be challenged on the same grounds as other forms of legislation made as a result of Westminster delegating its law-making powers to another body (see paras 3.16–3.17). Instead courts must respect the assessment made by a devolved legislature as to what is in the public interest for its own jurisdiction, unless that assessment is 'manifestly without reasonable foundations'. At one point the Supreme Court said that devolved legislation could be successfully

---

[21] Eg Gordon Anthony, *Judicial Review in Northern Ireland* (Oxford, Hart Publishing, 2008), 16–21.

[22] See his article 'Law and Democracy' [1995] *PL* 72 and his judgment in *Thoburn v Sunderland City Council* [2002] EWHC 195 (Admin), [2003] QB 151. For a critique, see John Griffith, 'The Brave New World of Sir John Laws' (2000) 63 *MLR* 159.

[23] [2011] UKSC 46, [2012] 1 AC 868.

challenged only if it was contrary to the rule of law, but it did not clarify exactly what it meant by that. It is likely that the Supreme Court would take the same attitude towards Acts of the Northern Ireland Assembly.

THE UNITED KINGDOM PARLIAMENT

2.16   Northern Ireland currently elects 18 MPs to the House of Commons in each general election.[24] At present a first-past-the-post voting system is used, whereas for all other elections in Northern Ireland (for the European Parliament, for the Northern Ireland Assembly and for local councils) the voting system is based on a form of proportional representation (the Single Transferable Vote system – STV). On 5 May 2011 a referendum was held throughout the UK on whether the voting system for general elections should be changed to the 'Alternative Vote' (AV) system, which is one where voters express their preferences between the candidates standing in their constituency and, by a process of elimination of the 'first preference' votes given to the least popular candidates, the person elected is the candidate who is the first to accumulate 50 per cent of the first and transferred preferences. In the referendum 32 per cent voted in favour of this change to the voting system but 68 per cent voted against. In Northern Ireland the respective figures were 44 per cent and 56 per cent (the highest percentage of 'yes' votes anywhere in the UK).

2.17   The law regulates the conduct of general elections in considerable detail. In 2010 the result of the election in the constituency of Fermanagh and South Tyrone was exceptionally close, with the Sinn Féin candidate getting just four more votes than the independent unionist candidate.[25] The Representation of the People Act 1983 allows a defeated candidate to challenge the result of an election if there are alleged irregularities, and that is what the independent unionist candidate did in this instance. But *In the Matter of the Parliamentary Election for Fermanagh and South Tyrone held on 6 May 2010*[26] the Divisional Court of Northern Ireland held that, even if there had been a breach of any of the rules governing elections, it had not affected the result in this case. There was also a challenge to the victory of a Labour MP in a constituency in England, the allegation being

---

[24] Although the Conservative Party is strongly in favour of reducing the overall number of MPs elected to the UK Parliament from 650 to 600 (including a reduction in those elected in Northern Ireland from 18 to 16), and legislation has been enacted permitting this to happen (see the Parliamentary Voting System and Constituencies Act 2011), the change is not going to be implemented prior to the next general election in 2015 because the Liberal Democrats, who are in a coalition government with the Conservatives, have not yet agreed to the proposed new electoral boundaries.

[25] 21,304 as opposed to 21,300.

[26] [2010] NIQB 113.

that he had told lies about an opponent in his election literature. Under the Representation of the People Act 1983 it is an illegal practice for an election candidate to make 'any false statement of fact in relation to the candidate's personal character or conduct' unless the candidate can show that he or she had reasonable grounds for believing the statement to be true.[27] For the first time in nearly 100 years a court upheld such a challenge and the MP in question, Phil Woolas, was stripped of the seat and banned from standing for election for three years.[28] A bye-election was then held to fill the vacancy.

2.18   In 2009–10 a huge scandal rocked the UK Parliament when it came to light that large numbers of MPs had been abusing the expenses system by claiming for items that were not remotely connected to their duties as an MP. The fault lay partly in the complexity and generosity of the expenses system, but also in the greed and deceitfulness of some MPs. A small group of MPs were prosecuted for their deception (the alleged crime being 'false accounting'). Initially they tried to argue that they could not be tried in an ordinary court because what they had done related to the proceedings of Parliament and, according to article 9 of the Bill of Rights of 1689, 'freedom of speech and debates or proceedings in Parliament ought not to be impeached or questioned in any court or place out of Parliament'. The issue eventually went to the Supreme Court, where nine justices unanimously held, in *R v Chaytor*,[29] that article 9 did not cover the kind of actions which these MPs were accused of. They were subsequently tried and convicted. Parliament itself took action to try to prevent future abuses of the expenses system by passing the Parliamentary Standards Act 2009, which established the Independent Parliamentary Standards Authority. In March 2011, in the face of criticism that the system it was operating was too strict, the Authority announced that it would be relaxing some of the restrictions, especially to make it easier for MPs living in the London area to carry out their functions without being out of pocket.

THE NORTHERN IRELAND AFFAIRS COMMITTEE

2.19   The UK Parliament has a large number of committees, one of which is the Northern Ireland Affairs Committee. This is a Select Committee of the House of Commons that comprises 14 MPs, five of whom represent constituencies in Northern Ireland. The Committee's main role is to scrutinise the work of the Northern Ireland Office and its associated public bodies, the Northern Ireland Office being the department within the UK Government which has responsibility for matters in Northern Ireland that

---

[27] s 106(1).
[28] *R (Woolas) v Speaker of the House of Commons* [2010] EWHC (Admin) 3169.
[29] [2010] UKSC 52, [2011] 1 AC 684.

have not been transferred to the Northern Ireland Assembly (see paras 2.50–2.51). The Committee usually operates through conducting inquiries into subjects that are of interest to it, soliciting written and oral evidence from those who have experience of the field. It then issues reports, with findings and recommendations.[30] The Government is supposed to respond to these recommendations within two months. In 2011 and 2012 the Committee published reports on corporation tax and on fuel laundering in Northern Ireland. In 2010 it reported on the Forensic Science Agency and television broadcasting.

THE STATUS OF NORTHERN IRELAND

2.20 Even though there are three legal jurisdictions within the UK (England and Wales, Scotland and Northern Ireland), the UK is still a unitary, not a federal, State. The arrangements for the devolution of powers to those jurisdictions are laid down in Acts of the Westminster Parliament. For Wales and Scotland those Acts are the Government of Wales Acts 1998 and 2006 and the Scotland Act 1998. For Northern Ireland they are the Northern Ireland Act 1998, the Northern Ireland (St Andrews Agreement) Acts 2006 and 2007, and the Northern Ireland Act 2009. The Northern Ireland Act 1998 is the Act which implements large parts of the Belfast (Good Friday) Agreement of April 1998, so it is therefore, in some sense, the most important constitutional document for Northern Ireland today. Prior to that Agreement the main constitutional documents for Northern Ireland were the Government of Ireland Act 1920 and then (after the Parliament of Northern Ireland was suspended in 1972 and abolished altogether in 1974) the Northern Ireland (Temporary Provisions) Act 1972 and the Northern Ireland Act 1974.[31]

2.21 As alluded to in the previous chapter (see para 1.29), section 1 of the Northern Ireland Act 1998 declares that:

> Northern Ireland in its entirety remains part of the United Kingdom and shall not cease to be so without the consent of a majority of the people of Northern Ireland voting in a poll held for the purposes of this section in accordance with Schedule 1.

---

[30] These are all available at www.parliament.uk/business/committees/committees-a-z/commons-select/northern-ireland-affairs-committee/Publications.

[31] For earlier accounts of constitutional law in Northern Ireland see H Calvert, *Constitutional Law in Northern Ireland: A Study in Regional Government* (London, Stevens, 1968); D Watt (ed), *The Constitution of Northern Ireland: Problems and Prospects* (London, Heinemann, 1981); and B Hadfield, *The Constitution of Northern Ireland* (Belfast, SLS Legal Publications, 1989). See also C Palley, 'The Evolution, Disintegration and Possible Reconstruction of the Northern Ireland Constitution' (1972) 1 *Anglo-American L Rev* 368.

Schedule 1 then provides that the Secretary of State for Northern Ireland *may* order the holding of such a poll on a specified date, but that he or she *must* order it 'if at any time it appears likely to him [or her[32]] that a majority of those voting would express a wish that Northern Ireland should cease to be part of the UK and form part of a united Ireland'. At least seven years must elapse between the holding of two such polls. Section 1 goes on to say that, if the wish expressed by a majority in such a poll is that Northern Ireland should form part of a united Ireland, the Secretary of State *must* then lay before the UK Parliament proposals to that effect which have been agreed by the governments of the UK and Ireland.

2.22   These provisions in the 1998 Act replace section 1(2) of the Ireland Act 1949, which was passed at Westminster mainly to recognize the change in status of what was previously called Ireland and was from then on to be called the Republic of Ireland, an area no longer 'part of His Majesty's dominions'. Section 1(2) said that 'in no event will Northern Ireland or any part thereof cease to be part of His Majesty's dominions and of the UK without the consent of the Parliament of Northern Ireland'. The significance of the form of words used in the 1998 Act, therefore, is that the power to change the status of Northern Ireland has effectively been transferred from 'the Parliament of Northern Ireland' to 'the people of Northern Ireland' and the only option available if Northern Ireland ceases to be part of the UK is that it becomes part of a united Ireland – the possibility of Northern Ireland becoming an independent state in its own right has been ruled out.

2.23   An opinion poll in March 2010 showed that approximately 55 per cent of people in Northern Ireland wanted it to remain part of the UK, a figure which included 25 per cent of Catholic respondents.[33] On the other hand, one quarter of Protestant respondents thought that there would be a united Ireland by 2021, the centenary of partition. A poll conducted for the BBC in January 2013 revealed that, when people were asked how they would vote if there was a border poll tomorrow, 65 per cent said they would vote for Northern Ireland to remain within the United Kingdom and 17 per cent said they would vote for Northern Ireland to join the Republic of Ireland (the remainder said they would not vote or did not know how they would vote). Interestingly, the poll found that more Catholics would vote for Northern Ireland to remain within the United Kingdom (38 per cent) than would vote for a united Ireland (35 per cent).

---

[32] Legislation at Westminster continues to be worded as if all people are men, but the Interpretation Act 1978, s 6, says that 'unless the contrary intention appears...words importing the masculine gender include the feminine'.

[33] *Belfast Telegraph*, 15 March 2010. For earlier polls see R MacGinty, 'Public attitudes to constitutional options in the context of devolution' in P Carmichael, C Knox and R Osborne (eds), *Devolution and Constitutional Change in Northern Ireland* (Manchester, Manchester UP, 2007), 31–46.

The right to self-determination

2.24   In debates over the constitutional status of Northern Ireland reference is often made to 'the right to self-determination'. This is a phrase used in international law, and is included at the beginning of each of two main international treaties on human rights agreed by the United Nations in 1966, the International Covenant on Civil and Political Rights and the International Cvenant on Economic, Social and Cultural Rights. But, as we shall see in Chapter 5, international law is often not enforceable, especially in national courts, and anyhow there is great disagreement amongst international lawyers as to when and how the right to self-determination can be invoked. In relation to Northern Ireland, for example, there is no consensus as to who should definitively exercise the right to determine its status; is it the people currently living in Northern Ireland, the people on the island of Ireland as a whole, the people living in the UK, or the people in both islands?[34]

THE NORTHERN IRELAND ASSEMBLY

2.25   The Northern Ireland Assembly has 108 Members (known as Members of the Legislative Assembly – MLAs). They are elected every four years[35] on the basis of 'single transferable vote proportional representation' (STV-PR), six representatives being elected for each of the 18 parliamentary constituencies in Northern Ireland. If an MLA dies or retires while in office the party he or she represents can choose a replacement representative without having to contest a bye-election, and between the 2007 and 2011 elections such replacements were chosen on no fewer than 14 occasions. There is currently no law against MLAs also serving as MPs, but all of the political parties in Northern Ireland are trying to move away from such dual mandates.[36] Members of the House of Lords (who, of course, are all unelected) can also be elected as MLAs.[37]

2.26   The first business of each newly elected Northern Ireland Assembly is to elect from among the MLAs a Presiding Officer and deputies.[38] The function of the Presiding Officer is to act as an independent chairperson at sittings of the Assembly, just as the Speaker of the House of Commons

---

[34] See, generally, C Bell and K Cavanaugh "Constructive Ambiguity' or internal self-determination? Self-determination, group accommodation and the Belfast Agreement' (1999) *Fordham International LJ* 1345.

[35] On the first Thursday in May of the year in question: Northern Ireland Act 1998, s. 31(1). Clause 7(2) of the Northern Ireland (Miscellaneous Provisions) Bill currently before the UK Parliament, extends to the life of each Assembly for five years.

[36] But Alasdair McDonnell, the leader of the SDLP is still both an MLA and an MP, as are Sammy Wilson and Gregory Campbell of the DUP.

[37] A current example is Lord Morrow MLA, of the DUP.

[38] Northern Ireland Act 1998, s 39(1).

does at Westminster. The election has to be with cross-community support, a concept which is crucial to the effective functioning of the power-sharing arrangements that were agreed in the Belfast (Good Friday) Agreement. It is defined in the Northern Ireland Act 1998 as meaning either:

(a) the support of a majority of the members voting, a majority of the designated Nationalists voting and a majority of the designated Unionists voting; or

(b) the support of 60 per cent of the members voting, 40 per cent of the designated Nationalists and 40 per cent of the designated Unionists voting.[39]

If 30 MLAs lodge a 'petition of concern' in relation to any matter which is to be voted on by the Assembly, the vote then requires cross-community support.[40]

2.27   A body called the Assembly Commission has been created, comprising a small group of MLAs who ensure that the Assembly is provided with the property, services and staff it requires.[41] It is the Assembly Commission which determines the terms and conditions of appointment of the staff of the Assembly and which authorises the use of the Assembly's premises for events.

Transferred, excepted and reserved matters

2.28   The Northern Ireland Act 1998 stipulates that the Northern Ireland Assembly and Northern Ireland Executive can deal with any 'transferred matter', which is a term defined as 'any matter which is not an excepted or reserved matter'.[42] Excepted matters are listed in the 22 paragraphs of Schedule 2 to the Act and include elections, international relations, immigration, most taxes, coinage, and national security. These are all matters which it is not envisaged will ever be transferred under the devolution arrangements for Northern Ireland. Reserved matters are listed in the 42 paragraphs of Schedule 3 to the 1998 Act and include civil defence, import and export controls, the minimum wage, financial services and banking, intellectual property, human genetics, consumer safety in relation to goods, and data protection. These are matters which may one day be transferred to Northern Ireland. Indeed some reserved matters which were included in the original list have subsequently been transferred, most notably the criminal

---

[39] s 4(5). The Assembly's Standing Orders prescribe the designation system. MLAs can choose to designate themselves as 'Others' – as Alliance Party MLAs do – but the effect of that is to reduce their influence on cross-community votes. See A Schwartz, 'How unfair is cross-community consent? Voting power in the Northern Ireland Assembly' (2010) 61 *NILQ* 349.
[40] Northern Ireland Act 1998, s 42(1)
[41] Northern Ireland Act 1998, s 40 and Sch 5.
[42] s 4(2).

law, prosecutions, the maintenance of public order, and the control of the police (see paras 2.32 and 7.3). The Acts regulating devolution to Scotland and Wales do not adopt the distinction between excepted and reserved matters. In Scotland there is simply a list of reserved matters (many of which overlap with matters listed as either excepted or reserved in Northern Ireland).[43] In Wales, the categories of excepted and reserved matters are not used at all. The legislation simply lists the fields and matters in relation to which the Assembly can make laws (called 'Measures').[44]

2.29 It is important to note that the Northern Ireland Assembly is not absolutely prohibited from legislating for excepted and reserved matters. It can do so if it first secures the consent of the Secretary of State for Northern Ireland and, in addition, any provision dealing with an excepted matter must be 'ancillary to other provisions (whether in the Bill or previously enacted) dealing with reserved or transferred matters'.[45] At the same time, while responsibility for social security, child support and pensions is a transferred matter, the 1998 Act requires the relevant Minister in Northern Ireland to consult with the Secretary of State with a view to securing that single systems apply on these issues throughout the UK.[46] Pending their devolution to the Northern Ireland Assembly, reserved matters can be legislated for by Orders in Council at Westminster.[47]

2.30 The 1998 Act imposes five further constraints on the legislative competence of the Assembly.[48] These absolutely prohibit the Assembly from legislating:

(1) for a country or territory other than Northern Ireland;
(2) in a way that is incompatible with rights listed in the Human Rights Act 1998;
(3) in a way that is incompatible with European Union law;
(4) in a way that discriminates against any person or class of person on the ground of religious belief or political opinion; and
(5) in a way that modifies the Human Rights Act 1998, parts of the European Communities Act 1972, or parts of the Northern Ireland Act 1998 itself.

---

[43] Scotland Act 1998, Sch 5.
[44] Government of Wales Act 2006, s 94 and Sch 5. The 2006 Act amended the 1998 Act of the same name so as to confer wider law-making powers on the Welsh Assembly if the people of Wales approved of that development in a referendum. A referendum was held on 3 March 2011 and 63 per cent of those voting did express their approval. The very first Measure proposed by the Welsh Assembly (on the making of local government by-laws) was referred to the Supreme Court by the Attorney General for England and Wales on the ground it might exceed the Assembly's new powers, but the Supreme Court rejected the challenge: see *Attorney General v National Assembly for Wales Commission* [2012] UKSC 53, [2012] 3 WLR 1294.
[45] s 8(a).
[46] s 87(1).
[47] s 87.
[48] s 6(2).

Controls on the legislative competence of the Northern Ireland Assembly

2.31 The Northern Ireland Act 1998 provides no fewer than seven different mechanisms for ensuring that legislation made by the Assembly falls within the competence of that body. The first three are general in nature, while the last four relate specifically to human rights. They are as follows:

(1) the Minister introducing the legislation must publish a statement that the Bill is within the Assembly's competence;

(2) the Presiding Officer can refuse to allow a Bill to be introduced if he or she decides that it is not within the Assembly's competence;

(3) the Attorney General for Northern Ireland can refer a Bill for consideration by the UK Supreme Court;[49]

(4) the Attorney General can also initiate court proceedings challenging the legislation's compatibility with 'Convention rights', ie those rights listed in the European Convention on Human Rights which were made part of domestic law throughout the UK by the Human Rights Act 1998 (see paras 5.38–5.40);

(5) the Secretary of State for Northern Ireland can refuse to submit a Bill for Royal Assent if he or she thinks it is incompatible with international human rights obligations;

(6) the Northern Ireland Human Rights Commission has power to advise the Assembly that a Bill is incompatible with human rights; and

(7) the compatibility of legislation with human rights can be challenged during current court proceedings or by way of parallel court proceedings.[50]

The residual power of the UK Parliament

2.32 Although the Northern Ireland Assembly has been given the power to make laws on transferred matters, this does not affect the residual power of the UK Parliament to make laws for Northern Ireland on any matter. However there is a constitutional 'convention' (ie tradition) whereby the UK Parliament will not make laws on transferred matters without first receiving, through a 'legislative consent motion', the agreement of the legislature to which it has devolved responsibility for those matters. (This convention also applied during the days of the Stormont Parliament, and was even extended to prevent debates at Westminster about transferred matters in Northern Ireland; this meant that the UK Parliament did not intervene early enough

---

[49] This is the power which the Attorney General for England and Wales exercised in the Welsh case mentioned in n 44 above.

[50] For further details, see B Dickson in A Lester, D Pannick and J Herberg (eds), *Human Rights Law and Practice* (London, Lexis Nexis, 3rd edn, 2009), 742–6.

when the Stormont Parliament failed to react appropriately to calls for reform concerning allegations of religious and political discrimination in Northern Ireland.)

THE NORTHERN IRELAND EXECUTIVE

2.33   Each newly elected Assembly must, within six weeks of its first meeting, elect from among its members the First Minister and Deputy First Minister. The candidates for these posts must stand jointly, so that if one of them fails to be elected the other fails also. The election requires cross-community support in the first of the two senses (set out in para 2.26 above). The political party which has the most MLAs has the right to nominate the First Minister, and the largest party of the other political designation then nominates the Deputy First Minister.[51] This is the election that was at issue in the *Robinson* case discussed above (para 2.5). The First and Deputy First Ministers have exercised their right under the 1998 Act to appoint junior Ministers (two in number). Together these four Ministers run the Office of the First Minister and Deputy First Minister (OFMDFM). The main responsibilities that have been assumed by this Office include liaison with the Assembly, the North-South Ministerial Council and British-Irish Council (described below, paras 2.46–2.48), the Executive's Programme for Government, equality of opportunity and good community relations, tackling poverty and social exclusion, the needs of children and young people and of victims and survivors, sustainable development, and emergency planning.

2.34   Once elected, the First and Deputy First Ministers must decide how many other ministerial offices are to be held and what functions should be exercisable by the holder of each office, but the maximum permissible number of such offices is 11.[52] The offices, except for the Department of Justice, are then distributed in accordance with the so-called d'Hondt formula, which is named after a Belgian mathematician Viktor d'Hondt. This formula requires the number of seats held by each party in the Assembly to be divided first by one, then by two, then by three, and so on. After each division, the party with the highest resulting number is allowed to choose a Department.[53] In the wake of the Assembly elections held in May 2011, the 10 departments distributed in this way were allocated as follows:

[51] Northern Ireland Act 1998, s 16C(6), inserted by the Northern Ireland (St Andrews Agreement) Act 2006, s 8.
[52] Northern Ireland Act 1998, s 17(4) and Departments (NI) Order 1999, Sch 1, as amended by the Department of Justice Act (NI) 2010, s 1.
[53] Ibid s 18(2)–(6).

(1)   Department of Agriculture and Rural Development: Sinn Féin
(2)   Department of Culture, Arts and Leisure: Sinn Féin
(3)   Department of Education: Sinn Féin
(4)   Department of Employment and Learning: Alliance
(5)   Department of Enterprise, Trade and Investment: DUP
(6)   Department of the Environment: SDLP
(7)   Department of Finance and Personnel: DUP
(8)   Department of Health, Social Services and Public Safety: DUP
(9)   Department for Regional Development: Ulster Unionist Party
(10) Department for Social Development: DUP

2.35   The Department of Justice, because it was created only after lengthy negotiations which culminated in the Hillsborough Castle Agreement of 5 February 2010,[54] is allocated on a cross-community vote basis, not in accordance with the d'Hondt formula (see para 1.33).[55] The Minister is currently an MLA from the Alliance Party. The selection system will change when the Northern Ireland (Miscellaneous Provisions) Bill becomes law.

2.36   Taken together, the First Minister, the Deputy First Minister, and all the other Ministers (except the junior Ministers) form the Executive Committee of the Assembly. There is, in other words, a mandatory coalition in Northern Ireland – compulsory power-sharing. Political scientists refer to this form of government as 'consociationalism'.[56] According to the Belfast (Good Friday) Agreement, which in this respect has been expressly incorporated into law by reference being made in the Northern Ireland Act 1998 to the relevant paragraphs of the Agreement,[57] the Executive 'will provide a forum for the discussion of, and agreement on, issues which cut across the responsibilities of two or more Ministers, for prioritising executive and legislative proposals and for recommending a common position where necessary'.[58] It must also seek to agree each year 'a programme incorporating an agreed budget linked to policies and programmes, subject to approval by the Assembly, after scrutiny in Assembly Committees, on a cross-community basis'.[59] Following the St Andrews Agreement of 2006, the Executive Committee was given the additional function of discussing and agreeing upon 'significant or controversial matters that are clearly outside the scope of the agreed programme' or that the First and Deputy First Ministers jointly determine should be considered by the Executive Committee.[60]

---

[54] www.nidirect.gov.uk/castle_final_agreement15__2_-3.pdf.
[55] Northern Ireland Act 1998, s 21A(3), inserted by the Northern Ireland (Miscellaneous Provisions) Act 2006, s 17(1); and Department of Justice Act (NI) 2010, s 2(1).
[56] See J McGarry and B O'Leary, *The Northern Ireland Conflict: Consociational engagements* (Oxford, Oxford UP, 2004).
[57] s 20(3).
[58] Strand One of the Agreement, para 19.
[59] Ibid para 20.
[60] Northern Ireland Act 1998, s 20(4), inserted by the Northern Ireland (St Andrews Agreement) Act 2006, s 5(1). For useful accounts of how the devolution arrangements in

2.37 Each government department in Northern Ireland obviously has a wide variety of matters to administer and each will encounter legal problems on very many points. Like all other individuals and organisations, however, they are not permitted to defy the law, even though they may often be instrumental in having the law changed. That is a consequence of the rule of law idea, which was discussed at the start of this chapter. Just as the Northern Ireland Act 1998 prohibits the Assembly from acting outside its legislative competence, so it also states that ministers and departments have no power to make any subordinate legislation, or to do any act, which is incompatible with the rights set out in the Human Rights Act 1998, incompatible with EU law, discriminatory against any person or class of person on the ground of religious belief or political opinion, or an attempt to modify certain 'entrenched' Acts of Parliament.[61]

The Crown prerogative

2.38 The Northern Ireland Act 1998 specifically retains the prerogative power of the Crown.[62] Technically this is vested in the monarch, but in practice it is exercised by the Government (see too para 3.50). To the extent that the prerogative power relates to transferred matters, it is exercisable by the relevant Minister or Northern Ireland department, except that, if it relates to the Northern Ireland Civil Service or the Commissioner for Public Appointments, it is exercisable by the First Minister and Deputy First Minister acting jointly.[63] The extent of the First and Deputy First Minister's prerogative powers became apparent in the case of *An Application for Judicial Review by Michelle Williamson*,[64] where the two Ministers had decided to appoint not just one Victims' Commissioner, as envisaged by the Victims and Survivors (NI) Order 2006, but four. Gillen J held that they had the power to do so, although he said it was unnecessary to decide if this was because of the ministers' prerogative powers or a 'third source' of power, which, according to some precedents, allows government ministers to carry out the ordinary business that a natural person would carry out.[65] In a case that came before the House of Lords in 2008, *R (Bancoult) v Secretary of State for Foreign and Commonwealth Affairs*,[66] the Law Lords were split

Northern Ireland have fared, see the *Devolution Monitoring Report*s by R Wilford and R Wilson, available on the website of The Constitution Unit at University College London: www.ucl.ac.uk/constitution-unit.

[61] s 24(1).
[62] Ibid s 23(1).
[63] Ibid s 23(2) and (3).
[64] [2009] NIQB 63.
[65] Ibid at [48]–[51].
[66] [2008] UKHL 61, [2009] 1 AC 453.

three to two on whether the UK government had acted within its prerogative powers when it prevented the inhabitants of the Chagos Islands in the Indian Ocean from returning to their homeland after being evacuated many years earlier when the USA took over the main island, Diego Garcia, as a military base. Disturbingly, the majority held that such treatment was lawful because it did not offend any fundamental principle of English common law.

THE PLEDGE OF OFFICE AND CODES OF CONDUCT

2.39   No minister is allowed to take up office in Northern Ireland until he or she has affirmed the terms of the pledge of office,[67] which, together with the code of conduct to which it refers, is set out in Annex A to Strand One to the Belfast (Good Friday) Agreement and also in Schedule 4 to the 1998 Act. The pledge of office requires ministers to, amongst other things, discharge all the duties of the office in good faith, commit to non-violence and exclusively peaceful and democratic means, serve all the people of Northern Ireland equally, and support and act in accordance with all decisions of the Executive and the Assembly. Under the code of conduct ministers must, for example:

> observe the highest standards of propriety and regularity involving impartiality, integrity and objectivity in relationship to their stewardship of public funds, ensure all reasonable requests for information are complied with, operate in a way that is conducive to promoting good community relations, and declare any personal or business interests which may conflict with their responsibilities.

In addition to the code of conduct referred to in Schedule 4 to the 1998 Act, the Executive Committee of the Assembly adopted a separate, and more detailed, Ministerial Code in 2007, another consequence of the St Andrews Agreement of 2006. This is given the force of law by section 28A of the Northern Ireland Act 1998, which was inserted into that Act by the Northern Ireland (St Andrews Agreement) Act 2006.[68] If a Minister takes a decision which appears to be contrary to the Ministerial Code, and the Presiding Officer certifies that it relates to a matter of public importance, the decision can be referred by 30 MLAs to the Executive Committee for re-consideration.[69]

2.40   If the Assembly resolves that a minister no longer enjoys the confidence of the Assembly because of his or her failure to observe any term of the pledge of office, that minister is excluded from holding office as

[67] Northern Ireland Act 1998, ss 16(4)(a) and 18(8).
[68] s 5(2). For a copy of the Code see www.northernireland.gov.uk/pc1952_ni_exec_min_code.pdf.
[69] Northern Ireland Act 1998, s 28B, inserted by the Northern Ireland (St Andrews Agreement) Act 2006, s 6.

a minister for a 12-month period.[70] Likewise, if the Assembly resolves that a political party does not enjoy the confidence of the Assembly because it is not committed to non-violence or to its ministerial members observing the other terms of the pledge of office, members of that party are excluded from holding ministerial office for a 12-month period.[71] Such exclusions can be extended for further 12-month periods.[72] A proposal to exclude a minister or party members has to be moved in the Assembly by at least 30 MLAs, by the First and Deputy First Ministers, or by the Assembly's Presiding Officer,[73] and the resolution has to be passed with cross-community support (see para 2.26).[74] These powers to exclude have not yet been exercised. During the difficult negotiations over restoration of the suspended Assembly in 2002 there were calls from some unionists that Sinn Féin MLAs should be excluded from the Assembly because of perceived republican dilly-dallying over the decommissioning of IRA weapons, but no such resolution was ever actually proposed. Likewise, in 2008, after it emerged that Ian Paisley Jr was on his father's payroll as a researcher while also serving as an MLA and a Junior Minister in the OFMDFM, he resigned from his post as Junior Minister before any proposal to exclude him could be made in the Assembly.

Legal constraints on ministerial behaviour

2.41 Ministers must try to avoid punishing their political opponents in some way other than by having them excluded for breaching the pledge of office or code of conduct. When, in 2000, the then First and Deputy First Ministers decided not to circulate an Executive paper to two DUP ministers because they were not, allegedly, fulfilling their office duties in good faith, the two DUP politicians sought and obtained a declaration from a High Court judge that the First and Deputy First Ministers had acted unlawfully in not circulating the Executive paper.[75]

2.42 Ministers must also be particularly careful not to commit contempt of court by prejudging or seeking to improperly influence a decision that has yet to be taken by some judicial or quasi-judicial body. In one instance, a senior judge upbraided the Minister for the Environment for comments he made on a BBC Radio Ulster phone-in programme about pending litigation

---

[70] Northern Ireland Act 1998, s 30(1).
[71] Ibid s 30(2).
[72] Ibid s 30(3).
[73] Ibid s 30(5).
[74] Ibid s 30(8).
[75] *In the Matter of an Application by Maurice Morrow and Gregory Campbell for Judicial Review* [2002] NIQB 4.

in which his Department was involved.[76] The judge invited the Attorney General to consider initiating contempt of court proceedings (see para 11.4), but in due course the Attorney General stated that no such proceedings would be commenced.[77]

2.43 If the Executive decides that an issue should be dealt with in accordance with a certain procedure, a Minister who does not then follow that procedure will be acting unlawfully. This occurred in 2007, when the then Minister for Social Development halted government funding for a group called the Conflict Transformation Initiative after the Ulster Defence Association had failed to meet the Minister's deadline for the commencement of weapon decommissioning. An employee of the initiative was successful in obtaining a court order quashing the decision to withdraw funding because Margaret Ritchie, the Minister in question, had not followed the procedures agreed at a meeting of the Executive a week earlier.[78] It was a breach of the Ministerial Code for a Minister not to support and act in accordance with all decisions of the Executive Committee.[79]

ASSEMBLY COMMITTEES

2.44 The Northern Ireland Act 1998 (still under the heading 'Executive Authorities'[80]) requires Assembly committees to be established (called 'statutory committees') 'to advise and assist each Northern Ireland Minister in the formulation of policy with respect to matters within his [*sic*] responsibilities as a Minister'.[81] These committees have a scrutiny, policy development and consultation role with respect to the various government departments, including the OFMDFM.[82] They can take the Committee stage of relevant primary legislation (ie Assembly Bills), approve relevant secondary legislation, call for persons to appear before them and for papers to be provided to them, initiate inquiries, and make reports.[83] The role of chairperson and deputy chairperson for each committee is allocated in accordance with the d'Hondt formula, in the same way as departments are allocated (see para 2.34).[84]

---

[76] *In the Matter of an Application by House of Fraser Ltd for Leave to Apply for Judicial Review* [2010] NIQB 105.

[77] www.bbc.co.uk/news/uk-northern-ireland-11643954 (28 October 2010).

[78] *In the Matter of an Application by Solinas* [2009] NIQB 43.

[79] Ibid at [33].

[80] Ie Part III of the Act (ss 16–30).

[81] s 29(1).

[82] Ibid, as amended by the Northern Ireland (St Andrews Agreement) Act 2006, s 10(2).

[83] Strand One of the Agreement, para 9, as incorporated into law by the Northern Ireland Act 1998, s 29(1)(c).

[84] For a while a Northern Ireland Civic Forum was also established, paid for by Northern Ireland's Department of Finance and Personnel, but this body was suspended at the same time

2.45 The 1998 Act also provides for the establishment of 'standing committees', which are permanent committees with specific roles allocated by the Standing Orders.[85] At present these committees include the Assembly and Executive Review Committee, the Audit Committee, the Business Committee, the Committee on Procedures, the Committee on Standards and Privileges, and the Public Accounts Committee. These perform very important functions in ensuring that the Assembly acts effectively and with probity. The Review Committee was especially to the fore during the period when plans were being laid for the devolution of policing and justice; it issued long reports on this matter in 2008, 2009 and 2010. In 2011 it published its views on whether the system for electing the First Minister and Deputy First Minister should be changed.[86] The Committee on Standards and Privileges maintains and publishes online the Register of Members' Interests. The Standing Orders also permit the Assembly to set up *ad hoc* committees with specific time-bound terms of reference, and committees may sit jointly on some matters. *Ad hoc* committees were created to look, for example, at local postal services in Northern Ireland and at the draft Sexual Offences (NI) Order 2008 (legislation being considered at Westminster). In November 2012, for the first time, an *Ad Hoc* Committee on Equality Requirements was set up to examine the equality and human rights aspects of the Welfare Reform Bill. The chairpersons of all the statutory and standing committees meet also as a group from time to time.

NORTH-SOUTH AND EAST-WEST BODIES

2.46 The Belfast (Good Friday) Agreement provided for a number of other institutions apart from the Northern Ireland Assembly and the Executive Committee.[87] The Northern Ireland Act 1998, as a consequence, creates North-South and East-West bodies such as the North-South Ministerial Council and the British-Irish Council,[88] but none of those has any executive power. In addition it provides for the Northern Ireland Human Rights Commission[89] and the Equality Commission for Northern Ireland,[90] the

as the Assembly in 2002, and it has not been revived. It had 60 members and its function was to serve as a consultative body on issues that were of significance in Northern Ireland. It could not make any laws or take any executive actions.

[85] Standing Orders 51, 52 and 54–59.
[86] *Review of the Operation of Sections 16A to 16C of the Northern Ireland Act 1998*, 18 January 2011.
[87] For comments on the North-South strand in the Agreement see C McCall, 'From Barrier to Bridge: Reconfiguring the Irish Border after the Belfast Good Friday Agreement' (2002) 53 *NILQ* 479.
[88] s 52.
[89] ss 68–72 and Sch 7.
[90] ss 73–78 and Sch 8.

former being a replacement for the Standing Advisory Commission on Human Rights and the latter a replacement for four pre-existing bodies dealing with different types of discrimination.[91] The two Commissions are primarily advisory bodies, but the Equality Commission also has considerable powers to enforce various pieces of anti-discrimination legislation.[92] They are considered further below (paras 7.28–7.31 and 7.39–7.53).

2.47   The North-South Ministerial Council,[93] like the Executive, had its first meeting in December 1999. Six North/South implementation bodies were established to implement the policies agreed by the Ministers at Council meetings.[94] These bodies are Waterways Ireland,[95] the Food Safety Promotion Board,[96] the Trade and Business Development Body,[97] the Special European Union Programmes Body,[98] the North-South Language Body[99] and the Foyle, Carlingford and Irish Lights Commission.[100] There is no North/South body dealing with justice issues, but the Department of Justice in Northern Ireland liaises closely with the Department of Justice and Equality in the Republic on matters such as organised crime: an annual seminar is held each year, where discussions take place between senior officers from the Police Service of Northern Ireland, An Garda Síochána (the Irish police), the Serious Organised Crime Agency (a UK body), the Criminal Assets Bureau in the Republic, and tax and customs officials from both jurisdictions.

2.48   The British-Irish Council (known too as the 'Council of the Isles') also meets regularly. It includes representatives not just from Ireland, Northern Ireland and England, but also from Scotland, Wales, the Isle of Man, Jersey and Guernsey. According to the Belfast (Good Friday) Agreement the purpose of the Council is 'to promote the harmonious and mutually beneficial development of the totality of relationships among the peoples of these islands'.[101] It seeks to achieve this by exchanging information and trying to reach agreement on co-operation on matters of mutual interest that are within the competence of the eight different administrations. The Council is mirrored at the legislative level by the British-Irish Parliamentary

---

[91] The Equal Opportunities Commission for Northern Ireland, the Fair Employment Commission, the Commission for Racial Equality in Northern Ireland and the Northern Ireland Disability Council.

[92] The function of these bodies is described in more detail at paras 6.47–6.61.

[93] Attendance from Northern Ireland is governed by s 52 of the Northern Ireland Act 1998. In 2001 two Sinn Féin MLAs successfully sought judicial review of David Trimble's refusal to nominate them for meetings of the North-South Ministerial Council: *In re De Brun and McGuinness' Application* [2001] 8 BNIL 12 (NICA).

[94] Northern Ireland Act 1998, s 55.

[95] www.waterwaysireland.org.

[96] www.safefoodonline.com.

[97] www.intertradeireland.com

[98] www.northsouthministerialcouncil.org/trade.htm.

[99] www.northsouthministerialcouncil.org/language.htm.

[100] www.northsouthministerialcouncil.org/aqua.htm.

[101] Strand Three of the Agreement, para 1.

Assembly,[102] a successor to the British-Irish Inter-Parliamentary Body. This Assembly comprises 25 representatives from each of the UK and Irish Parliaments, five representatives from each of the Scottish Parliament, the National Assembly of Wales and the Northern Ireland Assembly, and one representative from each of the States of Jersey, the States of Guernsey and the Tynwald of the Isle of Man. It holds two plenary sessions a year but its four committees (which look at sovereign matters between the Irish and Westminster parliaments, European affairs, economic matters, and the environment and social matters) meet several times a year. The Assembly's reports are sent to the various governments for comment.

2.49 There is, in addition, a British-Irish Inter-Governmental Conference, which replaced the Anglo-Irish Inter-Governmental Conference established under the Anglo-Irish Agreement 1985.[103] It focuses on promoting bilateral co-operation on matters of mutual interest between the UK and Irish governments, mainly, but not exclusively, in relation to Northern Ireland.

THE NORTHERN IRELAND OFFICE

2.50 The UK Government continues to play a role in Northern Ireland through the Northern Ireland Office (NIO), a department headed by the Secretary of State for Northern Ireland with offices in both London and Belfast. When the Secretary of State stays in Northern Ireland he resides at Hillsborough Castle in County Down. The NIO oversees the devolution settlement and represents the interests of Northern Ireland within the UK Government (and vice-versa). It is still the office responsible for appointing people to the Parades Commission of Northern Ireland and to the Northern Ireland Human Rights Commission. The Crown Solicitors Office in Belfast (see para 11.6 below), which provides legal services on Northern Ireland issues to UK government departments and other public bodies in Northern Ireland, is also part of the NIO.

2.51 The Secretary of State must comply with the law just like every other individual, but sometimes even a cabinet Minister can fall below the required standards. In *An Application for Judicial Review by Brenda Downes*,[104] for example, the Court of Appeal in Northern Ireland held that Peter Hain, the then Secretary of State, had failed to take into account a relevant consideration when appointing Mrs Bertha McDougall as the Interim Victims Commissioner for Northern Ireland in 2005: he had

---

[102] www.britishirish.org.

[103] By s 54(2) of the Northern Ireland Act 1998 the First and Deputy First Ministers must ensure that there is cross-community attendance by Ministers and junior Ministers at meetings of the Conference.

[104] [2009] NICA 26.

neglected to *take into account* the Code issued by the Commissioner for Public Appointments on how such appointments should be made in Northern Ireland, even though he was not legally obliged to *comply* with that Code.[105] To that extent the Code constrained the prerogative powers of the Secretary of State (see para 2.38). The court therefore declared the appointment to be unlawful, but as the office-holder's term of office had already expired by then the ruling had no practical effect, except to serve as a warning for the future (see too para 7.91).[106]

THE CIVIL SERVICE

2.52   It is the Northern Ireland Civil Service which staffs the various departments of government within Northern Ireland. The head of the Northern Ireland Civil Service co-ordinates the work of the 12 Northern Ireland departments and serves as the secretary to the Executive Committee, much as the most senior civil servant in the UK Civil Service acts as the Cabinet Secretary in London.[107] Officials working for the Northern Ireland Office are members of the UK Civil Service, not the Northern Ireland Civil Service, although the terms and conditions under which they are employed are very similar.[108]

2.53   The constitutional convention throughout the UK is that government Ministers take political responsibility for administrative errors committed by civil servants. On occasions this may lead to Ministers resigning, along with or in place of the senior civil servant involved in the mishap. Ministers can also be politically damaged if their 'Special Advisers' (SPADs) make mistakes. There are 19 SPADs in Northern Ireland – three for the First Minister, three for the Deputy First Minister, and one of each of all the other Ministers, including the two Junior Ministers in the OFMDFM. These advisers are appointed privately, not through a public competition, and they are not civil servants. Naturally there can often be significant tension between their role and that of senior civil servants. In 2011 a political row broke out when a Sinn Féin Minister appointed as a Special Adviser a woman who had been convicted of murdering the 22-year-old daughter of a resident magistrate in 1984. The Adviser was later replaced

---

[105] Ibid [12].

[106] In his subsequent memoirs Peter Hain severely criticised the judge in this case, Girvan J, but in the paperback version he later inserted a partial apology: *Outside In* (London, Biteback Publishing, 2012), 331–3 and 453–5.

[107] But the Cabinet Secretary is no longer 'Head of the Civil Service'.

[108] But see P Carmichael, 'The Northern Ireland Civil Service under Direct Rule and Devolution' (2003) 69 *International Review of Administrative Sciences* 205; D Birrell, 'The Reform Agenda in the Northern Ireland Civil Service: The influences of parity, integration, devolution and direct rule' (2007) 22 *Public Policy and Administration* 275.

and a Private Members Bill was introduced in the Assembly to disqualify people with serious criminal convictions from being appointed as Special Advisers in future.[109]

LOCAL GOVERNMENT

2.54 The present system of local government in Northern Ireland dates from 1973.[110] There are 26 local authorities: two city councils (Belfast and Derry[111]), 13 borough councils and 11 district councils. The 26 councils are subdivided into district electoral areas, which in turn are subdivided into 582 wards. Every four years between five and seven councillors are elected under a single transferable vote system to represent each district electoral area. City and borough councils may call the chairperson of their council the Mayor (in Belfast, the Lord Mayor) and may designate up to one quarter of their councillors as 'aldermen'; they may also confer the freedom of the city or borough on distinguished persons. Otherwise the powers and functions of all 26 authorities are the same. Councils can now pay basic allowances to councillors, as well as their expenses.[112]

2.55 The councils' powers are by no means as extensive as those given to local authorities in Great Britain. Housing, education, health, and social care, for instance, are no part of their concern, being handled instead by the Northern Ireland Housing Executive,[113] five Education and Library Boards (due to be replaced by a single Education and Skills Authority) and five Health and Social Care Trusts. But the councils still have responsibilities for, amongst other things, environmental health, noise, nuisances, consumer protection, litter prevention, the enforcement of building regulations and the licensing of street trading. The Anti-social Behaviour (NI) Order 2004 allows local authorities (as well as the Northern Ireland Housing Executive and the police) to apply to magistrates' courts for anti-social behaviour orders (ASBOs) in respect of any person over the age of 10 whose actions are such that others need to be protected against them. The Local Government (NI) Order 2005 further increased the powers of local councils by, for example, allowing them to regulate businesses carrying out cosmetic piercing or sun-tanning.

---

[109] At the time of writing the Civil Service (Special Advisers) Bill had just completed its Consideration Stage in the Assembly.

[110] Local Government Act (NI) 1972, as amended. This followed the report of the Review Body on Local Government in Northern Ireland (the Macrory Report), Cmd 546 (NI), 1970.

[111] The official name of the council is Derry City Council, but the county is still officially called Londonderry.

[112] Local Government (Payments to Councillors) Regs (NI) 1999 (SR 449).

[113] www.nihe.gov.uk.

2.56   In 2002, mindful that there were more than 150 public bodies in Northern Ireland for a population of less than 1.7 million, the UK Government initiated a Review of Public Administration in the province.[114] When this Review was completed in 2005 it recommended a rationalisation of education and health authorities as well as a reduction in the number of local councils. In the Programme for Government of the current Northern Ireland Executive, published in March 2012, there is a commitment to reduce the number of councils to 11, and the boundaries for the new council areas were provided for in secondary legislation later that year.[115] There is a plan to allow the new council areas to operate in shadow form prior to the next council elections in 2015. It is also possible that additional powers over matters such as housing and urban regeneration will be conferred on the councils before or at the time of the changeover.

2.57   Like central government departments, local councils and other public authorities dealing with matters such as education and health are not above the law: their decisions can often be challenged in a court or tribunal by way of applications for judicial review (paras 6.5–6.11). This was made clear in several court cases arising out of some councillors' opposition to Sinn Féin or to the Anglo-Irish Agreement of 1985.[116]

---

[114] www.rpani.gov.uk.
[115] Local Government (Boundaries) Order (NI) 2012 (SR 421).
[116] See, eg, *Re Curran and McCann's Application* [1985] NI 261 and *In re Neeson's Application* [1986] 13 NIJB 24. For further details, see B Hadfield, 'The Northern Ireland Constitution Act 1973: Lessons for Minority Rights', in P Cumper and S Wheatley (eds), *Minority Rights in the 'New' Europe* (The Hague, Martinus Nijhoff, 1999), 129–46.

3

Legislation in Northern Ireland

THE TWO SOURCES OF LAW

3.1 The legal system of Northern Ireland is a 'common law' system, which means that its laws are created not just by people who sit in legislatures but also by judges who make rulings in court cases. If and when a majority of the people living in Northern Ireland vote to leave the UK and to join the Republic of Ireland in a reunified Ireland, the nature of the legal system in the northern part of the island will not change significantly, for the Republic of Ireland's legal system is a common law system too. The UK and Ireland are the only common law countries in Europe. France and Germany, for example, are 'civil law' countries, which means that their laws ultimately derive from ancient Roman law and that they do not permit judges to issue rulings that make new laws: judges must simply apply the laws that have already been issued by the nation's legislature. Most of the predominantly English-speaking countries in the world have common law systems, but some, like South Africa, are considered to be 'mixed' systems.

3.2 The two main sources of law in Northern Ireland are, therefore, 'legislation' and 'case law'. This means that if you want to look up the law on a particular point you need to know how to trawl through the extensive body of legislation and court judgments that has accumulated over centuries. Now that we live in a digital age this task is much easier, with practically all the laws being available through the internet, mostly free of charge. But lawyers still use printed volumes to a considerable extent. This chapter will explain how to access both soft and hard copies of legislation relating to Northern Ireland, the emphasis being on making sure that the law which is accessed is fully up-to-date. Chapter 4 will explain case law and how to access it.

BASIC PRINCIPLES RELATING TO LEGISLATION

3.3 For the avoidance of confusion, it is important to clarify straightaway some basic principles governing the sources of law in Northern Ireland. In most countries the sources of law are regulated to some degree by the country's Constitution, which usually takes the form of a long single document that has been amended from time to time. The UK, as we know from Chapter 2, does not have such a single document. Instead its Constitution is scattered among a range of documents, including Acts of Parliament and judgments issued by courts, some of them issued many centuries ago. The five basic principles which follow are deduced from those documents.

(1)   In the UK, legislation issued as an Act of Parliament at Westminster is the highest form of law and takes precedence over all other forms. As explained in Chapter 2, lawyers describe this situation as 'the doctrine of parliamentary sovereignty', where the word 'sovereignty' is used to mean 'supremacy'. Acts of the UK Parliament are referred to as 'primary legislation'.

(2)   In general, the UK Parliament cannot prevent itself from acting differently in the future; it is not limited in what it can do by any higher constitutional principle than the doctrine of parliamentary sovereignty. Occasionally, however, Acts of the UK Parliament are considered to have a greater status than other Acts and courts can then rule that the other Acts must be interpreted in a way which complies with the Acts which have greater status. These special Acts are sometimes referred to today as 'constitutional Acts' (see para 2.14). Among them are the Bill of Rights 1689, the European Communities Act 1972, the Human Rights Act 1998 and (more controversially) the Northern Ireland Act 1998, which implemented the Belfast (Good Friday) Agreement.

(3)   In situations where courts are confronted with Acts of Parliament that appear to be inconsistent, and provided one of the Acts is not a so-called constitutional Act, the court must give priority to the Act which was passed more recently.

(4)   Legislation issued by some other authority, such as a government department, after it has been empowered to do so by an Act of the UK Parliament is in general a lower form of law than primary legislation but a higher form of law than case law. It is referred to as 'secondary', 'subordinate', or 'delegated' legislation. The only time a court can declare such secondary legislation to be illegal is when it purports to do something which the authority issuing it was not empowered by Parliament to do. Such illegal secondary legislation is then said to be '*ultra vires*', which is Latin for 'beyond the powers' (see para 2.4).

(5)   There is a constitutional convention (ie custom and practice) that legislation, whether primary or secondary, should not be retrospective in operation, but occasionally this is ignored, as when the government needs to validate some past or current activities which would otherwise be illegal. An example is the Northern Ireland Act 1972, which declared that from 1920 onwards the law was in fact different from what it was

said to be by the judges in *R (Hume) v Londonderry Justices* (1972).[1] In a more recent case a Northern Ireland judge said that if an Act is silent as to whether it is retrospective or not then a test of fairness has to be applied to see whether it should operate retrospectively.[2]

3.4 In the following sections of this chapter further details are given about the various types of legislation applicable in Northern Ireland and how to access the relevant documents.

ACTS OF THE UK PARLIAMENT

3.5 Acts of the UK Parliament, as noted, can be called primary legislation. The Scottish Parliament also issues Acts, as does the Northern Ireland Assembly, but strictly speaking these are all examples of secondary legislation (albeit an important type of that kind of legislation, as indicated at para 3.16 below) because they are made by an authority which has been empowered to do so by an Act of the UK Parliament. The UK Acts in question (which can be called 'enabling Acts' or 'parent Acts') are, respectively, the Scotland Act 1998 and the Northern Ireland Act 1998. Another word for Acts of Parliament, whichever body makes them, is 'statutes'. The phrase 'statute law' is sometimes used to refer to a collection of Acts of Parliament. When a new Act has been passed lawyers sometimes say it has been added to 'the statute book'.

3.6 The vast majority of Acts of the UK Parliament can also be referred to as 'public' Acts, because they potentially affect the whole of the general public. The number of public Acts enacted by the Westminster Parliament varies from year to year. In 2010 there were 41 Acts, in 2011 there were 25 and in 2012 there were 23. In addition to public Acts, some local, or private, Acts, are passed from time to time. These are statutes concerned only with a particular locality or company. In 2010 there were five local Acts, in 2011 there was none and in 2012 there were two.[3]

3.7 Local, or private, Acts should not be confused with Private Members' Bills, which are proposals for public Acts introduced and piloted through Parliament by an MP or peer who happens to do well in a parliamentary ballot. These are held in both Houses of Parliament – the Commons and the Lords – at the start of each parliamentary session. Usually only one or two of these Bills get passed into law each year, most of the others failing because they are opposed by the government. Famous examples of Private Members' Bills which did get passed are the Obscene Publications Act 1959,

---

[1] [1972] NI 91. See the discussion of this case at para 2.4.
[2] *Re Partition Acts 1868 and 1876, Ulster Bank Ltd v Carter* [1999] NI 93.
[3] The Bank of Ireland (UK) plc Act 2012 and the London Local Authorities Act 2012.

introduced by Roy Jenkins MP, and the Abortion Act 1967, introduced by David Steel MP. Only two Private Members' Bills have been successfully piloted through the House of Commons by Northern Ireland MPs. Gerry Fitt MP introduced what became the Chronically Sick and Disabled Persons (NI) Act 1978 and Martin Smyth MP introduced the Disabled Persons (NI) Act 1989. Both Acts largely reflect earlier legislation already in place for England and Wales.[4]

3.8   During the era of direct rule in Northern Ireland (when no legislature existed in Belfast), the UK Parliament continued to enact both public and local Acts for Northern Ireland, although these were both rare. If Acts were applied to Northern Ireland they usually applied as well to the rest of the UK, or at least to England and Wales. But exceptions were made when Westminster needed to deal with constitutional or electoral crises in Northern Ireland.[5] Acts of the UK Parliament that are confined in operation to Northern Ireland have the words 'Northern Ireland' either in the main part of the title of the Act or within brackets *before* the word 'Act'. Examples are the Northern Ireland (Emergency Provisions) Act 1987 and the Fair Employment (Northern Ireland) Act 1989. The words 'Northern Ireland' are often abbreviated to 'NI'. The main way in which legislation confined to Northern Ireland was passed during the period between the demise of the Stormont Parliament in 1972 and the establishment of the Northern Ireland Assembly in 1999 (and also during subsequent years when the Assembly was suspended, such as between 2002 and 2007), was by using the 'Order in Council procedure'. This was first authorised by the Northern Ireland (Temporary Provisions) Act 1972 and then by the Northern Ireland Acts 1974, 1998 and 2000. Orders in Council are an example of secondary legislation and are therefore described more fully later in this chapter (paras 3.23–3.31).

3.9   Sometimes Parliament at Westminster enacts an Act the purpose of which is to *consolidate* previous statutes, that is, to put into one Act all the various existing enactments already dealing with a particular matter. Examples of this are the Employment Protection (Consolidation) Act 1978 and the Social Security Contributions and Benefits (NI) Act 1993. Occasionally statutes are passed in order to *codify* existing statute and judge-made law on a topic. These statutes represent a fresh start on the topic and usually change the existing law significantly. An example is the Theft

---

[4] An example of a Private Members' Bill introduced in the House of Lords is the Criminal Cases Review (Insanity) Act 1999, which was prompted by the decision of the Court of Appeal in Northern Ireland in *Criminal Cases Review Commission's Reference under s 14(3) of the Criminal Appeal Act 1995* [1998] NI 275. It was introduced by Lord Ackner, a retired Law Lord. See too the Education (NI) Act 1978, which was introduced by Lord Dunleath in an attempt to bolster integrated education in Northern Ireland.

[5] Eg the Northern Ireland Constitution Act 1973, the Northern Ireland Acts 1974, 1998 and 2000, and the Electoral Registration (NI) Act 2005.

Act 1968. This Act applied only in England and Wales, but the Stormont Parliament passed a similar codifying Act for Northern Ireland – the Theft Act (NI) 1969 (see para 7.20).

HOW ACTS OF PARLIAMENT ARE MADE

3.10 Acts of the UK Parliament are made by being drafted as a Bill and then enacted as an Act. Officially they are made by 'The Queen in Parliament'. This means that they must be approved not only by the two Houses of Parliament (the House of Commons and the House of Lords) but also by the monarch. In 1911, by the Parliament Act of that year, Parliament curtailed the power of the House of Lords to block draft legislation that had already been agreed by the House of Commons, and in 1949 it curtailed it even further by another Parliament Act. The position today is that the House of Lords can delay a Bill only by a year; thereafter the House of Commons can enact the Bill notwithstanding the opposition of the Lords.[6] Recent examples of legislation passed in accordance with the Parliament Act 1949, that is, by the Commons alone and without the consent of the Lords, are the War Crimes Act 1991, the European Parliamentary Elections Act 1999 and the Hunting Act 2004. The monarch, moreover, no longer refuses to assent to an Act of Parliament presented to her.[7] As the House of Commons is usually dominated by MPs belonging to the political party which has formed the government, it is the government (and within that the Cabinet) which in practice decides what legislation should be passed. The government's intentions are made clear in the Queen's Speech at the beginning of each parliamentary session, which usually begins in November of each year, although there is no fixed date (in 2013 it began in May).

3.11 The great majority of public Acts start life as proposals put to the Cabinet, either by a Cabinet committee or by a particular government department through its representative on the Cabinet.[8] Often the proposals will have been preceded by a government White Paper on the topic, and perhaps by a Green Paper before that. From the Cabinet the proposals are sent in the form of departmental instructions to the Office of Parliamentary Counsel, whose expert staff have the task of actually drafting the legislation. Legislative drafting is a specialised skill. The policy instructions of the

---

[6] Parliament Act 1949, amending the Parliament Act 1911. The legality of the 1949 Act was confirmed in litigation brought by the Countryside Alliance in relation to the Hunting Act 2004: see para 2.11.

[7] There is now a constitutional convention that the Queen will not refuse the Royal Assent to a Bill passed by both Houses of Parliament, although it has been suggested that she has a personal human right to refuse to assent: R Blackburn, 'The Royal Assent to Legislation and a Monarch's Fundamental Human Rights' [2003] *PL* 205.

[8] See generally M Zander, *The Law Making Process* (6th edn, Cambridge, Cambridge UP, 2004) ch 1.

government department in question have to be translated into unambiguous legal language, with care being taken not to distort the intention behind the instructions or to leave any gaps or loopholes in the law. The Act must also be tied in with whatever legislation already exists on the topic. During the legislation's passage through Parliament the draftsperson will be at hand to advise Ministers and prepare any necessary amendments.

3.12   The passage of the draft legislation through Parliament at Westminster is usually a long and complicated process.[9] The standard procedure is for a Bill to be introduced into the House of Commons, where it is dealt with in five stages:

(1)   First Reading
(2)   Second Reading
(3)   Committee Stage
(4)   Report Stage
(5)   Third Reading.

The first reading is a formality. At the second reading stage the general principles of the Bill are discussed. It is at the committee and report stages that detailed amendments to the Bill are mostly considered. After the third reading the Bill is then sent to the House of Lords, where similar stages must be gone through, and if any amendments are suggested these must be returned to the House of Commons to be considered further.

3.13   A Bill which does not complete all of its stages during one parliamentary session (which usually runs from November of one year to October of the next) can be carried over to the following session, but a Bill cannot be carried over from one Parliament to the next: when a general election is called Parliament is dissolved and after the election the new Parliament starts its legislative programme from scratch. Once the parliamentary stages of a Bill are complete it is then accorded Royal Assent and immediately becomes an Act, although the date on which it comes into force will depend on what the Act itself says about its commencement (see para 3.15(7)). Acts are now published in conjunction with 'Explanatory Notes'. These explain in more simple language the intended effect of each section or group of sections in the Act, but they are not officially approved by Parliament.

3.14   The enactment of legislation at Westminster usually takes several months, although Bills which are really urgent can be dealt with in a day or two. The Northern Ireland Act 1972, for example, went through all of its stages within the space of five hours.[10] In 1974, following the Birmingham pub bombings, the Prevention of Terrorism (Temporary Provisions) Act

---

[9] Ibid ch 3.
[10] This is the Act which reversed the decision in *R (Hume) v Londonderry Justices*: see paras 2.4 and 3.3(5).

was passed in great haste too, as was the Criminal Justice (Terrorism and Conspiracy) Act 1998 in the wake of the Omagh atrocity in August 1998. The Anti-terrorism, Crime and Security Act 2001, enacted after the events on 9/11 in the United States, was rushed through the UK Parliament in just over three weeks during November and December 2001 – still a comparatively short timetable.

THE FORM OF ACTS OF PARLIAMENT

3.15   Today, Acts of the UK Parliament are set out in a traditional format, as illustrated by the Table of Contents from the Civil Aviation Act 2012, which is reproduced in Appendix 1 to this book. Having looked at the Table of Contents readers should try to access the full text of the Act online or in a law library (see paras 3.57 and 3.61). It displays most of the standard features of an Act of Parliament.

(1)   *The Chapter number* ('19'). This is the number given to the Act at the time of its publication; its purpose is simply to make identification of the Act easier when it is being looked up in a volume of statutes or online.

(2)   *The long title.* This provides a brief summary of the Act's purposes; it expands upon the Act's short title, on which see point (9) below.[11]

(3)   *The date* ('19th November 2012'). This comes immediately after the long title and is the date on which the Act was finally made, ie the date on which the Royal Assent was given. However, the granting of Royal Assent does not automatically bring an Act into force. This will be so only if the Act contains no other indication as to when or how it is to be brought into force (see point (7) below).

(4)   *The enacting words* ('Be it enacted...'). This is a standard formula placed at the beginning of all statutes of the UK Parliament, although the wording is slightly different for those statutes passed by the House of Commons alone.

(5)   *Parts, sections and subsections.* Most Acts have more than one Part, numbered 1, 2, 3 etc, with each Part dealing with a separate set of issues. Occasionally, Parts of statutes will be sub-divided into Chapters, and to help readers to find a particular provision, some very long Acts are now published with an index. Each Part or Chapter will contain several sections, which are also numbered 1, 2, 3, etc. Sections are in turn divided into subsections, which are numbered (1), (2), (3), etc. Subsections can then be split into paragraphs: (a), (b), (c)

---

[11] An Act's short title can be changed by a later Act; eg the Constitutional Reform Act 2005, Sch 11, para 1, changed the name of the Supreme Court Act 1981 to the Senior Courts Act 1981.

etc. The next subdivision, if needed, is called a subparagraph: (i), (ii), (iii), etc. Reference is made to a subparagraph by writing it as follows: s 32(2)(b)(i) (pronounced as 'section thirty-two, two, b, one'). While a statute is passing through Parliament it is called a Bill, not an Act, and its provisions are divided into clauses, not sections, but further subdivisions are still called subsections and paragraphs.

(6)   *The interpretation section.* Most statutes contain one or more sections defining more precisely some of the expressions used in the Act as a whole or in a Part of the Act. The Civil Aviation Act 2012, in section 72, defines some terms but also refers to Schedule 7 to the Act, where there is an index of all the terms defined throughout the Act. Note that a word like 'cargo' is defined in section 72 as 'including' mail; this is therefore not a complete definition of the term, so a judge may have to decide in a subsequent case whether some other item (eg a passenger's hand luggage) counts as 'cargo'.

(7)   *The commencement section* (s 110). Often the penultimate section of every Act, as here (s 31), contains a provision telling us when the Act is to come into force. Note that section 28 makes it clear that in this context the commencement orders issued by the Treasury are to take the form of statutory instruments (see para 3.32 below). In some cases Acts are not commenced until years after the granting of Royal Assent: the Equal Pay Act (NI) 1970, for instance, was not brought into force until 1976. The Easter Act 1928 (which provided for a fixed date for Easter), the Employment of Children Act 1973 (which further restricted the employment of children under the upper limit of school age) and the Smoke Detectors Act 1991 (which required all new dwellings to be fitted with smoke detectors) are examples of Acts where the mechanism for bringing them into force has *never* been activated.[12]

(8)   *The extent section.* This section (s 111) makes it clear in which parts of the UK the Act is to apply. Here it is clear that the Act is to apply in Northern Ireland.

(9)   *The short title section* (s 113). Every Act of the UK Parliament now ends with a section giving the short title of the Act. When a statute is passed that deals with a topic for which legislation already exists, it often states that the Acts can now be referred to together (eg the Fatal Accidents Acts 1959–1977).

(10) *Schedules.* Many Acts contain one or more Schedules setting out further details of matters mentioned in the body of the Act. The Civil Aviation Act contains 14 schedules, which together are almost as long (54 pages) as the main body of the Act (67 pages). If the Act is not making too many amendments to earlier legislation these may be set out in the body of the Act itself (as in s 76(1) and s 106(1) of the Civil

---

[12] *Current Law Statutes (Service File)* contains a useful loose-leaf table listing alphabetically the statutory provisions enacted since 1949 which are not yet in force.

Aviation Act 2012), otherwise they will be included in a schedule (as in Schedule 9 to this Act). Schedules are not self-enacting: somewhere in the Act there will be a provision stating that the Schedules are to have the force of law (see s 76 for Schedule 9 to this Act). Schedules can be divided into Parts, which are then divided into paragraphs, subparagraphs and sub-subparagraphs if required.

SECONDARY LEGISLATION

3.16   All pieces of secondary legislation are ultimately the offspring of a parent (or 'enabling') Act of Parliament. They are used in order to set out the law in more detail than that found in primary legislation, or where it would be too time-consuming to invoke the full Parliamentary law-making process just to make a fairly minor alteration to some existing legislative arrangements. The parent Act will give power to another law-making authority to issue the detailed laws on a particular matter. This law-making authority is usually the head of a government department (ie a Secretary of State) but it can also be, for instance, the Privy Council (which makes Orders in Council), a committee of judges and lawyers (which makes Rules of Court), or a district council or public authority (which makes local by-laws). The exact title of the particular piece of secondary legislation will depend on the wording of the parent Act; it may provide for an Order in Council, an order, regulations, rules, schemes, or by-laws. Nothing turns on the differences in title – all varieties of secondary legislation are equally binding as laws of the land, but not all of the documents will be equally easy to find: not all of them, for example, are published as 'statutory rules' (see para 3.35).

3.17   As already mentioned (see paras 2.4 and 3.3(4)), the most important legal difference between primary and secondary legislation is that secondary legislation *can* be declared by a court to be illegal, whereas primary legislation cannot. This can occur when the body or person which has issued the secondary legislation has acted beyond the powers conferred on that body or person by an Act of Parliament. Such secondary legislation is then *ultra vires* and is of no effect. Acts of the Northern Ireland Assembly, like Acts of the Stormont Parliament, are secondary legislation but so far no such Acts, or sections within them, have been declared illegal by a court for going beyond the law-making powers conferred on the regional legislature by the UK Parliament.[13]

---

[13] For a recent example of this concerning a Measure of the Welsh Assembly, see para 2.28, n 44).

ACTS OF THE NORTHERN IRELAND ASSEMBLY

3.18 Acts of the Northern Ireland Assembly are introduced into the Assembly by a member of the Northern Ireland Executive in the form of a Bill. Assembly Committees also have the power to introduce Bills, but to date they have not exercised it. The Executive will have already discussed the proposed Bill, and instructions on what the Bill needs to do will have been passed by the government department responsible for the Bill to professionals in the Office of the Legislative Draftsman in Belfast (the equivalent of the Office of Parliamentary Counsel in London: see para 3.11).

3.19 Bills in the Northern Ireland Assembly must go through even more stages than Bills at Westminster.[14] The Assembly's Standing Orders provide for the following:

(i)   First Stage, when the Bill is formally introduced by the Clerk of the Assembly reading its title[15]
(ii) Second Stage, when there is a general debate on the Bill's general principles
(iii) Committee Stage, when, normally within 30 days of the Second Stage, the details of the Bill are investigated by a committee of the Assembly and reported to the full Assembly together with proposals for amendments
(iv) Consideration Stage, when all Members of the Legislative Assembly (MLAs) can vote on the details of the Bill, including proposed amendments
(v)   Further Consideration Stage, when further such votes can take place
(vi) Final Stage, when the Bill is either passed or rejected without further amendment.

3.20 At any point before the Final Stage, the Bill can be referred to the Northern Ireland Human Rights Commission for advice on whether the Bill is compatible with human rights, and/or to an *ad hoc* Assembly Committee on Conformity with Equality Requirements for a report on whether the Bill complies with standards on equality and human rights.[16] After the Final Stage the Bill can be reconsidered by the Assembly if, for example, the Supreme Court has decided that part of it is not within the legislative competence of the Assembly (see para 2.28). Normally there must be an interval of five working days between each stage of a Bill; the stages can be accelerated but, contrary to the position at Westminster (see para 3.14), no Bill can pass through all of its stages in less than 10

[14] Northern Ireland Act 1998, s 13.
[15] An explanatory and financial memorandum must accompany the Bill on its introduction.
[16] To date the first type of referral has not occurred (although the Human Rights Commission has often volunteered its advice in any event). The second type of referral occurred for the first time in 2012, in relation to the proposed Welfare Reform Bill (see para 2.45).

days.[17] An uncompleted Bill can be carried forward from one Assembly session to the next if the Assembly so agrees, but not from one Assembly to a newly elected Assembly. A Bill is sent for Royal Assent once all the Assembly stages have been gone through.

3.21   As already explained (see para 3.5), Acts of the Northern Ireland Assembly are a type of secondary legislation, but by and large they have the same form as Acts of the UK Parliament and they are often referred to, albeit inaccurately, as primary legislation. Appendix 2 reproduces the opening of the Presumption of Death Act (NI) 2009, one of the nine Acts enacted by the Assembly in that year. Like the Act of the UK Parliament whose Table of Contents is reproduced in Appendix 1, this Act of the Northern Ireland Assembly has a Chapter number, a long title, a date indicating when Royal Assent was granted, and enacting words (rather more prosaic than in the Act of the UK Parliament). The sub-divisions used in Assembly Acts are the same as in Acts of the UK Parliament (ie parts, chapters, sections, subsections, paragraphs and subparagraphs). They also have sections dealing with interpretation, commencement and the short title, and they can contain Schedules. They do not contain an extent section because the Act will inevitably apply throughout the whole of Northern Ireland and nowhere else.

3.22   Acts of the Northern Ireland Assembly, like statutes of the old Stormont Parliament, which sat between 1921 and 1972, are distinguishable from statutes enacted by Parliament at Westminster because in their title the words 'Northern Ireland' appear *after* the word 'Act', as in the Justice Act (NI) 2011. In Acts of the UK Parliament which apply only, or mainly, in Northern Ireland the words 'Northern Ireland' appear *before* the word 'Act', as in the Justice (NI) Act 2004.

ORDERS IN COUNCIL

3.23   Legislation that is not made directly by the UK Parliament is termed 'secondary', 'subordinate' or 'delegated', legislation. All such legislation has to be actively or passively approved by Parliament, and some of it is actually debated there, but the time available for debates is strictly limited (usually to one-a-half hours) and neither House of Parliament has power to amend draft secondary legislation – it can only approve it or reject it in its entirety. There are several types of secondary legislation applicable in Northern Ireland but the most important category is Orders in Council. They are a sub-set of the category known as statutory instruments (see paras 3.32–3.34).

3.24   Orders in Council are viewed as the most important type of secondary legislation because they are formally made by the Queen on the

---

[17] Standing Orders of the Northern Ireland Assembly, Order 42 (5).

advice of her Privy Counsellors (ie senior government Ministers of the day). However in legal terms they carry no more weight than any other type of delegated legislation. There are a number of Acts providing for the making of Orders in Council which might apply in Northern Ireland as well as in other parts of the UK, but the reason for listing Orders in Council here as a separate type of secondary legislation is that, during the suspension and then abolition of the Northern Ireland Parliament in the period 1972 to 1999, and at intervals since then, when the Northern Ireland Assembly was suspended and direct rule re-imposed, there have been a number of enabling Acts which have allowed legislation to be made in the form of Orders in Council on matters that would previously have been dealt with by an Act of the Northern Ireland Parliament or Assembly. These enabling Acts, which succeeded one another, are the Northern Ireland (Temporary Provisions) Act 1972, the Northern Ireland Act 1974, the Northern Ireland Act 1998, and the Northern Ireland Act 2000.

3.25 For example, Orders in Council made under the Northern Ireland Act 1974 created laws for Northern Ireland on subjects which, being 'transferred matters' under the Northern Ireland Constitution Act 1973, would have been legislated for by the Northern Ireland Assembly if that body had survived the first few months of 1974 (see para 1.24). 'Reserved matters' under the Northern Ireland Constitution Act 1973 were also dealt with by Orders in Council. Only 'excepted matters' had to be legislated for by an Act of Parliament at Westminster. 'Law and order' was a reserved matter but 'terrorism' was an excepted matter, which is why there were various Criminal Evidence (NI) *Orders* but Northern Ireland (Emergency Provisions) *Acts*.

Orders in Council during devolution

3.26 When powers were devolved to the Northern Ireland Assembly in 1999, the Order in Council procedure provided for in the Northern Ireland Act 1974 was abolished. The position reverted, more or less, to what it had been prior to the abolition of the Stormont Parliament in 1972. Some Acts governing Northern Ireland were then made in Belfast, while others were made in London, and likewise some pieces of secondary legislation governing Northern Ireland were made in Belfast (in the form of statutory rules – see para 3.35), while others were made in London (in the form of statutory instruments – see para 3.32). The categories of 'transferred', 'reserved' and 'excepted' matters are not the same under the Northern Ireland Act 1998 as they were under the Northern Ireland Constitution Act 1973 or under the Government of Ireland Act 1920. But partly because the range of 'reserved' matters is greater in the 1998 Act than it was in the 1973 Act, the 1998

Act keeps in place the Privy Council's power to make Orders in Council for Northern Ireland.[18] More particularly, it allows Orders in Council to be made which amend existing Northern Ireland legislation on reserved matters; drafts of these Orders have to be referred to the Northern Ireland Assembly for its consideration and if the Assembly reports its views to the Secretary of State the latter must submit a copy of this report along with a draft of the Order to both Houses of Parliament at Westminster.[19] This was the procedure adopted, for example, for the Sexual Offences (NI) Order 2008, which amended various previous Orders (and Acts). Since criminal justice was devolved to the Assembly in 2010 this kind of Order in Council has become a rarity. In fact no Order in Council at all has been made for Northern Ireland since 2009.

3.27 When the Northern Ireland Assembly was suspended in February 2000 (for what turned out to be about four months), the power to make Orders in Council at Westminster was revived by virtue of the Northern Ireland Act 2000.[20] The Equality (Disability, etc) (NI) Order 2000 and the Flags (NI) Order 2000 were made during this period. Through judicial review proceedings (see paras 6.5–6.11) a Sinn Féin MLA challenged the Secretary of State's right to place the Flags (NI) Order before Parliament for its consideration, but the challenge failed.[21] When the Assembly was again suspended at midnight on 14 October 2002, the Northern Ireland Act 2000 operated to restore the power to make Orders in Council. In the four calendar years which elapsed before the Assembly was restored again in May 2007 a total of 84 Orders in Council were made under the 2000 Act.

The nature and validity of Orders in Council

3.28 Orders in Council are published and numbered as UK statutory instruments, a separate 'NI' number being given to them for publication in annual collections of Northern Ireland 'statutes'. These collections continue the series known as 'Acts of the Northern Ireland Parliament'. Although they are not Acts, Orders in Council do display two important features which are otherwise reserved for Acts. First, they often delegate law-making powers to other authorities, even though the general rule for secondary legislation is that such sub-delegation of powers is not possible.[22] Second, Orders in Council often amend or repeal Acts, which again is contrary to the normal rule for secondary legislation. Sections in legislation which allow subsequent secondary legislation to amend existing primary legislation are

---

[18] ss 84–86.
[19] s 85(4)–(6).
[20] Para 1(1) of the Schedule.
[21] *In re Murphy's Application* [2001] 8 BNIL 11.
[22] The Latin maxim is *delegatus non potest delegare*.

called 'Henry VIII clauses', because they were much used during that king's reign (1509–47).[23]

3.29   One respect in which Orders in Council made under the Northern Ireland Acts are clearly different from primary legislation is that they can be invalidated by the courts if they violate any of the European Convention rights set out in the Human Rights Act 1998. This follows implicitly from section 3 of the Act, when read together with the definition of 'subordinate legislation' in section 21(1). In one recent case, *In re G (Adoption: Unmarried Couple)*,[24] the House of Lords held that Article 14 of the Adoption (NI) Order 1987, which prevented unmarried couples in Northern Ireland from applying jointly to adopt a child, was invalid and could be ignored. The prohibition was deemed to violate the rule in Article 14 of the European Convention on Human Rights that unmarried people cannot be discriminated against in comparison with married people if the discrimination relates to one of the other Convention rights such as the right to a family life guaranteed by Article 8. Likewise, in *Re ES's Application*,[25] where a mother complained that a provision in the Children (NI) Order 1995[26] prevented her for at least 72 hours from challenging a court order requiring her child to be taken into emergency protection (see para 9.137(4)), the judge held that this was invalid because it violated the mother's rights under both Articles 6 and 8 of the European Convention.[27]

3.30   Extracts from a typical Order in Council, the Theft (NI) Order 1978, are set out in Appendix 3 to this book. The following typical features may be noted:

(1)   *Its number* ('23'). Each Order in Council made for Northern Ireland under the Northern Ireland Acts is given both a UK statutory instrument number (here it is 1251) and also a Northern Ireland Order in Council number (here it is 23). Statutory instruments are explained below (see para 3.32).

(2)   *Dates* ('29 September 1978'). The date on which an Order in Council is made is the date on which the Queen assents to her Privy Counsellors' recommendations. The date on which the Order comes into force is provided for in the body of the Order itself (see article 1 of the Theft (NI) Order); sometimes it does not come into force until a further statutory commencement order has been made naming an appointed day.

---

[23] See N Barber and A Young, 'The Rise of Prospective Henry VIII Clauses and their Implications for Sovereignty' [2003] *PL* 113. If they are widely worded they will often be objected to by opposition politicians in Parliament, who will be reluctant to delegate very extensive delegated powers to government ministers.

[24] [2008] UKHL 38, [2009] 1 AC 173.

[25] [2007] NIQB 58 (Gillen J).

[26] Art 64(8).

[27] Art 6 protects the right to a fair trial.

(3) *The enacting words* ('Now, therefore, Her Majesty...'). This is another example of a standard formula; the preliminary phrase beginning 'Whereas a draft...' is called the preamble.

(4) *Articles.* Each Order is divided into articles (not sections), with the further subdivisions being referred to as paragraphs and subparagraphs. The numbering and lettering systems are the same as for statutes, for example 'article 2(3)(b)'. (International treaties are also divided into Articles, and the custom is to capitalise the initial letter of the word in that context.)

(5) *The first articles.* These are devoted to setting out the title of the Order, its commencement date (if known), and the meaning of expressions used in it. In statutes, by contrast, these matters are usually dealt with by sections at the end.

(6) *Explanatory note.* This is provided at the very end of all secondary legislation in order to give a brief indication of the effects of the legislation. It is comparable to the long title of a statute (rather than to the explanatory memorandum which now accompanies statutes) but, unlike the long title, it forms no part of the actual enactment and should not be used as an aid to interpretation of the legislation.

3.31 It should be noted that not every item of legislation given the title 'Order' is in fact an Order in Council. Many enabling Acts authorise a government minister to do something 'by order'. Examples are the commencement orders referred to at para 3.15(7) above. The term 'Order' is also used for some pieces of legislation issued under the Crown prerogative: see para 3.50 below.

STATUTORY INSTRUMENTS

3.32 In England and Wales most of the secondary legislation is published in the form of consecutively numbered 'statutory instruments' (SIs). There were 3,328 of these issued in 2012, including 325 just for Wales (these are given an additional number starting with 'W'). A further 360 Scottish Statutory Instruments were made (SSIs). As already indicated (see para 3.31), a common type of statutory instrument is a 'commencement order', which stipulates when an Act, or a certain section of an Act, is to come into force. Commencement orders are now given a separate 'C' number when published (standing for 'commencement'), as well as an 'SI' number. Today, well over half of each year's SIs deal with the prohibition or restriction of traffic so that works can be carried out on roads.

3.33 Some statutory instruments, being made under the authority of a parent Act which extends beyond England and Wales, are applicable in Northern Ireland. Thus, for example, the Immigration and Nationality

(Fees) Regulations 2010[28] apply in Northern Ireland because the enabling Act is a statute in force throughout the UK, namely the Immigration, Asylum and Nationality Act 2002. But the Anti-Slavery Day Act 2010 (Specified Date) Order 2010[29] does not apply in Northern Ireland because the enabling Act (the Anti-Slavery Act 2010) does not apply outside England and Wales. Unfortunately it is not always possible to tell from the title of a statutory instrument whether it applies in Northern Ireland; you have to read the statutory instrument itself or look back at the enabling Act. Some statutory instruments are made in order to comply with the UK's obligations as a member of the European Union: section 2(2) of the European Communities Act 1972 is one of the most important enabling provisions in our law. Some of these SIs apply in Northern Ireland as well as in the other parts of the UK; a recent example is the Measuring Instruments (Non-Prescribed Instruments) Regulations 2006.[30]

3.34   As some Westminster statutes have effect only in Northern Ireland, the legislative powers delegated by such Acts can be effective only in Northern Ireland too. Their title contains the words 'Northern Ireland' *before* the word 'Rules', 'Regulations', 'Order', etc. An example is the Northern Ireland Assembly (Minimum Period) Order 2010,[31] made by the Secretary of State for Northern Ireland under the authority of section 31(6) of the Northern Ireland Act 1998. This Order stipulated that the Assembly had to be dissolved at least 26 days prior to the Assembly elections in 2011.

STATUTORY RULES

3.35   Statutory rules are made by law-making authorities in Northern Ireland under a power conferred by an Act of the UK Parliament, an Act of the Northern Ireland Parliament or Assembly, or by an Order in Council made under the Northern Ireland Acts 1974, 1998 or 2000. They are really Northern Ireland equivalents to the statutory instruments made for the rest of the UK. Sometimes they differ from the corresponding statutory instruments in title alone, the actual content remaining virtually identical. The title will always contain the words 'Northern Ireland' placed in brackets *after* the words 'Rules', 'Regulations', 'Order', 'Scheme', etc. A typical illustration of statutory rules would be the Waste Regulations (NI) 2011,[32] which were made by the Department of the Environment in Northern Ireland acting in exercise of the powers conferred upon it by section 2(2) of the European Communities Act 1972 and various articles in the Waste and Contaminated

[28] SI 778.
[29] SI 2325.
[30] SI 1270.
[31] SI 2944.
[32] SR 127.

Land (NI) Order 1997. The Waste Regulations (NI) 2011 are roughly equivalent to the Waste (England and Wales) Regulations 2011, a statutory instrument.

3.36 As in the case of Orders, not all laws with the title 'Rules' are in fact what they seem. They may not be statutory rules at all but statutory instruments issued just for Northern Ireland on a reserved or excepted matter. An example is the Northern Ireland (Sentences) Act 1998 (Sentence Review Commissioners) Rules 1998.[33] Such statutory instruments are recognisable from the position of the words 'Northern Ireland' *before* the word 'Rules'. It is worth repeating, however, that the difference in title does not affect the legislation's legal status.

3.37 In 2012 there were 461 statutory rules made for Northern Ireland. They were issued by over a dozen rule-making bodies, particularly by the Department of Agriculture and Rural Development and the Department of the Environment, and they dealt with a huge range of subjects. As in the case of statutory instruments, there are types of statutory rules which recur frequently, such as commencement orders and those setting new financial amounts to keep pace with inflation. Respective examples would be the Justice (2011 Act) (Commencement No 5) Order (NI) 2012[34] and the General Register Office (Fees) Order (NI) 2012.[35]

3.38 A typical statutory rule is reproduced in Appendix 4 to this book. It is the Misuse of Drugs (Amendment) Regulations (NI) 2010,[36] made by the Department of Health, Social Services and Public Safety in exercise of powers conferred by the Misuse of Drugs Act 1971 and after consultation with the Advisory Council on the Misuse of Drugs. These days a high proportion of all the statutory rules issued are ones which amend existing rules. There are no special features of this particular statutory rule which require highlighting. We can see that its number in the collection of statutory rules for 2010 is 148, and the attached explanatory note is helpful in placing the rule in context. Note that, even though it is a statutory rule, its title refers to 'Regulations'; this is because the Misuse of Drugs Act 1971, the enabling legislation in this case, says that the Department concerned may do certain things 'by regulation'. Each particular provision can therefore be termed a regulation. If the enabling legislation had authorised the issuing of Rules, or an Order, then each particular provision would have been termed, respectively, a rule or an article.

---

[33] SI 1859, made under the Northern Ireland (Sentences) Act 1998, Sch 2, para 1. These rules regulate the proceedings of the Sentence Review Commissioners in relation to the release on licence and recall of prisoners following the Belfast (Good Friday) Agreement 1998. See para 7.71.
[34] SR 449.
[35] SR 443.
[36] SR 148.

3.39 Many statutory rules, like statutory instruments, deal with local matters such as road traffic or railways. A recent example is the Motor Hackney Carriages (Belfast) (Amendment) By-laws (NI) 2008,[37] made by the Department of the Environment in exercise of powers conferred by article 65 of the Road Traffic (NI) Order 1981. It sets out how much licensed taxi drivers in Belfast can charge their customers. By-laws, incidentally, can also be made by many other public authorities, such as the Fisheries Conservancy Board for Northern Ireland, the Trustees of the Ulster Folk and Transport Museum, and Northern Ireland Railways. By-laws made by district councils are not published as statutory rules but they have the same legal status as such rules.

HOW SECONDARY LEGISLATION IS MADE

3.40 Secondary legislation is invariably drafted only after a period of consultation with interested parties. The final drafting is usually performed by civil servants within the legal branches of the government department concerned, not, as is the case with primary legislation, by parliamentary or legislative counsel (ie experts trained in drafting). But Orders in Council *are* drafted by experts in the Office of the Legislative Draftsman in Belfast.

3.41 Speaking very generally, the precise method of creating secondary legislation depends on the importance of the secondary legislation in question. In all cases, however, the legislation must be approved by Parliament (or the Northern Ireland Assembly) in its entirety; it cannot be amended while it is being debated, although it can be withdrawn and re-laid in a revised form. The Northern Ireland Act 1998 does not specify exactly what procedures are to be followed whenever a Minister of the Executive Committee wishes to issue secondary legislation,[38] but the Assembly's Standing Orders provide that they are to be scrutinised by Assembly Committees.[39]

3.42 Usually the most important pieces of secondary legislation must actually be affirmed by Parliament or the Assembly, a process which puts the onus on the government or Northern Ireland Executive to find time for debates. This is known as 'the affirmative resolution procedure' and if no debate takes place then the secondary legislation cannot come into operation. Secondary legislation which is urgent, and for which no time is immediately available for a parliamentary debate, can be made without first being laid before Parliament or the Assembly, but it must cease to have effect if it is not approved within a specified period, usually 28 or 40 days. This is known as 'the confirmatory resolution procedure'. A third alternative is

---

[37] SR 245.
[38] See in particular ss 22–25.
[39] Standing Order No 41.

'the negative procedure', whereby the secondary legislation takes effect, or continues to have effect if already made, unless a 'prayer' in either House of Parliament (or in the Northern Ireland Assembly) specifically annuls it within 40 days. Given the quantity of secondary legislation requiring to be made, this is the preferred method of proceeding. There is simply not enough time for debates on every proposed statutory instrument or rule.

3.43 Less important secondary legislation may be required to be laid before Parliament or the Assembly but it is not subject to the affirmative, confirmatory or negative procedure. Such legislation cannot be debated, but ministerial questions can be asked about it, and because it must be laid it cannot usually come into force before it has been laid. The least important secondary legislation need not be laid before Parliament or the Assembly at all, although again questions can be asked about it if an MP, peer or MLA happens to have his or her attention drawn to it. The statutory instruments which are afforded this most cursory treatment are mostly local in nature.

3.44 It should be noted, finally, that the making of secondary legislation is not the same as the bringing of it into force. That usually occurs some time later, as provided for in the secondary legislation itself.

FURTHER CONTROLS ON SECONDARY LEGISLATION

3.45 The validity of secondary legislation is controlled both by technical oversight and, if necessary, by the courts. All UK statutory instruments (except Orders in Council made under the Northern Ireland Acts) can be scrutinised from a technical, rather than a merit point of view, by the Joint Committee on Statutory Instruments, composed of 12 representatives from both the House of Commons and the House of Lords. This Committee consults the law-making authority concerned if it thinks that the instrument is technically defective, and the attention of Parliament can then be drawn to the matter.

3.46 The inspection of Northern Ireland secondary legislation, to see if it is technically defective, is carried out by a Statutory Committee in the Assembly or by an official called the Examiner of Statutory Rules.[40] Either body can draw the attention of the Assembly (or of Parliament if the Assembly is suspended) to those statutory rules which are in some way questionable because, for example, they impose a charge on the public revenues (which only Acts can do), they purport to have retrospective effect without any justification, they have been unjustifiably delayed, they appear to be *ultra vires* (ie beyond the powers conferred by the parent Act), they are unclear, or they are defectively drafted. The Examiner of Statutory Rules generally

---

[40] All of the reports of the Examiner of Statutory Rules are available online.

complains if there is a gap of less than 21 days between the laying of a statutory rule and its coming into force, but in practice he or she finds fault with only a tiny minority of the rules examined. Whenever the Examiner complains that a rule may be *ultra vires*, the appropriate law-making authority either lobbies to have the parent Act extended or issues a further rule repealing the offending provision.

3.47 Control by the courts over secondary legislation is sometimes described as 'judicial review', which is described in more detail in Chapter 6 (paras 6.5–6.11). It takes the form of a court decision that a piece of secondary legislation of whatever nature is *ultra vires*. Whether this is the case or not can often be a very controversial legal issue, as is illustrated by the conflicting speeches of the Law Lords in the Northern Ireland case of *McEldowney v Forde*.[41] In that case the issue arose indirectly and not in judicial review proceedings properly so called, but the difficulty of the point was nonetheless considerable. The question was whether the Minister of Home Affairs for Northern Ireland was acting *ultra vires* the Civil Authorities (Special Powers) Act (NI) 1922 when he added 'republican clubs and any like organisation howsoever described' to the list of associations which were unlawful under that Act. The decision turned on whether the Minister's action was 'for the preservation of the peace and maintenance of order' (this being how the 1922 Act limited the Minister's law-making power). By a majority of three to two the Law Lords held that it was.

3.48 The scope of the powers conferred by a parent Act was also in issue (again indirectly) in *R (Hume) v Londonderry Justices*.[42] There, as we saw at paras 2.4 and 3.3, the Divisional Court decided that the granting of power to an army officer to order an assembly of persons to disperse was beyond the power of the Stormont Parliament (and its delegates) because the Government of Ireland Act 1920 said that the Parliament of Northern Ireland was not to have power to make laws 'in respect of the army'. In *Dunkley v Evans*[43] an English court held that the West Coast Herring (Prohibition of Fishing) Order 1978,[44] which was made under the Sea Fish (Conservation) Act 1967 and prohibited herring fishing within a defined area, was partly invalid in that the defined area included an area of the sea adjacent to the coast of Northern Ireland, which was expressly excluded from the scope of the 1967 Act; the Order remained valid as regards the other areas mentioned.

---

[41] [1971] AC 633. See H Calvert 'The 'Republican Clubs' Case' (1970) 21 *NILQ* 191 and (on the Court of Appeal's decision) 'Special Powers Extraordinary' (1969) 20 *NILQ* 1; D N MacCormick, 'Delegated Legislation and Civil Liberty' (1970) 86 *LQR* 171.

[42] [1972] NI 91. Interestingly, the incident at issue in this case occurred before Bloody Sunday on 30 January 1972 but the decision was announced thereafter. The effect was to make some of the army's actions on that day illegal but the hastily enacted Northern Ireland Act 1972 retrospectively validated all such actions.

[43] [1981] 1 WLR 1523.

[44] SI 930.

3.49 These are all instances of secondary legislation being challenged for substantive violation of the parent Act. Procedural violations, such as failure to consult the appropriate authorities before making the statutory rule, or including a provision which prevents the courts from pronouncing on the rule's validity (a so-called 'ouster clause'), are also grounds for judicial review. In *An Application for Judicial Review by the Christian Institute*,[45] for example, a judge quashed (ie invalidated) a provision in the Equality Act (Sexual Orientation) Regulations (NI) 2006[46] dealing with harassment on the ground that there had not been proper consultation about this part of the secondary legislation before it was made. If a piece of secondary legislation is ambiguous to the point of absurdity judges are able to add, omit or substitute words to correct the obvious drafting error.[47]

PREROGATIVE LEGISLATION

3.50 Apart from primary and secondary legislation there is a third type of legislation which requires to be mentioned in passing: legislation created under the Crown's prerogative.[48] This takes the form of prerogative Orders in Council, whereby the Queen simply assents to proposals put before her by senior Ministers who have been appointed Privy Counsellors. The matters regulated by the Crown's prerogative in this way are now limited to particular fields such as the civil service, the armed forces and coinage. In 1984, when Prime Minister Margaret Thatcher wished to ban trade unions at Government Communications Headquarters at Cheltenham (GCHQ), she issued a ruling under a power conferred on her by a prerogative Order in Council, namely the Civil Service Order 1983. The legitimacy of the Order was the subject of considerable litigation, but it survived all challenges.[49]

3.51 Prerogative Orders with a legislative character are inserted in an appendix to the annual volumes of UK statutory instruments (see para 3.65 below) but they are quite different from Parliamentary Orders in Council, which are made under the authority of an Act of Parliament. They are not given a statutory instrument number. Moreover, under the Human Rights Act 1998, prerogative Orders in Council cannot be invalidated by reason

---

[45] [2007] NIQB 66 (Weatherup J).
[46] SR 439.
[47] *R (Confederation of Passenger Transport UK) v Humber Bridge Board* [2004] QB 310, where the Court of Appeal added words to an SI, thereby allowing tolls on the Humber Bridge to be levied even on buses carrying more than 16 passengers.
[48] In 2009 the then Labour Government in the UK published a review of executive Crown prerogative powers (*The Governance of Britain*) and concluded that major reform was unnecessary and inappropriate. See too House of Commons Library Note SN/PC/03861 (30 December 2009).
[49] *Council of Civil Service Unions v Minister for the Civil Service* [1985] AC 374.

of being incompatible with the European Convention on Human Rights,[50] whereas most Parliamentary Orders in Council, including those made under the Northern Ireland Acts, can be (see para 3.29).

OTHER LEGAL DOCUMENTS

3.52   There are various official documents which the lay person often believes have the full force of law but which in fact do not. Even though they are sometimes issued pursuant to a power conferred by an Act of Parliament, they can only influence, not dictate, the judges' views on what the law is. Such publications include the *Highway Code* (published by the Department of the Environment but only some of the rules it contains are actually legal requirements), the *Code of Practice on Picketing* (issued by the Department for Employment and Learning), the *Guide to the Statutory Duties in Section 75 of the Northern Ireland Act 1998* (issued by the Equality Commission for Northern Ireland), the codes of practice agreed to by various trade associations, and the codes of practice issued by the Department of Justice in Northern Ireland under the Police and Criminal Evidence (NI) Order 1989. Indeed codes of practice are becoming common in all sorts of fields.

3.53   Her Majesty's Revenue and Customs frequently issues policy statements which are treated by the courts as having a semi-legislative status: the statements declare that the Revenue and Customs will make extra-statutory concessions, that is, not charge tax on certain specified payments. Statements of practice published by insurance companies, and circulars put out by the Home Office and other government departments on a wide range of legal matters are also in this category. Judges, Masters and Registrars announce what are called 'Practice Directions' in order to provide for better organisation of proceedings within the courts.[51]

HOW TO FIND LEGISLATION

3.54   Even if you can recognise and read a piece of primary or secondary legislation when you find it, this skill will not be much use to you unless you know how to look for the legislation in the first place. The trouble is that most legislation is designed to operate prospectively, that is, for the future and not the past. When new legislation is enacted, it often makes amendments to

---

[50]   P Billings and B Pontin, 'Prerogative Powers and the Human Rights Act: Elevating the Status of Orders in Council' [2001] *PL* 21.

[51]   These are available on the website of the Northern Ireland Courts and Tribunals Service (under 'Judicial Decisions') and are reprinted in the *Bulletin of Northern Ireland Law* (see para 4.53).

legislation which is already in force. The earlier legislation is not re-enacted, or reprinted, in its new form; you have to read it in its original form and then read what the amending legislation has said. Amendments to primary legislation can be introduced by Acts which have very little in common with the original statute, for example by a Criminal Justice (Miscellaneous Provisions) Act or an Administration of Justice Act.[52] They can even be introduced by secondary legislation such as Orders in Council. Occasionally the up-to-date version of a heavily amended statute will be reproduced in a collection of legislation on a particular subject published for use by law students[53] and, of course, the internet is now of help in this context too (see para 3.57), but it can still often be difficult to discover the current legal position on a certain matter if there are several pieces of legislation purporting to deal with it, some dating back a long time.

3.55 In Northern Ireland the problems are accentuated by the fact that there have been so many legislatures claiming the power to legislate for the area which is now Northern Ireland. They are:

(i)   the Parliament of England, from 1226 to 1707
(ii)   the Parliament of Ireland, from 1310 to 1800
(iii)   the Parliament of Great Britain, from 1707 to 1800
(iv)   the Parliament of the United Kingdom, from 1801 to the present
(v)   the Parliament of Northern Ireland, from 1921 to 1972
(vi)   the Northern Ireland Assembly, in 1974[54]
(vii)   the Northern Ireland Assembly, from 1999 to the present.

3.56 Many of the statutes passed by these legislatures remain in force, or partly in force, even though they are of virtually no significance in practice. Seventy-eight Acts of the Parliament of England still apply, at least in part, as do 11 Acts of the Parliament of Ireland, 58 Acts of the Parliament of Great Britain, and no fewer than 797 Acts of the UK Parliament enacted during the nineteenth century.[55] From time to time an Act is passed with the specific purpose of repealing earlier statutes which have become superfluous, especially local and private Acts; an example is the Statute Law (Repeals) Act 2013, which extends to Northern Ireland.[56] Sometimes statutory provisions are repealed even before they have been brought into

---

[52] Eg the Employment Rights (NI) Order 1996 was amended through the insertion of arts 67A–67L by the Public Interest Disclosure (NI) Order 1998, art 3, and then again by the insertion of art 67KA by the Police (NI) Act 2003, s 26(1).

[53] Eg the series of *Blackstone's Statutes*, published by Oxford University Press, some of which are renewed annually.

[54] The enactments of this Assembly were called Measures, not Acts.

[55] See the sections headed 'Acts of the Old Irish Parliament', 'Acts of English Parliament' and 'Acts of Parliament of Great Britain' on www.legislation.gov.uk/browse/ni.

[56] Such Acts are usually the outcome of reviews carried out by the Law Commissions (see para 3.67).

force,[57] and occasionally an Act even contains a provision repealing some of its own provisions![58]

LEGISLATION ON THE INTERNET

3.57   If you are simply interested in looking up the text of a particular piece of legislation which you already know exists, the easiest way to do so is through the internet. The site maintained by the National Archives, *www. legislation.gov.uk*, has the full text of all legislation made anywhere in the UK since 1988. Most of the pre-1988 primary legislation is also available on the site, but in some instances it appears only in its original version, not as later amended (this is particularly so if the legislation was wholly repealed before 1991). Some of the post-1988 primary legislation is also still awaiting the insertion of amendments, but warnings are given on the screen when this is the case. The database does not contain secondary legislation made before 1988. All in all, this is the site where legislation made just for Northern Ireland is most easily found: there are separate databases for Northern Ireland Orders in Council, Acts of the Northern Ireland Assembly, Measures of the Northern Ireland Assembly of 1974, Acts of the Northern Ireland Parliament from 1921 to 1972, and Acts of the Irish Parliament from 1495 to 1800. It also contains a complete set of Northern Ireland Statutory Rules from 1991. When searching the *legislation.gov.uk* website it helps if you know the year in which the piece of legislation was made, as the site primarily organizes the data on a calendar year basis.

3.58   The website of the British and Irish Legal Information Institute (*www. bailii.org*), which can, like the site just mentioned, be accessed completely free of charge, carries the full text of all Acts passed at Westminster. However, some of the statutes enacted after 1987 appear in their unamended form while many of the statutes enacted prior to then appear in their amended form. The site also contains the full text of all statutory instruments since 2002, and some earlier SIs made between 1987 and 2002 (all in unamended form), which means that some Orders in Council made under the Northern Ireland Acts are included. But the site does not contain any legislation made by the Northern Ireland Parliament or Assembly.

3.59   Legislation can also be accessed through commercial information systems, such as Lexis or Westlaw UK.[59] While these are available only on a subscription basis, most university libraries in the UK and Ireland

---

[57] Eg s 44 of the Criminal Procedure and Investigations Act 1996 repealed some sections of the Criminal Justice and Public Order Act 1994 before they were commenced and reinstated some provisions which had been repealed by the 1994 Act.

[58] Eg Sch 13 to the Justice (NI) Act 2002 repealed (or 'revoked') ss 9(10) and (13) of the Act itself. Presumably these reflect last minute changes to the Act.

[59] Another, less popular, database, is Justis UK Statutes.

subscribe on behalf of all of their students. On both the Lexis and Westlaw UK databases the versions of primary legislation displayed are the amended versions, and comments or annotations are provided to explain when and how the amendments occurred. Lexis has all the Acts passed at Westminster which are still in force, all statutory instruments from 1940, and a selection of statutory instruments from before 1940. Westlaw UK contains all the Acts passed at Westminster after 1267 which were still in force in 1991, all such Acts enacted since that year, and all statutory instruments made since 1948. But, as with the BAILII website, neither the Lexis nor the Westlaw UK database includes any primary or secondary legislation made by the Northern Ireland Parliament or Assembly. Westlaw UK facilitates access to both primary and secondary legislation on the basis both of the year the legislation was made and its title. For some provisions, through tabs in the left-hand margin, it provides lists of cases and journal articles where the provisions in question have been discussed. While not always comprehensive, these citations can be a very useful starting point for deeper research into the effects of the legislation.

3.60 When accessing legislation on the internet care should be taken to ensure not only that the provisions in question have not been repealed but that they were actually brought into force in the first place. It also pays to read the advice of an expert so that you can get the most out of the technology available. An excellent book in this regard is *Effective Legal Research*, by John Knowles (the Law Librarian at Queen's University Belfast).[60]

PRINTED VOLUMES

3.61 All UK statutes, as well as being published singly and in annual collections, are indexed by the two-volume *Index to the Statutes* published every two years. Two private publishing companies also produce versions of these statutes with comments and annotations: *Halsbury's Statutes* and *Current Law Statutes*. Some of these, of course, are statutes which apply primarily in Northern Ireland, such as the Northern Ireland Act 1998, so the annotations can be a useful source for lawyers who are trying to understand the full import of that legislation. *Current Law Statutes* now includes an index at the end of each statute. A series called *Statutes in Force* provides the same service for England and Wales which *Statutes Revised* provides for Northern Ireland (see para 3.62); it comprises scores of loose-leaf volumes.

3.62 Acts of the Northern Ireland Assembly are now published in the series 'Northern Ireland Statutes' (see para 3.28), which previously reproduced the Acts of the Stormont Parliament and the Orders in Council made under

---

[60] London, Sweet & Maxwell, 3rd edn, 2012. See in particular ch 4.

various Northern Ireland Acts (see para 3.24). *Statutes Revised, Northern Ireland* is a 16-volume collection of the public Acts of the Parliaments of England, Ireland, Great Britain, the UK and Northern Ireland which affected Northern Ireland up to 1950. The texts are reprinted as amended, with the amending and repealing schedules therefore excluded. In 1982 a loose-leaf second edition of *Statutes Revised* was published in nine volumes, setting out in chronological order the text, also amended, of Acts and Orders affecting Northern Ireland between 1921 and 1981 but with the exception of the relevant UK statutes enacted during that period; a four-volume series (A-D) appended to the edition reprints the amended texts of all pre-1921 legislation, from whatever parliamentary source, still in force in Northern Ireland. Cumulative supplements to *Statutes Revised* are published annually to show what changes have occurred during the past year, but these take quite a long time to appear (usually longer than another year).

3.63   The Stationery Office publishes every three years or so an index to all the statutory provisions currently in force in Northern Ireland, arranged under distinct subject-headings. Another volume is published in loose-leaf form listing all the statute law which affects, or has affected, Northern Ireland, this time arranged in chronological order and with amendments and repeals noted. By the times these volumes appear, however, another year or so of legislation will have been published. They are all weighty tomes (in fact the index is in two volumes), but they are nevertheless very useful because they include references to statutes passed for the whole of the UK. They permit you to tell at a glance what primary legislation currently exists on any matter in Northern Ireland. The position can be so complicated, however, that even in these volumes mistakes and omissions are far from unheard of.

3.64   As with statutes, secondary legislation is published singly as well as collectively in annual bound volumes. Orders in Council made under the Northern Ireland Acts can be found in the series known as 'Northern Ireland Statutes'. Each of the volumes containing Orders in Council also includes tables showing the UK and Northern Ireland Acts (and previous Orders in Council) which have been repealed, amended or otherwise affected by Orders in Council made during the year. Further tables indicate the UK Acts passed during the year which apply in Northern Ireland and the effects of these Acts on previous Acts and Orders in Council. The consequences for earlier Acts and Orders of the statutory instruments and statutory rules made during the year are also tabulated.

3.65   The last volume for each year of the statutory rules for Northern Ireland contains a list of that year's UK statutory instruments which affect Northern Ireland (other than Orders in Council made under the Northern Ireland Acts) and there is an index categorising the rules on the basis of the authorities which made them. Further tables supply lists of the changes made by the year's statutory rules not just to earlier Acts and Orders (information which is also given in the annual volume of Orders in Council) but also to earlier statutory rules. A large loose-leaf index to all the statutory rules in force, arranged under subject headings, is now updated every year, but it does not give details of the amendments which later statutory rules may have made to earlier ones: the fully amended text can be gleaned only from reading all of the relevant rules together. Of course UK statutory instruments are also published in multiple volumes each year.

LAW REFORM[61]

3.66 We have seen that legislation, along with case law, is one of the two main sources of law in Northern Ireland. Case law (the subject of the next chapter) is obviously an unsatisfactory medium for making changes to the law because it comes into being only when persons choose to take particular disputes to court, and judges have neither the time nor the authority to expound on parts of the law which are not the precise subject of the litigation before them. Legislation is therefore the preferred medium for law reform and to help Parliament and the government to design new legislation various law reform agencies have been created.

The Northern Ireland Law Commission

3.67 This body has been in existence since 2007.[62] It is chaired by a High Court judge and has four other Commissioners, all appointed by the Minister of Justice. These include a barrister, a solicitor and a university law teacher. The Commission has a duty to keep under review the law of Northern Ireland with a view to its systematic development and reform, including its simplification and modernisation, but in performing this duty the Commission has to consult with the Law Commission of England and Wales, the Scottish Law Commission and the Law Reform Commission of Ireland. In addition the Act requires the Commission to consider any proposals for the reform of law in Northern Ireland referred to it. The Commission must submit a programme of law reform to the Department of Justice and that Department must in turn consult the Attorney General for Northern Ireland before approving any such programme. Annual reports on the Law Commission's work must be laid before Parliament at Westminster.

---

[61] See generally M Zander, *The Law-Making Process* (Cambridge, Cambridge UP, 6th edn, 2004) ch 9.

[62] Justice (NI) Act 2002, ss 50–52 and Sch 9. It is currently undergoing a review, so the legislation governing it may soon be amended in some ways.

3.68 The Commission operates by first producing a consultation paper setting out the possible reform options for the particular area of law in question. After considering the responses to this paper the Commission publishes a full report, together with recommendations and, where appropriate, draft legislation. It is then for the Minister of Justice to decide if, and how, the Commission's recommendations should be implemented. The Commission is keen to point out that it does not investigate complaints about solicitors or government departments, or give legal advice to individuals.

3.69 The topics identified for reform in the Commission's First Programme of Law Reform, which ran from 2009 until 2012, were land law, bail law, business tenancies law, the law relating to vulnerable witnesses in civil cases, and the law relating to multi-unit domestic apartments. By the end of 2012 it had completed its reports (and draft legislation) on the first four of these topics. Its report on land law actually contains two draft Bills, a general one (the Land Law Reform Bill (NI)) and a more specific one (the Ground Rents (Amendment) Bill (NI)). The land law of Northern Ireland has been in dire need of reform for many decades (having missed out on the reforms first introduced for England and Wales in the 1920s), so if the first of these Bills is eventually enacted it will be a significant achievement for the Commission (see para 9.3). In its consultation paper on its Second Programme of Law Reform the Commission did not indicate any particular areas of law that it was minded to reform but called for proposals from others. The Commission's Second Programme of Law Reform, for 2012–15, will cover multi-unit domestic apartments, the regulation of health care and pharmaceutical professionals, aspects of landlord and tenant law, the unfitness of an accused person to plead, the availability of the defence of insanity, and the initiation of criminal prosecutions. Three further projects which the Law Commission had wanted to conduct were not approved by the Minister of Justice. These were on the law relating to coroners and inquests, to family provision upon intestacy, and to re-registration of births and parental responsibility.

Other bodies

3.70 Prior to the creation of the Northern Ireland Law Commission there was no body outside the Northern Ireland Office charged with considering reform of the criminal law during the period of direct rule in Northern Ireland. But there were two earlier law reform bodies. One was the Law Reform Advisory Committee, which was created in 1989. Its remit was to scrutinise civil law matters which were not 'excepted' or 'reserved' under the Northern Ireland Constitution Act 1973 (see para 1.22). Its work paved the way for the

Business Tenancies (NI) Order 1996, the Civil Evidence (NI) Order 1997 and for part of the Law Reform (Miscellaneous Proceedings) (NI) Order 2005. The Committee was complemented by the Office of Law Reform (OLR), which was originally constituted in 1965 as a separate branch of the Office of the Legislative Draftsman in Northern Ireland, that being the year when the Law Commissions for England and Scotland were established. During its first five years the OLR was instrumental in having legislation enacted on matters such as theft, compensation for criminal injuries, preliminary enquiries in committal proceedings, misrepresentations, the age of majority and the enforcement of judgments. In 2003 it consulted on new rights for transsexual people and on partnerships between same-sex couples (in each case because reforms on these topics were already in the pipeline for England and Wales). Today the role of the OLR is fulfilled by the Civil Law Reform Division of the Departmental Solicitor's Office in the Department of Finance and Personnel. This Division is largely responsible for aspects of civil law reform such as family law, trusts and property law, tort law, contract law and private international law (for the meaning of this term see para 5.5).

3.71 On occasions a body is appointed by the UK Government or Northern Ireland Executive to look into matters of specific or of general concern. The best example of the latter type is a Royal Commission, which will conduct a large-scale inquiry into an issue with wide-ranging social and legal implications. Such Commissions are usually chaired by judges or high-ranking public servants. A good example is the Commission on Criminal Justice, chaired by Lord Runciman, which reported in 1993. An example of a less formal investigation is the Independent Commission on Policing in Northern Ireland, chaired by Chris (now Lord) Patten, which reported in 1999 (see para 7.44), and the Review of the Criminal Justice System in Northern Ireland which reported in 2000 (see para 7.2). Commissions are sometimes set up under what used to be the Tribunals of Inquiry (Evidence) Act 1921 and is now the Inquiries Act 2005. The Bloody Sunday Inquiry, chaired by Lord Saville, which lasted from 1998 until 2010, is an example of such an inquiry,[63] as is the Leveson Inquiry into the Culture, Practices and Ethics of the Press, the first part of which was concluded in 2012.[64] In 2012 the Northern Ireland Executive set up an inquiry into the institutional abuse of children in Northern Ireland occurring between 1922 and 1995; it is chaired by a retired High Court judge, Sir Anthony Hart.[65]

3.72 There is a Law Commission for England and Wales too.[66] Many of its reports influence the development of law in Northern Ireland, because

[63] www.bloody-sunday-inquiry.org.uk.
[64] www.levesoninquiry.org.uk.
[65] www.hiainquiry.org. See the Inquiry into Historical Abuse Act (NI) 2013.
[66] www.lawcom.gov.uk. There is also a Scottish Law Commission and in the Republic of Ireland there is a Law Reform Commission.

reforms introduced in England and Wales on the back of reports are often mirrored in Northern Ireland at a later date. In addition to proposing substantive legal reforms, the English Law Commission makes suggestions for tidying up the statute book. It drafts Statute Law (Repeals) Bills, which since 1965 have repealed over 5,000 enactments. The Commission also makes recommendations for the codification of law. It was responsible, for example, for the Income and Corporation Taxes Act 1988, which has more than 1,000 pages and applies as much in Northern Ireland as in the rest of the UK. The Commission's considerable efforts to codify the criminal law have not yet met with the same degree of governmental and parliamentary approval.

4

Courts and Case Law in Northern Ireland

INTRODUCTION

4.1   This chapter begins by explaining how the present system of courts in Northern Ireland has come to be as it is and then proceeds to describe how those courts 'make law'. It looks in particular at how the courts use legislation, which remains the primary source of law. Finally the chapter gives advice on how to look up case law.

COURTS IN IRELAND BEFORE 1921

4.2   When the Normans established themselves in Ireland they introduced a system of courts modelled on the English system. Accordingly the 'Four Courts' were set up in Dublin, on a site where the building still bears that name today, although the judges who served in those courts went round Ireland twice a year to hear cases more locally (they were then said to be 'on Assizes'). The first three of these courts were:

(1)   the Court of King's Bench, which dealt with cases involving the King's interest in the maintenance of law and order

(2)   the Court of Exchequer, which dealt with cases about taxation, and

(3)   the Court of Common Pleas, which dealt with disputes involving only private individuals.

Cases in these courts were decided by one judge, usually sitting with a jury of 12 'true and honest' men.

Courts of equity

4.3   The fourth court was called the Court of Chancery and it dealt with disputes which could not be dealt with in the other three courts. They were handled by the King's Chancellor, usually at that time an influential cleric, who was required to do justice 'according to the conscience of the case'. Through time the justice dispensed by the Court of Chancery became known as 'equity', to distinguish it from the justice dispensed by the King's other three courts, known as 'common law'. Amazingly, it was not until 1877 in Ireland (1875 in England)[1] that common law and equity could be administered in one and the same court. Until then the two types of law had to be kept quite separate. A person might, for instance, lose a case in a common law court but then take it to a court of equity and win.[2] After the fusion of equity and common law in the 1870s, all courts could apply both sets of principles, and in the event of a conflict the 'equitable' as opposed to the 'legal' principles were to prevail.[3] Today, law students still have to study 'Equity', because it is the origin for most of our modern rules on when and how property can be held under the device known as a 'trust' (see paras 9.20–9.23).

The rationalisation of the courts in the 1870s

4.4   Over time other courts were established in Ireland to deal with special types of case and with appeals.[4] To the four 'superior' courts were added five more:

(1)   a Court of Admiralty, to deal with shipping cases
(2)   a Court of Bankruptcy and Insolvency
(3)   a Court of Probate, to deal with disputes concerning wills
(4)   a Court for Matrimonial Causes, and
(5)   a Landed Estates Court, which handled disputes concerning the right to use land.

Two appeal courts, called the Court of Exchequer Chamber and the Court of Appeal in Chancery, were also created. For cases involving claims to small amounts of money there was a system of 'civil bill courts', also known as 'county courts', and power to try less serious criminal cases was given to magistrates' courts. By the 1870s, therefore, the court structure in Ireland had become rather complex and was not operating very efficiently.

4.5   In 1877 a thorough reorganisation of the superior courts took place in Ireland, again along English lines. The nine courts were amalgamated into

---

[1] Supreme Court of Judicature Act (Ir) 1877 and Supreme Court of Judicature Act 1873 respectively.

[2] A Burrows, 'We Do This at Common Law but That in Equity' (2002) 22 *OJLS* 1.

[3] For further details on the history of the Court of Chancery and equity, see P Pettit, *Equity and the Law of Trusts* (Oxford, Oxford UP, 12th edn, 2012), ch 1.

[4] See generally F Newark, 'Notes on Irish Legal History' (1947) 7 *NILQ* 121, reprinted in an updated form in F McIvor (ed), *Elegantia Juris: Selected Writings of F. H. Newark* (NILQ, 1973).

one High Court, which by 1900 came to have just two divisions: (1) the Chancery Division, which took over the work of two of the old courts – the Court of Chancery and the Landed Estates Court, and (2) the Queen's Bench Division, which took over the work of the other seven courts. The appeal courts were amalgamated into one Court of Appeal. The new High Court and Court of Appeal together constituted the Supreme Court of Judicature – a rather misleading title, since it remained possible to lodge a further appeal from the Court of Appeal in Dublin to the real 'supreme' court for the whole of the UK, the Appellate Committee of the House of Lords in London.

THE COURT OF JUDICATURE OF NORTHERN IRELAND

4.6 When the Government of Ireland Act of 1920 created separate court structures for the two parts of Ireland, the existing court system was closely followed in the North. A Supreme Court of Judicature of Northern Ireland was set up, comprising a High Court and a Court of Appeal. A Court of Criminal Appeal was added in 1930. Further changes were made in the 1970s. By the Judicature (NI) Act 1978 a third division of the High Court, the Family Division, was created, the Crown Court replaced the old system of Assizes, and the Court of Criminal Appeal was merged with the Court of Appeal. In 2009, to make room for the creation of the UK Supreme Court, the Supreme Court of Judicature of Northern Ireland was renamed the Court of Judicature of Northern Ireland.[5]

4.7 The High Court of Northern Ireland also contains what is termed a Divisional Court, which is a special court within the Queen's Bench Division that usually comprises two judges and mainly hears applications for judicial review in criminal cases.[6] In England and Wales the Queen's Bench Divisional Court plays a much more important part in the legal system, since it also deals with appeals on pure points of law in criminal cases that have first been heard in the magistrates' courts or the Crown Court. In Northern Ireland these appeals go to the Court of Appeal.

4.8 The High Court and Court of Appeal always sit in Belfast, in the Royal Courts of Justice in Chichester Street. The Crown Court sits not only in Belfast but also in 12 other towns in Northern Ireland. Beneath these courts there are a number of 'inferior' courts. There are county courts in 17 towns, which are grouped into seven county court divisions;[7] four of these courts are also 'Family Care Centres' handling important family law disputes. The county courts for Derry/Londonderry and for Belfast are called Recorder's

[5] Constitutional Reform Act 2005, s 59(2).
[6] See, eg, *R (Hume) v Londonderry Justices* [1972] NI 91, explained at paras 2.4 and 3.3.
[7] These divisions are Antrim, Ards, Armagh and South Down, Belfast, Craigavon, Fermanagh and Tyrone, and Derry/Londonderry.

courts, but their powers do not differ from those of other county courts. There are magistrates' courts in 20 towns, each of which is at the centre of what is called a 'petty sessions district'; these courts deal with minor criminal cases, though seven of them can handle minor family law disputes too. Figure 4.1 below shows how the various courts in Northern Ireland relate to one another; the arrows in the figure represent typical appeal routes. There is a map of court locations on the website of the Northern Ireland Courts and Tribunals Service.[8]

THE JUDICIARY IN NORTHERN IRELAND

4.9   The men and women who take decisions in the courts that have just been mentioned are usually called judges, but those who decide cases in magistrates' courts are called District Judges (Magistrates' Courts) if they are presiding and otherwise lay magistrates. Collectively all of these people are known as 'the judiciary'. Table 4.1 sets out the official titles given to these decision-makers, the number of them that can be in office at any one time, the qualifications they need to have in order to be appointed, how they should be addressed in court, and what their salary was in March 2013. Salaries have not risen for the last three years. The current rule is that members of the judiciary must retire when they reach the age of 70.

---

[8] www.courtsni.gov.uk/en-GB/ContactDetails/Pages/default.aspx.

Figure 4.1: The court and tribunal system in Northern Ireland

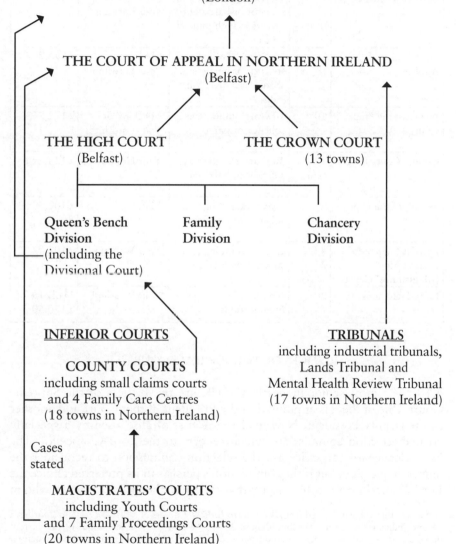

SUPERIOR COURTS

THE UNITED KINGDOM SUPREME COURT
(London)

THE COURT OF APPEAL IN NORTHERN IRELAND
(Belfast)

THE HIGH COURT
(Belfast)

THE CROWN COURT
(13 towns)

Queen's Bench
Division
(including the
Divisional Court)

Family
Division

Chancery
Division

INFERIOR COURTS

COUNTY COURTS
including small claims courts
and 4 Family Care Centres
(18 towns in Northern Ireland)

TRIBUNALS
including industrial tribunals,
Lands Tribunal and
Mental Health Review Tribunal
(17 towns in Northern Ireland)

Cases
stated

MAGISTRATES' COURTS
including Youth Courts
and 7 Family Proceedings Courts
(20 towns in Northern Ireland)

Table 4.1: The judiciary in Northern Ireland[9]

Official title	In post (Deps)	Qualifications for the post	How they should be addressed	Salary
Lord Chief Justice	1	15 years' standing as a solicitor or barrister or 2 years in high judicial office	'My Lord' or 'Your Lordship'	£214,165
Lord Justice of Appeal	3	15 years' standing as a solicitor or barrister or service as a high court judge	'My Lord' or 'Your Lordship'	£196,707
Justice of the High Court	10	10 years' standing as a solicitor or barrister	'My Lord' or 'Your Lordship'	£172,753
County Court Judge	17 (26)	10 years' standing as a solicitor or barrister	'Your Honour'	£128, 296[10]
Master of the High Court	7	7 years' standing as a solicitor or barrister	'Master'	£102,921[11]
District Judge and District Judge (Magistrates' Courts)	4 (4) 21 (21)	7 years' standing as a solicitor or barrister	'Your Worship'	£102,921
Lay Magistrates	208	No formal qualifications	'Your Worship'	Daily fee of £170.50

JUSTICES OF THE SUPREME COURT[12]

4.10   The most senior judges in the UK are the Justices of the Supreme Court. One of these is appointed as the President of that Court and another as the Deputy President. New justices are first of all chosen by a specially created selection commission, which reports to the Lord Chancellor. The Lord Chancellor can twice ask the selection commission to reconsider the names in question, but if the commission's persists in its preferred choice the Lord Chancellor must then notify that choice to the Prime Minister, who in

[9] Most of this Table is derived from *A Guide to Judicial Careers in Northern Ireland* (Northern Ireland Judicial Appointments Commission, 2011), 58 and 61. For the names of the current members of the judiciary see: www.courtsni.gov.uk/en-GB/AboutUs/OrganisationalStructure/Pages/Judiciary-of-Northern-Ireland.aspx.

[10] This is also the salary of the Presidents of the Appeal Tribunals, the Lands Tribunal, and the Industrial Tribunals and Fair Employment Tribunal.

[11] This is also the salary of coroners and of the Chairs of Industrial Tribunals and the Fair Employment Tribunal.

[12] For further details see www.supremecourt.gov.uk.

turn must recommend that person to the Queen for appointment.[13] There is also scope for appointing acting judges,[14] a supplementary panel of retired judges,[15] and even specially qualified advisers.[16] The Supreme Court also has a Chief Executive, who prepares an annual report on the Court's activities. The Court is located in a specially converted building in Parliament Square in London, very close to both the Palace of Westminster and Westminster Abbey. It took over the role of the top UK court from the Appellate Committee of the House of Lords in 2009. The same judges sometimes sit in the Judicial Committee of the Privy Council, which is housed in the same building. This hears appeals from some small Commonwealth countries, including several in the Caribbean but also Gibraltar, Jersey and Mauritius.[17]

4.11   Before being appointed, Justices of the Supreme Court must have been in possession of a 'Supreme Court qualification' for at least 15 years, which means that during that period they must have had the right to speak on behalf of clients in all proceedings in the superior courts of England and Wales or in the top courts of Scotland. A person from Northern Ireland can be appointed if he or she has served as a judge of the High Court or Court of Appeal for two years or as a barrister or solicitor for 15 years. In addition, anyone can be appointed to the Supreme Court if they meet the 'judicial-appointment eligibility condition', which means that they must have a legal qualification and have been engaged in law-related activities (such as teaching law or advising people about the law) for 15 years.[18] Only five people have ever been appointed from Northern Ireland to this level of court in the UK: Lord MacDermott in 1947, Lord Lowry in 1988, Lord Hutton in 1997, Lord Carswell in 2004, and Lord Kerr in 2009. Lord Kerr, who served as Lord Chief Justice of Northern Ireland from 2004 to 2009, is the judge who ensures that today's Supreme Court has knowledge and experience of the law of Northern Ireland, as statute requires.[19] Justices must retire when they reach the age of 70, although those who were first appointed as judges in lower courts before April 1995 can continue in a judicial role until they reach the age of 75, if they so wish.[20] As Lord Kerr was first appointed as a judge in 1993, he can remain as a Justice of the Supreme Court, if he so wishes, until he reaches the age of 75 in 2023.

4.12   There can be 12 Justices of the Supreme Court at any one time and they each currently earn £206,857.[21] The first and so far only woman to

[13] Constitutional Reform Act 2005, ss 26–31.
[14] Ibid s 38.
[15] Ibid s 39.
[16] Ibid s 44.
[17] For judgments of the Privy Council see www.jcpc.gov.uk/decided-cases/index.html.
[18] Constitutional Reform Act 2005, s 25(1) and (2); Tribunals, Courts and Enforcement Act 2007, ss 50–2.
[19] Constitutional Reform Act 2005, s 27(8).
[20] Judicial Pensions and Retirement Act 1993, s 26 and Sch 7.
[21] The President of the Supreme Court is paid slightly more, £214,165.

hold the post, Lady Hale, was appointed in 2004. The current President of the Court is Lord Neuberger of Abbotsbury and the Deputy President is Lord Hope (who is die to retire in June 2013).

4.13 Decisions on whether to grant permission for a case to be appealed to the Supreme Court are usually taken by a panel of three Justices, but detailed reasons are not given for the decisions. In general the Supreme Court will grant permission only if it thinks that the appeal involves a point of law of general public importance that ought to be heard by the Supreme Court at that time. When hearing appeals the Supreme Court usually sits as a bench of five judges, and never with a jury. Very important cases are sometimes heard by seven justices,[22] and extremely important cases are heard by nine justices.[23]

4.14 Many legal disputes occurring in Northern Ireland may in theory proceed as far as the Supreme Court, but in practice very few do – on average, only two or three a year.[24] The Attorney General of Northern Ireland can refer Assembly legislation to the Supreme Court if he or she thinks it might be outside the Assembly's competence to make (see paras 2.31 and 11.5).[25] For civil cases that are first heard in the magistrates' courts or county courts of Northern Ireland the final court to which the dispute can be taken is generally the Court of Appeal in Northern Ireland; appeals to the Supreme Court are possible only if the case involves 'a decision of any question as to the validity of any provision made by or under an Act of the Parliament of Northern Ireland or a Measure of the Northern Ireland Assembly.'[26] In some instances it is possible to take a case beyond the Supreme Court, to either the Court of Justice of the European Union in Luxembourg or the European Court of Human Rights in Strasbourg but, as will be explained later (see paras 5.26 and 5.40), those courts are not hearing 'appeals' so much as giving rulings on how the law should be applied within the UK.

JUDGES OF THE SUPERIOR COURTS[27]

4.15 In Northern Ireland the Lord Chief Justice and Lords Justices of Appeal are appointed by the Queen on the recommendation of the Prime Minister of the UK, but before making a recommendation the Prime Minister

---

[22] Eg *Assange v Swedish Prosecution Authority* [2012] UKSC 22, [2012] 2 AC 471 (on whether a European Arrest Warrant relating to Julian Assange, the founder of Wikileaks, was valid).

[23] Eg *R (Smith) v Oxfordshire Assistant Deputy Coroner* [2010] UKSC 29, [2011] 1 AC 1 (on whether UK soldiers are entitled to the protection of the Human Rights Act 1998 when they are serving abroad).

[24] In 2012 there were no such appeals.

[25] Northern Ireland Act 1998, s 11(1).

[26] Judicature (NI) Act 1978, s 42(6). Oddly, only Measures of the 1974 Assembly are mentioned here, not Acts of the current Northern Ireland Assembly.

[27] Ibid ss 1–15.

must consult both the current Lord Chief Justice of Northern Ireland (or, if that office is vacant, the longest serving of the current Lords Justices of Appeal) and the Northern Ireland Judicial Appointments Commission (see para 4.33).[28] Judges of the High Court are appointed by the Queen on the recommendation of the Lord Chancellor, but the Lord Chancellor *must* now recommend the person selected by the Northern Ireland Judicial Appointments Commission.[29] Since 1921 there have been 48 such judges in Northern Ireland. Three of the judges had fathers who were judges. As yet, astonishingly, not one woman has been appointed to the role.[30] In days gone by judges were often former Unionist politicians,[31] but such 'political' appointments are today unthinkable.

4.16 Only solicitors or barristers who have practised for at least 10 years are eligible for appointment as judges of the High Court of Northern Ireland. Vacancies on the bench are now advertised.[32] These senior judges can be removed from office if both Houses of Parliament so recommend,[33] but this has never occurred anywhere in the UK in modern times. Removal of senior judges appointed before the devolution of justice to Northern Ireland on 12 April 2010 also requires a recommendation to that effect from a tribunal convened by and reporting to the Lord Chancellor,[34] while removal of senior judges appointed after devolution requires such a recommendation from a tribunal convened by and reporting to the Lord Chief Justice of Northern Ireland.[35]

4.17 The most important judge in Northern Ireland is the Lord Chief Justice, currently Sir Declan Morgan, who was appointed in July 2009. The office replaced that of the Lord Chancellor of Ireland in 1921. The Lord Chief Justice is President of the Court of Appeal, the High Court and the

[28] Ibid s 12, as substituted by the Northern Ireland Act 2009, s 2(1) and Sch 2.

[29] Justice (NI) Act 2002, Sch 3, para 2, as substituted by the Northern Ireland Act 2009, s 2(2) and Sch 3, para 13. Prior to this change in the law (effective from 12 April 2010), the Lord Chancellor could veto a recommendation made by the Northern Ireland Judicial Appointments Commission. Controversially this occurred when Mark Orr QC was recommended for appointment in 2009: see www.newsletter.co.uk/news/local/london-blocks-judge-selection-ulster-qc-1-2813850.

[30] In defence of the current position the Northern Ireland Judicial Appointments Commission (see para 4.33) points out that four of the 17 county court judges are women and that women constitute approximately 44 per cent of tribunal membership and 54 per cent of the lay magistrates.

[31] According to D McKittrick and D McVea, in *Making Sense of the Troubles* (Belfast, Blackstaff Press, 2000), 11, between 1937 and 1968 13 sitting Unionist MPs were appointed judges (not all, of course, in the High Court).

[32] The first High Court judge to be appointed in this way was McLaughlin J in 1999. He was also the first to be sworn in during a public ceremony.

[33] Judicature (NI) Act 1978, s 12B, inserted by the Constitutional Reform Act 2005, s 133.

[34] Ibid s 12C, inserted by the Northern Ireland Act 2009, s 2(1) and Sch 2.

[35] Ibid s 12C(16); Justice (NI) Act 2002, ss 7 and 8, as amended by the Northern Ireland Act 2009, s 2(2) and Sch 3, paras 6 and 7; and the Justice (NI) Act 2002 (Commencement No 14) Order 2010 (SR 113).

Crown Court and in this capacity assigns work to the judges of the various courts and has a number of other administrative responsibilities. In England the Lord Chief Justice acts as President of the Criminal Division of the Court of Appeal, while the President of the Civil Division is a judge holding the title Master of the Rolls. There is no Master of the Rolls in Northern Ireland.

4.18   The Court of Appeal of Northern Ireland consists of the Lord Chief Justice and three other judges called Lords Justices of Appeal. The Lord Chief Justice can also ask judges of the High Court to sit as judges of the Court of Appeal, or Lords Justices of Appeal to sit as judges in the High Court. Lords Justices are invariably promoted to the Court of Appeal from the High Court and are made members of the Privy Council at that point, which is why they are referred to as 'the Right Honourable Lord Justice X'. A case in the Court of Appeal will usually be heard by three judges, always sitting in Belfast, but some matters may be dealt with by a two-judge bench and some (incidental matters) by one judge sitting alone. Occasionally a retired judge will be asked to assist in the Court of Appeal.[36] A jury is never involved.

4.19   The High Court of Northern Ireland consists of the Lord Chief Justice and up to 10 other judges.[37] These judges are officially called 'puisne' (pronounced 'puny') judges and are referred to as 'Mr Justice...' Knighthoods have been automatically conferred on High Court judges who agree to accept them since 1988. To ease the burden on High Court judges, the Lord Chancellor may from time to time request a county court judge to sit as a judge of the High Court. Today High Court judges may sit in any of the Divisions of the High Court, but six are formally allocated to the Queen's Bench Division, one to the Chancery Division and one to the Family Division. One judge is asked to specialise in judicial review proceedings within the Queen's Bench Division (see paras 6.5–6.11). Except for hearings in the Divisional Court (see para 4.7), a High Court case will involve only one judge, always sitting in Belfast. Juries (consisting of just seven persons, not 12 as in England) are used very rarely, mainly in libel cases. The work of the High Court is almost exclusively civil in nature, though it has to deal with criminal matters when considering applications for bail. When the Divisional Court is hearing a criminal cause or matter it must sit with two or three judges.[38]

---

[36] In *Praxis Care Group v Hope* [2012] NICA 8, an employment case, two of the three appeal judges were retired.

[37] The number was increased from 9 in 2004. See the Maximum Number of Judges (NI) Order 2004 (SI 1985). As of March 2013 there was one vacancy amongst the ten posts.

[38] Rules of the Court of Judicature (NI) 1980 (SR 346), Ord 53, r 2. See, eg, *In re Carter's Application* [2011] NIQB 15, [2011] 4 BNIL 68.

JUDGES OF THE INFERIOR COURTS

4.20 County court judges, of whom there are now 17 (including 4 women), with 26 deputies, sit throughout Northern Ireland. Again, at least 10 years' practice as a solicitor or barrister is required before a person can be considered for appointment. There are also four District Judges (and four deputies), who assist the county court judges and exercise an important jurisdiction in the 'small claims courts' (see paras 10.8–10.14). To be appointed as a District Judge one must have practised as a solicitor or barrister for at least seven years.

4.21 One of the major differences between the legal systems of Northern Ireland and England is that in Northern Ireland the responsibility for trying less serious criminal offences lies with full-time, legally qualified people now called 'District Judges' (Magistrates' Courts), formerly known as 'Resident Magistrates' (or 'RMs'). In England much of this work is still done by part-time justices who have no formal legal qualifications, although they undergo periodic training after they are appointed. Only in larger towns and cities are there full-time magistrates in England (where they are called 'stipendiary' magistrates, to indicate that they receive a stipend, or salary). Only barristers and solicitors of seven years' standing are eligible for appointment as District Judges (Magistrates' Courts). In addition to trying comparatively minor criminal offences, they conduct committal proceedings in the more serious criminal cases (see paras 8.62–8.65). They also deal with some civil law disputes, especially in matrimonial matters, and are responsible for a number of issues which might be said to be more administrative in nature than judicial, such as the renewal of licences for public houses.

4.22 According to the Justice (NI) Act 2002,[39] as amended by the Northern Ireland Act 2009,[40] a person who holds a judicial office other than as a judge of a superior court may be removed from office (and suspended from office pending a decision whether to remove him or her) only if the Lord Chief Justice so orders having first considered the recommendation made by a tribunal convened for the purpose of deciding whether the judge should be removed on the ground of misbehaviour or inability to perform the functions of the office. This process could be set in train if, for example, a county court judge were to be convicted of driving a car while under the influence of alcohol.

[39] ss 7 and 8.
[40] s 2(2) and Sch 3, paras 6 and 7.

Lay magistrates

4.23   The people who serve as lay magistrates in Northern Ireland were formerly referred to as Justices of the Peace (JPs).[41] The office is a very ancient one, first established in Ireland (as in England) in the fourteenth century. In England and Wales, JPs still act as full-scale magistrates but in Northern Ireland their powers have been severely limited since 1935. Persons become lay magistrates by replying to public advertisements and going through a rigorous selection process. They must reside or work within 15 miles of the county court division to which their appointment relates and they must not hold certain specified offices or occupations (eg as a solicitor).[42] Although they do not have to be legally qualified, they are nevertheless members of the judiciary in Northern Ireland. They are each appointed for a five-year term, renewable until they reach the age of 70. At present there are more than 200 in post. They get paid an attendance fee for each day, or half-day, that they sit in court. They are often required to sign summonses, warrants and various official forms, such as those relating to state pensions. Summonses are documents which direct people to appear in court on a certain day in order to answer a particular allegation. Warrants are documents authorising the police to arrest someone who is suspected of having committed a crime or to search premises where, for instance, stolen goods are thought to be hidden; or they may take the form of written authorisation for extending a person's detention or committing a person for trial or to prison on remand.

4.24   District Judges (Magistrates' Courts) and lay magistrates retain the somewhat controversial power to 'bind over' persons to keep the peace or be of good behaviour. This power, which derives from the common law and the Justices of the Peace Act 1361, enables magistrates to require people to forfeit a sum of money or serve a period of imprisonment if they break a promise to keep the peace or be of good behaviour during a stipulated period, which must not exceed two years. Such persons do not first have to be convicted of a criminal offence. On at least one occasion in England the power has been exercised in a way which has been held to contravene the European Convention on Human Rights (because of its vagueness),[43] so reform of the law may be imminent.

MASTERS AND CLERKS

4.25   The Northern Ireland Judicial Appointments Commission (see para 4.33) also recommends for appointment by the Lord Chancellor certain

---

[41] Justice (NI) Act 2002, ss 9–11.
[42] Lay Magistrates (Eligibility) (NI) Order 2004 (SI 246).
[43] *Hashman and Harrap v UK* (1999) 30 EHRR 241; but see, by way of contrast, *Steel v UK* (1998) 28 EHRR 604.

'statutory officers'. These include up to eight Masters.[44] Masters (and their deputies) are former legal practitioners of seven years' standing whose job is to deal with a variety of procedural and relatively minor substantive issues before a dispute reaches a High Court judge. An appeal against their decisions usually lies to such a judge. The title 'Master' is used even though the post-holder may be a woman.

4.26   Of the eight Masters, two assist the Queen's Bench Division, two assist the Chancery Division, and two assist the Family Division (dealing with probate and matrimonial work and with the care and protection of children and mental patients). In addition there is a Master who assesses lawyers' costs in certain cases (the Taxing Master) and a Master responsible for the enforcement of judgments. Being, in effect, junior High Court judges, decisions taken by Masters cannot be judicially reviewed (see paras 6.5–6.11).[45]

4.27   The main administrators in county court divisions are called chief clerks (formerly Clerks of the Crown and Peace), while those in magistrates' courts are called clerks of petty sessions. They do not have to be legally qualified because they play no role in adjudications within those courts. They are not members of the judiciary.

MEMBERS OF TRIBUNALS

4.28   Northern Ireland, like the rest of the UK, has a range of specialised tribunals which deal with disputes over many different subjects. Nearly all of them, about 20 in number, now operate under the auspices of the Northern Ireland Courts and Tribunals Service, and they handle approximately 30,000 disputes each year. The responsibility for recruiting people to serve as the Presidents or Vice-Presidents of tribunals is largely the responsibility of the Judicial Appointments Commission (see para 4.33), with the President of each tribunal being a member of the Tribunal Presidents' Group, which is chaired by a Lord Justice of Appeal. Other 'ordinary' members of tribunals are often appointed by the department of government responsible for the area of law dealt with by the tribunal (eg the Department for Employment and Learning appoints members of industrial tribunals: see para 9.106).

4.29   The commonest and best known tribunals are the Appeal Tribunals and the industrial tribunals. Appeal Tribunals hear appeals in towns all over Northern Ireland against decisions taken on claims for welfare benefits by bodies such as the Social Security Agency, the Northern Ireland Housing Executive, Land and Property Services, and Her Majesty's Revenue and Customs (see paras 6.72–6.73). They also handle appeals by people who

---

[44] Judicature (NI) Act 1978, s 70 and Sch 3.
[45] *Re Rice's Application* [1998] NI 265.

are claiming compensation for injuries suffered as a result of vaccinations, and appeals by insurance companies which are claiming reimbursement of money paid to persons injured in accidents (eg to cover hospital charges) if those people have later received compensation from the party responsible for the accident. There is a full-time President of Appeal Tribunals and one full-time Chairman. The rest of the membership comprises persons appointed to serve on part-time basis, some of whom are legally qualified but most of whom are not. If one side is unhappy with the decision reached by an Appeal Tribunal it can take a further appeal, though only on a point of law rather than a point of fact, to the Social Security Commissioners or Child Support Commissioners.

4.30   Industrial tribunals, which are called employment tribunals in Great Britain, deal with disputes brought by employees against their employers (see para 9.106). One section, the Fair Employment Tribunal, confines its attention to claims alleging discrimination on the basis of political opinion or religious belief (see paras 6.55 and 9.109). Each sitting tribunal will have a Chairperson, who will be legally qualified, one member with a trade union background and another member who has experience of business or personnel matters.

4.31   Amongst the many other tribunals that exist in Northern Ireland, and about which there is little space to say much in this book, are the following.[46]

(1)   the Lands Tribunal, dealing mainly with disputes about the use to which land can be put: see para 9.18
(2)   the Valuation Tribunal, hearing appeals regarding domestic rates
(3)   the Rent Assessment Panel, which decides what rents would be appropriate for properties in the private sector which are 'controlled' under the Rent (NI) Order 1978 (see para 6.84)
(4)   the Charity Tribunal, dealing with complaints that the Charity Commission will not register an organisation as a charity: see para 9.23
(5)   the Mental Health Review Tribunal, dealing with disputes over whether someone's detention in a mental hospital is necessary
(6)   the Special Educational Needs and Disability Tribunal, handling disputes over the provision being made for a child's special educational needs
(7)   the Care Tribunal, hearing appeals against decisions relating to the regulation of various kinds of care homes, including who is disqualified from working there

---

[46] See too the relevant section of the website of the Northern Ireland Courts and Tribunals Service: www.courtsni.gov.uk/en-GB/Tribunals/Pages/Tribunals.aspx. Some matters decided in Northern Ireland, such as decisions of the Department of the Environment in relation to road transport issues, are appealed to the Upper Tribunal sitting in England: [2012] 5 BNIL 103.

(8) the Pensions Appeal Tribunal, which deals with appeals from ex-servicemen or women whose claim for a war pension has been rejected by the Ministry of Defence

(9) the Immigration and Asylum Chamber of the First-tier Tribunal, which sits in Northern Ireland from time to time to hear appeals against the Home Secretary's decisions in immigration, asylum and nationality disputes, but which is administered by Her Majesty's Courts and Tribunals Service in London[47]

(10) the Northern Ireland Traffic Penalty Tribunal, which hears appeals against penalty charge notices (ie parking fines) issued on behalf of the Roads Service to people who have breached a parking restriction.

4.32 The website of the Northern Ireland Courts and Tribunals Service has a whole section devoted to tribunals. It also carries information about reform of the tribunal system. In 2010 the Service published a Tribunals Modernisation Strategy and Action Plan,[48] which indicated that, following devolution of policing and justice to the Northern Ireland Assembly, responsibility for industrial tribunals (including the Fair Employment Tribunal) and for the Planning Appeals Commission (see paras 6.86–6.89) would be transferred to the Courts and Tribunals Service. As of March 2013, however, that transfer had not yet occurred. In 2009–10 the Nuffield Foundation funded interesting work on how tribunals were operating in Northern Ireland, prompted by the suggestion that users of tribunals in Northern Ireland did not have as good an experience as their counterparts in Great Britain. After conducting many interviews the researchers concluded that, in general, people did not know what to expect from tribunals prior to the hearing, that good quality specialist advice and representation was very beneficial but was not available to all users, and that enhanced oversight is needed to maintain standards across tribunals.[49]

THE JUDICAL APPOINTMENTS COMMISSION

4.33 The Northern Ireland Judicial Appointments Commission was created in 2005,[50] its chairperson being the Lord Chief Justice. It mirrors the UK Judicial Appointments Commission, established under the Constitutional

---

[47] See, generally, F Connolly, *Immigration Law in Northern Ireland* (Belfast, SLS Legal Publications, 2011).

[48] Available on the website of the Northern Ireland Courts and Tribunals Service.

[49] See G McKeever and B Thompson, *Redressing Users' Disadvantage: Proposals for Tribunal Reform in Northern Ireland* (Belfast, Law Centre (NI), 2010). See too B Thomspon, *Structural Tribunal Reform in Northern Ireland* (Liverpool, University of Liverpool, 2011) and G McKeever, *Supporting Tribunal Users, Pre-hearing Information, Advice and Support in Northern Ireland* (Jordanstown, University of Ulster, 2011).

[50] See Justice (NI) Act 2002, s 3 and Sch 2, and Justice (NI) Act 2004, ss 1–4; also www.nijac.org.

Reform Act 2005,[51] which selects candidates for judicial office in England and Wales as well as for some tribunals operating in Northern Ireland. The creation of the Northern Ireland Commission was recommended by the Report of the Criminal Justice Review in 2000, partly to reassure those who felt that during the years of conflict in Northern Ireland the judiciary was not always impartial. It conducts the selection and appointments process for judicial posts and passes its views to the Lord Chancellor (solely on the basis of merit) for appointments up to and including the level of High Court judge. In addition the Commission engages in programmes of action to ensure that those holding judicial office in Northern Ireland, and those available for consideration for appointment, are reflective of the community there (meaning, in particular, that they reflect the different religious backgrounds present in the community). In 2008 and 2013 the Commission published research into the barriers to judicial office in Northern Ireland and the definition of 'merit' in the appointments process.[52]

4.34   The 2005 Act also confirms in explicit terms that government ministers throughout the UK must uphold the independence of the judiciary.[53] The Lord Chancellor, for example, must not seek to influence particular judicial decisions through any special access to the judiciary.[54] Additional guarantees are provided exclusively for the judiciary in Northern Ireland[55] and the Lord Chief Justice of Northern Ireland has the power to lay matters relating to any aspect of the administration of justice before Parliament at Westminster or the Assembly at Stormont if they appear to be of importance.[56]

4.35   The Constitutional Reform Act 2005 provided for the appointment of a Northern Ireland Judicial Appointments Ombudsman,[57] but this person's role is limited to dealing with complaints made by people unhappy with the process for appointments to judicial office. He or she cannot deal with complaints about judicial behaviour. In England and Wales, by contrast, there is an Office of Judicial Complaints to consider such matters,[58] from where they can be referred to the Judicial Appointments and Conduct Ombudsman for the UK.[59] That Office focuses primarily on 'maladministration', which embraces behaviour such as delay, rudeness, bias, faulty procedures, refusal to answer questions and unfair treatment. Unfortunately there is no equivalent office in Northern Ireland.

---

[51] s 61 and Sch 12.
[52] *Propensity to Apply for Judicial Office under the New Northern Ireland Judicial Appointments System* (2008) and *Rewarding Merit in Judicial Appointments?* (2013).
[53] s 3(1).
[54] s 3(5).
[55] Justice (NI) Act 2002, s 1, as amended by the Constitutional Reform Act 2005, s 4(1).
[56] Constitutional Reform Act 2005, ss 5 and 6.
[57] s 124 and Sch 15, inserting Sch 3A into the Justice (NI) Act 2002. See www.nijao.gov.uk.
[58] www.judicialcomplaints.gov.uk.
[59] www.judicialombudsman.gov.uk. See Constitutional Reform Act 2005, s 62 and Sch 13.

CONFLICTS OF INTEREST AND IMMUNITY FROM SUIT

4.36 Judges undertake to 'do right to all manner of people without fear or favour, affection or ill will according to the laws and usages of this realm'.[60] If a judge has a conflict of interest in a case (eg he or she has an account with the bank which is being sued) this must be declared to all the parties to the case, any of whom can then ask the judge to 'recuse' him [as in para 9.80] or herself (ie withdraw from the case). A judge's decision in a case can be challenged on appeal not only if there was actual bias but also if an observer might have reasonably suspected bias. This famously happened to Lord Hoffmann, one of the Law Lords hearing the *Pinochet* case,[61] because of his links to Amnesty International, which had been allowed to intervene in the case to give the court the benefit of its views on the issues at stake.

4.37 On account of their reputation for independence, judges are also sometimes appointed to conduct important inquiries (see para 3.71). Lord Saville, for instance, a Lord of Appeal in the House of Lords, chaired the Bloody Sunday Inquiry from 1998 to 2010. Senior judges also chair the Judicial Studies Board for Northern Ireland (which arranges training sessions for all members of the judiciary) and the Northern Ireland Law Commission (see para 3.67).

4.38 Judges in superior courts enjoy what is called 'immunity from suit' when doing their job in court. This means that they cannot be sued for compensation even if they have obviously taken a wrong decision, or said something, which has caused monetary loss or damage to a person's reputation. Judges in inferior courts do not have immunity to quite the same extent, but they can be sued only if they can be shown to have acted out of personal malice, which is *extremely* difficult to prove. District Judges (Magistrates' Courts) are immune from being sued for causing loss to litigants unless they act entirely 'without jurisdiction' (ie they exceed their powers entirely). This was affirmed in *McC v Mullan*, a case from Northern Ireland that reached the House of Lords.[62]

COURT INSPECTIONS

4.39 The Criminal Justice Review in Northern Ireland, which was called for in the Belfast (Good Friday) Agreement in 1998, was completed in 2000

---

[60] Justice and Security (NI) Act 2002, s 19.

[61] *R v Bow Street Metropolitan Stipendiary Magistrate, ex parte Pinochet Ugarte (No 2)* [2000] 1 AC 119, where the House of Lords granted a petition to set aside its earlier decision in the case. When the case was re-heard a slightly different conclusion was reached: see [2000] 1 AC 147. See D Woodhouse (ed), *The Pinochet Case: A Legal and Constitutional Analysis* (Oxford, Hart Publishing, 2000).

[62] [1985] AC 528.

and recommended that courts in Northern Ireland, like courts in England and Wales, should be periodically inspected to ensure that they are providing a satisfactory service to members of the public. Under the Courts Act 2003 a body called Her Majesty's Inspectorate of Court Administration was established. It inspects the systems that support the Crown Court, county courts, magistrates' courts, and Children and Family Court Advisory and Support Service (CAFCASS) in England and Wales, and it can inspect the courts in Northern Ireland if invited to do so. All the inspection reports so far produced on Northern Ireland are available through the Inspectorate's website.[63]

BASIC PRINCIPLES RELATING TO CASE LAW

4.40   In any common law system courts are almost as important a source of law as Parliament. The law which they create is sometimes referred to as case law, to distinguish it from legislation. Indeed the phrase common law is sometimes used as a synonym for judge-made law. Generally speaking, new law is created by courts in two types of situation:

(1)   where existing legislation has nothing at all to say about the point at issue, and
(2)   where what is said about the point at issue in legislation is unclear and needs to be interpreted.

4.41   Just as we did when looking at legislation as a source of law, it is sensible to begin by stating upfront some basic principles concerning case law in Northern Ireland.[64]

(1)   Not all judgments issued by courts in Northern Ireland create new law – the vast majority simply decide what actually happened in the dispute in question and apply the existing law to those facts. In situations where the judgments do make new law the part of the judgment that becomes law is that part which contains the reasoning underlying the decision (sometimes called the '*ratio decidendi*', which is Latin for 'the reason for the decision').[65] Judges may make other remarks in passing during the course of their judgments, but these do not constitute binding law. Such remarks are referred to as '*obiter dicta*', which is Latin for 'things said by the way'.
(2)   The judgments of courts higher up the judicial hierarchy are more authoritative than those of courts lower down. So, new law made by

---

[63] www.hmica.gov.uk/NICtSrep.htm.
[64] See M Zander, *The Law Making Process* (Cambridge, Cambridge UP, 6th edn, 2004), chs 5 and 6 and T Ingman, *The English Legal Process* (Oxford, Oxford UP, 13th edn, 2010), ch 5. See too F Newark, 'Law and Precedent in Northern Ireland' (1972) 23 *NILQ* 100.
[65] I McLeod, *Legal Method* (London, Palgrave Macmillan, 8th edn, 2011), ch 9.

the UK's Supreme Court is binding on the Court of Appeal in Northern Ireland, as it is on all other courts throughout the UK,[66] and new law made by the Court of Appeal in Northern Ireland is binding on the High Court in Northern Ireland. Decisions by all of these courts are binding on the inferior courts in Northern Ireland. This is known as 'the doctrine of precedent'.

(3) Courts at the same level in the judicial hierarchy are not absolutely bound to follow each other's judgments, but such judgments are considered to be very persuasive and only in exceptional circumstances will they not be followed. For example, in situations where there is no possibility of a further appeal to the UK's Supreme Court (as for nearly all civil cases begun in Northern Ireland's magistrates' courts or county courts) the Court of Appeal in Northern Ireland may disregard one of its own previous decisions if it considers that it was plainly wrong or too vague and that to follow it would be unjust or unfair. The UK Supreme Court will not follow one of its own previous decisions, or a decision by the House of Lords, if the criteria set out in the House of Lords' Practice Statement of 1966 are satisfied.[67] These allow a previous decision not to be followed if 'it appears to be right to do so', bearing in mind 'the danger of disturbing retrospectively the basis on which contracts, settlement of property, and fiscal arrangements have been entered into and also the especial need for certainty as to the criminal law'. There has to be at least this measure of flexibility, as otherwise the law would stagnate.

(4) Courts in Northern Ireland, strictly speaking, are not bound to apply the law laid down by courts in England and Wales (except for the UK Supreme Court), but they very frequently do so.

(5) Within one court the views of all the judges sitting in that court are given equal value. Judgments of the Lord Chief Justice, for example, are not any more binding on lower courts than judgments of other judges.

(6) While courts have to apply the doctrine of precedent, part of the skill of being a lawyer is being able to persuade a court that the facts of the case it is dealing with are sufficiently different from those of earlier cases to justify the court 'distinguishing' the earlier cases and issuing a new ruling covering the new facts. Likewise, an earlier decision may be distinguished on the basis that the earlier court reached it without giving proper consideration to other cases or legislation pointing the other way (in legal language such a decision is said to have been taken '*per incuriam*', ie 'without full care').

---

[66] Except that the UK Supreme Court cannot make new criminal law for Scotland, unless the issue in question can be classified as a 'devolution issue'.

[67] [1966] 1 WLR 1234. See *Austin v Southwark LBC* [2010] UKSC 28, [2011] 1 AC 355, at [25], per Lord Hope.

(7)   A higher court can overrule a previous decision by a lower court, but this just means that the higher court is changing the law from that time onwards, not that the losing party in the earlier decision (which may have been taken years previously) can now have that decision reversed. Courts throughout the UK have not so far applied the doctrine of 'prospective overruling', according to which a court decide the cases before it by applying the existing law but rules that from then on the law should be changed.[68]

HOW COURTS INTERPRET LEGISLATION[69]

4.42   However elaborately it is phrased, no rule embodied in primary or secondary legislation can hope to cater for all the circumstances which may arise for consideration. Administrators and judges will inevitably need to interpret the legislation in order to decide whether or not it applies to a given situation. Indeed the task of statutory interpretation occupies a great deal of our judges' time, and the majority of reported cases involve an issue of interpretation at some point. An example is the case of *R v Z*, where Girvan J. had to decide whether the term 'Irish Republican Army', which was listed as an illegal organisation for the purposes of the Terrorism Act 2000, included 'the Real IRA'. He held that it did not, but the Court of Appeal, and then the House of Lords, reversed his decision.[70]

4.43   The interpretation placed by judges on certain words in one piece of legislation will not necessarily be the same as the interpretation placed on the same words in a different piece of legislation. But there are certain approaches to the process of interpretation which judges tend to apply to all legislation, a selection of which is set out below. They range from what are general philosophies concerning judicial activity to what are quite specific presumptions.

(1)   The court will try to ascertain the intention of the legislator when it drafted the particular provision. Until very recently judges were obstructed in their efforts to do this by the rule that reports of proceedings in the UK's Parliament (*Hansard*) could not be looked at to see what the MPs and peers who voted on the provision thought it meant. But in *Pepper v Hart*[71]

---

[68] In *In re Spectrum Plus Ltd* [2005] UKHL 41, [2005] 2 AC 680 the House of Lords accepted that in an appropriate case it could apply the doctrine of prospective overruling, but it refused to do so in that case. See too *In re T (Children) (Care Proceedings: Costs)* [2012] UKSC 36, [2012] 1 WLR 2281.

[69] See McLeod, n 65 above, chs 18 and 19; Zander, n 64 above, ch 3; Ingman, n 64 above, 139–180. The bible in this area is F Bennion, *Statutory Interpretation* (London, LexisNexis, 5th edn, 2008).

[70] [2004] NICA 23, [2005] NI 106 and [2005] UKHL 35, [2005] 2 AC 645. Girvan J's decision is unreported.

[71] [1993] AC 593.

the House of Lords finally accepted that that rule should be relaxed so as to allow judges, when faced with an ambiguity in legislation, to refer to clear statements made by a Minister or other promoter of the legislation and to other parliamentary material which was necessary to understand those statements and their effects.

(2) The intention of Parliament can also be deduced from the long title of the Act, the unambiguous wording of other provisions in the Act, the omissions from the Act, the state of the pre-existing law, official reports preceding the enactment of the legislation, and the practical consequences of preferring one interpretation over another. Today the government issues 'Explanatory Notes' at the same time as it publishes new Bills. These are helpful in conveying in ordinary language what the effects of the Bill's provisions are, but because they are prepared by civil servants, not legislators, they will rarely be relied upon by judges as a guide to the interpretation of particular provisions.[72] The most important indication of Parliament's intention is the ordinary meaning of the words themselves: if one of the interpretations being contended for is at variance with that ordinary meaning, the court will usually prefer to adopt the ordinary meaning. To that extent a purely literal approach to interpretation is shunned. Instead a 'purposive' approach – one which asks 'What was Parliament really getting at here?' is adopted.

(3) Judges will follow conventional maxims of interpretation which it must be assumed the person who drafted the Act was aware of when it was written. One of these is that legislation which creates a criminal offence must be interpreted as narrowly as possible so as to preserve a person's freedom of action. Another is that the express mention of one of a class of things excludes by implication other items of the same class. For example, if at one point an Act refers to a 'vehicle' as 'a machine on wheels' it will be assumed that a machine which is not on wheels cannot be a vehicle for the purposes of any part of that Act. On some matters these maxims of interpretation are so well embedded in our law that they have ceased to be merely arguments to be taken into account by judges and have become obligations requiring the judges to decide the case in a certain way. An example of this is the principle that a person cannot take advantage of his or her illegal act in order to claim a right conferred by legislation.[73] For instance, a murderess cannot claim a widow's pension if the person she murdered was her husband.

(4) Some questions of interpretation recur so frequently that Parliament has provided set solutions to them. These are laid out in the Interpretation

---

[72] For a case in which an Explanatory Note *was* used as an aid to interpretation, see *In re Olchov's Application* [2011] NIQB 31, [2011] 5 BNIL 90.

[73] This is sometimes put in Latin as *ex turpi causa non oritur actio* ('no claim can arise from an unworthy foundation').

Act (NI) 1954 and the Interpretation Act 1978. The former covers the interpretation of Acts of the Northern Ireland Parliament and the Northern Ireland Assembly, as well as Orders in Council. The 1978 Act covers Westminster legislation applying in Northern Ireland. Both Acts deal with problems such as the meaning of 'month', whether 'man' includes 'woman', and whether the singular includes the plural.

HOW TO FIND CASE LAW

4.44   Most court decisions are given orally, in public, and there is no official written record of the reasons for the decision. But those that raise novel points of law are almost invariably written down as formal judgments of the court. A lot of these (but not all) are then put on websites, most of which are freely accessible to members of the public. In addition, there are still several series of printed law reports, which reproduce the most important of the judgments available online. Records of decisions which are unavailable online or in hard copy are said to be unreported, but some of them are still accessible to lawyers in specialist libraries. It should be remembered that judgments are records of the judges' reasons for coming to their conclusions. They are not records of everything that was said during the hearing of the case, whether by the judges, the lawyers, the witnesses, or the parties. Such records are called 'transcripts' and are based on audio recordings, the work of court stenographers or the judge's notes. Transcripts can be made available to lawyers and members of the public by the Northern Ireland Courts and Tribunals Service, but there will usually be a considerable charge for this service.

CASE LAW ON THE INTERNET

4.45   Records of important decisions taken in the Crown Court, High Court and Court of Appeal in Northern Ireland are now made available more or less as soon as they have been delivered on the website of the Northern Ireland Courts and Tribunals Service, and occasionally a judgment issued by a county court judge, a district judge or a Master will be found there too.[74] They can be accessed by clicking on 'Judicial decisions' on the home page of the website: lists of judgments issued during 12-month periods going back to 1999 will then appear. In a typical year there are no more than 200 new cases reported in Northern Ireland. In England there could be as many as 2,500.

4.46   Each case uploaded on to the Courts and Tribunals Service website is given a 'neutral citation'. For example, [2011] NICA 3 refers to the third

---

[74] www.courtsni.gov.uk.

judgment or set of judgments issued by the Court of Appeal in Northern Ireland during 2011. The abbreviations used for other courts are NIQB, NICh, NIFam, NICC (ie Crown Court), NIMaster, NICty and NIMag. The search engine on the Courts and Tribunals Service's website is not very reliable, so unless you know the exact name or date of a case you may not find it too easily. If you happen to know the neutral citation for the case, the quickest way to access it may be to search for that citation using a general search engine such as Google. However not every case for which you happen to have the neutral citation will itself be available online. Judgments issued by the UK's Supreme Court, including those in appeals coming from Northern Ireland, are available on the website of that court on the day they are delivered, and a press summary is published alongside the judgments.[75] The neutral citation abbreviation for that court is UKSC.

Bailii

4.47   A very good website for British and Irish case law is that of the British and Irish Legal Information Institute.[76] On the left-hand side of its home page this website lists various 'Bailii Resources', including seven databases, one of which is labelled 'Northern Ireland'. Clicking on this will take you to a further list of Northern Irish cases, arranged in accordance with the court that decided them. This list includes some judgments issued by the Social Security and Child Support Commissioners, Industrial Tribunals and the Fair Employment Tribunal, and many are cases that were decided before 1999. Clicking on any category of judgment on this list will allow you to search for a particular case by entering its name or by skimming the names of all the cases decided during the same year as that case. The results thrown up by a search based on the name of one of the parties will include cases where that same name occurred at some place during the judgment in question – it may well not be the particular case you are searching for.

4.48   The website of the Northern Ireland Courts and Tribunals Service and the British and Irish Legal Information Institute are freely available to everyone. If you are a law student at a university, or a practising solicitor or barrister, you may also have access to databases which are available on subscription. The best known of these, as explained in Chapter 3 in relation to access to legislation (see para 3.59), are probably Lexis and Westlaw UK. The latter does not contain much case law that is from Northern Ireland but the former has a database labelled 'Northern Ireland Unreported Judgments', which actually includes many cases that *are* reported as well as cases decided before the internet became available and which are otherwise

[75] www.supremecourt.gov.uk.
[76] www.bailii.org.

not easily accessible. You can easily search within that database for the name of one of the parties to a case you are trying to find or for terms that you think may have been used during the reporting of that case. You can also search on the basis of the judge or court that decided the case. If you do not find the case you are looking for, do not assume that it does not exist: it may be available in one of the series of printed law reports (see para 4.49) that has not yet been made digitally available.

PRINTED LAW REPORTS

4.49   In Northern Ireland there are two main series of printed law reports: the *Northern Ireland Law Reports* and the *Northern Ireland Judgments Bulletin*. Both are now published by a commercial firm (Butterworths) under the auspices of the Incorporated Council of Law Reporting for Northern Ireland. The former is the senior series because it began in 1925, but the reports in both series are checked by the judge in question before they are published to make sure that they accurately reproduce what the judge wrote in the judgment. A case in this series of law reports would be cited as, for example, '[2001] NI 165', where 'NI' stands for 'Northern Ireland Law Reports' and '165' is the page in that year's volume at which the report of the case begins. The *Northern Ireland Law Reports* now appear in two parts per year and contain cases decided in the High Court and Court of Appeal in Northern Ireland as well as cases from Northern Ireland that are taken on appeal to the Supreme Court. Some of the Supreme Court's decisions in appeals from Northern Ireland, like those previously taken by the House of Lords, are also included in series of law reports published primarily for England and Wales, such as the Weekly Law Reports, the All England Law Reports and Appeal Cases. They may also be included in the series of short reports included in some quality newspapers, the most respected of which is the *The Times' Law Reports*.

4.50   The *Northern Ireland Judgments Bulletin*, previously called the Bluebook from the colour of its cover, has been published since 1970, and now also appears twice a year. It reproduces the judges' judgments without including an editor's summary of the facts and the decision (in what is called a 'headnote') or a list of the other cases cited in the judgments. Otherwise there is little to choose between the two series of reports and one has to wonder why they cannot be merged. A case reported in the *Judgments Bulletin* will be cited thus: '[2000] NIJB 248'. Until about 20 years ago some cases reported in the *Judgments Bulletin* were later reported in the *Northern Ireland Law Reports* too, but this no longer occurs.

4.51 An index to all Northern Ireland cases reported in printed series between 1921 and 1997 was published in 1998 but it is not, unfortunately, available online and there is no index of the more recently reported cases.

4.52 Appendix 5 to this book reproduces the case of *Robinson (Iris) v Sunday Newspapers Ltd*[77], in which the judgment of the Court of Appeal in Northern Ireland was issued on 24 May 2011. The court allowed Mrs Robinson's appeal and directed that the application for the continuation of the injunction she was seeking should be heard in private. In order to avoid revealing the very information which it was ruling was private, the court redacted (ie edited) the published version of its judgment by removing some of the text, and the judgment indicates where that has occurred. Reading the case will show you how judges structure their judgments, what sorts of legal arguments they consider, how they deal with previous case law relevant to the legal points at issue (most of which is English case law), and the ways in which they couch their reasoning and conclusions. Unusually, no legislation is mentioned in this particular judgment, but Articles 2, 3 and 8 of the European Convention on Human Rights were considered because they are part of the law of Northern Ireland by virtue of the Human Rights Act 1998. The court must have thought that that was too obvious a point to require explicit explanation.

4.53 In some fields of law special series of law reports have been devised to help publicise lower courts' decisions as well as decisions of higher courts which would not otherwise qualify for inclusion in one of the major series. In Northern Ireland there are special series of this sort for decisions of the Lands Tribunal, industrial tribunals and social security appeal tribunals. Decisions of courts and tribunals which might not otherwise have been reported but which might nevertheless be of some legal interest were frequently noted in the *Bulletin of Northern Ireland Law*, a publication produced 10 times per year by a company called SLS (Legal Publications) Ltd at Queen's University Belfast. Unfortunately this ceased publication at the end of 2012. It attempted to list all developments of legal interest to Northern Ireland and its absence will be sorely missed.[78]

---

[77] [2001] NICA 13, [2011] 6 BNIL 72.

[78] The Bulletin summarised all new legislation applying in Northern Ireland (including commencement orders), all written judgments delivered by the Court of Appeal, High Court and county courts, selected decisions of tribunals, all personal injury awards in the High Court, notices issued by the Northern Ireland Courts and Tribunals Service (including judicial appointments), Practice Directions, many consultation documents or proposals for legislation and some developments in EU law and in the law of England and Wales.

5

International Law in Northern Ireland

INTERNATIONAL LAW

5.1 International law – or at any rate public international law – is the law which governs relationships between States. It derives from five sources:

(1) international treaties
(2) international custom and practice
(3) general principles of law recognized by civilized nations
(4) judicial decisions and
(5) the teachings of the most highly qualified writers.[1]

5.2 In general, international law is not itself a source of law in Northern Ireland. This means that the Northern Ireland Assembly, when legislating, and judges, when deciding cases, do not have to have any regard to international law. They have to do so only if the international law has already become part of the law of Northern Ireland through legislation. If judges were to apply international law when the national law is already quite clear on the point at issue, this would be a breach of their constitutional duty to apply the law of the land. But when the existing national law is unclear, perhaps because relevant legislation is ambiguous, judges are free to adopt an interpretation of the law which coincides with that preferred by international law, especially if the Government has already indicated its intention to abide by that law. An example of this occurring in Northern Ireland is the case of *R v Deery*,[2] which concerned a man who had been found guilty of possessing an unlicensed firearm. Between the date on which he was caught with the firearm and the date on which he was sentenced for the offence, new legislation had entered into force increasing the punishment

---

[1] See Art 38 of the Statute of the International Court of Justice (para 5.4 below), annexed to the Charter of the United Nations (1945), which is generally considered to reflect international consensus on the sources of international law.
[2] [1977] NI 164 (CA).

for the offence. The question for the court was whether this new legislation should be interpreted as applying to people whose offences were committed before it came into force or only to people whose offences were committed after that date. In preferring the latter interpretation Lord Lowry CJ cited Article 7 of the European Convention on Human Rights (1950), which says that no-one should be punished for a crime in a way that was not possible at the time the crime was committed. At the time, the European Convention had not yet been made part of Northern Ireland's law through legislation.[3]

Soft law standards

5.3   International law also recognises what are often called 'soft law' standards, which are standards laid down not in treaties but in documents headed 'Declarations', 'Basic Principles', or 'Standard Minimum Rules', etc. These are really statements of best practice which the General Assembly of the United Nations or some other internationally respected body has set out in an attempt to raise the level of treatment accorded to people by governments. Again, they are not binding on any domestic court, unless they have become so generally accepted as to amount to international custom and practice, but they may be referred to by judges as aids to the interpretation of ambiguous legislation or when the existing judge-made law of the land is uncertain. In recent years top UK courts have begun to pay more attention to both hard and soft international law as a source of domestic national law. They did so when ruling that General Pinochet could be extradited to Chile[4] and that a court could not rely on evidence that might have been obtained through the use of torture.[5]

5.4   It is beyond the scope of this book to explain the workings of international law and of its growing number of sub-branches such as international criminal law, international humanitarian law (sometimes referred to as the law of war), international human rights law and international environmental law. But it is worth mentioning that there are now a number of international courts that issue rulings on a wide variety of issues, which in appropriate circumstances could be cited in Northern Ireland's courts as evidence of current international legal standards.[6] These courts include:

---

[3] This only occurred when the Human Rights Act 1998 came fully into force on 2 October 2000.

[4] *R v Bow Street Stipendiary Magistrate, ex parte Pinochet Ugarte (No 3)* [2000] 1 AC 147. In the end the UK Government refused to extradite Pinochet to Spain because he was supposedly too ill to stand trial. Instead he returned to his native Chile.

[5] *A v Secretary of State for the Home Department (No 2)* [2005] UKHL 71, [2006] 2 AC 221.

[6] For a very readable account of contemporary international law issues, see Philippe Sands, *Lawless World* (London, Allen Lane, 2005).

(1)   The International Court of Justice (ICJ) at The Hague, which handles disputes between States (if they accept the jurisdiction of the Court) and issues Advisory Opinions when asked to do so by the General Assembly of the United Nations (UN). In 2010, for example, the ICJ issued an Advisory Opinion in answer to a question from the General Assembly about whether Kosovo's unilateral declaration of independence from Serbia was in accordance with international law.

(2)   The International Criminal Court (ICC), also based at The Hague, which tries individuals for war crimes, crimes against humanity and genocide.[7] Charles Taylor, the former President of Liberia, was convicted by the ICC in 2012 of aiding and abetting rebels in Sierra Leone during the 1991–2002 civil war in that country. He was sentenced to 50 years in prison.

(3)   The International Criminal Tribunal for the former Yugoslavia (ICTY), again at The Hague, which tries individuals for alleged war crimes, crimes against humanity and genocide committed during the conflicts in Bosnia-Herzegovina, Serbia and Croatia in the 1990s. Radovan Karadzic, the former leader of Bosnian Serbs, is currently under trial at the ICTY.

(4)   The Inter-American Court of Human Rights, located in San José, Costa Rica. This Court hears cases brought under the American Convention on Human Rights of 1969 and has issued important judgments dealing with issues arising out of the many conflicts that occurred in Latin and South America in the 1970s and 1980s. In its judgment in *Barrios Altos v Peru* in 2001 the Court found that Peru had to pay compensation to the families of 14 people who were killed by death squads composed of members of the Peruvian army in 1991.[8] It has also ruled that amnesty laws, passed to prevent prosecutions of those involved in serious civil unrest or its suppression, cannot apply to people who have committed 'crimes against humanity'.

(5)   The Court of Justice of the Economic Community of West African States (ECOWAS), situated in Abuja, Nigeria. In 2008 this court issued a landmark ruling when it held that the Government of Niger was guilty of not protecting a woman against slavery despite having domestic laws abolishing servitude. The Court ordered Niger to pay the claimant almost 20,000 US dollars by way of compensation.

(6)   The Panel and Appellate Body of the World Trade Organization, based in Geneva. In 1998 the Appellate Body ruled that in principle the USA was entitled to ban the import of shrimps from countries such as India if the shrimps were fished in a way which endangered migratory sea turtles, a protected species. But it held that, on the facts, the ban in this

---

[7] For more details see W Schabas, *The International Criminal Court: A Commentary on the Rome Statute* (Oxford, Oxford UP, 2010).

[8] (2001) IACHR Series C Nos 83 and 87.

case was invalid because it had been posed only on imports from some countries but not others.

Other very important international courts operate within the framework of the European Union and the Council of Europe. These are explained in separate sections below (see paras 5.10–5.43). At present there is no regional court for the Asia-Pacific area, whether in human rights or in any other field.

5.5   As well as public international law there is a body of law known as private international law, or the conflict of laws, which comes into play when disputes arise between individuals or companies based in different countries. Each country has its own rules on what rules to apply in such disputes, but there is a growing consensus as to what those rules should be, especially as States have entered into many treaties to try to harmonise them. Nevertheless, difficulties can still arise when, for example, a person does something in one country that harms people in a number of other countries, or when a dispute over the custody of children breaks out between parents living in different countries. The rules that apply in Northern Ireland are almost without exception the same as those which apply in England and Wales.[9]

TREATIES

5.6   When countries enter into treaties with other countries those treaties are considered to be comparable to contracts drawn up between private individuals or companies. Indeed a specific treaty has been agreed which sets out how other treaties should be interpreted.[10] For a treaty to be made a part of international law it has to be 'ratified' by States, with the treaty itself usually specifying how many States have to ratify it before it will come into force (for those States). States differ as to what is necessary under their own constitutional arrangements in order to ratify a treaty, but in the UK, under the Constitutional Reform and Governance Act 2010, ratification is normally taken to have occurred after the treaty, once signed by the Government, has been published and laid before Parliament for 21 days.[11] Very important treaties, such as the Maastricht Treaty of European Union of 1992, are usually submitted to Parliament for its express approval, or they

[9] For further details see a standard textbook such as Cheshire, North and Fawcett, *Private International Law* (Oxford, Oxford UP, 14th edn, 2008).
[10] See the Vienna Convention on the Law of Treaties (1969). This was invoked by the UK Supreme Court when rejecting the challenge by Julian Assange, of Wikileaks, to a European Arrest Warrant: *Assange v Swedish Prosecution Authority* [2012] UKSC 22, [2012] 2 AC 471. For a Northern Ireland case on a European Arrest Warrant see *De Juana Chaos v Kingdom of Spain* [2012] NIQB 32, [2012] 7 BNIL 23.
[11] s 20.

might even be put before the people in a referendum. A treaty providing for an increase in the powers of the European Parliament, or amending the founding treaties of the European Union, cannot be ratified unless it has been approved by an Act of the UK Parliament.[12]

The dualist approach

5.7 Most countries, including the UK and Ireland, do not consider treaties to be part of their national law unless they have been formally incorporated into that law by the national Parliament. This so-called 'dualist' approach to international agreements is justified on the basis that, if the position were otherwise, governments could change the national law of their country without first seeking parliamentary or judicial approval, which would be a clear breach of the doctrine of separation of powers (see para 2.12). That doctrine is intended to prevent law-making power residing in the hands of the executive branch of the State. Treaties that have been ratified but not yet incorporated into domestic law are not binding on any judge in the UK.[13] Examples of such treaties are the UN's International Covenant on Economic, Social and Cultural rights (1966) and the UN's Convention on the Rights of the Child (1989). 'Covenant' and 'Convention', by the way, are just alternative words for a treaty. One of the 'excepted matters' which the Northern Ireland Assembly has no power to deal with is 'relations with territories outside the UK', but one of the exceptions to that exclusion is 'observing and implementing international obligations'.[14] This means that the Assembly could, if it wished, incorporate the provisions of a ratified treaty into the law of Northern Ireland (provided they otherwise relate to a 'transferred matter': see para 2.28). This power also resided in the old Parliament of Northern Ireland; an example of its exercise is the Adoption (Hague Convention) Act (NI) 1969, which deals with inter-country adoptions.

5.8 Examples of domestic statutes incorporating treaties, or parts of treaties, into the law of Northern Ireland (and into the law of other parts of the UK at the same time) are the Carriage of Passengers by Road Act 1974, the State Immunity Act 1978,[15] the Human Rights Act 1998 and the International Criminal Court Act 2001.[16] These Acts, in effect, implemented

---

[12] s 23(1). See the European Union Act 2011, ss 1-14.

[13] *Maclaine Watson & Co Ltd v Department of Trade and Industry* [1990] 2 AC 418 (the International Tin Council case); but see the comments of Lord Steyn in *Re McKerr* [2004] UKHL 12, [2004] 1 WLR 807, at [48]–[50], where he thought the time might soon come for the orthodox approach to be altered.

[14] Northern Ireland Act 1998, Sch 2, para 3.

[15] This was the Act in dispute during the court cases in England on whether ex-President Pinochet of Chile could be brought to justice.

[16] Technically, the Human Rights Act 1998 did not 'incorporate' the 1950 European Convention on Human Rights. It merely made some of the rights set out in that Convention part

treaties which were concluded, respectively, in 1968, 1973, 1950 and 1998, each by a particular international agency. Sometimes the actual text of the treaty will be included in a Schedule to the Act of Parliament, at other times its provisions will be reworded but with more or less the same effect. Under the United Nations Act 1946,[17] if the UN Security Council calls upon the UK Government[18] to take measures not involving the use of armed force to give effect to a Security Council decision, the UK Government can issue an Order in Council to take those measures, even if they involve the apprehension, trial and punishment of people who breach the Order. But the UK Government needs to be careful to take only those measures which are strictly within its authority to take under this provision; if it does not, the Order in Council can be invalidated as being *ultra vires*.[19]

OTHER SOURCES OF INTERNATIONAL LAW

5.9   The four other sources of international law mentioned in paragraph 5.1 are less easily identified because they are rather vague. There is no consensus around the world as to what are the precise legal rules which can be derived from international custom and practice, the general principles recognized by civilized nations, judicial decisions, and the teachings of the most highly qualified writers. The views of the International Court of Justice are considered to be very authoritative in this regard, but no international body, official or unofficial, has yet succeeded in producing a code of the resulting rules which has been universally accepted. The best effort has been made by the International Law Commission (ILC), whose very raison d'être is to promote and codify international law.[20] Many of the ILC's reports have later resulted in Conventions agreed within the UN itself.[21] Some rules of international law have acquired such an elevated status over the years that they are now known as '*ius cogens*', or 'peremptory norms'. This means that they must always be applied by an international court, whatever the circumstances. Examples are the prohibitions on genocide, piracy and slavery.

of domestic UK law. In *Re McKerr* [2004] UKHL 12, [2004] 1 WLR 807 this distinction was used to justify the non-retrospectivity of the Human Rights Act 1998, but in *In re McCaughey* [2011] UKSC 20, [2012] 1 AC 725 the Supreme Court declined to follow *Re McKerr* because of a subsequent decision by the European Court of Human Rights which seemed to contradict it (*Šilih v Slovenia* (2009) 49 EHRR 37). See too para 6.35.

   [17] s 1(1).
   [18] Under Art 41 of the UN's Charter.
   [19] In *Ahmed v HM Treasury* [2010] UKSC 2, [2010] 2 AC 534 two anti-terrorism Orders were invalidated by the Supreme Court on this basis.
   [20] Statute of the International Law Commission, Art 1(1). This Statute was adopted by the General Assembly of the United Nations in 1947.
   [21] See the list at www.un.org/law/ilc.

EUROPEAN UNION LAW[22]

5.10 When the UK joined the European Economic Community (the EEC, also known at that time as the Common Market), the European Atomic Energy Community (Euratom) and the European Coal and Steel Community (ECSC) on 1 January 1973, the Treaties establishing those Communities were incorporated into UK law by an Act of the Westminster Parliament, the European Communities Act 1972. Subsequent amendments to the founding Treaties have also been incorporated. The principal milestones are as follows:

(1) ECSC Treaty 1951 (expired in 2002) → European Communities Act 1972
(2) Treaty of Rome 1957 (the EEC Treaty, and the Euratom Treaty) → European Communities Act 1972
(3) Single European Act 1986 (an amending Treaty, despite its name) →European Communities (Amendment) Act 1986
(4) Treaty of Maastricht 1992 (the Treaty on European Union) → European Communities (Amendment) Act 1993
(5) Treaty of Amsterdam 1997 → European Communities (Amendment) Act 1998
(6) Treaty of Nice 2001 → European Communities (Amendment) Act 2002
(7) Treaty of Lisbon 2007 → European Union (Amendment) Act 2008.

5.11 When the Treaty of Maastricht came into force in 1993, the European Union (EU) comprised three 'pillars'. The first pillar dealt with the establishment and the functioning of the internal market, which ensured the free movement of goods, persons, services and capital, undistorted competition and related economic, social, environmental or other Community policies. It embraced and supplemented the areas which had previously been the concern of the EEC, introduced the co-decision procedure, which gave the European Parliament for the first time the power to legislate in tandem with the Council (now called 'ordinary legislative procedure'), and renamed the EEC as the European Community (EC). The second pillar was concerned with the common foreign and security policy, and the third with police and judicial co-operation; these two pillars remained inter-governmental responsibilities. Only the EC, which exercised supranational powers under the first pillar, had 'legal personality', in the

---

[22] See generally T C Hartley, *The Foundations of European Union Law* (Oxford., Oxford UP, 7th edn, 2010; D Chalmers, G Davies and G Monti, *European Union Law* (Cambridge, Cambridge UP, 2nd edn, 2010); P Craig and G de Búrca, *EU Law – Text, Cases and Materials* (Oxford, Oxford UP, 5th edn, 2011); L Woods and P Watson, *Steiner and Woods' EU Law* (Oxford Oxford UP, 11th edn, 2012); I McLeod, *Legal Method* (London, Palgrave Macmillan, 8th edn, 2011), ch 5.

sense that it could act on behalf of all the EU's Member States in respect of the matters covered by the first pillar, including the adoption of binding legislation.

5.12 When the Treaty of Lisbon entered into force in 2009, the pillar structure was abandoned; the common foreign and security policy, and police and judicial co-operation in criminal matters were brought within the ambit of the EU, and legal personality was conferred on the whole of the EU, which replaced the EC. The EU can now speak for the Member States on all the matters that were previously distributed among the three pillars. The Union can also enter into international treaties with third countries or international organisations, and those treaties will then be binding on both the Union institutions and the Member States and thus have primacy over EU secondary legislation and national laws. Although the EU has not itself become a State, it has evolved as a 'supranational' community with constitutional characteristics into an integrated legal order which confers rights on private parties and involves the autonomous exercise of public power subject to controls analogous to those in a State. The Lisbon Treaty has maintained the balance between the two polar forces of 'supranationalism' and 'intergovernmentalism'.[23] The official name of the original 1957 Treaty, as amended, is now the Treaty on the Functioning of the European Union (TFEU). It exists side-by-side with the Treaty on European Union (TEU), which includes general provisions on the Union's objectives, principles and institutions, as well as its external action and common foreign and security policy. The TEU also provides for the first time for the Member States' right to withdraw from the Union. All the relevant documents are of course available online, but you can also buy the full texts of these two treaties, together with other important EU legislation, in book form.[24]

5.13 According to the most commonly accepted interpretation of the UK's 1972 and subsequent European Communities Acts, the common law of the three UK legal systems (England and Wales, Scotland and Northern Ireland), as well as existing and future UK legislation, all have effect subject to EU law. In other words, EU law is a 'higher' source of law in Northern Ireland, although only because the UK Parliament has said so. To that extent the theory of parliamentary sovereignty (see para 2.12) is not compromised. Thus the supremacy of EU law over conflicting national law is based on the will of Parliament, which voluntarily accepted limitations on its sovereignty when it adopted the European Communities Act 1972 and its subsequent amendments. The European Union Act 2011 confirms that directly applicable or directly effective EU law (see paras 5.16 and 5.20) is law in

---

[23] See D Doukas, 'The Verdict of the German Federal Constitutional Court on the Lisbon Treaty: Not Guilty but Don't Do it Again!' (2009) 34 *European Law Review* 866, at 871–2 and 886–7.

[24] See, eg, Blackstone's EU Treaties and Legislation 2012–2013 (Oxford, Oxford UP, 2012).

the UK only because Parliament has so provided in the 1972 Act and later Acts.[25] The 2011 Act also provides that if in future there is a proposal to alter an EU treaty in a way which would transfer more powers from the UK to the EU there will have to be a referendum on that proposal in the UK.[26]

5.14 It is therefore important to know who makes EU laws, and how. The principal law-making and political institutions are the following:

(1) *The European Commission.* This is, in a sense, the 'cabinet' of the EU, comprising a President, seven Vice-Presidents, and 19 other Commissioners, all of whom have offices in Brussels. It is the Union's executive and the 'guardian of the treaties' which proposes EU legislation and represents the Union's interests as a whole and independently of national governments. It may also adopt legislation when exercising legislative powers delegated by the Council and/or the European Parliament. Each of the 27 Member States of the EU is therefore represented on the Commission[27] by someone who has a particular portfolio (eg external affairs, competition, energy, trade, transport), although obviously the Commissioners are there to work on behalf of the EU as a whole and not for their own country's interests. The Vice-Presidents and Commissioners are not directly elected to their posts but are chosen by the President of the Commission, who is elected by the European Parliament after having been nominated by the European Council. The President and the members of the Commission must be approved as a body by the European Parliament before they can be formally appointed for five years by the European Council.

(2) *The European Parliament.* This is a body that since 1979 has been directly elected by the people of Europe every five years. There are now 754 Members of the European Parliament (MEPs), three of whom represent Northern Ireland. The Parliament sits mainly in Brussels, but sometimes in Strasbourg (France) and Luxembourg. It cannot itself initiate legislation, a function reserved for the European Commission, but it can consider proposals for legislation drawn up by the Commission. On the overwhelming majority of matters EU legislation can only be adopted if Parliament, as well as the Council consent – a process known as the 'ordinary legislative procedure' (formerly known as 'co-decision'). However, on a few other, more politically sensitive matters, such as excise duties and other forms of indirect taxation, the European Parliament has only a consultative role and the legislation can be adopted by the Council acting unanimously even if the Parliament does not consent. The Parliament also shares

---

[25] European Union Act 2011, s 18.
[26] Ibid ss 2, 3 and 6.
[27] The total number of Commissioners is likely to rise to 28 as Croatia is set to become the 28th Member State of the EU on 1 July 2013.

responsibility with the Council for drafting and adopting the Union's budget. It can further dismiss the entire Commission by a motion of censure.

(3) *The Council of the European Union* (or *Council of Ministers* or *Council*) is probably the most important of the EU's decision-making bodies because it comprises government Ministers from each of the 27 Member States who together pass legislation (usually by qualified majority and jointly with the European Parliament in the 'ordinary legislative procedure', but sometimes unanimously and on its own), approve the EU's annual budget (again in conjunction with the Parliament), co-ordinate the national economic policies, conclude international agreements on behalf of the Union and adopt measures in the fields of foreign affairs, or security and justice (in the latter field, in conjunction or in consultation with the Parliament). The national Ministers who attend the Council meetings will differ depending on the subject under discussion at the meeting in question.

(4) *The European Council.* Confusingly, there is also a body known as the European Council, which is made up of the heads of State or government of the 27 Member States as well as the President of the European Union and the President of the European Commission. It is assisted by the Union's High Representative for Foreign Affairs, who is also one of the Commission's two Vice-Presidents. The European Council represents the Member States' interests at the highest level and usually meets two or three times a year (in what are called 'EU summits'), mainly to discuss and decide on macro-political issues and strategic priorities, and give the necessary impetus for the development of the Union. It does not have any formal law-making powers of its own.

5.15   EU law falls into three categories:

(1) The provisions of the Treaties setting up the Community and the Union, and amendments to those Treaties, as well as the Charter of Fundamental Rights of the EU (see para 5.23); all of these can be said to constitute the primary legislation of the EU, binding not only on the EU's own institutions but on the Member States too.

(2) Regulations, Directives, Decisions, or other legally binding acts (and Recommendations, Opinions or other legally non-binding or soft law acts[28]) adopted by the EU's institutions, that is, the Council of the European Union, the European Parliament and, in terms of delegated legislation, the European Commission; all of these acts can be referred to as the secondary legislation of the EU.

---

[28] Recommendations and Opinions are, technically, non-binding, but the Court of Justice of the European Union has held that the former can be taken into account when interpreting national laws adopted to implement EU measures. It is therefore possible to argue that Recommendations and Opinions are persuasive authorities in Northern Ireland's courts.

(3)   Rulings and decisions of the Court of Justice of the European Union, which actually comprises three courts: the Court of Justice (formerly known as the Court of Justice of the European Communities), the General Court (formerly known as the Court of First Instance) and the Civil Service Tribunal.

5.16   Some of the legislative acts in the second category (namely, Regulations and most Decisions) are 'directly applicable' in all 27 of the Member States of the EU, which means that they have the force of law in each of those countries without the need for any further national legislation. They are said to be 'self-executing'. Regulations are binding in their entirety on all Member States, while Decisions are binding only on those States, corporations or individuals to whom they are addressed.

5.17   Sometimes Regulations do require Member States to adopt national measures to implement them. Council Regulation 1257/99, for example, required Member States to introduce measures to create rural development plans. It may also be necessary to put in place administrative measures to give effect to the rights created by Regulations, but in such cases the Regulations still remain directly applicable, so if the administrative measures are not adopted in time, people can still rely directly upon the Regulations in any legal dispute in national courts.

5.18   Decisions of the EU's institutions are always binding on the people or bodies to whom they are addressed without the need for any further implementation. They are designed to deal with specific situations, such as whether a Member State should be allocated structural funding for a specific project or whether a company is in breach of competition law. The addressees of such decisions (or any other persons who can prove that they are directly and individually concerned) have the standing to challenge the decisions before the Court of Justice.[29] Decisions are also used by the Council and the European Parliament to set out policy positions. For instance, the Sixth Environmental Action Plan, which was laid down in Decision 1600/2002, set out the EU's priorities in environmental law for the period 2002 to 2012 (a Seventh Plan is still under discussion). These sorts of decisions are not addressed to anyone in particular and require implementing measures, so they cannot be challenged by individuals in the Court of Justice.

---

[29] Under art 263(4) TFEU, any natural or legal person may bring an action of annulment 'against an act addressed to that person or which is of direct and individual concern to them, and against a regulatory act which is of direct concern to them and does not entail implementing measures'.

Directives

5.19   Directives, despite their name, are not directly applicable; they are binding only as to the result to be achieved by them and each Member State is free to decide upon the means for giving the Directives legal and administrative effect (ie for 'transposing' them into national law). A Directive will, however, set a time limit for the implementation of its provisions. Thus, by Directive 2008/104 of 19 November 2008 ([2008] OJ L327/9) Member States had to alter their law on the protection of temporary agency workers within three years. This was done for England, Wales and Scotland through the Agency Workers Regulations 2010, made by the Department of Business, Innovation and Skills.[30] Every now and then the government issues a European Communities (Designation) Order to indicate the authorities in the UK which, under section 2(2) of the European Communities Act 1972, are empowered to make UK regulations giving effect to EU law.[31] Often a Directive is implemented in Northern Ireland through statutory rules issued by a department of the Northern Ireland Executive.[32] Because employment law is a devolved matter in Northern Ireland (unlike in Scotland), separate Agency Workers Regulations (NI) 2011 were issued by the Department for Employment and Learning in Northern Ireland.[33] Directives constitute the principal means of co-ordination or harmonisation of national laws. Failure to properly implement them within the given deadline may give rise to infringement proceedings brought by the European Commission against the recalcitrant Member State (see para 5.28), and to the application of the doctrines of direct or indirect effect, and State liability.

5.20   While most types of EU legislation (except Regulations) are not directly applicable, the jurisprudence has developed a similar concept – 'direct effect', to allow them to be of benefit to individuals living within the EU. The concept was first developed by the Court of Justice in 1963, in the case of *Van Gend en Loos*.[34] There the Court held that an Article in the Treaty of Rome requiring the abolition of customs duties (now Art 30 TFEU) could be used as a defence by someone who was being prosecuted for not paying an import tariff in the Netherlands. Today any provision of EU legislation is, in principle, capable of having direct effect so long as it is clearly and precisely worded, unconditional (that is, not subject to any reservations or limits), and not dependent on any further action being taken. (The last requirement has

---

[30] SI 93.

[31] Eg the European Communities (Designation) (No 5) Order 2010 (SI 2690).

[32] Eg the Cross-Border Mediation Regs (NI) 2011 (SR 157), which implement Directive 2008/52/EC on aspects of mediation in civil and commercial matters applying to cross-border disputes.

[33] SR 350.

[34] Case 26/62, [1963] ECR 1; [1963] CMLR 105.

been relaxed with regard to Directives, which may claim direct effect even after their implementation deadline has expired.) Usually the direct effect operates 'vertically', allowing individuals and companies to argue that the legislation imposes obligations on the State; sometimes (mainly in the case of Treaty provisions, but not Directives) it operates 'horizontally', allowing individuals and companies to make use of the EU legislation in their own private disputes. A claimant may be able to get round the non-availability of the direct effect concept at the horizontal level by arguing instead that the other party to the dispute should be regarded as an 'emanation of the State' and thus bound to act in accordance with the EU legislation. In *Foster v British Gas plc*,[35] for example, a woman employee who was required by her employer to retire at 60 years of age, while male employees could continue working until they were 65 years of age, won her case because British Gas was at that time a nationalised industry and so ultimately the responsibility of the British Government (the *Foster* criteria may however also be satisfied in case of privatised utilities or private entities entrusted by the State with the provision of a public service and special powers).

5.21 If a Member State fails to implement an EU Directive by the given deadline, or if it implements it incorrectly or incompletely, individuals may still be able to rely on the Directive's provisions in national court proceedings against State bodies or any other 'emanation of the State'. The State's failure to properly implement a Directive and that Directive's failure to produce vertical direct effect may give rise to an indirect effect in that national courts must, according to the established case law of the Court of Justice, do their best to interpret national laws in a way which complies with the Directive.[36] This is essentially a rule of statutory interpretation, the effectiveness of which depends on the capacity of national judges to interpret national legislation in accordance with EU legislation so far as is possible, that is, without distorting the clear meaning of national legislation.[37] In addition, if a provision of EU law (whether in a Treaty or a Directive) clearly aims to confer rights and duties on individuals, a person who suffers losses as a result of a Member State's failure to comply with that provision may be able to sue the government in question to recover compensation for the losses suffered (in a so-called '*Francovich* action').[38] This occurred in a case in Northern Ireland involving the Government's failure to implement the Working Time Directive.[39] But the breach of EU law has to be sufficiently

---

[35] Case C-188/89, [1990] ECR I–3313.
[36] Case 14/83, *Von Colson and Kamann* [1984] ECR 1981 and Case C-106/89, *Marleasing* [1990] ECR I-4135.
[37] *Webb v EMO Air Cargo* [1992] 4 All ER 929.
[38] *Francovich v Italy* [1992] IRLR 85.
[39] *Re Burns' Application* [1999] NI 175. The Working Time Directive was issued in 1993 (93/104/EC) and was supposed to have been implemented within three years. The Working Time Regulations 1998 eventually implemented the Directive two years late.

serious.[40] This is presumed to be the case if it has clearly been established by infringement proceedings or by a preliminary ruling of the Court of Justice, or if it can be established on the basis of settled case law. There will also be a sufficiently serious breach if the Member State enjoys no or very little legislative discretion in the matter or if it manifestly and gravely disregards the limits of that discretion. Exceptionally, if the highest appeal court in a Member State manifestly infringes EU law, especially if it is settled case law of the Court of Justice, that too could constitute a sufficiently serious breach for this purpose. State liability may serve as either an additional or alternative remedy, available for breaches of both directly and non-directly effective EU law rights.

5.22   It is now clear that courts throughout the UK can refuse to apply even an Act of Parliament if the judges are of the view that the Act conflicts with EU law. In the *Factortame* case[41] the House of Lords, following a ruling by the Court of Justice, held that provisions in the Merchant Shipping Act 1988, and regulations made thereunder, should be 'disapplied'. Much the same conclusion was reached by the House of Lords itself (this time without needing a prior determination by the Court of Justice) in a later case concerning a provision in the Employment Protection (Consolidation) Act 1978: see *R v Secretary of State for Employment, ex parte the Equal Opportunities Commission*.[42] For a case where a court in Northern Ireland disapplied provisions in legislation because of their inconsistency with EU law, see *Perceval-Price v Department of Economic Development*.[43]

THE EU CHARTER OF FUNDAMENTAL RIGHTS

5.23   With the coming into force of the Treaty of Lisbon in 2009 a document called the Charter of Fundamental Rights, first agreed by EU Member States in 2000, and revised and re-proclaimed in 2007, also came into effect. This supplements the general principles of EU law, and the Union's obligation under Article 6(2) of the TEU to accede to the European Convention on Human Rights. Article 6(1) of the TEU states that the EU 'recognises the rights, freedoms and principles set out in the Charter of Fundamental Rights' and adds that the Charter has the same legal value as the EU Treaties. It goes on to say, however, that the Charter does not extend in any way the competences of the EU as defined in the Treaties. The Charter, with its six substantive sections headed Dignity, Freedoms, Equality, Solidarity, Citizens' Rights and Justice, is probably the most

---

[40] Joined Cases C-46/93 and C-48/93, *Brasserie du Pêcheur v Germany* and *R v Secretary of State for Transport, ex parte Factortame Ltd (No 3)* [1996] ECR I-1029.
[41] *Factortame Ltd v Secretary of State for Transport (No 2)* [1991] 1 AC 603.
[42] [1995] 1 AC 1.
[43] [2000] NI 141.

comprehensive 'Bill of Rights' in the world, but it only applies within EU Member States in the fields where the EU has some competence or EU law applies. While it is binding on EU institutions, it is only binding on EU Member States when they are implementing EU law.[44] Moreover the UK insisted on qualifying its acceptance of the Charter; Protocol 30 to the TFEU says that the Charter does not extend the ability of the Court of Justice of the European Union or of any court in the UK 'to find that the law, regulations or administrative provisions, practices or action...of the UK are inconsistent with the fundamental rights, freedoms and principle that it reaffirms'. The exact significance of these words has still to be explored in the UK courts. The first occasion on which the UK Supreme Court considered the scope of a provision in the EU Charter (it was Article 8, which guarantees the protection of personal data) was in *Rugby Football Union v Consolidated Information Services Ltd*.[45] The Court held that on the facts of that case Article 8 had not been violated.

THE COURT OF JUSTICE OF THE EUROPEAN UNION[46]

5.24   The Court of Justice of the European Union (CJEU), which sits in Luxembourg and was known until 2009 as the European Court of Justice, is staffed by 27 judges and eight Advocates-General, all of whom are chosen by the governments of the 27 Member States[47] after consultation with a seven-member panel consisting of former members of the Court of Justice or the General Court, members of national supreme courts and lawyers of recognised competence. The judges are selected from the people who are eligible for appointment to the highest judicial posts in their own countries or who are jurists of recognised competence, and whose independence is beyond doubt. The judges, who are appointed for a renewable six-year term of office, elect their own President, for a renewable three-year term. The Court may sit in chambers of three or five judges, as a Grand Chamber of 15 judges or, very rarely, as a full court of 27 judges. Most cases are heard by a chamber, but a Member State or a Union institution that is a party to proceedings can request that a case be heard by a Grand Chamber.

5.25   Advocates-General are similar to the court advisers used in continental legal systems but unfamiliar in common law countries. One of them is

[44] Art 51 of the Charter.

[45] [2012] UKSC 55, [2010] 1 WLR 3333.

[46] www.curia.eu.int. See T Ingman, *The English Legal Process* (Oxford, Oxford UP, 13th edn, 2010) 91–98.

[47] These are Belgium, Cyprus, the Czech Republic, Denmark, Estonia, Finland, France, Germany, Greece, Hungary, Ireland, Italy, Latvia, Lithuania, Luxembourg, Malta, the Netherlands, Poland, Portugal, Slovakia, Slovenia, Spain, Sweden and the United Kingdom. Croatia is due to become the 28th member of the EU on 1 July 2013; the Court of Justice and the General Court will then each have 28 judges.

allocated to each case coming before the Court of Justice. In reporting to the judges their task is threefold:

(1)   to suggest a solution to the case
(2)   to relate that solution to the existing law
(3)   to set out the likely future developments in the law.

But the Advocates-General do not actually participate in the drafting of the Court's judgments, nor even in the discussions which lead to the Court's decisions. Although their submissions are not binding on the Court, they are made public before the Court issues its judgment (which is usually rather terse and will not include any dissenting opinions) and are often largely adopted by the Court. They certainly serve as useful background material explicating the judgment and often as persuasive authorities. Since 1973 the Court's judgments have been published in English in the European Court Reports, volumes I (for the Court of Justice) and II (for the General Court). Every decision (since the Court began operating in 1953) is also available online.[48]

References for preliminary rulings

5.26   The Court of Justice has jurisdiction to hear many different types of cases involving EU law, but the most important are probably those concerned with the interpretation of EU primary law, or the validity or interpretation of acts of the EU's institutions. If such matters arise during the course of a case before any national court or tribunal of a Member State, they can be referred to the Court under what is now Article 267 of the TFEU. The opinion of the Court is then handed back to the domestic court so that it can be applied to the facts of the particular case. Courts and tribunals 'of last instance', that is, from which there is no further appeal, are obliged to refer such matters to the Court of Justice unless the correct interpretation is so clear that it leaves no room for any reasonable doubt. The Court of Appeal in Northen Ireland is a court of last instance in several matters and so is affected by this obligation. This Article 267 reference procedure could well take a couple of years to complete in any particular case.

5.27   Examples of preliminary references made from Northern Ireland to the Court of Justice are those by the Resident Magistrate in *Pigs Marketing Board (NI) v Redmond*,[49] by the President of Industrial Tribunals in *Johnston v Chief Constable of the RUC*[50] and by the Court of Appeal in *Gillespie v Northern Health and Social Services Board*.[51] The *Johnston* case illustrates well the

---

[48]   www.curia.eu.int/en/content/juris/index.htm. See also http://eur-lex.europa.eu/RECH_naturel.do.
[49]   [1978] NI 73.
[50]   [1987] QB 129.
[51]   [1997] NI 190.

significance of the preliminary reference procedure. In that case 31 female police reservists complained to an industrial tribunal that the Chief Constable had discriminated against them on gender grounds when he refused to renew their contracts on the basis that he did not want women police officers to carry guns. The Chief Constable then secured a certificate from the Secretary of State declaring the matter to be one of national security and therefore outside the purview of a tribunal. The industrial tribunal referred the matter to the Court of Justice, which delivered its judgment in 1986, ruling that it was contrary to EU law to deny access to justice in such a way.[52] The case was then sent back to be considered by a tribunal in Northern Ireland, which held in favour of the claimants and, most unusually for a tribunal case, ordered the respondent Chief Constable to pay the applicants' legal costs. The decision led to a settlement payment of £1.2 million and resulted in the making of the Sex Discrimination (Amendment) (NI) Order 1988, which changed the Sex Discrimination (NI) Order 1976 so as not to allow a claim of national security to automatically prevent any future legal action based on sex discrimination.

Infringement proceedings

5.28 Another important category of case dealt with by the Court of Justice are 'infringement proceedings', which occur when the European Commission, using powers conferred by Article 258 of the TFEU, takes a case against a Member State for not fully complying with its obligations under EU law. The UK has been on the receiving end of such proceedings on many occasions. In 1982 it was held to be in breach of the Equal Pay Directive of 1975 because it was not ensuring equal pay for work of equal value,[53] and in 2006 it was found in breach of its obligations under the Working Time Directive of 1993 when it did not ensure that the workers' right to benefit from effective rest was observed.[54] On the other hand, the UK Government won the case brought against it for limiting the scope of the duty on employers to protect the health and safety of their employees to whatever was reasonably practicable.[55] Under EU competition law, the European Commission can also take infringement proceedings against companies before the General Court for operating illegal cartels or 'abusing their dominant position' in the market. In 2004, for example, as a result of the General Court's ruling in *Microsoft Corp v Commission*,[56] the giant US company was required to pay a fine of 497 million euros.[57]

[52] Case 222/84, *Johnston v Chief Constable of the RUC* [1986] ECR 1651.
[53] Case 61/81, *European Commission v UK* [1982] ICR 578.
[54] Case C–484/04, *European Commission v UK* [2007] ICR 592.
[55] Case C–127/05, *European Commission v UK* [2007] IRLR 720.
[56] Case T–201/04, [2007] ECR II-3601, [2007] 5 CMLR 11.
[57] In 2012, a periodic penalty payment imposed on Microsoft by the Commission was reduced by the General Court from 899 to 860 million euros (Case T–167/08, *Microsoft Corp v European Commission*, judgment of 27 June 2012).

Judicial review

5.29   The Court of Justice has jurisdiction over actions for annulment brought against EU legislation (Art 263 TFEU) or actions concerning an EU institution's failure to act (Art 265 TFEU) brought by a Member State or another EU institution. Direct challenges made by individuals or legal entities against EU legislation or an EU institution's failure to act, as well as actions brought by a Member State against acts of the Commission or acts of the Council in the field of competition law (eg prohibition of illegal state aids) are decided at first instance by the General Court. There is, however, a very tight deadline (of two months) for all such judicial review applications. Should an action for annulment succeed, EU legislation will be declared null and void (Art 264 TFEU).

Advisory Opinions

5.30   The Court of Justice of the EU, like the International Court of Justice (see para 5.4) and the European Court of Human Rights (see para 5.4(1)) can also issue Opinions when asked to do so – in this case by an EU Member State, the Commission, the Parliament or the Council. But the power applies only in relation to questions as to whether an international agreement envisaged by the EU is compatible with the TEU and TFEU. In the event of an adverse Opinion being issued, the agreement cannot then be entered into unless the Treaty is amended.[58] The best known example of such an Opinion is that issued in 1994 in which the Court of Justice expressed the clear view that the (then) European Community had no competence, under existing law, to accede to the Council of Europe's Convention on Human Rights.[59] Following the amendments brought about by the Treaty of Lisbon, the TEU now provides a sound legal basis for the EU's 'obligation' to accede to that Convention.[60]

5.31   The judgments of the Court of Justice are binding on the national courts and authorities of all 27 EU countries. If the national authorities continue to breach EU law, the Court cannot hold conflicting national law to be void but it can impose financial penalties on the Member State in question, often amounting to quite substantial sums.[61] In the vast majority of cases, of course, the national authorities do eventually comply with the Court's judgments.

---

[58] Art 218(11) TFEU.
[59] Opinion 2/94 on Accession by the Community to the ECHR [1996] ECR I-1759. See too n 65 below.
[60] Art 6(2) TEU.
[61] Art 260(2) TFEU.

5.32 In line with the practice followed in the civil law countries, which constitute the majority of EU Member States, the Court of Justice adopts what to British and Irish lawyers seems an unashamedly creative attitude when faced with problems of statutory interpretation.[62] However, judges in the UK now often imitate their European counterparts when EU legislation requires interpretation. They tend to use a more 'purposive' approach to the interpretation of national legislation as well (see para 4.43(2)). The Court of Justice is also much less committed than British courts to the notion of binding precedent: it can refuse to follow its own previous decisions, although in practice it largely follows or builds on its established line of case law. The accumulated case law created by the Court of Justice, in conjunction with EU legislation, is sometimes referred to as the *acquis communautaire* ('the Community's accepted law').

OTHER EU COURTS

5.33 Apart from the judicial review applications mentioned above (para 5.29), the General Court hears disputes over damages caused by the EU institutions or their staff, disputes over Community trademarks, and appeals against decisions of the EU Civil Service Tribunal. Appeals lie to the Court of Justice on points of law or, exceptionally, where there is a serious risk of the unity or consistency of Union law being affected (Art 256 TFEU). As with the Court of Justice, the General Court comprises 27 judges,[63] each appointed for renewable six year terms, but there are no separate Advocates-General to assist these judges. Usually cases are dealt with by chambers of three or five judges, while less frequently the General Court may sit as a single judge, or as a Grand Chamber of 13 judges or as a full court.

5.34 The Treaty of Nice 2001 provided for the creation of a third tier of courts, called 'judicial panels', and the Treaty of Lisbon 2009 provided for 'specialised courts' (Art 257 TFEU). In 2004 the first of these additional courts was established by the Council and attached to the Court of Justice; it was named the Civil Service Tribunal[64] and comprised seven judges. No other specialised court has yet been established, although there is a long-standing proposal to set up a European and Community Patents Court. In 2011, however, the Court of Justice ruled, in an Advisory Opinion that setting up such a Patents Court would not currently be within the powers of the EU.[65]

[62] As in the *Van Gend en Loos* case, where the concept of direct effect was created: see para 5.20.
[63] On Croatia's membership, see n 27 above.
[64] Council Decision 2004/752, [2004] OJ L333/7.
[65] Opinion 1/09 [2011] ECR I-1137. This was a decision of the Full Court, comprising all 27 judges.

5.35   The function of the Court of Auditors of the EU,[66] which is not a court in the usual English sense of the word, is to check that the EU's budget is being properly managed. It has the power to investigate any EU institution or agency which handles EU money, if necessary carrying out on-the-spot checks in Member States, including on the premises of an entity which is in receipt of payments from the EU budget, and it will draw the attention of the European Commission to any problems it uncovers. Every year it presents an overall report on the previous financial year to the European Parliament and the Council; a report which is very influential in helping the Parliament to decide whether to approve the Commission's handling of the budget. The Court of Auditors is also asked for its opinion before the EU's financial regulations are adopted. Although it can comment on other matters at any time, it does not have any legal powers of its own: it merely transmits relevant information to other EU bodies which must then decide what, if any, action to take.

HOW TO FIND EU LAW

5.36   The best way in which to access general information about the EU is through the EU's own Europa website, www.europa.eu. For access to EU legislation (ie Treaties, Directives, Regulations etc) you should go first to the EU's EUR-Lex website, www.eur-lex.europa.eu. On this you can search for documents by word, date, number or by their 'OJ' reference (every piece of EU legislation is printed in the Official Journal of the European Union, the full text of which is contained on the EUR-Lex website). The consolidated (ie updated) texts of the TEU and TFEU are there as well, of course. Under the heading 'Collections' you can look for whatever legislation is currently in force under 20 main categories, most of which are sub-divided into a number of more specific categories, and perhaps further sub-divided, with the relevant legislation then being listed in chronological order. You can therefore see at a glance whether there has been a recent piece of EU legislation on an area that interests you. Under the sub-sub-heading 'Protection of workers', for example, there will be more than 60 separate documents listed, comprising Decisions, Recommendations, Opinions, Resolutions, Directives and Regulations. The site also contains all 'preparatory documents', meaning, for example, Commission legislative proposals, Council common positions, and legislative and budgetary resolutions of the Parliament. To supplement this, there is a directory of EU legislation in preparation.

5.37   The EUR-Lex site also contains a full database of all decisions taken by the Court of Justice, the General Court and the Civil Service Tribunal. If

---

[66] Art 285 TFEU. More information can be found at http://www.eca.europa.eu.

you know the name of one of the parties to the case, you can search for it by using the word search facility. If you know the year of the decision and the case number, you can search by those features too. There are of course printed versions of the decisions of the Court. The best known series is the European Court Reports. Occasionally decisions in UK cases which have gone to the Court of Justice will also be reported in a UK law report, such as the *All England Law Reports* or *Weekly Law Reports*. Information on how properly to cite EU sources, how to check if EU legislation is in force, how to trace whether a Directive has already been implemented in the UK (and a wealth of other useful information) can be obtained by consulting *Effective Legal Research* by John Knowles.[67]

THE EUROPEAN CONVENTION ON HUMAN RIGHTS

5.38 The European Court of Justice should not be confused with the European Court of Human Rights, which sits at Strasbourg in France. The Court of Human Rights has the job of interpreting the European Convention for the Protection of Human Rights and Fundamental Freedoms, which is a treaty drawn up by the Council of Europe in 1950. The Council of Europe is an international organisation formed in 1949 which now comprises 47 European states (every country except Belarus). It is distinct from the European Union, being more active on social and cultural fronts than on economic and political matters.

5.39 The UK was one of the first countries to ratify the Convention on Human Rights in 1951 and the Convention entered into force at the international level in 1953. This meant that from that date other countries could take cases against the UK complaining about human rights abuses it was allegedly committing. Greece took advantage of this in the 1950s when it complained about the way British forces were treating insurgents in Cyprus and in 1971 the Republic of Ireland brought a case against the UK complaining about the use of internment without trial in Northern Ireland and the mistreatment of detainees. The cases about Cyprus were settled out of court;[68] the case about Northern Ireland led to a finding that internment was justified but that some detainees had been subjected to inhuman and degrading treatment (but not torture).[69] Generally speaking a State is not liable for actions it commits in a country which is not party to the Convention[70] and a person who is outside a

[67] London, Sweet & Maxwell, 3rd edn, 2012.
[68] *Greece v UK* (1956–57) 1 Ybk 128; (1958–59) 2 Ybk 175.
[69] *Ireland v UK* (1979–80) 2 EHRR 25.
[70] *Bankovic and others v Belgium and others* (2007) 44 EHRR SE5, where the Court declared inadmissible a complaint by Serbs over the bombing of Yugoslavia by NATO countries in 1999. For a trenchant critique see E Roxstrom, M Gibney and T Einarsen, 'The NATO bombing case

State cannot claim that that State has breached his or her Convention rights.[71]

5.40   The UK Government did not permit individuals in the UK to take cases against it to Strasbourg until 1966, and it did not take legislative action to make Convention rights part of the domestic law of the UK until the Human Rights Act was enacted in 1998.[72] That Act came into force on 2 October 2000, but in the previous year the Acts which had devolved powers to administrations in Edinburgh, Cardiff and Belfast had already forbidden those authorities from doing anything which contravenes the Convention.[73] It is important to remember that when individuals take cases to the European Court of Human Rights they are not actually appealing against the decision of a domestic court; they are simply asking the Court to rule whether the domestic law of the UK is in violation of the European Convention on Human Rights. Victory is Strasbourg does not necessarily mean that the remedies sought in the domestic court will then be made available to the applicant.

How the European Court of Human Rights operates

5.41   Until 1998 complaints to Strasbourg had first to be considered by the European Commission of Human Rights, which decided whether they were 'admissible' within the terms of the Convention. In that year, however, the Commission was merged with the European Court of Human Rights, which then became a full-time body.[74] Today admissibility questions are usually decided by a three-judge committee of the Court. Complaints will not be admissible, for example, if all avenues for redress in the national courts have not yet been exhausted or if more than six months have elapsed since the date of the final decision in the national courts. If the complaints are admissible (about 95 per cent are held not to be) the Court will carry out an inquiry and seek to bring about a friendly settlement. If no such settlement is possible, the case will be referred to a Chamber of the Court (comprising seven judges) for full

and the limits of Western human rights protection' (2005) 23 *Boston University International LJ* 55. In two more recent cases the Court held that the UK was responsible for violating the human rights of individuals in Iraq: *Al-Skeini v UK* (2011) 53 EHRR 18 and *Al-Jedda v UK* (2011) 53 EHRR 23.

[71] *In re Doherty's Application* [2004] NIQB 41, where a prisoner in Ireland failed in his claim against the Northern Ireland Prison Service over its refusal to transfer him to Northern Ireland.
[72] The last Member State of the Council of Europe to incorporate the European Convention into its domestic Law was Ireland, which did so from 31 December 2003 by virtue of the European Convention on Human Rights Act 2003.
[73] See now the Scotland Act 1998, s 29(2)(d); the Government of Wales Act 2006, s 81; and the Northern Ireland Act 1998, s 24(1)(a).
[74] This was a result of Protocol 11 to the Convention.

consideration and a decision.[75] In some rare cases there will be an oral hearing, but it will be short (less than a day). Before or after a Chamber deals with a case it can be referred to the Grand Chamber (comprising 17 judges) if it is deemed to be particularly important. All inter-state cases must now go to the Grand Chamber.

5.42 There are as many judges eligible to sit in the European Court of Human Rights as there are Member States of the Council of Europe. The judges are now appointed for one term of up to nine years and must retire when they reach the age of 70. Decisions taken by the Court are binding on all the States involved in the case, although in practice States wait some time before altering their national law to bring it into line with the pronouncements of the Court. On occasions the Court may order a national government to pay compensation to an aggrieved party, but in most cases the decision that the Convention has been breached is deemed by the Court to be a sufficient remedy. The ultimate responsibility for ensuring that the Court's decisions are complied with in the Member States belongs to the Committee of Ministers of the Council of Europe.[76] This Committee is a political rather than a legal body and can reach a decision only if two-thirds of the delegates agree.

5.43 The Court of Human Rights is creaking under the weight of applications made to it.[77] In 2012, 65,162 applications were allocated to a single judge or chamber, including 1,734 from the UK.[78] The number of judgments issued was 1,093, the lowest since 2004, but the Court also issued 1,800 decisions on admissibility. A further 81,700 applications were declared inadmissible or struck out of the list by single judges. The number of pending applications, which had topped 160,000 in 2011, was reduced to 128,000 by the end of 2012, but it is still a huge figure.[79] Suggestions are now being made that if the Court is to continue to fulfil its potential as the most important court for some 800 million Europeans it will need to be much more selective in the cases it chooses to consider. Following High Level Conferences on the future of the European Court of Human Rights at Interlaken, Izmir and (in 2012) Brighton, steps are finally being taken to make the workload of the Court more manageable.[80]

---

[75] The Court's Registrar issues press releases on many judgments; they are available on the Court's website.

[76] A Council of Europe website is devoted to the execution of the Court's judgments: www. coe.int/T/E/Human_rights/execution.

[77] The statistics cited here are available on the Council of Europe's website: www.coe.int (under 'Reports').

[78] The Court cannot say how many of these applicants had addresses in Northern Ireland.

[79] Just 4 countries were the source of more than half the pending applications: Russia, Turkey, Ukraine and Romania.

[80] See the Foreword to the Annual Report for 2012 by Dean Spielmann, the President of the Court, and 11–15.

THE CONVENTION'S IMPACT ON LAW IN NORTHERN IRELAND[81]

5.44   The European Court of Human Rights has held against the UK in scores of cases, ever since the first such decision in 1975.[82] Over the years, as a result of the Court's decisions, the UK Government has had to change the law on (amongst other things) contempt of court, the 'closed shop' in workplaces, courts-martial, immigration, telephone tapping, prisoners' rights, defamation law and corporal punishment in schools. In one recent case, for example, two young people in England who were sued for libel by McDonalds were held to have had their rights breached when they could not get access to legal aid to defend themselves.[83] But only a very small proportion of applications lodged in Strasbourg by people living in the UK are ultimately successful. In 2012 only 21 such applications were declared admissible and only 24 judgments were issued in cases brought against the UK. In those 24 cases there was a finding that a Convention right had been violated in only 10 of them.

5.45   Over the years there have been many cases brought against the UK Government by people living in Northern Ireland. Following the partially substantiated complaint by the Irish Government in the 1970s (see para 5.39), instructions to security forces in Northern Ireland with regard to interrogation techniques were altered, and a complaint by an individual led to homosexuality being decriminalised.[84] However, a challenge to the legality of the use of plastic bullets in Northern Ireland failed before the European Commission,[85] as did an application alleging that the police had not properly protected people's human rights during the 'protest' at Holy Cross Primary School in 2001.[86]

The rights to liberty, life and a fair trial

5.46   In 1988 the Court held in *Brogan v UK*[87] that administrative detention for more than four days and six hours, on the order of a government Minister acting under the Prevention of Terrorism (Temporary Provisions) Act 1984, was a breach of Article 5(3) of the Convention, which requires detainees to be brought promptly before a judge. The Government then

---

[81] See also B Dickson, *The European Convention on Human Rights and the Conflict in Northern Ireland* (Oxford, Oxford UP, 2010) and B Dickson, 'Northern Ireland', in A. Lester, D Pannick and J Herberg (eds), *Human Rights Law and Practice* (London, LexisNexis Butterworths, 3rd edn, 2009) ch 6.
[82] *Golder v UK* (1979–80) 1 EHRR 525.
[83] *Steel and Morris v UK* (2005) 41 EHRR 403.
[84] *Dudgeon v UK* (1982) 4 EHRR 149. See the Homosexual Offences (NI) Order 1982.
[85] *Stewart v UK* (1985) 7 EHRR 453.
[86] *PF and EF v UK*, App No 28326/09, decision of 23 November 2010.
[87] (1989) 11 EHRR 117.

officially 'derogated' from (ie opted out of) the Convention in this respect, as it claimed to be allowed to do under Article 15 of the Convention. In a subsequent challenge to this derogation the Court held that it was indeed valid under Article 15 because there was 'a public emergency threatening the life of the nation' and the steps taken were not more than those 'strictly required by the exigencies of the situation'.[88]

5.47   The UK Government was condemned by the Court for not properly protecting people's right to life when three members of the IRA who were on a reconnaissance mission to plan the planting of a car bomb were shot dead in Gibraltar in 1988 without proper consideration having been given by British security forces to whether they could have been taken alive.[89] This was a very significant decision (by 10 judges to nine) in that it has since required security forces all over Europe to be much more careful when planning operations to trap violent criminals.

5.48   In 1996 a partially successful challenge was mounted to the then law in Northern Ireland which allowed inferences of guilt to be drawn from the silence of someone who had been arrested and questioned by the police under anti-terrorist powers but who had not had the benefit of a solicitor's advice.[90] Two decisions of the Court in 2000 further condemned the unavailability of legal advice in situations where inferences of guilt could be drawn.[91] At no point, though, did the European Court say that all persons arrested by the police should be allowed to have their solicitors present while they were being interviewed by the police. In 1998 the UK Government lost another case when it tried to prevent two applicants from challenging the Secretary of State's decision that they had no right to claim that they had been discriminated against on religious or political grounds in the allocation of a public sector contract.[92]

5.49   In 2001 the European Court held that Article 2 of the Convention (which protects the right to life) had been breached in relation to 11 individuals who had been shot by the police or army in Northern Ireland (and one by the UDA) because there had not been thorough, prompt and impartial investigations into the killings.[93] As a result the Government had to make changes to the inquest and prosecution systems in Northern Ireland. Whether enough has been done to comply with these and subsequent judgments in the same vein is still, 12 years later, being considered by the Council of Europe's Committee of Ministers.

---

[88] *Brannigan and McBride v UK* (1994) 17 EHRR 539.
[89] *McCann v UK* (1996) 21 EHRR 97.
[90] *Murray (John) v UK* (1996) 22 EHRR 29. See too *Brennan v UK* (2002) 34 EHRR 18.
[91] *Averill v UK* (2000) 8 BHRC 430 and *Magee v UK* (2001) 31 EHRR 35.
[92] *Tinnelly and McElduff v UK* (1999) 27 EHRR 249. This decision was later applied in two similar cases, *Devenney v UK* (2002) 35 EHRR 643 and *Devlin v UK* (2002) 34 EHRR 1029.
[93] *Jordan v UK* (2003) 37 EHRR 52; *Kelly v UK* App No 30054/96; *McKerr v UK* (2002) 34 EHRR 20; *Shanaghan v UK* App 37715/97.

Rights in the future

5.50   The Standing Advisory Commission on Human Rights in Northern Ireland recommended as long ago as 1977 that a Bill of Rights based on the European Convention should be enacted for the whole of the UK[94] and various bodies, most notably the Northern Ireland Human Rights Commission (see para 6.28), have since published proposals for a Bill of Rights for Northern Ireland which draw heavily on the European Convention while going substantially beyond it in several important respects.[95] However the UK Government has signalled that it does not favour such a comprehensive Bill of Rights for Northern Ireland. In 2011 the Government established a Commission to look into the options regarding a UK Bill of Rights, but in 2012 that Commission issued a report which failed to arrive at a consensus position on that issue.[96]

5.51   As explained above (para 5.23), the EU's Charter of Fundamental Rights is now part of EU law. That Charter includes the rights set out in the European Convention on Human Rights but adds to them significantly, especially in the field of 'solidarity' where protection of workers' rights[97] is guaranteed, as is entitlement to social security benefits and access to preventive health care. Discrimination based on genetic features is also banned.[98] The Treaty of Lisbon also allows the European Union to become a party to the European Convention, but arrangements to bring that about are still not fully in place.

---

[94] Cmnd 7009; 1977.
[95] The Belfast (Good Friday) Agreement 1998 contains provisions requiring the Commission 'to consult and to advise on the scope for defining, in Westminster legislation, rights supplementary to those in the European Convention on Human Rights, to reflect the particular circumstances of Northern Ireland, drawing as appropriate on international instruments and experience [and reflecting] the principles of mutual respect for the identity and ethos of both communities and parity of esteem'.
[96] See www.justice.gov.uk/about/cbr/index.htm.
[97] Arts 27–31, 34 and 35.
[98] Art 21.

6

Public Law in Northern Ireland

PUBLIC LAW AND PRIVATE LAW

6.1 Law can be divided into a number of different branches. One fundamental distinction is between law which governs the behaviour of the State (and its various agencies), which is generally known as public law, and law which governs the behaviour of private individuals and companies, which is generally known as private law. In this chapter we will look at some of the basic principles of public law. In the following chapter we will focus on another type of law where the State plays a prominent role – criminal law and in Chapter 8 we will explain the agencies involved in operating that law. Chapters 9 and 10 will then look at the content and procedures of private law.

6.2 Public law can itself be sub-divided into a number of branches, some of which are described below. We will look in turn at administrative law, human rights law, equality law, welfare law, housing law and planning law. Where appropriate we will also examine the specialist public bodies in Northern Ireland which enforce the law in these fields. But first a few words need to be said about the concept of 'public authorities'.

PUBLIC AUTHORITIES

6.3 Public law, by definition, concerns itself with the actions and inactions of public authorities, though the lists of bodies that qualify as public authorities sometimes differ depending on the context. For the purposes of applications for judicial review (paras 6.5–6.11) the definition of public authorities is very broad: courts are prepared to review the decisions of virtually any organisation which performs a public or semi-public function provided those decisions affect the public interest in some way. Even a business cooperative empowered to issue fishing licences has been held to be amenable to judicial review,[1] as has Northern Ireland Electricity, a privatised company which was performing the vital public function of supplying electricity.[2] But the bodies that are public authorities for the purposes of the Ombudsman's jurisdiction (paras 6.12–6.21), the Human Rights Act 1998 (paras 6.22–6.27), the Freedom of Information Act 2000 (paras 6.45–6.46), and the equality duties (paras 6.58–6.61) are not always the same, even though there is a great deal of overlap between those categories and all of the bodies would be subject to applications for judicial review unless acting in a purely private law capacity (such as an employer).

6.4   This book cannot begin to explain the functions, or even provide a comprehensive list, of all the public authorities in Northern Ireland. There are well over 150 of them. A few are given greater attention later in this chapter and in other chapters.

ADMINISTRATIVE LAW AND JUDICIAL REVIEW[3]

6.5   Administrative law is the name given to the legal rules and principles which control the way the 'executive' arm of the State (including central government, local government and a wide range of other public bodies) is permitted to go about its business. It is a branch of law which has developed greatly in the past 50 years, the mainspring for this being the legal procedure known as 'an application for judicial review'. This was a procedure invented by the courts themselves (ie it is a 'common law' development), but it has since been recognised, and to some extent regulated, by Parliament.[4] It takes the form of an application to the High Court claiming that a public body has not acted lawfully. It must be brought to the court promptly, and usually no later than three months after the occurrence of the act which is being complained about.[5] If it relates to a criminal cause or matter it will be dealt with by at least two judges sitting in the Divisional Court, and an appeal may go from there directly to the Supreme Court. If it relates to a civil cause or matter it can be dealt with by a single High Court judge, and an appeal

---

[1] *Re Kirkpatrick's Application* [2004] NIJB 15 (but not on the facts of that case, because an alternative remedy was available).

[2] *Re Sherlock and Morris's Application* [1996] NIJB 80. For further discussion of this and related cases see Anthony, n 3 below, 40–44.

[3] This is one of the few areas of law in which there is not one but two books specifically focusing on the legal rules applicable in Northern Ireland: see G Anthony, *Judicial Review in Northern Ireland* (Oxford, Hart Publishing, 2008) and J Larkin and D Scoffield, *Judicial Review in Northern Ireland: A Practitioner's Guide* (Belfast, SLS Legal Publications, 2007).

[4] Judicature (NI) Act 1978, ss 18–25.

[5] Rules of the Court of Judicature, Order 53. The procedures which lawyers need to comply with when involved in applications for judicial review are set out in Practice Note 1/2008, available on the website of the Courts and Tribunals Service: www.courtsni.gov.uk.

may go to the Court of Appeal in Northern Ireland and thereafter to the Supreme Court.[6] If there is an alternative remedy available to someone who is dissatisfied with a public authority's decision, the courts will expect that route to be pursued before an application for judicial review is considered. Moreover, before an application can proceed to a full hearing, a judge has to give permission for the case to continue because it raises an arguable point.[7] Judges in Northern Ireland seem quite willing to grant such permission, more so than their colleagues in England and Wales. At the full hearing the application is usually dealt with without any witnesses being called in person; instead written statements that have been sworn in advance by these witnesses are submitted to the judge for his or her consideration. These statements are called 'affidavits'. In a case from Northern Ireland decided by the House of Lords the judges liberalised the rules concerning the disclosure of other documents in judicial review applications.[8]

Which actions can be judicially reviewed?

6.6   Applications for judicial review can be brought only in relation to actions taken by public bodies, or actions taken by private bodies for public purposes.[9] They may also cover inactions (ie omissions to act) by such bodies. Depending on the context of the dispute, courts in England and Wales tend to decide what actions are amenable to judicial review by asking whether the action was taken under a statutory power, whether the matter involved is a 'public law issue', and (most important of all) whether the body in question is performing a 'public function'. In Northern Ireland, however, the courts tend to pay more attention to whether the matter involved is one 'of public interest', meaning that it is an issue which affects the public generally rather than just one individual or a group of individuals. This is a laxer test, which means that some actions may be subject to judicial review in Northern Ireland when they would not be in England and Wales. On the other hand, in situations where there is an alternative course of action open to an applicant for judicial review, judges in Northern Ireland are often more reluctant to allow the application to proceed than judges in England and Wales might be.[10]

---

[6] See the principles set out in *Re JR27* [2010] NIQB 12, [2010] 4 BNIL 74, as applied in *In re Canning's Application* [2012] NIQB 49, [2012] 9 BNIL 58.

[7] If the application for leave fails, an appeal can be lodged in the Court of Appeal without seeking any further permission: *In re McNamee and McDonnell* [2011] NICA 40, [2011] 10 BNIL 53.

[8] *Tweed v Parades Commission for Northern Ireland* [2006] UKHL 53, [2007] 1 AC 650.

[9] If the action in question is a clinical judgment there will be limited scope for intervention by way of judicial review: *In re JR52's Application* [2011] NIQB 64, [2011] 9 BNIL 58.

[10] Contrast, eg *Re Neill's Application* [2005] NICA 5 with *R (AC) v Secretary of State for Justice* [2008] EWHC 171 (Admin).

On what grounds can actions be judicially reviewed?

6.7   The grounds on which an application for judicial review can be made are the same in Northern Ireland as they are in England and Wales. Today it is customary to say that there are four grounds on which an application can be based if it is to have a chance of success. The first three were clarified by the House of Lords in the famous litigation concerning Mrs Thatcher's efforts to control the trade unions at Government Communications Headquarters in England (the *GCHQ* case[11]). The first is that the decision being complained about was not within the powers of the body making it – ie it was *ultra vires*. The second is that the decision was taken in an improper way, perhaps because no prior warning was given that it was going to be taken or because it runs counter to the expectations which people affected by it had legitimately raised in their own minds. The third is that the action taken was one which no reasonable public body of that description could have taken, a ground which is sometimes called '*Wednesbury* unreasonableness' after the name of a case in the 1940s where the principle was first enunciated.[12] A handy way of remembering these grounds for judicial review is to think of three words beginning with 'i' – illegality, impropriety and irrationality.[13] In a sense, though, all three are instances of illegality or unlawfulness in a broader sense. The fourth ground on which an application for judicial review can now be based is 'lack of proportionality', which refers to situations where, putting it colloquially, a sledgehammer has been used to crack a nut. The availability of this ground was confirmed by the House of Lords in *R (Daly) v Secretary of State for the Home Department*.[14]

Judicial review focuses on process, not substance

6.8   The orthodox view is that applications for judicial review are meant to focus on the processes used by a public body when coming to its decision to act, not on the substance (ie merits) of that decision. If judges could always substitute their own views for those of administrators there would be breach of the separation of powers doctrine (see para 2.12). Attention therefore focuses on issues such as whether the public body has properly consulted people before taking actions that affect them, whether the public body has closed its mind (or 'fettered its discretion') in relation to the options available to it for dealing with certain issues, whether the public body has been biased in its approach or unfair in the way it has engaged with people, and whether the action it has taken was proportionate to the purpose it

---

[11] *Council of Civil Service Unions v Minister of the Civil Service* [1985] AC 674.
[12] *Associated Provincial Picture Houses Ltd v Wednesbury Corporation* [1948] 1 KB 223.
[13] These were the terms used by Lord Diplock in the GCHQ case, n 11 above.
[14] [2001] UKHL 26, [2001] 2 AC 532.

was trying to achieve. The intensity of the scrutiny which judges will apply when considering applications for judicial review will increase if the human rights of the applicant are alleged to have been breached but will diminish if the action in question is one which relates to a matter of national security or to a highly sensitive political issue. It is very unlikely, for example, that a successful application for judicial review could be taken in relation to a decision by the Prime Minister to merge two government departments or to impose financial sanctions on a foreign government.

6.9 As a consequence of their reluctance to step into the shoes of administrative bodies, judges who grant applications for judicial review do not always 'quash' (ie annul) the decision being complained about and order a different decision to be taken instead. If they do do that, the name of the remedies they award are *'certiorari'* (ie to quash) and *'mandamus'* (ie to order). But instead they might just send the decision back to the body in question so that it can be reconsidered in the light of remarks made by the judges. Moreover, contrary to popular belief, judicial review applications, even if successful, very rarely result in someone receiving compensation for the injustice they claim to have suffered. The purpose of judicial review is not to provide compensation or to punish anyone. It is to ensure that administrative bodies perform their tasks in as fair and just a way as possible.

An example of judicial review

6.10 An example of an application for judicial review, and of the limitations to the procedure, is *Re Williamson's Application*.[15] Here, the daughter of a married couple who were killed by a bomb planted by the IRA in a fish shop on Belfast's Shankill Road in 1993, applied for judicial review of the decision taken in 1999 by the Secretary of State for Northern Ireland, Dr Mo Mowlam, that the IRA was still maintaining a complete and unequivocal ceasefire, which meant that its prisoners could still be released early under the terms of the Belfast (Good Friday) Agreement, as implemented by the Northern Ireland (Sentences) Act 1998. Kerr J, as he then was,[16] dismissed the application, and the Court of Appeal affirmed that decision, holding that the Secretary of State had applied the correct test when deciding whether the IRA had maintained its ceasefire. The Court of Appeal said:

> It is not for us in a court of law to intervene unless it is established that the Secretary of State has gone wrong in law. We cannot repeat too often or too clearly that a judicial review is not an appeal against the merits of the decision

---

[15] [2000] NICA 7, [2000] NI 281.
[16] He later became Lord Chief Justice Kerr and then Lord Kerr. He is now a Justice of the UK Supreme Court.

under review. It is our function only to ascertain whether the decider has taken into account the correct considerations and made the decision within the proper parameters by correct application of the law. If we so hold, it is not for us to form or express any view on the quality or merits of the decision, and nothing we say in this judgment should be taken in any way as an attempt to do so. The area with which the 1998 Act is concerned is delicate and sensitive, and it is hardly surprising that strong views should be held on it or that decisions within this area should give rise to serious differences of opinion. It is part of the democratic process that such decisions should be taken by a minister responsible to Parliament, and so long as the manner in which they are taken is in accordance with the proper principles the courts should not and will not step outside their proper function of review.

6.11 Nevertheless, despite their limited potential, applications for judicial review are still very common in Northern Ireland. Many civil society organisations resort to them almost as a campaigning tool. In 2011, the High Court in Northern Ireland disposed of 197 applications for leave to apply for judicial review. In 100 (51 per cent) of these applications, leave was granted. Of the 89 actual applications for judicial review disposed of in the same year, 20 (22 per cent) were granted.[17] The figures are roughly in line with those for 2009 and 2010.

THE OMBUDSMAN

6.12 Quite apart from the control which judges are able to exercise over public bodies through applications for judicial review, there is another very important type of redress which people who are dissatisfied with public bodies can explore. They can raise a complaint with the Ombudsman, whose job it is to investigate allegations of 'maladministration'. In Northern Ireland there are actually two ombudsman posts, but both have always been held by the same person. One post is that of the Assembly Ombudsman (formerly known as the Northern Ireland Parliamentary Commissioner for Administration[18]) and the other is the Commissioner for Complaints.[19] In 2010 the Assembly's Committee for the OFMDFM issued a consultation paper on proposals to reform the office of the Northern Ireland Ombudsman.[20] Amongst other things, it suggested the creation of a unified Public Services Ombudsman for Northern Ireland. This could take

---

[17] *Northern Ireland Court Service Judicial Statistics 2011*, Table B.18. The statistics are available on www.courtsni.gov.uk.
[18] Ombudsman (NI) Order 1996, art 3(1). Pending devolution the holder was also entitled to be called the Parliamentary Ombudsman for Northern Ireland: art 3(3).
[19] Commissioner for Complaints (NI) Order 1996.
[20] See http://archive.niassembly.gov.uk/centre/2007mandate/public/pn_Update_leg_ni_ombud. htm, and also the report by the Northern Ireland Assembly's Research and Library Service, *The Office of the Northern Ireland Ombudsman* (NIAR 145–11, 2011).

over the functions of the existing bodies but also have a power to conduct investigations or systemic reviews on its own initiative, without having to wait for a complaint to be lodged. As yet, no legislation has been tabled at the Assembly to take forward such reforms.

6.13 Currently, no matter which of the two hats is being worn, and just as in applications for judicial review, the Ombudsman's job is to examine the procedures by which decisions are reached by public bodies, not to assess the merits of those decisions in the absence of maladministration. The term 'maladministration' is not defined in the legislation, but it does not simply mean a mistake and nor is it limited to the type of behaviour that would be a ground for judicial review. It refers to action which has been influenced by improper considerations, is totally unreasonable, or is incompetent, malicious, discriminatory or negligent. The Ombudsman does not usually investigate complaints in respect of which the complainant has a right to take proceedings in a court of law or tribunal (apart from applications for judicial review),[21] and for this purpose the Equality Commission for Northern Ireland (see para 6.47) and the Police Ombudsman (see para 7.61) are considered to be tribunals. Someone who is complaining about being refused a welfare benefit, for instance, must take the grievance to an Appeal Tribunal (see para 4.29). Only if he or she is unhappy with the manner in which the claim was processed before or after the decision was made (and if there is no point of law involved that can form the subject of an appeal to a Social Security Commissioner: see para 4.29) will a complaint to the Ombudsman be permissible.

Assembly Ombudsman

6.14 The function of the Assembly Ombudsman is to investigate written complaints about maladministration within any of the Northern Ireland government departments and several other bodies, including government agencies like the Child Support Agency and the Planning Service.[22] Unlike the ombudsmen in Great Britain, the Assembly Ombudsman in Northern Ireland also has the power to investigate complaints about personnel matters in the civil service.[23] As the Northern Ireland Office is a department of the UK Government, complaints about its decisions or action should be sent to the UK Parliamentary Commissioner for Administration, who is based in London.[24] The same applies to national public bodies such as HM Revenue

[21] Ombudsman (NI) Order 1996, art 10(3).
[22] The full list is set out in Sch 2 to the Ombudsman (NI) Order 1996, as amended, and is available on the Ombudsman's website.
[23] The power to deal with personnel issues is unique in these islands and is one which the current Ombudsman would be happy to give up.
[24] www.ombudsman.org.uk.

and Customs and the Post Office, and to bodies which are themselves accountable to the Northern Ireland Office, such as the Northern Ireland Human Rights Commission.[25]

6.15   Complaints about maladministration can be made to the Assembly Ombudsman by anyone who claims to have sustained injustice as a result of the maladministration. In the first instance the complaint should be made to a Member of the Legislative Assembly (MLA),[26] who should then pass it on to the Ombudsman, but if the Ombudsman receives a complaint which has not first been passed through an MLA, the Ombudsman will in practice refer it to an MLA nominated by the complainant and ask the latter to act as a sponsor for the complaint.

6.16   A complaint must normally be made within 12 months of the date when the aggrieved person first had notice of the matters alleged in the complaint.[27] The Ombudsman may, however, investigate a complaint made at a later date if he or she thinks there is a special justification for doing so.[28] In all cases except those which clearly fall outside his or her jurisdiction, or which are withdrawn, the Commissioner invites the comments of the body complained about, examines relevant documents, and interviews persons privately. He or she has all the powers of a High Court judge to secure the examination of witnesses and the production of documents,[29] and, most importantly, no-one can refuse to supply information because of some other legal obligation to maintain secrecy or some legal right to claim 'privilege' (see para 8.106).[30]

6.17   The Ombudsman sends a report on the investigation to the MLA who has sponsored the complaint, to the body complained about and to any person involved in the allegations made in the complaint. If the Ombudsman finds that a complaint is justified, he or she will seek to obtain a settlement of the grievance on the complainant's behalf. This may involve the granting of an apology, the remedying of some situation or even the payment of compensation. But if no settlement can be reached the complainant cannot take the matter any further, except through judicial review proceedings (see paras 6.5–6.11). Like all the official Ombudsmen in the UK, the Assembly Ombudsman has the power to make a special report to Parliament, but this power is very rarely exercised.

---

[25] For the full list of bodies subject to the UK Parliamentary Commissioner, see the Parliamentary Commissioner Order 2010 (SI 239).
[26] Ombudsman (NI) Order 1996, art 9(2). Before devolution the complaints had to be sent through an MP.
[27] Ibid art 11(5).
[28] Ibid art 11(6).
[29] Ibid art 14(2).
[30] Ibid art 14(3) and (4).

Commissioner for Complaints

6.18 The function of the Commissioner for Complaints is to investigate written complaints made directly by persons claiming to have suffered injustice through maladministration on the part of public bodies other than those of, or sponsored by, central government. The office therefore covers such bodies as Education and Library Boards, Health and Social Services Trusts, district councils and the Labour Relations Agency.[31] It too was first created in 1969.[32] It has a similar, but by no means identical, role to that of the Local Administration Ombudsmen in Great Britain. Among the matters which cannot be investigated are the conduct of legal proceedings, the behaviour of the police, and the financial interests of district councillors.[33]

6.19 This kind of complaint does not have to be processed through an MLA, but it still usually needs to be made within 12 months of the complainant getting to know of the action he or she is complaining about.[34] Investigations are conducted in the same way as described above in relation to the Assembly Ombudsman, with reports made to the complainant, the body concerned and any other person involved in the complaint. An important difference between the two procedures, however, is that if the Commissioner for Complaints upholds a grievance but is unable to obtain a satisfactory settlement, the complainant can then apply to a county court for compensation.[35] The Commissioner for Complaints may also ask the Attorney General to seek an injunction or declaration in the High Court to restrain a public body from persisting in action which has been found to amount to maladministration.[36] Such remedies are not available in Great Britain.

6.20 In 1997 the Commissioner for Complaints acquired the right to deal with complaints against health service providers, including complaints about clinical judgments and hospital and community nursing services.[37] The work of dentists, opticians and chemists is included too. The equivalent post in Great Britain is that of the Health Service Ombudsman.

6.21 In England and Wales there is a statutory Legal Services Ombudsman, but no such post yet exists in Northern Ireland (see para 11.17). Northern Ireland does, however, have a Judicial Appointments Ombudsman (see para 4.35), a Police Ombudsman (see para 7.61) and a Prisoner Ombudsman

---

[31] The full list of bodies which are subject to the Commissioner's oversight is provided in the Commissioner for Complaints (NI) Order 1996, Sch 2, as amended. See too the office's website: www.ni-ombudsman.org.uk.
[32] By the Commissioner for Complaints Act (NI) 1969.
[33] The full list is in the Commissioner for Complaints (NI) Order 1996, Sch 3, as amended.
[34] Commissioner for Complaints (NI) Order 1996, art 10(6).
[35] Ibid art 16.
[36] Ibid art 17.
[37] Commissioner for Complaints (Amendment) (NI) Order 1996.

(see para 7.83). Helpful information about the full range of Ombudsmen operating throughout the UK and Ireland can be obtained from the British and Irish Ombudsman Association.[38]

HUMAN RIGHTS LAW

6.22   In 1998 the UK Parliament enacted the Human Rights Act, which allows people to bring public authorities in the UK to court if they are alleged to be violating the rights conferred on people by the European Convention on Human Rights, a treaty ratified by the UK Government as long ago as 1951 (see para 5.39). The Act marked a real turning-point in human rights law in the UK. Before then people's rights were usually considered under the topic of 'civil liberties', the law on which was more commonly explained in textbooks on constitutional law rather than in freestanding books on human rights law.

6.23   The Human Rights Act 1998 makes it clear that it is not restricting any rights or freedoms conferred on people in the UK by any other law.[39] But it provides special procedures for people who feel that their Convention rights have been violated. The Convention rights are the standard civil and political rights that one would expect any liberal democracy to protect, namely:

- the right to life (Article 2)
- the right not to be ill-treated (Article 3)
- the right not to be enslaved (Article 4)
- the right to liberty (Article 5)
- the right to a fair trial (Article 6)
- the right not to be tried for something that was not an offence when it was done (Article 7)
- the right to a private and family life (Article 8)
- the right to freedom of belief (Article 9)
- the right to freedom of expression (Article 10)
- the right to freedom of assembly and association Article 11)
- the right to marry (Article 12)
- the right not to be improperly discriminated against (Article 14)
- the right to not to have one's property interfered with (Article 1 of Protocol 1)
- the right to education (Article 2 of Protocol 1)
- the right to free elections (Article 1 of Protocol 1).

[38] www.bioa.org.uk.
[39] s 11.

The Convention rights do not include some social and economic rights which many people now think are every bit as important as civil and political rights. These include the right to health care, the right to an adequate standard of living and the right to housing. Some of these rights are already guaranteed, to some extent, by other laws, such as Acts of Parliament dealing with the National Health Service, the social security system and homelessness. There are also laws guaranteeing the right to a national minimum wage and the right not to be dismissed unfairly from employment. Many people would like to see all rights brought together in a Bill of Rights, the name traditionally given to a document which guarantees rights at a constitutional level. Whether this should be a Bill of Rights for the whole of the UK, or just for Northern Ireland, is a sub-question in that debate, one that has long exercised the Northern Ireland Human Rights Commission (see paras 5.50, 6.28 and 6.31).

Section 2 of the Human Rights Act

6.24   There are four sections in the Human Rights Act which are worthy of particular note, namely sections 2, 3, 4 and 7. As regards section 2, a court in the UK which is dealing with a question about a Convention right must 'take into account' the case law of the European Court of Human Rights. This does not mean that the UK court has to decide the case in the same way as it thinks the European Court would decide it, but at the very least it must give clear reasons why it wishes to deviate from the principles laid down by the European Court's case law. So far the top UK court has always followed a decision of the Grand Chamber of the European Court, even if sometimes it has had difficulty in interpreting exactly what the Grand Chamber meant.[40]

Section 3 of the Human Rights Act

6.25   By section 3, when anyone in the UK is considering the meaning of legislation he or she must, 'so far as it is possible to do so', give effect to the legislation in a way which is compatible with Convention rights. A good example of this happening in Northern Ireland is *Re King's Application*,[41] where a court read words into the Life Sentences (NI) Order 2001 in order to make it apply to prisoners currently serving life sentences as well as to those who might receive such sentences in the future. Section 3 also permits a court to ignore secondary legislation if it is incompatible with Convention

---

[40] A good example is the Supreme Court's decision in *In re McGaughey* [2011] UKSC 20, [2012] 1 AC 725, an appeal from Northern Ireland.
[41] [2003] NI 43.

rights. This is in line with the traditional doctrine of separation of powers, which allows courts to strike down secondary legislation if it has not been made in accordance with proper procedures. Two examples of this occurring in relation to legislation made specifically for Northern Ireland were given in Chapter 3 (see para 3.29).

Section 4 of the Human Rights Act

6.26   By section 4 of the Human Rights Act, if it is just not possible to interpret a piece of primary legislation in a way that is compatible with Convention rights, the High Court (or any higher court) can declare it to be incompatible with Convention rights. This does not make the piece of primary legislation in any way invalid, nor does it affect the legal position of the parties to the court proceedings in question, but it does allow the UK government to amend the legislation at a later time by making a 'remedial order'.[42] So far there has been only one declaration of incompatibility issued by a court in Northern Ireland. This was in *Re McR's Application*,[43] where a man had been charged with attempting consensual anal intercourse with a woman, in breach of the Offences against the Person Act 1861.[44] Kerr J, as he then was, declared the legislation to be incompatible with the right to a private life, as guaranteed by Article 8 of the European Convention on Human Rights.

Section 7 of the Human Rights Act

6.27   By section 7, a person who claims that a public authority has acted, or is proposing to act, in a way which is incompatible with a Convention right, can sue that authority provided that he or she is, or would be, a victim of that act. The proceedings can take the form of an application for judicial review (see paras 6.5–6.11),[45] but they do not have to. In effect, a new statutory 'tort' (see para 9.78) of 'acting incompatibly with Convention rights' has been created, just as when Parliament made discrimination unlawful through, for example, the Sex Discrimination (NI) Order 1976 and the Fair Employment (NI) Act 1976 (see para 6.50). Proceedings under section 7 have to be brought within a year of the date on which the act complained of took place, although a court has a discretion to prolong that period if it considers this to be 'equitable having regard to all the

---

[42] Human Rights Act 1998, s 10 and Sch 2.
[43] [2003] NI 1.
[44] s 62.
[45] Eg *In re W's Application* [2012] NIQB 37, [2012] 7 BNIL 30, where a woman unsuccessfully claimed that the decision not to treat her as a trafficked person was in breach of art 4 of the European Convention (see para 6.23).

circumstances'.[46] There are also two further exceptions to the one year rule: if the proceedings are in the form of an application for judicial review they must adhere to the three months time limit applying in such cases, and if the proceedings are against the Northern Ireland Government for acting incompatibly with Convention rights the proceedings can be brought even after one year (although the law is unclear as to what longer time limit applies).[47]

THE NORTHERN IRELAND HUMAN RIGHTS COMMISSION[48]

6.28   The Northern Ireland Human Rights Commission (NIHRC) is an institution foreshadowed in the Belfast (Good Friday) Agreement of 1998. The parties to that Agreement wanted to set up a Commission which had more teeth than the existing Standing Advisory Commission on Human Rights (SACHR), a body which had been operating with limited powers since 1973[49] and whose views on human rights had been largely ignored by successive UK governments. SACHR did play a significant role in improving the laws on religious and political discrimination in Northern Ireland (see para 6.50) and in its final few years it looked closely at the use of lethal force by members of the security forces, the system for handling complaints against the police, the rights of prisoners, arrangements for supporting victims of crime, plans for improving community relations, access to education, legal aid, inquests, abortion, race relations and the rights of persons with disabilities. SACHR also undertook significant work on whether there should be a Bill of Rights for Northern Ireland, its 1977 report remaining one of the best studies of that topic.[50] Its view at that time was that a Bill for the UK as a whole, based on the European Convention on Human Rights, should be introduced as a matter of urgency, but in 1992 it changed its position so as to advocate a Bill of Rights for Northern Ireland alone, again based on the European Convention, even if no such Bill was enacted for the whole nation. When the Human Rights Act was passed in 1998 this in effect satisfied SACHR's earlier recommendation.

[46] Human Rights Act 1998, s 7(5).
[47] See *Somerville v Scottish Ministers* [2007] UKHL 44, [2007] 1 WLR 2734. This decision was reversed by statute in Scotland, but it still represents the legal position in Northern Ireland.
[48] See, generally, C Harvey, 'Building a Human Rights Culture in a Political Democracy: The Role of the Northern Ireland Human Rights Commission' in C Harvey (ed), *Human Rights, Equality and Democratic Renewal in Northern Ireland* (Oxford, Hart Publishing, 2001), ch 6. The Commission's website address is www.nihrc.org.
[49] Northern Ireland Constitution Act 1973, s 20.
[50] *The Protection of Human Rights by Law in Northern Ireland*, Cmnd 7009.

The Commission's duties and powers

6.29   The NIHRC was established in 1999, under section 68 of the Northern Ireland Act 1998.[51] The Act does not specify how many Commissioners there should be, but appointments are made by the Secretary of State after shortlisted applicants have been interviewed. It is answerable to the Secretary of State for Northern Ireland, not to a Minister in the Northern Ireland Executive, and its annual reports are tabled at the UK Parliament. Its main duties are to promote understanding and awareness of the importance of human rights in Northern Ireland, advise the Secretary of State and the Executive Committee of the Northern Ireland Assembly of the measures which ought to be taken to protect human rights, advise the Assembly whether a Bill is compatible with human rights (see para 3.20), and advise the Secretary of State on what should be contained in a Bill of Rights for Northern Ireland.[52] The NIHRC also has at least three important powers: to assist individuals with court or tribunal proceedings involving the protection of human rights, to bring proceedings of this nature itself, and to conduct investigations. These duties and powers were enhanced by the Justice and Security (NI) Act 2007. It is now clear that when the NIHRC is taking cases to court it can rely upon Convention rights even though it is not itself a victim or potential victim of the unlawful act to which the proceedings relate.[53] And when it is investigating situations existing on or after July 2007 the NIHRC may require a person to supply information to it, provided it has first concluded that no-one else has sufficiently investigated the matter.[54] It may also enter places of detention if it first concludes that entry is required because the matter being investigated has not been sufficiently investigated by anyone else.[55]

6.30   The Commission can assist individual applicants with their court or tribunal cases and can take cases in its own name. It can also apply to intervene in cases as a third party. To win this right to intervene it had to take the issue as far as the House of Lords.[56] Amongst matters investigated by the Commission have been the rights of children held in juvenile justice centres, the rights of women and girls in prison, the rights of detained immigrants, the rights of homeless people who have no recourse to public

---

[51] See generally A Lester, D Pannick and J Herberg (eds), *Human Rights Law and Practice* (London, LexisNexis Butterworths, 3rd edn, 2009) 746–751.

[52] There is also a Joint Committee between the NIHRC and the Irish Human Rights Commission, which was established in 2001.

[53] Northern Ireland Act 1998, s 71(2A), (2B) and (2C), inserted by the Justice and Security (NI) Act 2007, s 14(2). A similar power was conferred on the Equality and Human Rights Commission in Great Britain by the Equality Act 2006, s 30(3).

[54] Northern Ireland Act 1998, ss 69A and 69B, inserted by the Justice and Security (NI) Act 2007, s 16.

[55] Ibid s 69C, inserted by the Justice and Security (NI) Act 2007, s 16.

[56] *Re Northern Ireland Human Rights Commission* [2002] UKHL 25, [2002] NI 236.

funds, and the rights of older persons in nursing homes.[57] The Commission has also submitted numerous papers commenting on proposed changes to law and policy suggested by various government departments, but its experience has been similar to that of SACHR in that the Governments in London and Belfast tend to pay little heed to the recommendations it makes. The Commission is probably more effective on the international plain,[58] where interventions can be made at the UN Human Rights Council and at various UN treaty-monitoring bodies such as the Committee Against Torture, the Committee on the Rights of the Child and the Committee on the Elimination of Racial Discrimination.

Advice on a Bill of Rights

6.31   For most of its first ten years of existence the NIHRC's focus was on producing advice to the Secretary of State for Northern Ireland on what should be contained in a Bill of Rights for Northern Ireland, a duty derived from the Belfast (Good Friday) Agreement 1998. Its advice was finally transmitted in 2008. A year later the Northern Ireland Office issued a consultation paper on its own views concerning a Bill of Rights, which were very far removed from those of the Commission. Debates in the Northern Ireland Assembly have highlighted the wide gulf that also exists between the views of unionist and nationalist politicians on this issue.[59] The Belfast (Good Friday) Agreement requires any Bill of Rights for Northern Ireland to go beyond what is already contained in the European Convention on Human Rights, to reflect 'the particular circumstances of Northern Ireland, drawing as appropriate on international instruments and experience', and to reflect 'the principles of mutual respect for the identity and ethos of both communities and parity of esteem'.[60] As mentioned above (para 6.23), there is also a debate as to whether, if there is to be a Bill of Rights for Northern Ireland, it should form part of a UK Bill of Rights.[61] In 2011 the UK Government set up a Commission to examine whether there should be a UK Bill of Rights, but its final report, published in 2012, is inconclusive on the

---

[57] *In Our Care* (2002) and *Still In Our Care* (2006); *The Hurt Inside* (2004); *Our Hidden Borders* (2009); *No Home From Home* (2009); *In Defence of Dignity* (2012).

[58] B Dickson, 'The Contribution of Human Rights Commissions to the Protection of Human Rights' [2003] *PL* 272. The NIHRC has sometimes sent submissions to the European Court of Human Rights when cases from Northern Ireland have been under consideration there. The current Chief Commissioner of the NIHRC, Professor Michael O'Flaherty, has been prominent in leading reform of the UN's human rights treaty-monitoring process.

[59] See the debates on 25 September 2001 and 1 March 2010, available on the website of the Assembly.

[60] Para 4 of the section headed 'Rights, Safeguards and Equality of Opportunity' in Strand Three of the Belfast (Good Friday) Agreement 1998.

[61] See, eg C Harvey and D Russell, 'A New Beginning for Human Rights Protection in Northern Ireland?' [2009] *EHRLR* 767.

matter. Two prominent human rights lawyers, Professor Philippe Sands and Baroness Helena Kennedy, thought that the time was not right for such a Bill because reaching agreement on its content might jeopardise the existing Human Rights Act.

CORONERS' COURTS[62]

6.32   Coroners' courts are not courts in the normal sense of the word, because they do not decide if someone is guilty of a crime or liable for a civil wrong. Instead they conduct 'inquests' (ie formal investigations) into certain deaths. They are run by coroners, who in Northern Ireland are appointed by the Lord Chancellor from among barristers or solicitors of five or more years' standing.[63] At present the Coroners Service is headed by a High Court judge and there is one Senior Coroner and two Coroners. The relevant legislation is the Coroners Act (NI) 1959 and the Coroners (Practice and Procedure) Rules (NI) 1963,[64] as amended.

6.33   Coroners investigate unexpected, unexplained, violent or suspicious deaths, the focus being on who the deceased person was, and when, where, by what means and in what circumstances he or she came to die.[65] To assist in this process the coroner can order a *post mortem* examination to be carried out by a government-approved doctor, and this occurs in almost half of the cases investigated. The coroner will decide to hold an inquest if it seems that death was due to an unnatural cause, even if no body has been found.[66] The police are under a continuing statutory duty to pass to the coroner all information they are able to obtain concerning the death.[67] In England and Wales and the Republic of Ireland an inquest can be held even though the death occurred abroad, provided that the body has since been returned to the coroner's district, but the law does not permit such an inquest to be held in Northern Ireland.

Inquests

6.34   Each year there are over 200 inquests held in Northern Ireland, representing between 5 per cent and 10 per cent of the deaths reported to

[62] See J Leckey and D Greer, *Coroners' Law and Practice in Northern Ireland* (Belfats, SLS Legal Publications, 1998) and the useful booklet prepared by the Northern Ireland Courts and Tribunals Service, *Coroners Service for Northern Ireland* (available online).

[63] Coroners Act (NI) 1959, s 2(3). There is a similar inquest system in England and Wales, but in Scotland 'fatal accident inquiries' are used instead.

[64] SR & O 199.

[65] Coroners Act (NI) 1959, s 31(1); *R (Sacker) v Coroner for West Yorkshire* [2004] 2 AC 182.

[66] *In re Howard's Application* [2011] NIQB 125, [2011] 10 BNIL 16.

[67] Ibid s 8; *McCaughey v Chief Constable of the PSNI* [2007] UKHL 14, [2007] 2 AC 226.

the coroner.[68] The inquests usually take place in recognised courthouses and do not normally involve a jury, but if the coroner has reason to suspect that the death occurred in prison, in an accident or in circumstances prejudicial to the safety of the public, a jury of between seven and 11 persons *must* be summoned.[69] The coroner plays a more leading role in an inquest than a judge would do in a regular court of law because he or she has a wide-ranging discretion as to which witnesses should be called (compelling their attendance if necessary) and will take an active part in examining them. The witnesses are placed under oath and may be questioned by other interested parties such as the family of the deceased person. There is no absolute right for these parties to be legally represented in the proceedings, but they do have the right to obtain copies of relevant evidence submitted to the coroner by the police in advance of the inquest.[70] Speeches cannot be made to the jury except by the coroner in his or her summing-up at the end of the inquest. Applications for financial help with preparing for an inquest can be made under the legal advice and assistance scheme (see para 11.33) and there is an extra-statutory scheme for covering the cost of representation in 'exceptional' cases.[71]

6.35   There have been many controversial inquests into deaths caused by members of the security forces in Northern Ireland[72] and in important decisions in 2001 the European Court of Human Rights ruled that inadequacies in the inquest system in such cases meant that there had been a breach of the procedural duty implied in Article 2 of the European Convention on Human Rights, which protects the right to life.[73] Some changes were accordingly made to the inquest system in Northern Ireland (eg the removal of a suspect's right not to give evidence at the inquest[74]) and a comprehensive review proposed that the coroners' system in Northern Ireland should be headed by a High Court judge.[75] However, in *Re McKerr*[76]

---

[68] For details see the annual *Judicial Statistics of Northern Ireland*. The website of the Northern Ireland Courts and Tribunals website has a good booklet entitled *Coroners Inquest* (2011).

[69] Coroners Act (NI) 1959, s 21. In England a jury must also be summoned if the death results from an injury supposedly caused by a police officer in the execution of his or her duty and inquest juries in that jurisdiction comprise 12 jurors.

[70] *Re Jordan's Application* [1996] 7 BNIL 15.

[71] The scope of the extra-statutory scheme was considered in *In re Hemsworth's Application* [2003] NIQB 5. The Justice (NI) Act 2002, s 76, allows the Lord Chancellor to direct that legal aid is to be available in connection with proceedings which are otherwise excluded from the state schemes. He so directed for the inquest into the Omagh bomb of August 1998, which took place in September 2000.

[72] *Inquests and Disputed Killings in Northern Ireland* (Committee on the Administration of Justice, Belfast, 1992).

[73] *Jordan v UK* (2003) 37 EHRR 52, *Kelly and others v UK* App No 30054/96, *McKerr v UK* (2002) 34 EHRR 553 and *Shanaghan v UK* App No 37715/97.

[74] Coroners (Practice and Procedure) (Amendment) Rules (NI) 2002 (SR 37).

[75] *Fundamental Review of Death Certification and Coroner Services in England, Wales and Northern Ireland*, Cm 5831; 2003 (the Luce Report).

[76] [2004] UKHL 12, [2004] 1 WLR 807.

the House of Lords ruled that deaths occurring prior to the date when the Human Rights Act 1998 came into force (ie 2 October 2000) did not have to be investigated in a way which fully complied with Article 2 of the European Convention. Then, in 2011, having taken into account a recent decision by the Grand Chamber of the European Court of Human Rights,[77] the Supreme Court departed from *Re McKerr* in *In re McCaughey*.[78] It ruled there that, if an inquest is held into a death which occurred before 2 October 2000, it must comply with the procedural requirements implicit in Article 2, at any rate so far as that is possible under domestic law.

The conclusions at an inquest

6.36 Proceedings before a coroner should not prejudice proceedings which might be taken in another court, and for this reason inquests are often delayed until any criminal proceedings connected with the death have run their course. In Northern Ireland delays in holding an inquest have often endured for years; even today there are still more than 30 so-called 'legacy inquests' still due to be held in relation to deaths which occurred during the troubles between 1968 and 1998. Coroners and juries at inquests in Northern Ireland issue 'findings', not 'verdicts', and they cannot express any opinions on questions of criminal or civil liability. More particularly, unlike in England and Wales, they cannot conclude that the death was due to an 'unlawful killing'.[79] Within five days of the end of the inquest the coroner must send the particulars of death to the appropriate registrar of deaths and where the circumstances appear to disclose that a criminal offence may have been committed the coroner must also furnish the Public Prosecution Service with a written report of those circumstances.[80]

Challenging the findings at an inquest

6.37 If a coroner decides not to hold an inquest, that decision can be judicially reviewed (see paras 6.5–6.11). Even without such a review, the earlier decision can be reversed by a coroner if new information comes to light.[81] There cannot be any appeal against the findings at a coroner's inquest, but the process can again be made the object of a judicial review application, which might lead to a new inquest if at the earlier one the coroner failed, for instance, to call a jury when one should have been called, or to properly

---

[77] *Šilih v Slovenia* (2009) 49 EHRR 996.
[78] [2011] UKSC 20, [2012] 1 AC 725. Lord Rodger strongly dissented.
[79] *Jordan v Lord Chancellor* [2007] UKHL 14, [2007] 2 AC 226.
[80] Justice (NI) Act 2002, s 33(3).
[81] *In the Matter of an Application by Michael Millar* [2005] NIQB 34.

sum up the evidence to the jury. In England, but not in Northern Ireland, the Attorney General retains a power to refer a coroner's inquest to the High Court, which can order a second inquest to be held.

Treasure

6.38   Coroners also have jurisdiction to hold inquests into the finding of treasure, that is:

- any object at least 300 years old which has metallic content of which at least 10 per cent by weight is precious metal or which is one of at least ten coins in the same find, and
- any object at least 200 years old which belongs to a class designated by the Secretary of State as being of outstanding historical, archaeological or cultural importance.[82]

6.39   When treasure is found, the finder must notify the Coroners Service of the find within 14 days. Failure to do so is a criminal offence.[83] A coroner proposing to conduct an inquest must notify the Department of the Environment and give any interested persons an opportunity to examine witnesses at the inquest.[84] A revised code of practice for treasure cases in Northern Ireland was published in 2002 by the Environment and Heritage Service of the Department of the Environment[85] and it provides for the close involvement of the Ulster Museum in any case involving treasure. Treasure normally belongs to the Crown, subject to any prior interests and rights deriving from the time when it was originally hidden or abandoned, but the Crown will usually donate the treasure to a museum. Before the transfer takes place, the Secretary of State must determine whether an *ex gratia* reward should be paid by the museum to any person involved in the find, or to any person who has an interest in the land on which the treasure was found.[86]

THE PARADES COMMISSION

6.40   The human right to freedom of assembly has been one of the most contentious issues in Northern Ireland, particularly in the 1990s when serious civil unrest broke out over the demand from the Orange Order that they had the right to march down the predominantly Catholic Garvaghy Road in Portadown. Special measures have therefore been introduced in

---

[82] Treasure Act 1996, ss 1 and 2. See also the Treasure (Designation) Order 2002 (SI 2666).
[83] Ibid s 8.
[84] Ibid s 9.
[85] *The Treasure Act 1996: Northern Ireland Code of Practice.*
[86] Treasure Act 1996 s 10(1) and (2).

an effort to reduce the risk of public disorder arising from parades and associated protests.[87] Prior to 1998, the relevant law was contained in the Public Order (NI) Order 1987. This conferred on the police the power to impose conditions on public processions if they reasonably believed that the circumstances in which a parade was being held might result in serious public disorder, serious damage to property or serious disruption to the life of the community.[88] These criteria, however, were widely criticised because they put tremendous pressure on the police to yield to the greatest threat of public disorder from whichever side that came.

6.41 In 1996, the UK Government established the Independent Review of Parades and Marches, chaired by Dr Peter North of the University of Oxford. This group recommended the establishment of an independent Parades Commission, which would take over the police's decision-making powers in relation to public processions, and an extension of the statutory criteria under which conditions could be imposed on parades. These recommendations were largely implemented by the Public Processions (NI) Act 1998. Today the Parades Commission comprises six persons.[89] In addition to issuing determinations relating to proposed parades, the Commission has a duty under section 2 of the 1998 Act to promote greater understanding about public processions and to facilitate mediation as a means of resolving disputes. The Act also requires the Commission to produce a Code of Conduct (providing guidance to persons organising public processions or protest meetings), a set of Procedural Rules (regulating the procedure which the Commission must follow in exercising its functions) and a Guidelines document (expanding on the statutory criteria in s 8(6) of the Act for imposing restrictions on a parade).[90] Following serious disturbances in Ardoyne in North Belfast on 12 July 2004,[91] the Public Processions (Amendment) (NI) Order 2005 extended the power of the Commission to impose conditions on both supporters of and objectors to a parade.

The Commission's duties and powers

6.42 Organisers of all public processions (except funerals and Salvation Army processions) are now required to give the police 28 days' notice[92] and organisers of any related protest must give 14 days' notice.[93] A copy of

---

[87] See further T Hadden and A Donnelly, *The Legal Control of Parades and Marches in Northern Ireland* (Belfast, Northern Ireland Community Relation Council, 1997).

[88] art 4.

[89] www.paradescommission.org.

[90] ss 3, 4 and 5.

[91] See *Report on the Policing of the Ardoyne Parades 12 July 2004*, prepared for the Northern Ireland Policing Board by Keir Starmer QC and Jane Gordon.

[92] The notice requirement had been 7 days until it was increased by the Public Order (NI) (Amendment) Order 1997.

[93] Public Processions (NI) Act 1998, ss 6 and 7.

these notices is then passed to the Parades Commission. Before it reaches a decision on contentious parades or protest meetings the Commission will invite written and oral evidence. If conditions need to be imposed on the parade or protest, it will aim to do so at least five days before the parade. The criteria which the Commission may consider when deciding whether or not to impose conditions are contained in sections 8(6) and 9A(6) of the Public Processions (NI) Act 1998. These refer (as well as to the potential for public disorder and disruption to the life of the community) to any impact which the procession may have on relationships within the community, any failure of the organiser of, or a participant in, any parade or protest meeting to comply with the Code of Conduct and (in the case of parades only) the desirability of allowing a procession customarily held along a particular route to be held along that route. The compatibility of these criteria with the European Convention on Human Rights was unsuccessfully challenged in a case concerning a proposed Orange Order parade in Dunloy in County Antrim.[94] In a more recent case the High Court allowed the Parades Commission, when imposing restrictions on the numbers of bands taking part in a parade, to take into account the unwillingness of the organisers of the parade to engage in dialogue with local residents since the previous year's parade.[95] The Commission has no power to ban a parade altogether, only to re-route it or to impose other conditions on how it proceeds.

6.43 The Parades Commission's Procedural Rules allow the Commission to amend or revoke a decision about a parade where fresh information has come to light. The Minister of Justice, too, may review a decision by the Parades Commission if requested by the Chief Constable to do so. The only other means of challenging a decision of the Commission is by way of judicial review (see paras 6.5–6.11). The Commission survived judicial reviews of its decision in 1999 to re-route a 'Civil Rights March' between Lurgan and Portadown[96] and to impose restrictions on a march in Portadown.[97] But in 2006 the Commission was ordered to disclose to a Lodge of the Orange Order police reports and other documents which the Commission had taken into account before banning a parade by the Lodge in Dunloy, County Antrim.[98]

6.44 In the Hillsborough Castle Agreement of 5 February 2010[99] (which paved the way for the devolution of policing and justice to the Northern Ireland Assembly two months later) provision was made for a working group to be set up to devise an improved framework for the management and regulation of public assemblies. The First Minister and Deputy First Minister were then

[94] *Re Tweed's Application* [2001] NI 165.
[95] *Re Ballymaconnolly Sons of Conquerors Flute Band* [2012] NIQB 63, [2012] 10 BNIL 77.
[96] *Re McConnell's Application* [2000] 4 BNIL 71.
[97] *Re Farrell's Application* [1999] NIJB 143.
[98] *Tweed v Parades Commission of Northern Ireland* [2006] UKHL 53, [2007] 1 AC 650.
[99] Available at www.nio.gov.uk.

to ensure that an Act resulting from the working group's proposals and the subsequent public consultation would be in place by the end of 2010. This timetable was not met and by May 2013 a Bill had still not been submitted to the Northern Ireland Assembly. Concerns were also growing that the requirement to seek permission from the Parades Commission to organise a procession was being widely flouted by loyalists who were gathering on the streets to object to the decision of Belfast City Council to fly the union flag at Belfast City Hall only on 18 designated days each year.

THE INFORMATION COMMISSIONER'S OFFICE

6.45 The rights to data privacy and to access to information are safeguarded in Northern Ireland by a branch of the UK's Information Commissioner's Office (ICO). The ICO upholds data privacy by overseeing the implementation of the Data Protection Act 1998 and the Privacy and Electronic Communications (EC Directive) Regulations 2003;[100] it upholds access to information by overseeing the implementation of the Freedom of Information Act 2000 (which did not come fully into force until 2005) and the Environmental Information Regulations 2004.[101] The Office publishes guidance to enable organisations to adopt good practices in the fields of data protection and access to information, it tries to resolve complaints from people who think that the legislation on these issues has been breached, it maintains a public register of all data controllers, it monitors the 'publication schemes' which must be adopted by all public authorities under the Freedom of Information Act (FoI), and it prosecutes people who commit offences under the legislation. If a person disagrees with a decision taken by the ICO he or she can appeal to the First-tier Tribunal (Information Rights) and from there to the Upper Tribunal (Administrative Appeals) and then, on points of law, to the Court of Appeal.[102] It is no exaggeration to say that FoI requests, as they are referred to, have revolutionised the culture of secrecy in public authorities. A request made under the FoI Act for information must in general be responded to within 20 days. There is usually no charge for the information provided, but an organisation can turn down a request if it thinks that dealing with the request will cost it more than £450 (or £600 if it is a central government organisation).[103] In his memoirs, however, Tony Blair expresses very strongly the view that the Act was a huge mistake because in government it inhibits the expression of people's opinions and the consideration of options.[104]

---

[100] SI 2426.
[101] SI 3391.
[102] Until 2011 appeals from the ICO went to the Information Tribunal and then to the High Court: see, eg, *Anderson v The Information Commissioner* [2011] NIQB 44, [2011] 6 BNIL 52.
[103] See, generally, www.gov.uk/make-a-freedom-of-information-request.
[104] Tony Blair, *A Journey* (London, Hutchinson, 2010), 516–7.

Data protection controversies

6.46   In an age when vast quantities of information are so easily transmitted, the role of the ICO is becoming increasingly important. Following a report by the House of Commons' Home Affairs Committee in 2010 entitled *A Surveillance Society?*,[105] the ICO produced its own report to Parliament on the state of surveillance in the United Kingdom.[106] This concluded by questioning 'whether the current legal instruments, at UK and European levels, including specific data protection legislation as well as broader human rights law, are robust enough to limit surveillance and curb the excesses of data collection'. During the period of the Labour governments in the UK between 1997 and 2010 there were several high-profile data losses,[107] as well as long-running controversies over the proposals to introduce identity cards and to retain indefinitely the DNA samples provided by people who have been arrested. In *R (S) v Chief Constable of South Yorkshire Police* five judges in the House of Lords held that the current retention policy for fingerprints and DNA samples was fully compliant with the European Convention on Human Rights,[108] but when the same case reached the Grand Chamber of the European Court of Human Rights all 17 judges thought that the retention policy was in breach of the right to privacy guaranteed by Article 8 of the Convention.[109] The law in England and Wales was eventually reformed by the Protection of Freedoms Act 2012.[110] In 2011 the Minister of Justice in Northern Ireland issued a consultation paper proposing changes to bring the law there into line with the European Court's requirements.[111] The law was eventually changed by section 9 of the Criminal Justice Act (NI) 2013.

EQUALITY LAW AND THE EQUALITY COMMISSION

6.47   Equality law could be seen as a sub-branch of human rights law, but it is useful to explain it separately because it is informed by principles that are very particular and in Northern Ireland it is enforced by a special agency, the Equality Commission.[112] This was formed in 1999 out of the merger of four existing bodies: the Equal Opportunities Commission (which dealt with gender discrimination), the Fair Employment Commission (which dealt with discrimination based on religious belief and political opinion),

[105] (2007–08) HC 58-1.
[106] Available at www.ico.gov.uk.
[107] Most notably the loss in November 2007 by HM Revenue and Customs of two discs carrying the personal details of 25 million people: http://news.bbc.co.uk/1/hi/7104945.stm.
[108] [2004] UKHL 39, [2004] 1 WLR 2196.
[109] *S and Marper v UK* (2009) 48 EHRR 50.
[110] ss 1–25.
[111] Available at www.dojni.gov.uk.
[112] See too C White, *Northern Ireland Social Work Law* (Dublin, Tottel Publishing, 2004), ch 4.

the Commission for Racial Equality and the Northern Ireland Disability Council.

The Commission's duties and powers

6.48   Members of the Equality Commission, like those of the NIHRC, are appointed by the Secretary of State after being shortlisted and interviewed, but the Commission is accountable to the Office of the First Minister and Deputy First Minister rather than to the Secretary of State for Northern Ireland. There can be up to 20 Commissioners at any one time. They are obliged to ensure that the Commission's resources are appropriately distributed between religious and political discrimination, sex discrimination, race discrimination and disability discrimination.[113] There is provision for the Commission to receive advice on the exercise of its functions from a 'consultative council', but no such body has yet been established.[114] As well as helping to enforce the laws on discrimination and equality, the Equality Commission has a significant educational and research role, trying to persuade employers and service providers of the economic, social and industrial advantages which can flow from fair and lawful practices in recruitment and promotion. The Commission also looks out for discriminatory advertisements: if it believes that an advertiser is likely to continue to publish such adverts it can apply to the High Court for an injunction restraining their publication.

The law on discrimination

6.49   The law in Northern Ireland on discrimination based on gender,[115] race,[116] disability,[117] sexual orientation[118] or age[119] is largely the same as that in Great Britain, but the law on religious and political discrimination is significantly more advanced in Northern Ireland because of the special problems that have arisen there since the partition

---

[113] Northern Ireland Act 1998, s 74(3)(a).

[114] Ibid s 74(3)(b) and (4). The Commission issued a consultation paper on the topic in 2004.

[115] See B Jones, 'Sex Discrimination', in B Dickson and B Gormally (eds), *Human Rights in Northern Ireland: The CAJ Handbook* (Belfast, Committee on the Administration of Justice, Belfast, 2013), ch 14. 'Gender Discrimination' refers here to treating a person of one sex less favourably than a person of the other sex solely because of the first person's sex, treating a person less favourably because he or she is changing or has changed their gender (see the Sex Discrimination (Gender Reassignment) Regs (NI) 1999, SR 311), and treating a married person less favourably than a single person solely because the first person is married. There is no protection for single persons as such.

[116] See C White, 'Race Discrimination', ibid, ch 15.

[117] See G Kilpatrick, 'Disability Discrimination', ibid, ch 16.

[118] See B Fitzpatrick, 'Sexual Orientation Discrimination', ibid, ch 18.

[119] See B Fitzpatrick, 'Age Discrimination', ibid, ch 17. See too para 6.64 below.

of Ireland.[120] It is therefore given special attention in this book (see para 6.50 below). In 2001 the Northern Ireland Executive promised to prioritise the passing of a so-called 'Single Equality Act', which would consolidate, simplify and enhance the existing legislation on equality in Northern Ireland. But although the Office of the First Minister and Deputy First Minister issued a consultation document on the issue in 2004, practically nothing has been heard of the proposal since then. Meanwhile Great Britain has forged ahead with the Equality Acts of 2006 and 2010, the combined effect of which is to make the protection of equality in Northern Ireland less comprehensive than in the rest of the UK. The Equality Commission has published papers highlighting the deficiencies in Northern Ireland's equality laws compared with those in Great Britain,[121] and the Northern Ireland Assembly's Research and Information Service has produced a useful 40-page review of equality and human rights legislation in Northern Ireland in the light of EU and international obligations.[122]

Religious and political discrimination

6.50 The Government of Ireland Act 1920 made it unlawful for either the Parliament or the Government of Northern Ireland to do anything that discriminated against people on the basis of their religious belief.[123] When the Northern Ireland Constitution Act 1973 was passed, in an attempt to create a power-sharing government in Northern Ireland in 1974, the ban on discrimination was extended to acts done on the basis of political opinion.[124] In 1976 further legislation was passed to deal with religious and political discrimination in the employment context.[125] Then the Fair Employment and Treatment (NI) Order 1998 extended protection against religious and political discrimination beyond the contexts of actions by Parliament, the government and employers into the context of the provision of goods, facilities and services by private businesses.[126]

6.51 None of this legislation made inequality of opportunity or unlawful discrimination on religious or political grounds a criminal offence, but

[120] See E Collins, 'Religious and Political Discrimination', in Dickson and Gormally, n 115 above, ch 13.

[121] See www.equalityni.org, under 'The Law' and then 'Pressing for reform'.

[122] NIAR 313-11; available at www.niassembly.gov.uk/researchandlibrary/2011/7511.pdf (August 2011).

[123] s 5(1) for the ban on Parliamentary action and s 8(6) for the ban on government action.

[124] ss 17 and 19.

[125] Fair Employment (NI) Act 1976. This was not mirrored in Great Britain until the Employment Equality (Religion or Belief) Regs 2003 (SI 1660), and even then discrimination on the grounds of political opinion was not included.

[126] This was achieved for Great Britain by the Equality Act 2010, ss 10 and 29.

the 1998 Order requires all private sector employers with more than 10 employees to register with the Equality Commission and it is a criminal offence to fail to register when required to do so. All public authorities are automatically registered. All registered employers must monitor the religious make-up of their workforce and send details of this to the Commission each year.[127] In addition, each public sector employer and each private sector employer with more than 250 employees must return information on the perceived religion of applicants for jobs.[128] The Commission then publishes an annual report summarising the returns. A registered employer must also review the employment practices within the firm at least once every three years. The aim of monitoring is to make it easier to identify job categories where there are fewer workers or applicants from one religious community than might otherwise be expected. It is a criminal offence to refuse to supply information to the Commission which must be monitored but, because the data is otherwise confidential, it is also an offence to disclose it to anyone other than the Commission.

Investigations and affirmative action

6.52   The Equality Commission has power under article 11 of the 1998 Order to investigate the employment practices of particular employers to see what action ought to be taken to promote equality of opportunity. Under this power the former Fair Employment Commission undertook dozens of investigations into private sector companies as well as several public bodies such as district councils and Education and Library Boards. If the Commission finds a failure to afford equality of opportunity it can determine what steps should be taken to secure it and can ask for undertakings from employers or give them directions.[129] If such directions are not complied with within a reasonable period the Commission can apply to the Fair Employment Tribunal (see para 6.55) for an enforcement order. If this in turn is not complied with, the Tribunal can fine the employer up to £30,000 and can disqualify the employer from eligibility for government grants and contracts (this is the notion of 'contract compliance'). It can even refer the employer's case to the High Court, which has greater powers to fine and can even imprison for contempt of court.

6.53   The Equality Commission often seeks to promote affirmative action programmes with employers. The sorts of measures recommended include the ending of informal selection methods (such as word of mouth recruitment), the establishment of a neutral or harmonious working environment as regards religious and political emblems, and the setting

---

[127] Fair Employment and Treatment (NI) Order 1998, art 52.
[128] Ibid art 54.
[129] Ibid arts 12–14.

of goals and timetables with respect to improvements to the religious balance of the workforce. There is some evidence that affirmative action programmes have had an effect in reducing inequality.[130] Of course some of these measures have to contend with the so-called 'chill factor' – some people are reluctant to apply for jobs in an environment where they might feel threatened.

6.54   It should be stressed that, even if an employer employs too few people to have to register or monitor the workforce, he or she is still bound by the law's requirement not to discriminate against a person on the grounds of religious belief or political opinion. However, certain forms of employment, such as serving as a cleric, a school-teacher or in a private household remain exempt from control.[131] The exemption for school-teaching is particularly controversial, as it is seen by some as a hindrance to the development of integrated education in Northern Ireland. The Equality Commission wants to see it removed.[132] The Commission supported the positive discrimination measure that was in place from 2001 to 2011 to ensure that at least 50 per cent of new recruits to the Police Service of Northern Ireland were Catholics.[133] A special opt-out from an EU Directive had to be negotiated to make this discrimination lawful in the eyes of EU law.[134] It was later challenged as a violation of the European Convention on Human Rights, but unsuccessfully.[135]

The Fair Employment Tribunal

6.55   The Equality Commission can receive complaints from any person claiming to be a victim of religious or political discrimination and can investigate the matter. The Fair Employment (NI) Act 1989 made indirect discrimination just as unlawful as direct discrimination, although no compensation is payable for the former unless it was intentional. If a person wants to seek compensation for the discrimination they have allegedly suffered, they must lodge a complaint with the Fair Employment Tribunal[136] (another product of the 1989 Act) within three months of the discrimination

---

[130] C McCrudden, R Ford and A Heath, 'Legal Regulation of Affirmative Action in Northern Ireland: An Empirical Assessment' (2004) 24 *OJLS* 363.

[131] Fair Employment and Treatment (NI) Order 1998, Pt VIII (arts 70–80).

[132] Ibid art 71. The investigation found that in controlled (state) schools 85% of the teachers were Protestants and 5% were Catholics, in maintained (Catholic) schools 98% were Catholic and 1% Protestant, and in integrated schools 48% were Protestants and 43% Catholic.

[133] Police (NI) Act 2000, s 46.

[134] Council Directive 2000/78/EC of 27 November 2000 establishing a general framework for equal treatment in employment and occupation, art 15(1). art 15(2) provides the exemption for the recruitment of teachers.

[135] *Re Parsons' Application for Judicial Review* [2003] NICA 20, [2004] NI 38.

[136] This is part of the Office of Industrial Tribunals and the Fair Employment Tribunal and is now governed by the Fair Employment and Treatment (NI) Order 1998, arts 81–90.

occurring. The Tribunal will first refer the complaint to the Labour Relations Agency (see para 9.112) to see if an amicable settlement can be reached. If it cannot, a hearing will take place before the Tribunal, where the procedures are essentially the same as in an industrial tribunal (see paras 4.30 and 9.106). As in other cases of alleged discrimination, the burden of proof on the complainant is relatively easy to discharge. No legal aid is available, but under the Fair Employment and Treatment (NI) Order 1998 the applicant can ask the Equality Commission not just for initial advice but also for free legal representation before the Fair Employment Tribunal.

6.56   The Fair Employment Tribunal can order unlimited compensation if it upholds the complaint, including an award for injured feelings,[137] something not allowable in non-discrimination cases heard by industrial tribunals. The Tribunal can also specify what other remedial action needs to be taken to correct the discrimination. An appeal lies on a point of law to the Court of Appeal. Under article 80 of the 1998 Order, investigations into individual complaints have to be curtailed if the Secretary of State for Northern Ireland issues a certificate that an allegedly discriminatory act has been done for the purpose of safeguarding national security or protecting public safety or public order. To deal with appeals against such certificates a special tribunal has been created, although it has never actually sat.[138]

6.57   As a whole, the laws on religious and political discrimination in Northern Ireland are widely viewed as the most radical employment equity laws anywhere in Europe.[139] They appear to have had some impact on the employment differential between Catholics and Protestants in Northern Ireland, but the unemployment differential remains stubbornly resistant to change. According to the Labour Force Survey, the religious composition of the population of working age in 2009 (including those available for, but not in, work) was 51 per cent Protestant and 49 per cent Catholic.[140] According to the Equality Commission's *Monitoring Report No. 20*, the overall composition of the actual workforce in that year was 54.6 per cent Protestant and 45.4 per cent Catholic. In early 2011 the unemployment rate for Catholics was just over 5 per cent while for Protestants it was just under 4 per cent.[141]

---

[137] Ibid art 39(4). Guidance on how much to award was given by the Court of Appeal in Northern Ireland in *Baird v Cookstown District Council* [1998] NI 88.

[138] Northern Ireland Act 1998, s 91 and Sch 11. Appeals from the tribunal go to the Court of Appeal: s 92.

[139] However dissatisfaction with the Fair Employment (NI) Act 1976 led to the formulation in 1984 of the so-called MacBride Principles, drawn up by a group of civil rights activists led by Sean MacBride, a Nobel Peace Prize laureate. The Principles were inspired by the Sullivan Principles, which were designed to encourage responsible employment practices by American firms operating in South Africa. Several state legislatures in America endorsed the MacBride Principles by threatening to disinvest from American companies which refused to abide by them. The UK government and the Fair Employment Commission strongly condemned the Principles.

[140] In Northern Ireland this survey is conducted by the Northern Ireland Research and Statistics Agency on behalf of the Department of Enterprise, Trade and Investment.

[141] See www.poverty.org.uk/i47/index.shtml.

Equality duties

6.58   The Northern Ireland Act 1998 entrusted that Equality Commission with the oversight of new equality duties imposed by section 75 of the Act. Section 75(1) requires public authorities, when carrying out functions relating to Northern Ireland, to have due regard to the need to promote equality of opportunity:

(1) between persons of different religious belief, political opinion, racial group, age, marital status or sexual orientation;
(2) between men and women generally;
(3) between persons with a disability and persons without; and
(4) between persons with dependants and persons without.

Under section 75(2), and without prejudicing their obligations under section 75(1), public authorities must also have regard to the desirability of promoting good relations between persons of different religious belief, political opinion or racial group.

6.59   Public authorities have to produce an 'equality scheme' demonstrating how they are complying with their duties. The scheme needs to be submitted to, and approved by, the Equality Commission. If the Equality Commission does not feel able to approve it, the scheme is referred to the Secretary of State for Northern Ireland, who has the powers to request the authority to make a revised scheme or to make a scheme him- or herself for the authority. To gain approval from the Equality Commission the scheme has to address a number of points. In particular, it has to state the authority's arrangements for assessing the likely impact (on equality of opportunity) of policies proposed to be adopted by the authority and for monitoring any adverse impact of policies which are adopted.

6.60   The Equality Commission has issued guidelines as to the desirable form and content of equality schemes,[142] and also practical guidance on equality impact assessment,[143] and in 2010 it even published a model scheme. It also has a guide on how to promote good relations, the section 75(2) duty.[144] If an equality scheme is breached a complaint can be lodged with the Commission and an investigation can be launched, but the Commission has limited powers to apply any sanctions if the complaint is substantiated. The courts, too, are reluctant to allow applications for judicial review in this context.[145] The Commission publishes annual reports on implementation of the section 75 duties.

---

[142] *Section 75 of the Northern Ireland Act 1998: A Guide for Public Authorities* (2010).
[143] *Section 75 of the Northern Ireland Act 1998 – Practical Guidance on Equality Impact Assessment* (2005).
[144] *Promoting Good Relations – A Guide for Public Authorities* (2007).
[145] *Re Neill's Application* [2005] NICA 5.

6.61   Although the section 75 duties were innovative at the time, they have been surpassed by developments in Great Britain, where the Equality Act 2010 has consolidated and developed the range of equality duties imposed on public authorities there. There is a provision in the Act, although not yet in force, which imposes a new public duty on public authorities, when making decisions of a strategic nature about how to exercise their functions, to have due regard to the desirability of exercising them in a way that is designed to reduce the inequalities of outcome which result from socio-economic disadvantage.[146] As yet no such duty exists in any legislation applying in Northern Ireland.

THE COMMISSIONER FOR CHILDREN AND YOUNG PEOPLE[147]

6.62   The Northern Ireland Commissioner for Children and Young People (NICCY) was created by the Commissioner for Children and Young People (NI) Order 2003.[148] The Commissioner has extensive powers to safeguard and promote the rights and best interests of Northern Ireland's children and young people, defined as those aged under 18,[149] and has a duty to review the adequacy and effectiveness of services and the law relating to children and young people and to advise Ministers accordingly. The document which inspires the Commissioner's policies is the United Nations' Convention on the Rights of the Child (1989), even though that international treaty has not been formally incorporated into the domestic law of any part of the UK. The Commissioner can help children and their parents or guardians with any complaints they might have about public services for children, can carry out formal or informal inquiries, and can conduct research.

6.63   A major research report on the state of children's rights in Northern Ireland was published by the Commissioner in 2004.[150] In that same year the Commissioner failed in an application for judicial review of the UK Government's decision to put before Parliament the proposed Anti-social Behaviour (NI) Order 2004,[151] and there was a subsequent failure to convince the Court of Appeal in Northern Ireland that the Government had not properly reformed the law on corporal punishment of children

---

[146] s 1(1).
[147] www.niccy.org.
[148] There are now similar commissioners in other jurisdictions in these islands, but their duties and powers differ significantly. The Derry Children's Commission is an unofficial body. There is a European network of the official bodies: see www.ombudsnet.org.
[149] But help can be given to young people with a disability, or those leaving care, up to the age of 21.
[150] Available on the Commissioner's website.
[151] *In re Northern Ireland Commissioner for Children and Young People's Application* [2004] NIQB 40.

following a ruling by the European Court of Human Rights on the subject.[152]

THE COMMISSIONER FOR OLDER PEOPLE

6.64 The Employment Equality (Age) Regulations (NI) 2006 protect people against age discrimination in the employment context and in some educational sectors, but unlike in Great Britain there is still no general protection against age discrimination in access to goods, facilities and services.[153] However, there is a draft EU Directive on this matter which may soon require the Northern Ireland Executive to extend protection to that sphere too. Unless such treatment can be objectively justified, it is no longer legal to compel an employee to retire at the age of 65.[154]

6.65 Northern Ireland is ahead of most other jurisdictions in that in 2011 the Assembly passed a Commissioner for Older People Act (NI).[155] The principal function of this Commissioner is to safeguard and promote the interests of older people. He or she has a range of duties and powers, including the power to conduct or commission research and educational activities, to assist older persons when they are making complaints against relevant authorities, and (if the complaint raises a question of principle and does not fall within an existing complaints system) to actually investigate complaints raised by older persons. Pending the appointment of a Commissioner in 2011, an Older People's Advocate worked on a part-time basis from 2006.

WELFARE LAW

6.66 Welfare law is the branch of public law which governs the way in which the State provides welfare benefits to those in need of them. Although it is a devolved matter, the Minister for Social Development in Northern Ireland is under a statutory duty to consult with the Secretary of State for Work and Pensions in the UK Government with a view to ensuring that there is one single legislative scheme throughout the UK for social security, child support and pensions.[156] It is customary, therefore, for legislation that

---

[152] *In re Northern Ireland Commissioner for Children and Young People's Application* [2009] NICA 10. The European Court of Human Rights case was *A v UK* (1998) 27 EHRR 611.

[153] See L Glennon and B Dickson, *Making Older People Equal: Reforming the Law on Access to Services in Northern Ireland* (Belfast, Changing Ageing Partnership, Queen's University Belfast, 2009).

[154] Employment Equality (Repeal of Retirement Age Provisions) Regs (NI) 2011 (SR 168).

[155] Wales also has a statutory Older People's Commissioner, an office created in 2006, but the Commissioner's powers are not as extensive as those of the Commissioner in Northern Ireland.

[156] Northern Ireland Act 1998, s 87(1) and (2).

has been passed in this field for Great Britain to be mirrored very shortly afterwards by legislation passed for Northern Ireland (formerly in the form of an Order in Council, now in the form of an Act of the Northern Ireland Assembly). There are, for example, the Pensions Act 2004 and the Pensions (NI) Order 2005, the Child Maintenance and Other Payments Act 2008 and the Child Maintenance Act (NI) 2008, and the Welfare Reform Act 2009 and the Welfare Reform Act (NI) 2010.

6.67   The content of the legislation applying in the two jurisdictions is largely identical, but the social security system in Northern Ireland is administered separately. Overall responsibility lies with the Department for Social Development, but it delegates this to the Social Security Agency, which has offices all around Northern Ireland. Her Majesty's Revenue and Customs also play a significant role as regards tax credits, child benefit and statutory sick pay, while the Department of the Environment, through the Northern Ireland Housing Executive and the Land and Property Services is responsible for the administration of housing benefit.

The benefits available

6.68   This book cannot go into the details of each and every benefit available under welfare law, for that would take a volume several times the size of this one. Most of the relevant law derives from the Social Security Contribution and Benefits Act (NI) Act 1992, as amended, and regulations made under the authority of that Act. A useful summary of the relevant conditions of entitlement has been written by Eileen Evason, a well-known local commentator on this area.[157] Local offices of the Social Security Agency or Child Maintenance and Enforcement Division can also provide information as to the conditions to be fulfilled for entitlement to any payment,[158] and if a claimant is dissatisfied with the service provided by either of those agencies he or she can ask for the matter to be investigated by an official called the Independent Case Examiner. There is also a wealth of information about welfare benefits, tax credits and pensions on the UK government's official website for citizens, *www.direct.gov.uk*. In addition, the Child Poverty Action Group produces a Welfare Benefits and Tax Credits Handbook each year.[159] Care should be taken when consulting these sources because the law in this area is constantly changing. In particular, the current UK government is planning extensive alterations to the welfare system between 2011 and 2013.

---

[157] *Social Security Law: A Short Guide* (Belfast, SLS Legal Publications, 2006).
[158] The website of the Department for Social Development carries electronic versions of the so-called Blue Volumes, *The Law Relating to Social Security for Northern Ireland*, and of the Orange Volume, *The Law Relating to Child Support*: www.dsdni.gov.uk/index/law_and_legislation.htm.
[159] Available through www.cpag.org.uk.

6.69   Welfare benefits can be contributory benefits (for which you help to pay through subscriptions to the national insurance fund deducted from your wages or salary), non-contributory benefits, or means-tested benefits. Contributory benefits include statutory sick pay (which is normally paid by an employer), statutory adoption, maternity and paternity pay, maternity allowance, bereavement allowance, contributory employment and support allowance, contributory jobseekers' allowance, industrial injuries disablement benefit and retirement pensions. Non-contributory benefits include child benefit, disability living allowance, attendance allowance and carer's allowance. The best known of the means-tested benefits is income-based jobseekers' allowance, which is designed to provide income to people who are not in full-time employment (but who are required to search for work) and whose income, if any, whether from other benefits or from private resources, is not enough to meet their requirements. Other means-tested benefits include housing benefit, income support, social fund payments, working tax credit and child tax credit.

How claims for benefits are processed

6.70   All benefit authorities should process a claim promptly. Indeed the Northern Ireland Housing Executive, once it has received all the information it needs, is legally required to process claims for housing benefit within 14 days, or as soon as practical thereafter. There are no similar statutory requirements on the Social Security Agency and Her Majesty's Revenue and Customs, though an interim payment can be made in certain circumstances where there is a delay in paying a social security benefit or tax credit. There is no right of appeal against a decision not to make an interim payment, but permission to make an application for judicial review can be sought (see para 6.5).

6.71   In most cases the claimant can ask for the official's decision to be revised on any grounds; the revision will be automatic if requested within one month of the original decision, otherwise specific grounds for the revision (such as an official error or a mistake about or ignorance of facts) must be provided. There is a right to appeal against a decision, including a revised decision, within a further month. After an appeal has been lodged the decision in question may be looked at again. If this happens and the decision is changed the appeal may lapse, even if the claimant has not got everything he or she wants. If still unhappy the claimant must appeal again.

Appeal Tribunals

6.72   Appeals are dealt with by what is called an 'Appeal Tribunal', which will usually be comprised of between one to three people depending on the benefit – a legally qualified chairperson and for some benefits two other people who have expertise in the type of issue being considered, such as disability (see too para 4.29). Chairpersons are appointed to their posts by the Lord Chancellor but the 'lay' members are drawn from a panel drawn up by the President of the Appeal Tribunals. Part of the President's role is to ensure that chairpersons and panel members are adequately trained and informed, that procedures are kept fair and easy to understand, and that the arrangements for holding tribunals are properly made. In status and salary the President is equal in rank to a county court judge. The Appeals Service is the name given to the office over which the President presides.

6.73   An appeal to a tribunal must be in writing and will usually be heard within two or three weeks of the tribunal receiving the papers. Tribunals in this sphere are meant to *be*, as well as to *seem*, completely independent of the Department for Social Development. The Appeals Service is now managed through the Northern Ireland Courts and Tribunals Service. For this reason the hearings are not conducted on Departmental premises; indeed court buildings are now frequently used. Members of the public can attend, just as they can attend hearings in a court of law, but they rarely do so. If intimate personal or financial circumstances or public security considerations are involved, the chairperson can require the hearing to be held in private. The proceedings are meant to be informal and uncomplicated, with the chairperson having a wide discretion as to how to run things. Claimants do not have to appear in person, but statistics show that they stand a better chance of winning the appeal if they both appear and bring a representative (such as an adviser from a Citizens' Advice Bureau).

The legal aid position

6.74   Most controversially, legal aid is not available to people who are too poor to pay to be represented by a solicitor at an Appeal Tribunal, although the legal advice and assistance scheme (see para 11.33) can make £88 worth of solicitor's help available short of actual representation, and this could cover most of the cost of the paperwork involved in preparing a case for hearing. Alternatively, or additionally, a Citizens' Advice Bureau worker, an independent advice centre worker, a friend or a relative is allowed to represent the claimant free of charge: in tribunals, unlike courts, there are no restrictions on who can act as a legal representative. Some people believe it is a good thing that legal aid is not available for representation because otherwise the proceedings would inevitably become too legalistic; others say that the denial of legal aid is blatant discrimination against the underprivileged. The whole issue was considered by the Review on Access to Justice, which reported to the Minister of Justice in 2011. He has since been reflecting on how to proceed.

6.75   A claimant can obtain reimbursement of travelling expenses and compensation for loss of wages incurred through attendance at a tribunal. Witnesses can be called and may be questioned by both sides, but a tribunal has no power, as a court of law would have, to compel the attendance of witnesses, the swearing of oaths or the production of documents. The tribunal's decision is given in a short note.

Social Security and Child Support Commissioners[160]

6.76   An appeal against an Appeals Tribunal's decision must be lodged within one month of the claimant receiving the full written decision from the tribunal, but the permission of the chairperson of the tribunal is required before an appeal can go ahead because in all cases there must be a question of law in dispute, not just a question of fact. If the chairperson refuses permission to appeal, a request can be put directly to a Commissioner.

6.77   Commissioners have to be barristers or solicitors of at least 10 years' standing, which puts them on a footing with county court judges. Apart from the Chief Commissioner there is one other full-time Social Security Commissioner in Northern Ireland. The Appeals Service has published an information leaflet describing what happens when an appeal is forwarded to the Service, and it is available online.[161] Child Support Commissioners are appointed under the Child Support Act 1991 and they hear appeals from Appeal Tribunals handling child support claims. In Northern Ireland the people who serve as Social Security Commissioners also serve as Child Support Commissioners.

6.78   A Social Security Commissioner may or may not hold an oral hearing into the case, but he or she must always fully reconsider the case and give a decision in writing.[162] This is normally supplied to the parties a few weeks after the oral hearing (if there is one). A new decision can be substituted for that of the original tribunal, or the case can be referred back to a tribunal with instructions as to how to determine it. Reports of some decisions by the Commissioners are published, and decisions by

---

[160] For general information on these posts see www.courtsni.gov.uk/en-GB/Tribunals/OSSC.
[161] www.dsdni.gov.uk/publications/documents/tas_information_leaflet(2).pdf.
[162] See the Social Security Commissioners (Procedure) Regs (NI) 1999 (SR 225), the Social Security Commissioners (Procedure) (Tax Credit Appeals) Regs (NI) 2003 (SR 18), and the Child Support Commissioners (Procedure) Regs (NI) 1999 (SR 226), all as amended.

Commissioners in Northern Ireland are binding on Appeal Tribunals, while decisions by Commissioners in Great Britain are not binding in Northern Ireland but are strongly persuasive. A few decisions are noted from time to time in the *Bulletin of Northern Ireland Law* (see para 4.53) and there is a selection available online through the websites of the Department for Social Development,[163] the Social Security Commissioners[164] and the British and Irish Legal Information Institute.[165]

6.79   A further appeal can lie from either kind of Commissioner, although again only with permission and on points of unclear law, to the Court of Appeal in Northern Ireland; usually only two or three of these arise each year. Some may even go as far as the UK Supreme Court (or its predecessor, the House of Lords).[166]

The Social Fund Commissioner[167]

6.80   In the case of discretionary social fund payments there can be no appeal to a Social Security Commissioner: in that area final decisions are taken by the Social Fund Commissioner, who is an official independent of government departments. Disputes about regulated payments under the Social Fund, such as funeral payments, Sure Start maternity grants and winter fuel payments, can be appealed to an Appeal Tribunal, and from there to a Social Security Commissioner. The Social Fund Commissioner also appoints social fund inspectors, monitors the quality of their decisions, gives advice to them on how to improve the standard of their decisions and arranges for their training. He or she must submit an annual report to the Department for Social Development.

The Social Security Advisory Committee[168]

6.81   The Social Security Advisory Committee (SSAC) was set up in 1980 for the whole of the UK, with one member being appointed from Northern Ireland. It is an independent statutory body charged with advising the Secretary of State for Work and Pensions, and the equivalent devolved departments, on social security matters. Although the chairperson and the dozen or so members are appointed by the Secretary of State for Work and Pensions, they do not automatically agree with the government line when giving an opinion on social security issues, which they do either at

---

[163] www.dsdni.gov.uk/benefitlaw/ni-caselaw-digest.asp.
[164] www.osscsc.gov.uk.
[165] www.bailii.org/recent-accessions-nie.html#nie/cases/NISSCSC.
[166] Eg *Zalewska v Department for Social Development* [2008] UKHL 67, [2008] 1 WLR 2602, an unsuccessful appeal supported by the Law Centre (NI).
[167] www.osfcni.org.uk.
[168] www.ssac.org.uk. There is also an Industrial Injuries Advisory Council

the Government's request or on their own initiative. Most social security regulations, when they are at the drafting stage, have to be submitted to the SSAC for its comments. Before producing a report on draft regulations the SSAC usually undertakes a public consultation exercise and the Government must publish the SSAC report when it lays the regulations before Parliament for consideration.

HOUSING LAW[169]

6.82 Responsibility for housing matters in Northern Ireland again largely lies with the Department for Social Development. It is mainly involved in regulating the social rented sector (sometimes referred to as social housing), but it also oversees the laws which regulate the private rented sector. As regards the owner-occupied sector, the Department of the Environment (because of its planning responsibilities: see para 6.86) can be considered more relevant.

6.83 The public rented sector comprises some 125,000 dwellings owned by the Northern Ireland Housing Executive, a centralised body formed in 1971 when responsibility for the allocation of social housing was taken away from district councils in Northern Ireland because of allegations of religious and political discrimination in the allocation processes. Today a further 25,000 dwellings are rented out by registered housing associations. Together the Housing Executive and housing associations are called 'social landlords'. They allocate accommodation in accordance with housing need, and that need is assessed by applying the criteria laid down in the Housing Selection Scheme.[170] This Scheme awards points to applicants depending on their personal circumstances. The applicants are then placed on a waiting list and are offered homes as and when they become available. When they accept a tenancy they must be given a copy of the tenancy agreement and a tenant's handbook. The tenancy agreement will specify, for example, the duties of the landlord and tenant with respect to repairs to the house. Normally the tenancy will be for a trial period of one year: only then does the tenant acquire security of tenure, which means that he or she cannot be required to leave the house unless one of the statutory grounds for repossession is satisfied and a court order has been obtained by the social landlord. The most commonly occurring grounds for repossession are non-payment of rent and causing a nuisance. Most tenants have the right to buy their home under the Housing Executive's House Sales Scheme,[171] provided

---

[169] See generally S Geary, 'Housing Rights' in B Dickson and B Gormally (eds), *Human Rights in Northern Ireland: The CAJ Handbook* (Belfast, Committee on the Administration of Justice, Belfast, 2013), ch 24.

[170] www.nihe.gov.uk/housing_selection_scheme.pdf.

[171] See the guide for tenants available on the website of the NIHE: www.nihe.gov.uk.

certain conditions are met. They also have the right to improve their homes, provided that they obtain written consent in advance, and they have a right to be compensated for the improvements at the end of the tenancy.

The private rented sector

6.84   Relatively speaking, the private rented sector is not regulated in detail by law. Most rental agreements are entirely private matters between the landlord and tenant, although every tenant has the right to a rent book,[172] the right to be free from harassment, and the right not to be evicted unless the landlord has obtained an order for possession from a court.[173] A relatively small number of private tenancies are 'controlled tenancies', which means, amongst other things, that the amount of rent the landlord can charge for the premises is limited by law and can be increased only if a Rent Assessment Panel approves of the increase. Special regulations apply to houses in multiple occupation (HMOs), particularly with regard to safety. In one well-known case the Landlords Association for Northern Ireland successfully applied for judicial review of the Registration Scheme for HMOs on the basis that it violated landlords' right to peaceful enjoyment of their property under the European Convention on Human Rights.[174]

6.85   Under the Housing (NI) Order 1988, as amended by the Housing (NI) Order 2003, the Northern Ireland Housing Executive is under a duty to provide help to people who are homeless or threatened with homelessness.[175] Priority is given to pregnant women, people with dependent children, people who are in fear of violence, people who have lost their homes through a disaster such as a fire or flood, people who are old or disabled, and people who are aged 16 to 21 and vulnerable to exploitation. The net result is that middle-aged single men and women often do not benefit from the homelessness legislation. In such cases the Housing Executive is simply under a duty to provide specific advice and assistance, not actual accommodation.[176]

---

[172] Private Tenancies (NI) Order 2006, art 5.

[173] Rent (NI) Order 1978, art 54, as amended by the Private Tenancies (NI) Order 2006, art 60. See the booklet *Protection Against Harassment and Illegal Eviction: A Guide for Private Landlords and Tenants in Northern Ireland* (2007), available on the Department's website: www.dsdni.gov.uk.

[174] *Re Landlords Association for Northern Ireland's Application* [2005] NIQB 22, [2006] NI 16.

[175] See, eg, *In re JM and WM's Application* [2011] NIQB 105, [2012] 1 BNIL 39.

[176] Housing (Amendment) Act (NI) 2010, s 4. See too the Homeless Persons Advice and Assistance Regs (NI) 2011 (SR 339).

PLANNING LAW

6.86   In Northern Ireland all applications for planning permission must be made to the Department of the Environment, rather than to a local authority as in England and Wales. The Department has an Executive Agency called the Planning Service,[177] which consults with district councils and other affected bodies before deciding whether to grant planning permission or not. If the permission is refused, or granted subject to conditions, the applicant may appeal to the Planning Appeals Commission (PAC) within six months (or such longer period as the Commission may allow). But anyone who objects to a planning application has, at present, no right to appeal against the granting of permission.[178]

6.87   The Planning Appeals Commission[179] is one of those bodies which, like Rent Assessment Committees, does not call itself a tribunal but in fact operates in much the same way as those which do. It was first established by the Planning (NI) Order 1972, although the relevant legislation is now the Planning (NI) Order 1991.[180] The PAC consists of a Chief Commissioner and as many other members as the Office of the First Minister and Deputy First Minister may determine (in May 2011 there were 37). An appeal is generally heard by one Commissioner appointed by the Chief Commissioner, and the hearing usually takes place at a venue near the location of the relevant land. The actual decision on the appeal, however, is taken by the PAC as a whole. Some of the more important decisions are noted in the *Bulletin of Northern Ireland Law* (see para 4.53).

The Commission's duties and powers

6.88   As full reasons for the refusal of planning permission are not always given at the time when the refusal is first announced, the hearing before a Commissioner may be the applicant's earliest opportunity to discover what the details of those reasons are. The Department consequently presents its case first at these hearings, even though it is technically the respondent. No official rules have been made to govern the conduct of proceedings at a hearing, but they are kept as informal as possible.[181] Legal aid is not

---

[177] www.planningni.gov.uk.

[178] *Re Ronald Foster's Application* [2004] NIQB 1.

[179] www.pacni.gov.uk. The PAC doubles up as the Water Appeals Commission, in which capacity it deals with matters such as appeals against decisions on sewerage services or trade effluent discharges.

[180] See further W Orbinson with A Farningham, *Northern Ireland Planning Policy, Vol 1 (Policy) and Vol 2 (Index)* (Belfast, SLS Legal Publications, 2003).

[181] Care needs to be taken that the informality is not such as to breach the right to a fair hearing guaranteed by art 6 of the European Convention on Human Rights: *In re Stewart's Application* [2003] NICA 4.

available. There is an alternative 'written representation' procedure available to appellants; this avoids the need for a hearing and is used for some of the apparently straightforward appeals. Approximately one-half of all planning appeals are allowed. The Commission's website lists all the appeals received during the previous three months as well as all the decisions made within the previous six months. If you know the PAC appeal reference number you can view the decision letters online. There can be no further appeal against a decision of the Planning Appeals Commission, only an application for judicial review (see paras 6.5–6.11).

6.89   The PAC also has a duty to conduct public local inquiries (in order to consider objections made against development plans) as well as hearings or inquiries which may arise from planning applications which the Department of the Environment judges to be of major significance. There are usually only two or three inquiries each year. Normally one member of the PAC will conduct the inquiry and then report to the PAC as a whole. Having considered the matter, the PAC will prepare its collective recommendations and submit them to the Department of the Environment. It is the Department which makes the final decision. Often these inquiries take a great deal of time. There have been many complaints about this, including by politicians and business leaders.[182]

6.90   The Northern Ireland Assembly passed the Planning Act (NI) 2011 in an attempt to reform the planning system. The Act transfers most planning functions away from the Department of the Environment to district councils, within a timetable to be agreed by the Northern Ireland Executive. It also brings forward a number of reforms which will improve the efficiency with which planning applications are dealt with. It expands the categories of people who must be consulted about planning applications, but it does not give objectors to applications any greater substantive rights than they had before.[183]

---

[182] Eg in 2010 Ryanair pulled out of its operations at Belfast City Airport because of delays in a public inquiry over an extension to the runway there: www.bbc.co.uk/news/uk-northern-ireland-11139463.

[183] Further information is available on the website of the Department of the Environment.

7

Criminal Law in
Northern Ireland

INTRODUCTION

7.1 Criminal law is that part of the law which prohibits acts contrary to public order or to the interests of society as a whole. It calls these acts 'offences' and prescribes a variety of punishments for any person who is convicted of committing them. A large number of public bodies are involved in administering the criminal justice system, which is now very largely a devolved matter in Northern Ireland. This chapter begins by explaining how the Belfast (Good Friday) Agreement in 1998 dealt with criminal justice and providing some information about the Department of Justice which since 2010 has had responsibility for criminal justice in Northern Ireland. It then sets out some of the basic principles underlying the criminal law in Northern Ireland and identifies the main elements of well-known offences. Next it outlines the legal measures taken to combat terrorist crime. It continues by considering the level of crime in Northern Ireland, including crime committed by paramilitary organisations. The chapter concludes by looking at the role played by key organisations which enforce the criminal law – the police, prison and probation services, for example. Chapter 8 will then explain how people are tried for criminal offences in Northern Ireland and will set out the rights of persons accused of crimes as they are processed through the criminal justice system.

THE DEPARTMENT OF JUSTICE

7.2 The Belfast (Good Friday) Agreement provided for the creation of a Criminal Justice Review Group. Having consulted widely, the Group issued its recommendations in 2000.[1] At the same time it published no fewer than

---

[1] www.nio.gov.uk/mainreport.pdf. J Jackson, 'Shaping the Future of Criminal Justice' in C Harvey (ed), *Human Rights, Equality and Democratic Renewal in Northern Ireland* (Oxford, Hart Publishing, 2001) ch 7.

18 research reports, which provided a huge amount of information about various aspects of the criminal justice system in Northern Ireland. The core message running through the main Review Group's recommendations was the need for the criminal justice system to protect human rights. Many of the specific recommendations have since been implemented by the Justice (NI) Acts 2002 and 2004.[2] For a while the implementation process was supervised by a Justice Oversight Commissioner, Lord Clyde. That post came to an end in 2006, but Lord Clyde's reports are still available on a website.[3] There is also a useful website providing general information about the criminal justice system in Northern Ireland.[4]

7.3   As explained in Chapter 1 (see para 1.33), responsibility for the criminal justice system in Northern Ireland was eventually transferred to the Department of Justice within the Northern Ireland Executive on 12 April 2010.[5] The delay from 1998 is a stark indicator of the sensitivity of the responsibilities that have been devolved, which include policing, prosecutions, the prison system, the operation of the courts, and the content of the criminal law. The role of the Department is to support the Minister of Justice, whose primary function is to keep the people of Northern Ireland safe. To that end he or she must publish a criminal justice plan every three years and set out how progress in meeting the plan will be measured. The Department also provides resources for the work of five executive agencies, namely, the Northern Ireland Courts and Tribunals Service, the Northern Ireland Prison Service, the Forensic Science Agency, the Youth Justice Agency, and the Compensation Agency. It has a close relationship with a number of other independent public bodies such as the Northern Ireland Policing Board and the Parole Commissioners for Northern Ireland.

7.4   Like other government departments, the Department of Justice issues consultation papers on most major issues before the Minister decides what changes to make to the justice system. At the time of writing, for example, consultations are still on-going into the future administration and structure of tribunals in Northern Ireland and into reform of the legal aid system in civil courts. Consultations which have recently concluded include those on a five-year strategy for improving access to justice for victims and witnesses of crime, a framework for reducing offending and proposals for reforming the law relating to those with mental incapacity. Soon after the Department was created the Minister set up review groups to examine the Northern

---

[2] See C Fox, 'New Hope for the Criminal Justice Review? A Commentary on the Implementation Process' (2003) 54 *NILQ* 437.

[3] www.cjsni.gov.uk/index.cfm/area/information/page/justiceoversightcommissioner.

[4] www.cjsni.org.uk.

[5] Department of Justice Act (NI) 2010. The precise duties and powers of the Department are set out in considerable detail in the Northern Ireland Act 1998 (Devolution of Policing and Justice Functions) Order 2010 (SI 976). For a helpful synopsis see G Anthony, 'The Devolution of Policing and Justice' (2011) 17 *EPL* 197.

Ireland Prison Service, access to justice and the youth justice system in Northern Ireland. Within a year of being appointed, the Minister piloted the Justice Act (NI) 2011 through the Assembly. Amongst other things, this Act imposes a new levy on offenders to be used for the improvement of victims' services and allows special measures to be taken to assist vulnerable victims and witnesses during court proceedings. It also changes the way community safety strategies are implemented (by allowing Policing and Community Safety Partnerships to be created at a local council level) and reforms the legal aid system. Later in 2013 the Minister intends to introduce in the Assembly a Faster, Faster Justice Bill.[6]

GENERAL PRINCIPLES OF CRIMINAL LAW

7.5   Criminal law has a different purpose from that which underlies civil law. Perhaps the best way to understand the difference is to consider the two types of legal proceedings that may be started after a road accident has occurred, where one person's careless driving has damaged another car and injured its driver. The careless driver may receive a summons from the police, which means that *criminal* proceedings are being taken in a magistrates' court with the object of punishing the driver if he or she is found guilty of the crime of careless driving. The aim of the criminal law relating to road traffic is to ensure that everyone on the roads remains safe; it does so by punishing those who endanger others. But such punishment will not help the other driver to pay for the repairs to his or her car or to get compensation for the injuries he or she has suffered. Even if the careless driver is fined by the magistrates' court, the money paid will go to the State, not to the other driver. Unless the careless driver or an insurance company pays up voluntarily, the other driver must commence *civil* proceedings against the careless driver in a county court or in the High Court (depending on the amount involved), claiming 'damages' to compensate for the cost of repairing the car and the personal injuries.

7.6   One incident, therefore, can give rise to both criminal and civil proceedings, but the person initiating the proceedings and the object of the proceedings are different, and the courts hearing the cases are also different (although the judges may be the same). Criminal courts do have some powers to award civil law remedies in the course of criminal proceedings, but these powers are limited and are not frequently exercised. In some situations there also exists a right to claim compensation from the State for losses suffered through a criminal's violent actions. This kind of claim must be processed through the *civil* courts and is described in more detail in Chapter 9 (see para 9.82).

---

[6] For an account of the achievements and intentions of the Department see the speech by the Minister delivered on 6 February 2013, available at www.dojni.gov.uk/index/media-centre/justice-for-everyone--minister_s-speech.pdf.

7.7   The criminal law of Northern Ireland, like that of England and Wales, rests on a number of fundamental principles. One of the most important is that any kind of behaviour is criminal only if it is *expressly* made an offence by the law. Most of the criminal law has been embodied in statutes. Only a few offences (the most prominent of which is murder) are still regulated primarily by judge-made law. Of course judges still have to interpret criminal law statutes whenever their provisions are ambiguous or unclear. A second, related, principle is that no-one can be convicted of a crime unless the behaviour in question was prohibited at the time it occurred.[7] Nor can a person be given a more severe sentence than that which was applicable when the offence was committed. In the case of *R v Deery* Lord Lowry LCJ applied this latter principle in a case concerning the possession of firearms.[8]

The burden and standard of proof

7.8   A third principle is that no accused person can be convicted of a crime unless the prosecution has proved his or her guilt. This is sometimes expressed in the phrase 'the burden of proof is on the prosecution' and it is most starkly illustrated by the famous English case of *Woolmington v DPP*,[9] where a 21-year-old man shot dead his 17-year-old wife in highly suspicious circumstances but nevertheless won his appeal against conviction (and the death penalty) because the judge had not directed the jury clearly enough that the burden of proving guilt rested with the prosecution. In criminal law, in other words, a court cannot jump to conclusions: it always has to decide cases in accordance with the evidence presented to it.

7.9   Moreover the standard, as opposed to the burden, of proof in a criminal case is 'beyond reasonable doubt'.[10] This means that the accused person must be presumed innocent until proved to be guilty[11] and must be acquitted if the court is not certain that he or she is guilty. There are rare occasions when, once the prosecution has proved certain basic facts, the burden of proving that he or she is not guilty rests on the accused.[12] In such cases, however, it is usually enough for the accused to prove this on 'the balance of probabilities'. This is a lower degree of proof than 'beyond reasonable doubt' and is the same standard as is required in all non-criminal litigation. It really means that the accused must prove that what he or she is saying is more likely to be true than not true. Examples occur when the

---

[7] This latter principle is also enshrined in art 7 of the European Convention on Human Rights, which is enforceable in the courts of Northern Ireland by virtue of the Human Rights Act 1998.
[8] [1977] NI 164. See too para 5.2.
[9] [1935] AC 462.
[10] Not, be it noted 'beyond *all* reasonable doubt'.
[11] This fundamental principle is protected under art 6(2) of the European Convention on Human Rights.
[12] See J Stannard, 'A Presumption and Four Burdens' (2000) 51 *NILQ* 560.

accused claims to have impaired mental responsibility or to be insane,[13] or when he or she has been charged with possessing certain prohibited articles, like a gun or heroin.[14]

Actus reus and mens rea

7.10 A fourth basic principle is that a person can be found guilty of a crime only if he or she not only did the act in question (called in law the *actus reus* – 'the guilty act') but also did it with a criminal mindset (*mens rea* – 'a guilty mind'). A few offences are said to be 'offences of strict liability', which means that proof that a person committed the *actus reus* is enough to convict that person. So, if you are caught driving while under the influence of drink or drugs you will be found guilty of that offence even though you did not know that you were under that influence because, for example, someone had put drugs into some food you had recently consumed.

7.11 More generally, being under the influence of drink or drugs cannot be raised as a defence if a person is charged with a criminal offence which requires just a 'basic intent', such as assault or criminal damage. It was a case that went to the House of Lords from Northern Ireland that established this general principle,[15] but a decade or so later the House decided that if a person is charged with a crime which requires a 'specific intent', such as murder, then intoxication *can* be a defence. Another case from Northern Ireland established the principle that 'automatism' can be a defence, as when someone damages property when having an epileptic seizure.[16] The House of Lords also decided, in *Director of Public Prosecutions for Northern Ireland v Lynch*,[17] that a person charged with murder can be acquitted if he or she has done the killing because of a threat to his or her own life, or the life of a member of his or her family (the defence of 'duress'). However in a later case the House of Lords changed its position on this issue.[18] Thus, under the law as it stands, if the Real IRA were to tell (A) that unless he shoots (B) the Real IRA will shoot (A) or (A)'s wife, (A) will not be allowed to plead the defence of duress if he shoots (B) and is charged with (B)'s murder.

---

[13] Criminal Justice Act (NI) 1966, ss 2(2) and 5(3).
[14] Eg Terrorism Act 2000, s 77.
[15] *Attorney General for Northern Ireland v Gallagher* [1963] AC 349.
[16] *Bratty v Attorney General for Northern Ireland* [1963] AC 386.
[17] [1975] AC 653.
[18] In *R v Howe* [1987] 1 AC 417. The House later denied the defence to a man charged with attempted murder: *R v Gotts* [1992] 2 AC 512.

Using force to prevent a crime

7.12   It is a defence under the common law that when one was acting in an allegedly criminal way, one was acting in self-defence. Once this suggestion is raised by the accused, the prosecution has to show beyond a reasonable doubt that he or she was not in fact acting in self-defence. A further important principle is that a person may use whatever force is reasonable in the circumstances when preventing a crime or when effecting or assisting in the lawful arrest of an offender, a suspected offender or a person unlawfully at large.[19] To take account of situations where, for example, a woman uses force against a violent partner, or a police officer uses force to deal with someone acting dangerously, the law has recently been amended to make it clear that the defendant in such situations is entitled to rely on his or her belief that certain circumstances existed provided it is determined that that belief was genuinely held, even if the belief was unreasonable or mistaken.[20] When deciding whether the degree of force used was reasonable a court must also bear in mind that 'a person acting for a legitimate purpose may not be able to weigh to a nicety the exact measure of any necessary action'.[21] Using such force will not in itself amount to a criminal offence. While the defence of using reasonable force to prevent a crime may seem a sensible general rule, the House of Lords applied it during Northern Ireland's troubles in a way which tended to give a great deal of freedom to members of the security forces to use lethal force in situations where some lesser use of force, or alternative actions altogether, might have been preferable. A notorious example is the case of *Attorney General's Reference No. 1*, also known as the *McElhone* case, where a soldier was accused of unlawfully shooting dead a man who, when challenged, had run away across a field. In the course of upholding the soldier's acquittal the House of Lords, through Lord Diplock, said that the shooting was justified because if the man had escaped he might have gone on to commit a terrorist offence.[22] In another controversial case, the conviction of a soldier for murdering a passenger in a car which had been driven through an army checkpoint near Belfast was overturned by the Court of Appeal because new evidence was produced to show that the lethal shot could not have been fired after the car had passed the soldier but only on its way towards him, which meant that the use of force was reasonable.[23]

---

[19] Criminal Law Act (NI) 1967, s 3(1).
[20] Criminal Justice and Immigration Act 2008, s 76(4).
[21] Ibid s 76(7)(a).
[22] *Attorney General for Northern Ireland's Reference (No 1 of 1975)* [1977] AC 105.
[23] *R v Clegg* [1995] 1 AC 482.

Principals and accessories[24]

7.13 Finally, a person can be convicted of a crime not only if he or she was the only person involved in actually committing it but also if he or she helped someone else to commit it (this is called 'aiding and abetting'), if he or she plotted with someone else to commit it ('conspiracy') or even if he or she tried but failed to commit it ('attempting'). The actual perpetrator of the crime is called the 'principal', while everyone else involved in the perpetration is called an 'accessory'. It can sometimes be difficult to draw the line between an act preparatory to a crime and an attempt to commit the crime: after Michael Stone was apprehended while entering Parliament Buildings at Stormont in 2006 he was eventually convicted of attempted murder because he had begun to embark on what was a carefully planned sequence of steps.[25] Usually the punishments available to courts when they are sentencing accessories to crimes are just as serious as those which can be imposed on the principal offenders. A person who accompanies another person on, say, a bank robbery, but who knows that the other person has a gun, which he intends to use to threaten anyone who gets in the way of the robbery, may well also be guilty of murder if the other person actually uses the gun and kills someone. This is known as the doctrine of common enterprise. It was applied when some individuals were charged with murder after becoming involved in the lynching of two British soldiers in West Belfast in 1988.[26] However if a person is enticed into committing a crime by an undercover police agent (provided the person would not in any event have committed that particular crime) he or she can raise the defence of 'entrapment'.[27] More generally, criminal courts have a discretion to dismiss a prosecution or allow an appeal if they think the prosecution was an abuse of process, as in *R v Mullen*,[28] where a man was forcibly returned to England from Zimbabwe to stand trial for committing offences on behalf of the IRA, without adherence to proper extradition procedures.

CRIMINAL OFFENCES

7.14 As in England and Wales, the range of criminal offences in the law of Northern Ireland is vast. The commonest way of classifying them is into fatal offences against the person (eg murder, manslaughter and infanticide),

[24] See generally the Criminal Attempts and Conspiracy (NI) Order 1983.
[25] *R v Stone* [2010] NICA 1.
[26] *R v Kane, Kelly and Timmons* (1991, unreported).
[27] As in *R v Kearns* [2010] NICC 32 (Hart J), where the prosecution of one defendant was stayed because he had been entrapped but the prosecution of another continued because he had not.
[28] [2000] QB 520. See too *In re Nolan's Application* [2011] NIQB 128 (Div Ct), where however no abuse of process was found.

non-fatal offences against the person (eg assault, battery, and aggravated assault), sexual offences, theft and deception offences, other offences against property (eg criminal damage), public order offences (eg rioting, harassment, and obstruction of the police), road traffic offences and offences against public morals (eg obscenity). But there are many other offences which do not fall into these main categories (eg weapons offences and drug offences). The detailed rules for all these offences are usually the same in Northern Ireland as in England and Wales, so the standard textbooks used in the former jurisdiction are just as useful in Northern Ireland.[29] Of course the name or date of the applicable legislation may differ. For example, the Sexual Offences Act 2003 is applicable in England and Wales, but the Sexual Offences (NI) Order 2008 is applicable in Northern Ireland. Given the constraints of space, only a brief flavour of what has to be proved for someone to be found guilty of some of these offences can be provided here.

Homicide

7.15   Whenever someone kills someone else it can be referred to as a homicide. But there is no specific crime of that name in either English or Northern Irish law.[30] Instead the crime is designated as murder, manslaughter, infanticide or causing death by dangerous driving. The crime of murder requires an act of killing coupled with 'malice aforethought', which means an intention either to kill or to cause grievous bodily harm. If the *mens rea* for murder cannot be proved, the person who kills another will instead be convicted of manslaughter. This also applies if the person is suffering from what is called 'diminished responsibility'.[31] The year 2012 saw the lowest number of victims or murder or manslaughter in Northern Ireland since before the troubles, with just 13 victims.[32] Until recently the defence of provocation had the same effect; that defence has now been replaced by the defence of loss of self-control, but it too, if accepted, will reduce the crime to manslaughter (provided another of the same sex and age as the defendant, with a normal degree of tolerance and self-restraint and placed in the same circumstances as the defendant, might have reacted in a similar way).[33]

7.16   The great difference between murder and manslaughter is that the only sentence that can be imposed for murder is life imprisonment (with a recommendation from the judge that the convicted person serve a certain

---

[29] Eg Michael Allen, *Textbook on Criminal Law* (Oxford, Oxford UP, 11th edn, 2011); Richard Card, *Card, Cross and James on Criminal Law* (Oxford, Oxford UP, 20th edn, 2012).
[30] But 'culpable homicide' is a specific crime in Scottish law.
[31] Coroners and Justice Act 2009, s 53.
[32] *Irish News*, 2 January 2013. The number of deaths on the roads in 2012 was the lowest since records began, at 48.
[33] Ibid ss 54-56.

number of years in prison – the 'tariff period'[34] – before being considered for parole), while the prison sentence imposed for manslaughter is at the discretion of the judge. This is why it can be so crucial to decide if a particular killing is murder or manslaughter. If someone kills another person as a 'mercy killing', in order to put the other person out of their misery, it will still usually amount to murder. If someone stands idly by while knowing that another person is killing someone else, and then does nothing to reveal the crime, that too will usually be murder.[35]

7.17 Juries are often reluctant to convict someone of murder because of the draconian sentence that inevitably ensues, and even the term manslaughter has connotations suggesting that the defendant was inherently a bad person. In some contexts, therefore, Parliament has created new offences targeted at actions that juries want to disapprove of but not categorise as evil. Examples are causing death by dangerous driving,[36] assisting a suicide,[37] infanticide,[38] unlawfully procuring an abortion,[39] and child destruction.[40]

Non-fatal offences against the person

7.18 As regards non-fatal offences against the person, the commonest charges relate to assault (ie causing someone to apprehend immediate and unlawful personal violence) and battery (ie the actual infliction of unlawful

---

[34] In *R v McCandless* [2004] NICA 269, [2004] 2 BNIL 101 the Court of Appeal in Northern Ireland said that courts in Northern Ireland should follow the Practice Statement issued by Lord Woolf CJ when fixing tariff periods. This suggests a normal starting point of 12 years and a higher starting point, in more serious cases, of 15 or 16 years.

[35] As in the case of Hazel Stewart, convicted in 2010 of murdering her former husband and another woman in 1991, even though the actual killings were carried out by her then lover, Colin Howell: *R v Stewart* [2011] NICC 10. In January 2013 she lost her appeal: www.belfasttelegraph.co.uk/news/local-national/northern-ireland/court-rejects-double-killer-appeal-29039465.html.

[36] Road Traffic (NI) Order 1995, art 9.

[37] Criminal Justice Act (NI) 1966, s 13. In 2010 the Public Prosecution Service in Northern Ireland issued guidelines as to the factors it will take into account when deciding whether to prosecute someone for this offence: *Policy on Prosecuting the Offence of Assisted Suicide*, available at www.ppsni.gov.uk, under 'Publications'.

[38] Infanticide Act (NI) 1939, s 1.

[39] Offences Against the Person Act 1861, ss 58 and 59. A woman can obtain an abortion in Northern Ireland only if her life would be at risk if the pregnancy were to continue, or if she would be a 'physical and mental wreck': *R v Bourne* [1939] 1 KB 687. See too para 9.139 and the guidance issued in April 2013 by the Department of Health, Social Services and Public Safety in Northern Ireland, available at www.dhsspsni.gov.uk/guidance-limited-circumstances-termination-pregnancy-april-2013.pdf. According to a written ministerial statement made to the Northern Ireland Assembly on 22 August 2012, there were 43 legal abortions in Northern Ireland in 2010–11. The Abortion Act 1967 applies only in England, Scotland and Wales.

[40] Criminal Justice Act (NI) 1945, s 25. The child in question must have died before it had an existence independent of its mother, but a person who causes the child to die cannot be convicted unless the prosecution proves that he or she did not act in good faith to preserve the life of the mother.

personal violence).[41] There are various forms of so-called 'aggravated assault', such as assault causing actual bodily harm (ABH),[42] wounding or inflicting grievous bodily harm (GBH),[43] wounding or inflicting GBH with intent,[44] administering poison,[45] assault with intent to rob,[46] assault on a constable in the exercise of his or her duty,[47] assault with intent to resist arrest,[48] and assault aggravated by hostility.[49]

7.19   The range of sexual offences in Northern Ireland is mostly laid out in the Sexual Offences (NI) Order 2008, which categorises them into non-consensual sexual offences (such as rape and sexual assault), sexual offences against children, sexual offences against persons with a mental disorder, prostitution, and miscellaneous offences (such as administering a substance with intent ('spiking'), having sex with an adult relative, exposure, and voyeurism). The 2008 Order reduced the age at which young people can lawfully engage in sexual intercourse to 16 (from 17). Only a man can commit rape,[50] but a person of either sex can commit assault by penetration;[51] both offences carry a maximum sentence of life imprisonment. Whether it is reasonable to believe that another person has consented to sexual activity is to be determined having regard to all the circumstances, including any steps the first person has taken to ascertain whether the other person consents.[52]

Theft and deception

7.20   Theft and deception offences are governed mostly by the Theft Act (NI) 1969, as amended by the Theft (NI) Order 1978. The core offences are theft, robbery and burglary. The 1969 Act defines theft (which is synonymous with stealing) as occurring when a person 'dishonestly appropriates property belonging to another with the intention of permanently depriving the other of it'.[53] No comprehensive definition of 'dishonestly' is provided by any piece of legislation, so this is for the judges and juries to work out on a case by case basis. The maximum prison sentence for theft is 10 years.[54] The Act goes on to define 'robbery' as occurring when a person steals, and

---

[41] Like murder, these are common law crimes – there is no statutory definition of them.
[42] Offences Against the Person Act 1861, s 47.
[43] Ibid s 20.
[44] Ibid s 18.
[45] Ibid s 23.
[46] Theft Act (NI) 1969, s 8(2).
[47] Police (NI) Act 1998, s 66(1)
[48] Offences Against the Person Act 1861, s 38.
[49] Criminal Justice (No 2) (NI) Order 2004, art 2.
[50] Sexual Offences (NI) Order 2008, art 5.
[51] Ibid art 6.
[52] Ibid arts 5(2), 6(2), 7(2) and 8(2).
[53] Theft Act (NI) 1969, s 1(1)
[54] Ibid s 7.

immediately before or at the time of doing so, and in order to do so, he or she uses force on any person or puts or seeks to put any person in fear of being then and there subjected to force.[55] The maximum sentence for robbery is life imprisonment. 'Burglary' is when a person enters a building as a trespasser and with intent to steal anything in the building, inflict GBH on any person in the building, or do unlawful damage in the building.[56] The maximum prison sentence for burglary is 14 years.[57]

7.21 Other theft and deception offences include taking a vehicle without authority (sometimes called TADA: taking and driving away),[58] abstracting electricity,[59] obtaining property by deception,[60] obtaining pecuniary advantage by deception,[61] false accounting,[62] blackmail (ie 'making unwarranted demands with menaces'),[63] handling stolen goods,[64] dishonestly retaining a wrongful credit,[65] and 'going equipped for stealing'.[66] Making off without payment is an offence under the Theft (NI) Order 1978.[67]

Offences against property

7.22 Apart from theft and associated offences, the main offence against property in the law of Northern Ireland is criminal damage, which is governed by the Criminal Damage (NI) Order 1977. This states that: 'A person who without lawful excuse destroys or damages any property belonging to another intending to destroy or damage any such property or being reckless as to whether any such property would be destroyed or damaged shall be guilty of an offence'[68] and the maximum sentence that can be imposed for that offence is 14 years in prison.[69] However, if the destruction or damage was caused with the intent to endanger the life of another or being reckless as to whether the life of another would be endangered the maximum sentence is life imprisonment.[70] Likewise, if the destruction or damage is caused by

---

[55] Ibid s 8(1).
[56] Ibid s 9(1).
[57] Ibid s 9(4).
[58] Ibid s 12.
[59] Ibid s 13.
[60] Ibid s 15.
[61] Ibid s 16.
[62] Ibid s 17. This is what some MPs were charged with in 2010 when they were 'fiddling' their parliamentary expenses.
[63] Ibid s 20.
[64] Ibid s 21.
[65] Ibid s 23A, inserted by the Theft (Amendment) (NI) Order 1997, art 4, and amended by the Fraud Act 2006.
[66] Ibid s 24.
[67] art 5. It carries a maximum prison sentence of 2 years: art 6(2)(b).
[68] Criminal Damage (NI) Order 1977, art 3(1).
[69] Ibid art 6(2).
[70] Ibid arts 3(2) and 6(1).

fire the offence is called arson and the maximum sentence again becomes life imprisonment.[71] The House of Lords has ruled that in this context a person can be said to have acted recklessly only if he or she was aware of the circumstance or risk in question: children, for example, would not always be aware of a risk that would be clear to an adult.[72]

Public order offences

7.23   Public order offences in Northern Ireland are provided for in the Public Order (NI) Order 1987 and some other pieces of legislation. The 1987 Order criminalises acts which are intended or likely to stir up hatred or arouse fear in relation to a group of persons defined by reference to religious belief, sexual orientation, disability, colour, race, nationality or ethnic or national origins.[73] It also creates the offences of riotous or disorderly behaviour in a public place,[74] provocative conduct in a public place,[75] obstructive sitting in a public place,[76] the wearing of uniforms in a public place,[77] and the carrying of an offensive weapon in a public place.[78] Harassment is not defined by legislation, but the Protection from Harassment (NI) Order 1997 says that a person who pursues a course of conduct which amounts to harassment (and which a reasonable person in possession of the same information would think amounts to harassment) is guilty of an offence and can be sent to prison for up to six months.[79] A person who obstructs or impedes a police officer in the execution of his or her duty is also committing an offence and can be sent to prison for up to two years if convicted.[80]

Road traffic offences

7.24   The Road Traffic (NI) Orders 1981, 1995 and 2007 regulate road traffic offences in Northern Ireland, amongst the many of which are causing death or GBH by dangerous driving,[81] dangerous driving,[82] careless or inconsiderate driving,[83] driving when under the influence of drink or

---

[71] Ibid arts 3(3) and 6(1).
[72] *R v G* [2003] UKHL 50, [2004] 1 AC 1034, overruling the House's earlier decision in *R v Caldwell* [1982] AC 341.
[73] Public Order (NI) Order 1987, arts 8-17.
[74] Ibid art 18.
[75] Ibid art 19.
[76] Ibid art 20.
[77] Ibid art 21.
[78] Ibid art 22.
[79] Protection from Harassment (NI) Order 1997, arts 3 and 4.
[80] Police (NI) Act 1998, s 66.
[81] Road Traffic (NI) Order 1995, art 9.
[82] Ibid art 10.
[83] Ibid art 12.

drugs,[84] driving with an alcohol concentration above the prescribed limit, driving in contravention of the seat belts regulations or the safety helmets regulations,[85] causing danger to road users,[86] and contravening traffic signs.[87] The Criminal Justice (NI) Order 2008 created the additional offences of causing death by careless or inconsiderate driving and causing death when driving while disqualified or uninsured.[88] Under the Road Traffic (NI) Order 1981,[89] the Department of the Environment may issue a 'Highway Code' comprising directions for the guidance of persons using roads (see para 3.52). The 1995 Order makes it clear that:

> A failure on the part of any person to observe any provision of the Highway Code shall not of itself render that person liable to criminal proceedings of any kind, but any such failure may in any proceedings (whether civil or criminal, and including proceedings for an offence under the Road Traffic Orders) be relied upon by any party to the proceedings as tending to establish or to negative any liability which is in question in those proceedings.[90]

Offences against public morality

7.25   These days, criminal law in Northern Ireland tends not to interfere too much with personal morality. Homosexuality was decriminalised by the Homosexual Offences (NI) Order 1972 (see also para 5.45) and heterosexual anal intercourse was decriminalised by the High Court in *Re McR's Application*[91] (see para 6.26). However, while the crimes of blasphemy and blasphemous libel have been abolished in England and Wales,[92] they still exist in Northern Ireland, and the Obscene Publications Acts of 1959 and 1964, which applied in England and Wales, were never mirrored in Northern Ireland so that the offence of obscenity is regulated in Northern Ireland entirely by the common law. The common law considers material to be obscene if it has a tendency to 'deprave and corrupt',[93] and there is uncertainty as to whether the common law (like the Acts in England and Wales) would allow a defence based on what is for 'the public good'. The common law also recognizes an offence called conspiracy to corrupt public morals.

---

[84] Ibid art 15.
[85] Ibid arts 23(3) and 27(3).
[86] Ibid art 33.
[87] Ibid art 50.
[88] Ibid arts 52 and 53.
[89] Ibid art 130.
[90] Ibid art 51(6).
[91] [2003] NI 1.
[92] Criminal Justice and Immigration Act 2008, s 79(1).
[93] The test derives from what Cockburn LCJ said in *R v Hicklin* (1868) LR 3 QB 360, at 371.

TERRORISM LAW

7.26   There has been a long history of unrest in Ireland connected with what some would call the colonisation of the island by Britain. When Northern Ireland was formed in 1921 there were already numerous Acts of Parliament in place to try to deal with the unrest, but the new government in Northern Ireland immediately decided to reform those laws by passing the Civil Authorities (Special Powers) Act (NI) 1922. This conferred extensive powers on members of the security forces and on government ministers. It was renewed annually until 1928, when it was extended for a further five years. In 1933 it was made permanent legislation, although it was again amended in 1944. A good account of the how the Act was applied during the Stormont regime has been provided by Donohue.[94]

7.27   When a further bout of troubles broke out in Northern Ireland in the late 1960s (see para 1.18) it quickly became apparent that new laws would need to be devised to deal with them. Following an inquiry conducted by a committee chaired by an English Lord of Appeal, Lord Diplock, the first of what would turn out to be a long series of Northern Ireland (Emergency Provisions) Acts (known as EPAs) was passed at Westminster in 1973.[95] Following a series of pub bombings in England in 1974, further anti-terrorist laws were passed for the whole of the UK in the shape of the Prevention of Terrorism (Temporary Provisions) Act 1974, also the first of a series in later years – known as PTAs.[96]

7.28   There were seven main features of the anti-terrorist laws applying in Northern Ireland during the troubles. They were:

(1)   special powers to allow the police and army to stop and question people
(2)   special powers to allow the police and army to conduct searches and seize property
(3)   special powers to allow the police and army to arrest people
(4)   special powers to allow the police, army and the government to detain people
(5)   special powers to allow the government to proscribe (ie ban) terrorist organisations
(6)   special powers to allow the government to 'exclude' people from parts of the UK
(7)   special powers to allow the Attorney General to order that people accused of terrorism-related offences must be tried by a judge sitting without a jury (in so-called 'Diplock courts').[97]

---

[94] *Counter-Terrorist Law and Emergency Powers in the United Kingdom 1922-2000* (Dublin, Irish Academic Press, 2000), ch 2.
[95] Further EPAs were enacted in 1975, 1978, 1987, 1991, 1996, and 1998.
[96] Further PTAs were enacted in 1976, 1984, 1986, and 1989.
[97] See J Jackson, 'Many years on in Northern Ireland: the Diplock legacy' (2009) 60 *NILQ* 213.

Anti-terrorism law after the Belfast (Good Friday) Agreement

7.29   Following the Belfast (Good Friday) Agreement in 1998 the anti-terrorist laws were gradually scaled down, with the relevant EPA and PTA being repealed and replaced by the Terrorism Act 2000. This Act placed anti-terrorist laws on a permanent footing throughout the UK and broadened the definition of terrorism, so that it now means the use or threat of action where: (a) the action involves serious violence against a person, serious damage to property, the endangering of a person's life, a serious risk to the health or safety of a section of the public, or the serious disruption of an electronic system; (b) the use or threat is designed to influence the Government or intimidate a section of the public; and (c) the use or threat is made for the purpose of advancing a political, religious or ideological cause.[98] The 2000 Act confers a special arrest power: 'A constable may arrest without a warrant a person whom he reasonably suspects to be a terrorist'.[99] This then triggers special detention powers (see para 8.19).[100]

7.30   The 2000 Act preserved some special anti-terrorism powers just for Northern Ireland[101] and these remained in force until the end of July 2007. They were not allowed to disappear entirely, however, for some provisions in the Justice and Security (NI) Act 2007 replaced them. Sections 1 to 9 of that Act ensure that trials on indictment without a jury can still take place for 'certified' trials, that is, trials which the Director of Public Prosecutions certifies should be held without a jury because the offence in question appears to be connected to a proscribed organisation or to religious or political hostility of one person or group towards another person or group.[102] The DPP must also be satisfied that there is a risk that the administration of justice might be impaired if the trial were to be conducted with a jury. Judges are very reluctant to judicially review these decisions by the DPP because they depend on a consideration of security considerations.[103] The non-jury provisions were to endure for just two years, unless renewed.[104] They *were* renewed, both in 2009 and 2011,[105] and are likely to be again in 2013. Non-jury trials therefore continue to occur in Northern Ireland, because of the continuing risk that if jurors were involved in troubles-related cases they might be intimidated. Other hangovers from the old EPAs and PTAs also

[98] s 1(1) and (2). The Counter-Terrorism Act 2008, s 75, inserted 'racial cause' into this list of purposes.

[99] s 41(1).

[100] There are also codes of practice on how these powers (and anti-terrorism stop and search powers) should be exercised. They are available on the website of the Northern Ireland Office: www.nio.gov.uk.

[101] Pt VII (ss 65–113).

[102] Justice and Security (NI) Act 2007, s 1(2)–(6).

[103] See *In re Arthurs' Applications* [2010] NIQB 75.

[104] Justice and Security (NI) Act 2007, s 9.

[105] Justice and Security (NI) Act 2007 (Extension of duration of non-jury trial provisions) Order 2011 (SI 1720).

remain in force, such as the police and army power to stop any person for so long as is necessary to question him or her in order to ascertain his or her identity and movements.[106]

7.31 Even though the responsibility for policing and justice was devolved to the Department of Justice in Northern Ireland in April 2010, the responsibility for terrorism law still rests with the Ministry of Justice in London. Responsibility for national security in Northern Ireland remains with the Northern Ireland Office (see paras 2.50–2.51).

Internment and control orders after of 9/11

7.32 Since the events in the United States on 11 September 2001 and in London on 7 July 2005 additional anti-terrorist laws have been put in place for the whole of the UK, mainly through the Anti-terrorism, Crime and Security Act 2001, the Prevention of Terrorism Act 2005, the Terrorism Act 2006 and the Counter-Terrorism Act 2008. The 2001 Act allowed non-British people who were reasonably suspected of involvement in terrorism to be detained indefinitely without trial (ie interned). A group of such detainees, who were held in Belmarsh prison in London, challenged the compatibility of such detention with their rights under the European Convention on Human Rights and the House of Lords held, by eight votes to one, that the detention provisions were both disproportionate and discriminatory,[107] a decision later endorsed by the Grand Chamber of the European Court of Human Rights.[108] The decision by the House of Lords meant that the relevant section of the 2001 Act was not renewed when it was due to expire in February 2005 and instead the Government introduced the Prevention of Terrorism Act 2005 to provide for restrictions on liberty short of imprisonment, known as control orders. These could be imposed on any person, British or not, though the power to make them had to be approved by Parliament on an annual basis.

7.33 Following further criticism of control orders by senior judges and others, the coalition government announced in 2011 that it would be replacing control orders with new measures.[109] These were provided for by the Terrorism Prevention and Investigations Measures Act 2011. T-PIMs, as they are known, can last for up to two years before being considered for renewal but they allow curfews of only 10 hours at a time, not 16 hours as tolerated by the courts when they were reviewing control orders. The maximum pre-charge detention period for suspected terrorists has been

---

[106] Justice and Security (NI) Act 2007, s 21.
[107] *A v Secretary of State for the Home Department* [2004] UKHL 56, [2005] 2 AC 68.
[108] *A v UK* (2009) 49 EHRR 29.
[109] HC Debs, Vol 522, col 306 (26 January 2011).

reduced from 28 days to 14 days[110] and the draconian stop and search powers contained in the Terrorism Act 2000[111] have been replaced by more targeted and proportionate powers[112] which respond to another decision of the European Court of Human Rights holding that the former powers were a breach of the right to liberty that is guaranteed by Article 5 of the European Convention on Human Rights.[113]

Other counter-terrorism laws

7.34   The Terrorism Act 2000 contains many provisions on the proscribing of organisations, the seizure of terrorist property, the investigation of terrorist activity, and terrorist offences such as the provision of weapons training, the directing of terrorist organisations, and the collection of information useful to terrorists. The Terrorism Act 2006 creates still further offences, including the encouragement of terrorism, the dissemination of terrorist publications, the preparation of terrorist acts and attendance at a place used for terrorist training. The Counter-Terrorism Act 2008 confers new powers on the police concerning the removal of documents for examination and allows for the questioning of suspects even after they have been charged with an offence (although the latter provisions have not yet been brought into force). That Act also imposes requirements on terrorists released from imprisonment to notify the authorities of their whereabouts[114] (as sex offenders have to do) and   confers new powers on the UK government to direct financial institutions to take certain action regarding persons who may be involved in money laundering or terrorist financing.[115]

7.35   The Terrorism Act 2000 also requires the submission to Parliament of annual reports on how the Act has been operated.[116] For 10 years these were prepared by Lord Carlile of Berriew QC, who was also asked to report on the operation of the Prevention of Terrorism Act 2005. His reports are available on the website of the UK Ministry of Justice. The current independent reviewer is David Anderson QC. There is also an independent annual review of the provisions in the Justice and Security (NI) Act 2007, carried out by a separate reviewer, Robert Whalley. These are available on the website of the Northern Ireland Office. Since 2007 Lord Carlile has also reported annually to the Secretary of State for Northern Ireland, on a non-

---

[110] This is now provided for by the Protection of Freedoms Act 2012, s 57. Section 58 allows the Secretary of State to reimpose a maximum detention period of 28 days if an emergency arises at a time when Parliament has been dissolved (eg prior to a general election).

[111] ss 44-47.

[112] Protection of Freedoms Act 2012, ss 57-63.

[113] *Gillan and Quinton v UK* (2010) 50 EHRR 45.

[114] Pt 4, ss 40-61.

[115] s 62 and Sch 7.

[116] s 126.

statutory basis, on the operation of the arrangements for handling national security-related matters in Northern Ireland, but these reports are not made public.

LEVELS OF CRIME

7.36   Statistics on offences committed in Northern Ireland are made available through the annual reports of the Chief Constable and on the Police Service's website.[117] In 2012 the police published a booklet examining the trends in recorded crime in Northern Ireland between 1998-99 and 2011-12.[118] Statistics on the cases dealt with by criminal courts are published online by the Northern Ireland Courts and Tribunals Service through its quarterly court bulletins on the work of the magistrates' courts, the county courts, the High Court and the Court of Appeal, and also through its annual *Northern Ireland Judicial Statistics*. For its part, the Northern Ireland Statistics and Research Agency (NISRA) produces a *Digest of Information on the Northern Ireland Criminal Justice System*, now appearing at least once a year.[119] Occasionally NISRA publishes important supplementary information in booklets entitled *Research and Statistical Bulletins*. These include data from the Northern Ireland Crime Survey which is now conducted every year.[120] Also worth consulting is the *Security and Justice* chapter in NISRA's *Northern Ireland Annual Abstract of Statistics*.

7.37   Table 7.1, below, indicates the numbers of serious offences recorded during the past three years. Attempting, conspiring, inciting, aiding, abetting, causing or permitting an offence is generally included under the heading of the offence itself. It must be remembered that recorded crime is not the same thing as actual crime, becausse for various reasons many offences never come to the notice of the police. The Table also indicates the percentage of the crimes that were 'cleared' each year. In the police's eyes an offence is cleared if it is one for which a person has been charged, summonsed or cautioned, one which a court has taken into consideration when sentencing a person for another crime, or one which cannot be proceeded with because, although there is enough evidence of a person's guilt, that person is too young to be prosecuted or is dead. Cleared offences are *not* the offences for which persons have been found guilty and punished, nor those which

---

[117] www.psni.police.uk.

[118] See www.psni.police.uk/police_recorded_crime_in_northern_ireland_1998-99_to_2011-12.pdf.

[119] The last available edition was published in April 2012, and was updated in July 2012: see www.dojni.gov.uk.

[120] It is a household survey of about 4,000 people and has been running continuously since 2005. See S Toner and R Freel, *Experience of Crime: Findings from the 2011-12 Northern Ireland Crime Survey*, Research and Statistical Bulletin 1/2013. There is of course a separate Crime Survey for England and Wales.

have been admitted by offenders who have been diverted from the criminal justice system through, for example, restorative justice programmes.

Table 7.1: Recorded crime and clearance rates 2009-2012[121]

	2010-11	2011-12	2012-13
Sexual offences	2,120	1,836	1,948
Clearance rate	25.6%	26.9%	20.7%
Other offences against the person	29,437	30,922	30,701
Clearance rate	38.5%	36.2%	33.4%
Robbery	1,306	1,221	1,014
Clearance rate	19.9%	20.6%	21.3%
Burglary	11,942	10,580	9,581
Clearance rate	11.6%	12.6%	11.8%
Criminal damage	25,003	23,255	21,364
Clearance rate	12.9%	13.3%	13.0%
Drug offences	3,482	3,780	4,378
Clearance rate	83%	76.8%	80.5%
All offences[122]	**105,040**	**103,389**	100,389
Clearance rate	27.3%	26.3%	26.4%

7.38   Recorded crime in Northern Ireland is lower than at any time since the current counting rules were adopted in 1998-99, and the clearance rates are higher. But it is still the case that only about a quarter of all recorded crime is cleared up, with the clearance rate for robbery, burglary and criminal damage being significantly lower than that. However, compared with other parts of the UK, and indeed much of the rest of the world, crime rates in Northern Ireland are still low. The results of the 2011-12 Northern Ireland Crime Survey[123] showed that 11.2 per cent of the adult occupants in all households were victims of crime during the previous 12 months, while the comparable figure in the 2011-12 Crime Survey for England and Wales was 21.3 per cent. The only type of crime which, relatively speaking, is more common in Northern Ireland is 'assault with minor injury'. The biggest differences relate to household crime, vandalism and all vehicle-related crimes. Only 44 per

---

[121] Source: www.psni.police.uk. The figures are from the reports entitled 'Police Recorded Crime in Northern Ireland'. An accompanying User Guide explains what is meant by clearance (or 'sanction detection') rates.
[122] This row includes various other offences not listed in the rows above.
[123] See Toner and Freel, n 120 above.

cent of all the crimes recorded in the 2011-12 Northern Ireland Crime Survey were actually reported to the police, but this is still higher than the figure in England and Wales (43 per cent). The crime with the highest reporting rate was burglary (69 per cent). The persons most at risk of violent crime were young people aged between 16 and 24 (6.1 per cent).

Fear of crime

7.39   The latest figures on the fear of crime also date from the 2011-12 crime surveys.[124] As in previous years they show that, despite the lower rate of crime in Northern Ireland, respondents to the survey displayed higher levels of worry about crime than respondents in England and Wales. Thus, 19 per cent were worried about violent crime in Northern Ireland as opposed to 14 per cent in England and Wales, and 15 per cent were worried about being burgled in Northern Ireland as opposed to 11 per cent in England and Wales. Twelve per cent of respondents perceived the level of anti-social behaviour in their own local area to be high, compared with a figure of 15 per cent in England and Wales. Paradoxically, respondents in Northern Ireland were in some respects less likely to perceive themselves as being at risk of becoming a victim of crime. Nine per cent thought they were at risk of violent crime, compared with 13 per cent in England and Wales, while 15 per cent saw themselves at risk from car crime compared with 18 per cent in England and Wales. In fact the risk of being a victim of violent crime or car crime in Northern Ireland is just two per cent.

Organised crime

7.40   Organised crime is a serious problem in Northern Ireland, as in many other jurisdictions, which is why the Northern Ireland Office established the Organised Crime Task Force in 2000.[125] This comprises representatives from the Northern Ireland and UK governments, the police, HM Revenue and Customs, the Serious Organised Crime Agency and the National Criminal Intelligence Service. It has already identified hundreds of organised crime gangs based in Northern Ireland, many of which operate in the fields of drug trafficking, fuel fraud, extortion and counterfeiting. The majority of the top level groups are, says the Task Force, either associated with or controlled by paramilitary organisations, with cross-border smuggling being by far the most lucrative activity. The Task Force publishes an annual threat assessment of the scale and nature of the organised crime problem in Northern Ireland

---

[124] See P Campbell and R Freel, *Perceptions of Crime: Findings from the 2011–12 Northern Ireland Crime survey*, Research and Statistics Bulletin 2/2013.
[125] www.octf.gov.uk.

and its strategy for dealing with it. At the time of writing the future strategy for combating organised crime in Northern Ireland is a little uncertain because in Great Britain a new National Crime Agency is being created to undertake this task and there are ongoing negotiations concerning how those who conduct activities on behalf of this Agency in Northern Ireland can be held accountable for how they conduct themselves.[126]

PARAMILITARY CRIME

7.41   Table 7.2, below, gives a picture of the level of paramilitary crime in Northern Ireland since 1969, as compiled by the police.[127] The annual figures have been aggregated into seven periods, each of six years, followed by provisional figures for one two-year period (2011 and 2012). As can be seen, 3,381 people had died by the end of 2012, the worst years by far being the early 1970s. Approximately 60 per cent of all deaths were caused by republican paramilitaries, 30 per cent by loyalist paramilitaries and 10 per cent by members of the security forces.[128] The worst single atrocity in Northern Ireland was the 'Real IRA' bomb in Omagh in August 1998, which killed 29 people and unborn twins. Approximately 2,000 of the killings are still unsolved in the sense that no-one has been brought to justice for committing them. Table 7.2 does not include the many people who died in Great Britain, the Republic of Ireland or other parts of Europe. In that category there were 51 British soldiers killed.

7.42   During the troubles in Northern Ireland there were very many so-called 'punishment attacks' committed by members of paramilitary organisations against people supposedly responsible for 'anti-social behaviour' (mostly young men).[129] Nor did the incidence of these attacks decline in the immediate aftermath of the Belfast (Good Friday) Agreement in 1998, as can be seen from the Table. Even today there are dozens of victims of such attacks each year. Unfortunately, neither the police nor the Public Prosecution Service are able to say how many people have been charged with these offences over the years, let alone convicted for them. A request under the Freedom

---

[126] The relevant legislation is the Crime and Courts Act 2013. On 4 February 2013, after a 90-minute debate, the Northern Ireland Assembly failed to reach cross-community agreement on a 'legislative consent motion' (see para 2.32) whereby Westminster could have proceeded to include Northern Ireland within the provisions of the Crime and Courts Act.

[127] Other sources provide slightly different figures; see, eg D McKittrick, S Kelters, B Feeney, C Thornton and D McVea, *Lost Lives* (Edinburgh, Mainstream Publishing, rev ed, 2007).

[128] Ibid Appendix on Statistics.

[129] See, generally, J Darby 'The Effect of Violence on the Irish Peace Process' in C Harvey (ed), *Human Rights, Equality and Democratic Renewal in Northern Ireland* (Oxford, Hart Publishing, 2001); C Knox and R. Monaghan, *Informal Justice in Divided Societies: Northern Ireland and South Africa* (London, Palgrave Macmillan, 2002), and D Feenan, *Informal Criminal Justice* (Aldershot, Ashgate, 2002).

of Information Act 2000 has however revealed that of the 272 incidents which occurred in 2008, 2009 and 2010, only 12 had been 'cleared' by early 2011, a clearance rate of just over 4 per cent.[130] Moreover the Northern Ireland Housing Executive reports that in 2011-12 it spent £6.1 million on re-housing people who had been intimidated out of their homes.[131]

Table 7.2: Paramilitary crime 1969-2012

Years	All deaths[132]	Injuries	Punishment attack casualties	Shootings	Bombs and incendiaries
1969-74	1,155	12,517	n/a	20,900	6,451
1975-80	926	9,251	n/a	6,917	5,036
1981-86	455	5,617	338	3,077	2,140
1987-92	506	6,070	1,037	3,340	2,707
1993-98	247	6,894	1,308	1,435	1,093
1999-04	70	5,363	1,651	1,546	1,149
2005-10	19	1,859	583	481	377
2011-12	3	n/a	142	131	100
TOTALS	3,381	47,571	5,059	37,827	19,053

THE POLICE SERVICE

7.43   The police in Northern Ireland are now called the Police Service of Northern Ireland, the successor body to the Royal Ulster Constabulary (RUC). The RUC was formed in 1922 and during the troubles in Northern Ireland played a crucial role in combating terrorism. Between 1969 and 1998, 200 police officers and 102 police reservists were killed in terrorist incidents.[133] However several controversies dogged the RUC during those years.[134] In 1978 a Committee of Inquiry headed by an English county court judge made various recommendations for making police interrogation

---

[130] See http://faircop.org/component/k2/item/81-young-people-hardest-hit-by-punishment-beatings.

[131] *Northern Ireland Housing Executive Annual Report 2011-12*, 113 (under the 'SPED' scheme – Special Purchase of Evacuated Dwellings).

[132] Including deaths caused by members of the security forces when combating paramilitary activities.

[133] Each of the deaths is catalogued in C Ryder, *The RUC: A Force Under Fire* (London, Arrow Books, 2000). See also J Brewer and K Magee, *Inside the RUC: Routine Policing in a Divided Society* (Oxford, Oxford UP, 1991), Sir John Hermon, *Holding the Line: An Autobiography* (Dublin, Gill and Macmillan, 1997) and C Ryder, *The Fateful Split: Catholics and the RUC* (London, Methuen, 2004).

[134] See, generally, S Livingstone, 'Policing, Criminal Justice and the Rule of Law' in J Hayes and P O'Higgins (eds), *Lessons from Northern Ireland* (Belfast, SLS Legal Publications, 1990).

practices more acceptable;[135] alleged shoot-to-kill incidents in 1982 were the subject of the (still unpublished) Stalker-Sampson report in 1987; there were also extensive allegations that police officers colluded with loyalist paramilitaries,[136] that they issued threats to solicitors representing republicans,[137] that they harassed people on the streets and during searches,[138] and that they fabricated evidence or altered notes of interviews.[139] In several cases the courts ordered the police to pay exemplary damages to people mistreated while in police custody.[140]

The Patten Commission

7.44   The Belfast (Good Friday) Agreement of 1998 provided for the creation of a Commission on Policing to bring forward proposals for future policing arrangements that would enjoy widespread support from the community as a whole. The Commission was chaired by Chris (now Lord) Patten and reported in 1999.[141] Amongst the most controversial of its recommendations were that the RUC should be renamed, its badge altered, the Union flag no longer flown at police stations, and the focus of policing made the protection of human rights.[142] Many of the recommendations were translated into law by the Police (NI) Acts 2000 and 2003, and an Oversight Commissioner was appointed to ensure that implementation of all the recommendations was thorough.[143] The Police (NI) Act 2000 also

[135] *Committee of Inquiry into Police Interrogation Procedures in Northern Ireland*, Cmnd 7947, 1979 (the Bennett Report).

[136] A report on this by a senior police from England, Mr John Stevens (later the Commander of the Metropolitan Police), was completed in 1990, but only a summary of it was published. No police officer was charged as a result of the inquiry, only soldiers.

[137] Such as Rosemary Nelson, who was murdered by loyalist paramilitaries in 1999. A public inquiry into this killing ran from 2005 to 2011. It concluded that the police had not colluded with paramilitaries but that they had not done enough to ensure that Mrs Nelson was protected against attack: see www.rosemarynelsoninquiry.org.

[138] See R McVeigh, *It's Part of Life Here* (Belfast, Committee on the Administration of Justice, 1995).

[139] Eg in the case of the UDR Four, three of whom had their convictions quashed by the Court of Appeal in 1992. The fourth defendant's conviction was confirmed: *R v Latimer* [2004] NIJB 142.

[140] Eg *Adams v Chief Constable of the RUC* (1997, unreported).

[141] *A New Beginning: Policing in Northern Ireland*. See www.belfast.org.uk/ report.htm. For a review of developments in policing in Northern Ireland during the 10 years following the Patten Report, see J Doyle (ed), *Policing the Narrow Ground: Lessons from the Transformation of Policing in Northern Ireland* (Dublin, Royal Irish Academy, 2011) and J Murphy, *Policing for Peace in Northern Ireland: Change, Conflict and Community Confidence* (Basingstoke, Palgrave Macmillan, 2013).

[142] See too J McGarry and B O'Leary, *Policing Northern Ireland: Proposals for a new start* (Belfast, Blackstaff Press, 1999).

[143] Police (NI) Act 2000, ss 67–68 and Sch 4. The office was kept in place until May 2007, with 3 reports published each year. They provide fascinating detail on how the PSNI has come to be one of the most accountable police forces in the world. See www.oversightcommissioner.org, and T Constantine, 'The role of the Oversight Commissioner', ch 7 in Doyle (see n 141 above).

created a Northern Ireland Policing Board to replace the Police Authority for Northern Ireland (see para 7.54) and the Board was tasked with appointing District Policing Partnerships in every district council area (see para 7.58). Even before the Patten Commission reported, moves were afoot to create a Police Ombudsman's office (see para 7.61).

The Police Service of Northern Ireland

7.45   The Police Service of Northern Ireland officially came into being on 4 November 2001. Police officers who were at that time serving in the RUC simply switched to the PSNI, but a generous severance scheme allowed about 4,000 officers (and 1,000 reservists) to leave the police between 2001 and 2011, at a total cost to the taxpayer of more than £500 million. Recruitment and training of new officers began almost immediately after the PSNI was formed and the first batch of students to graduate as probationary constables of the new service did so in April 2002. By way of an exception to the law prohibiting discrimination on religious grounds, the PSNI was required for at least a three-year period to draw 50 per cent of its new recruits from the Catholic community.[144] This measure actually remained in place until March 2011, by which time the proportion of Catholic police officers had risen to 29 per cent. Police officers are also required to give notice of their membership of any organisation which might reasonably be seen as affecting their ability to perform their duties impartially. By April 2009, 225 officers had notified membership of an Orange lodge, the Royal Black Institution or the Apprentice Boys, while 352 had stated that they were freemasons.[145]

7.46   The maximum permitted size of the PSNI is 7,500 officers and there are currently just under 7,000 in post. The full-time Reserve was finally wound up in 2011. The police officers' representative bodies are, for lower ranks, the Police Federation for Northern Ireland and, for higher ranks, the Superintendents' Association of Northern Ireland. The Chief, Deputy Chief and five Assistant Chief Constables are members of ACPO, the Association of Chief Police Officers for England, Wales and Northern Ireland.[146] In 2004 plans were announced for a new training college for the police (and for the fire and rescue professions), to be built at Desertcreat near Cookstown, but this is not due to be completed until 2015 or 2016.

7.47   As in other legal systems, the primary role of the police in Northern Ireland is to prevent and detect crime. It costs more than £1 billion per

[144] Ibid s 46. This was expressly permitted by a provision in an EU Directive and a challenge based on the European Convention on Human Rights failed in the Court of Appeal: *Re Parsons' Application for Judicial Review* [2004] NI 37.
[145] *Annual Report of the Chief Constable 2008–09*, 7.
[146] www.acpo.police.uk.

year to achieve this. During the troubles, the RUC was assisted in its public order work by the British army, although the official policy after 1976 was that the police had an independent responsibility in all areas and the army would merely give support when this was called for. After the second IRA ceasefire in 1997, the need to call upon the army gradually disappeared. There are still several thousand soldiers housed in Northern Ireland, but they are largely confined to barracks.

7.48 It is to the PSNI that applications for firearm certificates are made, with appeals against a refusal lying to the Minister of Justice. There are well over 100,000 legally held firearms in Northern Ireland, approximately 150 registered firearms dealers and several dozen firearms clubs and approved ranges.[147]

7.49 The PSNI no longer has any powers to bring prosecutions, this being the preserve of the Public Prosecution Service (see para 8.34). The police's continuing monopoly over the official *investigation* of crimes will always, however, be a limiting factor on a prosecutor's autonomy. If an interested person feels aggrieved at the police's failure to investigate a crime, an application can be made to the High Court for an order compelling the police to carry out their duty.[148] It used to be thought that it was not possible for the victim of a crime, or his or her relative, to sue the police if the police were negligent in failing to prevent the crime,[149] but the European Court of Human Rights has held that such a blanket immunity from being sued is contrary to the right to a fair hearing conferred by Article 6 of the European Convention on Human Rights.[150] Still, there would need to be very clear evidence of negligence before such a claim for compensation would succeed.[151]

The Historical Enquiries Team

7.50 In 2005 the Historical Enquiries Team was established within the PSNI (but reporting directly to the Chief Constable) to re-examine all deaths occurring as a result of the security situation in Northern Ireland between 1969 and 1997. It was anticipated that such re-examinations would take six years, since there were 2,546 separate incidents to look at, involving 3,268 deaths. The review system is seen as one way of providing closure

---

[147] The relevant legislation is the Firearms (NI) Order 2004.
[148] *R v Commissioner for the Metropolitan Police, ex parte Blackburn* [1968] 2 QB 117.
[149] *Hill v Chief Constable of West Yorkshire* [1989] AC 53.
[150] *Osman v UK* (1998) 29 EHRR 245.
[151] The claim even failed in the two appeals reported as *Van Colle v Chief Constable for Hertfordshire* [2008] UKHL 50, [2009] 1 AC 225. Mr and Mrs Van Colle also lost when they took their case to the European Court of Human Rights: *Van Colle v UK* App No 7678/09, decision of 13 November 2012.

for some of the families who lost loved ones during the troubles, but it is a slow and relatively unproductive process for most. Occasionally, however, it has led to people being brought to justice for terrible crimes.[152] In 2010 the then Chief Constable, Matt Baggott, stated that he wanted to wind up the HET within three years, with some of the complex investigations then being moved back into the PSNI, subject to appropriate oversight, but this timescale has proved unrealistic. Funding is now set to continue until 2015.

Community policing

7.51 The PSNI's latest 'Policing with the Community Strategy' was agreed with the Policing Board in early 2011. It extends the pre-existing strategy, which was focused on setting up Neighbourhood Policing Teams, so that community policing becomes a responsibility of police officers in all positions. It makes commitments that the police will update the victims of crimes about the progress being made with the investigation of those crimes and pledges that there will be improvements to the way that contact between the police and members of the public is conducted. As part of their efforts to improve community relations among young people, the police continue to run camping trips and sports events. They interact with school pupils through road safety roadshows[153] and a programme called Citizenship and Safety Education (CASE). The Youth Diversion Scheme provides a framework within which the PSNI respond to all those below the age of 17 who come into contact with the police on account of their wayward behaviour. It supplies an opportunity for diversion through 'restorative' interventions such as warnings and cautions. Juvenile cautions are administered by means of a youth conferencing process run by the Youth Justice Agency (see para 8.91). A report published in 2010 by the Independent Commission on Youth Crime and Antisocial Behaviour recommended that the scheme used in Northern Ireland should be adopted in England and Wales too.[154]

National policing

7.52 The PSNI is occasionally assisted in its work by the Serious Organised Crime Agency (SOCA), which is based in England (see too para

---

[152] Eg on 14 February 2013, following a trial prompted by an HET report, Robert Rodgers was convicted of the murder of Eileen Doherty in Belfast in 1973: *R v Rodgers* [2013] NICC 2.
[153] In 2010 there were 55 deaths on the roads of Northern Ireland, a remarkable reduction of 60 on the 2009 figure.
[154] *Time for a Fresh Start*, available at www.youthcrimecommission.org.uk. See too the press statement issued by the Minister of Justice, David Ford, on 15 July 2010.

7.40).[155] The Agency works mainly on the smuggling of drugs, human trafficking, major gun crime, computer crime, and money laundering. It has similar powers to those of the Serious Fraud Office,[156] an independent UK government department which investigates and prosecutes cases of complex fraud, so it can compel individuals to answer questions during interviews and to produce documents on demand (on pain of being found guilty of a criminal offence). The Agency also houses the Child Exploitation and Online Protection Centre and is responsible for trying to recover assets from criminals; it took over that function from the Assets Recovery Agency (which had a branch in Northern Ireland) in 2007.[157] Given the prevalence of cross-border smuggling in Ireland, SOCA liaises closely with its sister body in the Republic, the Criminal Assets Bureau.[158] The Crime and Courts Act 2013 (see para 7.40) brings all the existing national crime organisations under the umbrella of one National Crime Agency but only in England, Wales and Scotland.[159]

7.53   'Crimestoppers' is a national charity which works in conjunction will all UK police forces to encourage people to provide information about suspected crimes, anonymously if they prefer. Its freephone number is 0800 555 111.[160] If you wish to access information about the levels, types and numbers of crimes being reported within a mile of any place in Northern Ireland, you can now do so by visiting www.nicrimemaps.org. There are also more than 750 accredited neighbourhood watch schemes in Northern Ireland. Research completed in 2012 showed that such schemes were proving effective in helping to reduce crime and make people feel safer.[161]

BODIES OVERSEEING THE POLICE

The Northern Ireland Policing Board

7.54   Until 1970 the RUC was exclusively accountable to the Minister of Home Affairs in the Northern Ireland Government, but the Police Act (NI) 1970 created a Police Authority, free of direct political influence, with the task of monitoring the RUC's activities. On the same day that the PSNI was formed in 2001, the Police Authority was replaced by the Northern Ireland Policing Board.[162] This has nine 'independent' members, including

---

[155] Established by the Serious Organised Crime and Police Act 2005. Its website is www.soca.gov.uk.

[156] www.sfo.gov.uk. The Director is appointed by and is accountable to the Attorney General for England and Wales.

[157] As a result of the Serious Crime Act 2007.

[158] Established under the Criminal Assets Bureau Act 1996.

[159] See www.homeoffice.gov.uk/crime/nca.

[160] See too www.crimestoppers-uk.org/in-your-area/northern-ireland.

[161] See www.nipolicingboard.org.uk/nw_evaluation_survey_-_final_report.pdf.

[162] www.nipolicingboard.org.uk. See too D Rea, D Bradley and B Gilligan, 'Public

the chairperson, and ten 'political' members drawn from local parties. Sinn Féin eventually agreed to take its seats on the Board in 2007. Since the devolution of policing to the Northern Ireland Assembly in 2010, it is the responsibility of the Minister of Justice (not the Secretary of State) to set long-term objectives for the police, after consulting with the Policing Board and others,[163] and the Minister must lay these objectives before the Assembly,[164] but the Policing Board sets shorter-term objectives which must be consistent with the Minister's objectives.[165] The Chief Constable must also submit to the Policing Board the draft of an annual policing plan; the Board itself reviews this draft and issues the final policing plan after consulting the Secretary of State.[166] The Board can require the Chief Constable to report on any issue relating to policing and can initiate an inquiry into any aspect of policing.

7.55 The Policing Board wasted little time in agreeing a new badge and uniform for the PSNI[167] and it has issued codes of practice relating to the functions of policing and community safety partnerships (see para 7.58). It has also produced an impressive Code of Ethics, which lays down standards of conduct and practice for police officers and makes them aware of the rights and duties arising out of the European Convention on Human Rights.[168] In addition the Board has set up a Performance Committee,[169] which oversees the monitoring of the PSNI's adherence to human rights standards and publishes an annual *Human Rights Report*. These reports make recommendations as to how the PSNI could improve its respect for human rights and assesses whether the previous year's recommendations have been implemented.[170] The report for 2012 reveals that since 2005 the PSNI has implemented 192 recommendations made in previous annual reports, as well as 61 recommendations made in various 'thematic' reports issued by the Policing Board on topics such as policing with young people or policing with people who are lesbian, gay, bisexual or transsexual.

accountability: the Policing Board and the District Policing Partnerships', ch 10 in Doyle (see n 141 above).

[163] Police (NI) Act 2003, s 1. The other consultees are the Chief Constable, the Northern Ireland Human Rights Commission and the Equality Commission for Northern Ireland.
[164] Police (NI) Act 2000, s 24.
[165] Ibid s 25.
[166] Ibid s 26.
[167] Ibid s 54.
[168] Ibid s 52. The code was made part of the discipline code for police officers by the PSNI (Conduct) Regs 2003 (SR 68).
[169] Before April 2013 this was called the Human Rights and Professional Standards Committee.
[170] See too G Lynch, 'Human rights and police reform', ch 3 in Doyle (n 141 above).

Views on police performance

7.56   According to the results of a survey conducted for the Policing Board in January 2013, 65 per cent of respondents thought that the PSNI was doing a very good or a fairly good job in the local area, up from 59 per cent a year earlier. The figure for Protestant respondents in January 2013 was 67 per cent, and for Catholic respondents it was 64 per cent. Ten per cent of respondents thought that the PSNI was doing a very poor or fairly poor job in their local area, and 26 per cent were very dissatisfied or fairly dissatisfied with the levels of police patrols in their area.[171] When opinions were asked for in relation to the work of the PSNI in Northern Ireland as a whole, the approval rate went up to 70 per cent and the disapproval rate went down to 10 per cent.[172] As many as 87 per cent had some, a lot or total confidence in the PSNI's ability to provide a day-to-day policing service for everyone in Northern Ireland, and a reassuring 91 per cent felt very or fairly safe in their local community.[173] The same survey shows that the Policing Board itself was known to 82 per cent of respondents, but only 31 per cent of those respondents thought that it was working well or very well. Surprisingly perhaps, more Catholic respondents (34 per cent) were of this view than Protestants respondents (27 per cent).

7.57   The PSNI can sometimes be its own fiercest critic. In 2009 an internal PSNI report, leaked to the press, suggested that officers were being overwhelmed by paperwork and needed to be freed up to fight crime. Noting that 61 per cent of officers' time was spent inside stations, the report feared that 'the successful, and undoubtedly important, implementation of the majority of the 175 recommendations in the Patten Report of 1999 has led to a compliance-based culture, in silos, where commanders and frontline officers can see limited evidence of strategic linkage or alignment'.[174] Shortly afterwards a new Chief Constable took up the reins at the PSNI and he has since made it his priority to reduce time spent by police officers on paperwork.

Policing and Community Safety Partnerships

7.58   One of the most innovative suggestions in the Patten Report was that the Policing Board should be complemented by district policing partnerships (DPPs) in each of the 26 district councils in Northern Ireland. These were duly created as committees of the district councils, a majority of their

---

[171] See www.nipolicingboard.org.uk/january_2013_omnibus_survey_publications.pdf, Tables 1 and 5.
[172] Ibid Table 2.
[173] Ibid Tables 4 and 10.
[174] www.u.tv/News/Leaked-report-criticises-PSNI/f51d1226-e127-43b4-b871-7fa949766 daa.

198 Criminal Law in Northern Ireland

members being elected councillors and the rest being chosen by the Policing Board after a stringent selection process. There were monthly meetings between the DPPs and the district police commanders and the DPPs' views had to be taken into account by the police and the Policing Board when policing plans and strategies were being formulated. In 2003 Community Safety Partnerships were also set up to advise the government and others on community safety policies. They comprised representatives from the police, district councils, voluntary and community organizations, the business sector, the Housing Executive and youth justice services. The Community Service Unit in the Northern Ireland Office helped to develop an overall strategy on community safety, funding projects in the field and supporting the community safety partnerships.[175]

7.59 There was obviously an overlap between the functions of the two types of partnerships, so one of the reforms brought about by the Justice Act (NI) 2011 was the merger of the bodies into Policing and Community Safety Partnerships (PCSPs).[176] These new partnerships – one for each of the 26 district council areas in Northern Ireland, with four additional District PCSPs to cover West, East, North and South Belfast – became effective on 1 April 2012. They are funded jointly by the Policing Board and the Department of Justice but they work in accordance with a Code of Practice developed by the Policing Board. The PCSPs consult and engage with the local community on issues of concern relating to policing and community safety, and a Policing Committee within each PCSP has distinct responsibilities to provide views to the relevant district commander as well as the Policing Board on policing matters, to monitor the performance of the police, and to work to gain the cooperation of the public with the police. Obviously each PCSP must also strive to reduce crime and enhance community safety in its area. To enhance their community safety work certain public bodies have been designated as organisations which are allowed to have representatives attend meetings of the partnerships. These bodies include the PSNI itself, the Northern Ireland Housing Executive, the Probation Board, Health Trusts and Education Boards. For more information about the PCSPs, consult the Policing Board's website.[177]

Independent Custody Visiting Scheme

7.60 The Policing Board has responsibility for the statutory visiting scheme in Northern Ireland.[178] This allows for the appointment of about

[175] See www.communitysafetyni.gov.uk.
[176] ss 20–35.
[177] See www.nipolicingboard.org.uk/index/our-work/policing_and_community_safety_partner ships.htm.
[178] Police (NI) Act 2000, s 73.

50 people who, in their spare time and for no payment except expenses, are entitled to visit any of the 'designated' police stations where people can be detained for between six and 36 hours under the Police and Criminal Evidence (NI) Order 1989 or for up to 48 hours under the Terrorism Act 2000. The custody visitors visit police stations in pairs at any time of the day or night. Their job is to ensure that detainees are being properly looked after in accordance with a Code of Practice issued under the 1989 Order. To that end they can speak with the detainees and examine their custody records (provided the detainee consents). After each visit a report is submitted both to the Policing Board and to the Chief Constable. The custody visitors cannot themselves investigate complaints, but they can draw them to the attention of the relevant authorities. Leaflets and surveys produced by the custody visitors, together with quarterly statistics about their visits to police stations, are available on the Policing Board's website.[179] On 4 September 2012 James McVeigh died while in police custody at Musgrave Police Station in Belfast; at the time of writing the circumstances surrounding the death were still being investigated.

The Police Ombudsman for Northern Ireland[180]

7.61 The system for dealing with complaints against the police in Northern Ireland was radically overhauled in 2000 when the office of the Police Ombudsman began operating. The predecessor body, the Independent Commission for Police Complaints (ICPC), could *supervise* investigations of complaints, but the actual investigations were conducted by police officers. It was following a widely acclaimed report on the subject by Dr Maurice Hayes,[181] a former Ombudsman for Northern Ireland, that new legislation was enacted.[182] The legislation was further developed in 2000 as a result of recommendations in the Patten report.[183]

7.62 The office of the Police Ombudsman is able to conduct its own, completely independent, investigations into complaints brought against the police. The standard of proof required is now on the balance of probabilities, not beyond reasonable doubt,[184] and although there can be no appeal against

---

[179] See www.nipolicingboard.org.uk/index/publications/custody-visitors.htm.
[180] See also M O'Rawe, 'Complaints Against the Police', in B Dickson and B Gormally (eds), *Human Rights in Northern Ireland: The CAJ Handbook* (Belfast, Committee on the Administration of Justice, 2013), ch 5; N O'Loan, 'The Police Ombudsman for Northern Ireland: Some reflections', ch 9 in Doyle (see n 141 above).
[181] *A Police Ombudsman for Northern Ireland? A Review of the Police Complaints System in Northern Ireland* (1997).
[182] Police (NI) Act 1998, ss 50–65.
[183] Police (NI) Act 2000, ss 62–66.
[184] RUC (Conduct) Regs 2000 (SR 315); RUC (Conduct) (Senior Officer) Regs 2000 (SR 320); RUC (Appeals) Regs 2000 (SR 317).

the Police Ombudsman's conclusions they can still be the object of an application for judicial review (see paras 6.5–6.11).[185] To allow complaints which are not serious to be settled, and provided that the complainant and the police officer involved agree, the Police Ombudsman can attempt to act as a mediator between the two parties.[186] The Ombudsman can also carry out research into, and send to the Chief Constable and to the Policing Board a report on, any matters concerning police practices and policies which come to his or her attention.[187] In grave and exceptional circumstances the Police Ombudsman will look into an issue which occurred more than a year before the complaint was made. In 2001, for example, a report was issued into the death of Samuel Devenny as long ago as 1969. One of the most controversial reports by the first Police Ombudsman, Nuala O'Loan, was into the PSNI's investigation of the Omagh bomb in 1998.[188] Published in 2001, the report accused the then Chief Constable and an Assistant Chief Constable of seriously flawed leadership, such that the chances of convicting the Omagh bombers 'have been significantly reduced'.[189]

7.63 In 2011 the Police Ombudsman's reports into police investigations of deaths at McGurk's Bar in Belfast in 1971 and at The Heights Bar in Loughinisland in 1994 led to considerable controversy, mainly over the definition of the term 'collusion' between police officers and loyalist paramilitaries. 'Collusion' is a not a word with any specific legal meaning, so people disagree as to when some reprehensible conduct actually qualifies for that description. As a result of the controversy the Ombudsman who was then in post decided to retire early from the position and a new Ombudsman took office in July 2012. He immediately gave a commitment that his investigations would be carried out in a completely independent manner, free from police, governmental or any sectional community interest. In January 2013 he announced that his office would resume its investigations into the 150 or so cases relating to police malpractices during 'the troubles' which have been referred to the Ombudsman's Office by the PSNI's Historical Enquiries Team (see para 7.50) or by members of the public. These had been put on hold as a result of doubts over the office's independence. Just a month later the Ombudsman issued an excoriating report into the PSNI's handling of a missing person's inquiry.[190]

7.64 The Ombudsman cannot, however, investigate complaints against officers who have retired from the police, nor any complaints against

---

[185] See eg *In re Montgomery's Application* [2011] NIQB 134, [2012] 3 BNIL 84.

[186] Police (NI) Act 1998, s 58A, inserted by Police (NI) Act 2000, s 62(1).

[187] Ibid ss 60A and 61A, inserted, respectively, by Police (NI) Act 2000, s 63(1) and Police (NI) Act 2003, s 13.

[188] See www.policeombudsman.org/Publicationsuploads/omaghreport.pdf.

[189] Ibid para 7.4.

[190] Press release, 21 February 2013 ('Police investigation 'a catalogue of mistake after mistake").

soldiers, even when they have been acting in support of the police. And if a complainant is the object of a criminal prosecution, the prosecution usually needs to be completed before the Police Ombudsman concludes an investigation of the complaint.[191] The Police Ombudsman does not have to disclose to complainants all the documents examined during the course of an investigation.[192] In 2012 the Minister of Justice consulted the public on what changes should be made to the future operation of the Ombudsman's Office,[193] but he has not yet announced his decisions on this matter.

7.65   The Ombudsman's office does not itself take disciplinary proceedings against police officers. This is left to the police themselves. Hearings usually take place before disciplinary boards consisting of three officers, one of whom must be an assistant chief constable or commander.[194] Hearings into the conduct of senior officers take place in a tribunal consisting of a single person appointed by the Policing Board (perhaps with one or more assessors to help).[195] The standard of proof required for a finding of guilt in all of these hearings is now the balance of probabilities.[196] Appeal tribunals can be set up to hear appeals from disciplinary boards.[197]

7.66   The annual reports of the Police Ombudsman provide details on the quantity and nature of complaints lodged, and on the resulting recommendations following investigations. In 2011–12, 72 per cent of matters investigated were not substantiated and 2 per cent were substantiated but no further action was recommended. Eighteen per cent of the cases were referred to the Public Prosecution Service because the allegation in question amounted to a criminal offence, but the Ombudsman recommended that no prosecution be brought in relation to them. In only 8 per cent of cases did the Ombudsman deem it necessary to recommend that some action be taken in the wake of the investigation. In six cases he recommended that a police officer should be prosecuted and in 19 cases he recommended to the Chief Constable that formal disciplinary proceedings should be taken against police officers. In a further 474 instances the Ombudsman recommended that the police officer be given advice and guidance, a written warning or some management attention.[198]

---

[191] *In re O'Callaghan's Application* [2003] NIQB 17.

[192] *In re an Application by the Committee on the Administration of Justice and Martin O'Brien* [2005] NIQB 25.

[193] The Department of Justice's website has both the consultation paper and a summary of the responses thereto.

[194] RUC (Discipline and Disciplinary Appeals) Regs 1988 (SR 10), Sch 4.

[195] RUC (Conduct) (Senior Officer) Regs 2000 (SR 320), reg 14.

[196] RUC (Complaints etc.) Regs 2001 (SR 318), reg 11.

[197] RUC (Appeals) Regs 2000 (SR 317), see especially reg 7.

[198] *Annual Statistical Bulletin for the Office of the Police Ombudsman for Northern Ireland 2010–11*, Tables 18, 20 and 21.

HM Inspectorate of Constabulary[199]

7.67   Her Majesty's Inspectorate of Constabulary for England and Wales acts as an advisory body to the Department of Justice in Northern Ireland regarding matters such as recruitment and equipment for the police. It also carries out regular inspections of the PSNI, and the PSNI is included in the Inspectorate's periodic thematic reports. Other inspection reports are produced by Criminal Justice Inspection Northern Ireland (see para 7.97). Occasionally the Northern Ireland Audit Office or the Public Accounts Committee of the Northern Ireland Assembly will also take an interest in the way the PSNI goes about its business.[200]

THE PRISON SERVICE[201]

The prison population

7.68   The prison population in Northern Ireland reached a peak of almost 3,000 in 1978. It declined leading up to and in the immediate aftermath of the Belfast (Good Friday) Agreement, but it has slowly risen again since 2001.[202] At the end of December 2012 it stood at 1,683. Of these, 1,205 (72 per cent) were sentenced prisoners, the rest being remand prisoners. They were distributed between the prisons as follows: 981 in Maghaberry Prison near Lisburn, 502 in Magilligan Prison on the North-West coast,[203] and 200 at Hydebank Wood Prison and Young Offenders Centre in South Belfast (including 50 women). As regards the length of sentences being served, at the end of December 2012 there were 369 prisoners serving two years or less, 648 serving more than two years but less than life, and 186 serving life. There is also a holding centre for up to 19 immigration detainees in the town of Larne, where they can be detained for up to seven days.[204] The proportion of people imprisoned compared to the population as a whole is significantly smaller in Northern Ireland than it is in Great Britain.

7.69   The Northern Ireland Prison Service is an executive agency within the Department of Justice.[205] In 2011–12 its running costs were £155

---

[199] www.homeoffice.gov.uk/hmic/hmic.htm
[200] Eg in relation to the PSNI's use of agency staff (NIAO Report of 2 October 2012; PAC Report due later in 2013).
[201] www.niprisonservice.gov.uk. See too J Challis, *The Prison Service in Northern Ireland 1900–1990* (Belfast, Prison Officers' Association, 1999).
[202] See the useful graph in the *Annual Report and Accounts of the Northern Ireland Prison Service 2011–12*, 40.
[203] This includes the Foyleview Unit, from which prisoners can go out to work in the community.
[204] It is called Larne House and is run by the UK Border Agency.
[205] Prison Act (NI) 1953, s 5.

million and the cost per prisoner that year was approximately £71,398
– considerably higher than the cost of imprisonment in Great Britain.[206]
Magilligan is a medium-security prison, housing mainly shorter-term
prisoners. Maghaberry is a high-security prison housing male long-term
prisoners as well as male remand prisoners; prisoners claiming allegiance
to paramilitary organisations are, at their own request, housed in separate
parts of the prison, away from each other as well as from other prisoners.[207]
Remand prisoners are held only at Maghaberry or Hydebank Wood; woman
prisoners are held only at Hydebank Wood. Prison officers are trained at the
Prison Service College in Millisle, County Down, and are unionised in the
Prison Officers' Association.

The prisons during the troubles

7.70   During the 30 years of the troubles in Northern Ireland, from 1969
to 1998, 29 prison officers were murdered by terrorists. There were also
particularly serious incidents within Northern Ireland's prisons during
the 1980s and 1990s. A hunger strike at the Maze Prison, following the
long-running 'blanket' and 'dirty' protests, led to the deaths of 10 republican
prisoners in 1981.[208] Some of the demands of the prisoners, such as the
right to wear their own clothes, were eventually conceded. In 1983 there
was a mass escape of 38 prisoners from the Maze Prison, the largest ever
escape in British penal history. In 1997 a loyalist prisoner, Billy Wright, was
murdered at the Maze Prison by republican paramilitaries[209] and in 1998
another prisoner, David Keys, was murdered by loyalist paramilitaries. In
2002, after staff contact details somehow fell into the hands of paramilitary
organisations, more than £30 million was spent by the Northern Ireland
Office in providing extra security measures for Prison Service staff. In
November 2012 dissident republicans murdered a prison officer, David
Black, as he drove along a motorway.

[206] See the *Annual Report and Accounts of the Northern Ireland Prison Service 2011–12*, pp
41–2. In *The Times* of 21 April 2011 (p 27) the cost per prisoner in England and Wales was put
at £40,000 and in Scotland at £31,000.

[207] The republican prisoners are housed in Roe House and the loyalists in Bush House. In
November 2012 the republicans called off a dirty protest provoked by what they claimed was
excessive strip-searching.

[208] The prison at Maze, also near Lisburn (and formerly known as Long Kesh), closed in 2000.
The prison on the Crumlin Road in Belfast closed in 1996. For the story of the hunger strikes,
see D Beresford, *Ten Men Dead* (London, Collins, 1987).

[209] The inquiry into this murder reported in 2010 and concluded that the murder was a
result of serious negligence by the prison authorities, but not of collusion with republican
paramilitaries: www.billywrightinquiry.org.

The 'accelerated' release of prisoners

7.71   Even before the Belfast (Good Friday) Agreement in 1998, prisoners convicted in Diplock courts (see para 7.28) were able to benefit from the generous rules in Northern Ireland regarding remission of sentences: they could be released after serving just one-half of their sentence, whereas in England prisoners had to serve at least two-thirds.[210] In the wake of the Agreement the Northern Ireland (Sentences) Act 1998 provided for the appointment of Sentence Review Commissioners,[211] to whom prisoners could apply for a declaration of eligibility for early release.[212] The preconditions were that the prisoner must have committed a scheduled offence prior to the Agreement, must have been sentenced to at least five years in prison, must not be supporting a paramilitary organisation that was not on ceasefire, must not be likely to become a supporter of such an organisation or to be concerned in acts of terrorism if released immediately, and, if currently serving a life sentence, must not be a danger to the public if released immediately. By July 2000 some 447 prisoners had been released (241 republicans, 194 loyalists and 12 'non-aligned' prisoners); a further 30 were released thereafter. Of all those released, 21 were later taken back into prison for breaking the terms of their licence.[213] Anyone convicted today of a scheduled offence committed before Good Friday 1998, and who was a member of a paramilitary organisation which is now on ceasefire, can be made to spend no more than two years in prison, including time spent on remand.[214] But there is not yet any law dealing with the so-called 'on the runs' (OTRs) – republicans who have fled justice.[215]

Prison conditions today[216]

7.72   The prison regime in Northern Ireland is regulated partly by legislation (the Prison Act (NI) 1953 and the Prison and Young Offenders Centre Rules (NI) 1995) and partly by Standing Orders issued to prison

[210] Northern Ireland (Remission of Sentences) Act 1995.
[211] www.sentencereview.org.uk.
[212] Ireland enacted the Criminal Justice (Release of Prisoners) Act 1998, which set up a Release of Prisoners Commission.
[213] *Annual Report of the Sentence Review Commissioners 2011–12*, p 25.
[214] See *R v McGeough* [2011] NICC 7 (Stephens J), where the defendant was convicted of attempted murder, possession of firearms and membership of the IRA in 1981. He was later sentenced to 20 years in prison, but was released In January 2013 on account of the early release provisions in the Good Friday Agreement of 1998.
[215] A government effort to deal with this issue by legislation in 2005 was abandoned.
[216] For a general survey of the law affecting prisoners in Northern Ireland, see J Monahan and A Jemphrey, 'Prisoners' Rights', in B Dickson and B Gormally (eds), *Human Rights in Northern Ireland: The CAJ Handbook* (Belfast, Committee on the Administration of Justice, 2013) ch 6.

governors by the Department of Justice.[217] Prisoners are categorised as being on a 'basic', 'standard' or 'enhanced' regime depending on how well they are adhering to the rules of the prison.[218] The rules require that prisoners should engage in useful work. Some are employed in servicing the prisons themselves, while others work in prison industries making items such as shoes, clothing and metalwork. Many prisoners enrol for education courses, ranging from the most basic to Open University level.

7.73 The Young Offenders Centre at Hydebank Wood, which opened in 1979, has places for 300 young men, mainly aged 18 to 21, who have been sentenced to less than three years in custody. The few females in this category are housed in a separate unit at the same establishment. The regime is officially described as 'brisk', with the inmates gaining privileges by using their time in a positive and constructive way. The Centre offers extensive education, vocational training and physical recreation facilities. In 2012 the Minister of Justice ended the practice whereby some young people below the age of 18 could be held at Hydebank Wood if they were certified as being unruly or guilty of serious misconduct.[219]

Discipline and welfare

7.74 Discipline in the prisons is now primarily the responsibility of the governors, but the most serious punishment which a governor can impose is loss of privileges or cellular confinement for up to 14 days. Any offence which a governor believes requires a more severe punishment may be referred to the police. It used to be the case that the prison governor or responsible Minister could impose a penalty of loss of remission, but this is no longer possible because the European Court of Human Rights ruled that in such cases prisoners would need to be given legal representation and the UK government did not want such an expense to be incurred. Legal aid is available for prisoners to make applications for judicial review of decisions taken in the prisons (see paras 6.5–6.11), but few of these are ultimately successful.[220]

7.75 Voluntary groups active in the area of prisoners' welfare include the Northern Ireland Association for the Care and Resettlement of Offenders, the Extern Organisation and the Prison Fellowship of Northern Ireland. There are also organisations working on behalf of 'political' ex-prisoners, notably Coiste na n-Iarchimí[221] for republicans and EPIC (the Ex-Prisoners' Interpretive Centre) for loyalists.

[217] The Standing Orders are available on the Prison Service's website.
[218] This is known as the Progressive Regimes and Earned Privileges Scheme (PREPS); see, eg, *In re Harbinson's (Mark) Application* [2012] NIQB 38, [2012] 7 BNIL 43.
[219] Department of Justice Press Release, 28 June 2012.
[220] A typical example is *Application by (Ivan) Foden for Judicial Review* [2013] NIQB 2.
[221] This is, loosely, Irish for 'Association of Ex-Prisoners'.

7.76 Periodic inspections of the prisons are conducted by Criminal Justice Inspection Northern Ireland (see para 7.97), and in the past by HM Inspectorate of Prisons. In 2009 a particularly negative report was published on the back of an unannounced inspection of Maghaberry Prison; the prison was found to be performing 'poorly' as regards safety and purposeful activities and 'not sufficiently well' as regards respect and resettlement. A further inspection of Maghaberry conducted in 2012 showed that there had been improvements, but that there was still a long way to go.[222] There have also been occasional reports by the Council of Europe's Committee for the Prevention of Torture[223] and research reports published by the Northern Ireland Human Rights Commission, especially on the plight of women prisoners.[224] As in England, there is a high rate of suicides in Northern Ireland's prisons, and the Prisoner Ombudsman (see para 7.83) has been critical of prison staff in this context.[225]

7.77 On the back of quite damning criticisms of the Northern Ireland Prison Service contained in various inspection reports, the Minister of Justice ordered a review of the Service. An interim report of the Review Team was published in February 2011 and was very critical of the way the Service operates. It called for 'a high-level and well-resourced change programme, with political support, leadership and direction, to equip the service to meet the needs and challenges that now face it'. The Review Team's final report was published in October 2011 and contained 40 recommendations. One of these was that there should be an early retirement scheme which would allow a significant number of prison officers to leave and new staff to be recruited, alongside a training and development programme, externally delivered, for those who remain or join. Another was that there should be a new code of ethics and values, and new disciplinary and appraisal systems based on the code.[226] The Minister subsequently put in place an early retirement scheme and in February 2013 he announced that 544 members prison officers had applied to leave the Prison Service under the terms of the scheme. To date approval had been given for just 360 to leave, but he was hoping to be able to extend approval to cover all who initially applied.[227]

---

[222] Like all its other reports these reports on Maghaberry are available on the CJI's website: www.cjini.org.

[223] www.cpt.coe.int/en/default.htm.

[224] See, generally, L Moore and P Scraton, *The Hurt Inside* (rev ed, 2005) and *The Prison Within: The Imprisonment of Women at Hydebank Wood 2004–06* (2007), both published by the Northern Ireland Human Rights Commission.

[225] See the Ombudsman's report into the death of Colin Bell, published 9 January 2009 (available on the Ombudsman's website).

[226] Recommendations 26 and 27.

[227] NIA Debs, Vol 81, p 34; 5 February 2013.

Lifers

7.78   The court which imposes a life sentence must in most cases specify the 'tariff period' which has to be served in order to satisfy the requirements of retribution and deterrence, having regard to the seriousness of the offence. On occasions the trial judge will sit with the Lord Chief Justice to hear arguments from barristers as to what the appropriate tariff period should be,[228] and an appeal lies to the Court of Appeal against the term set.[229] Judges in Northern Ireland follow the guidelines on tariffs set out by the Lord Chief Justice of England and Wales in 2002, where he talked of a 'normal' starting point of 12 years and a 'higher' starting point of 15–16 years.[230] In some particularly serious cases no such tariff period is set (so that a life sentence really means 'for life'), but the Minister of Justice can (and, in cases where the offender was under 18 years of age when he or she committed the offence, must) at a later stage direct when the release provisions are to apply.[231]

7.79   After the tariff period has expired the prisoner can apply to Parole Commissioners for a release date.[232] In taking their decisions the Commissioners must have 'due regard' to the need to protect the public from serious harm.[233] A release date is usually notified about a year in advance so that during the pre-release period the prisoner can take part in a scheme of work and home leave. After release the prisoner remains on licence for the rest of his or her life and can be recalled to prison when the Minister of Justice considers this necessary to avoid danger to the public. If the Minister does revoke an ex-prisoner's licence the matter is referred to the Parole Commissioners for a decision on whether to maintain the revocation or to release the prisoner.[234] In deciding not to release the prisoner the Parole Commissioners must be careful not to base their decision only on material that was not disclosed to the prisoner, otherwise there will be a violation of Article 5(4) of the European Convention on Human Rights.[235]

7.80   As mentioned in para 7.68 above, at the end of 2012 there were 186 lifers in Northern Ireland, some 11 per cent of the prison population. A

---

[228] See, eg *R v Larmour* [2004] NICC 4, *R v McParland* [2004] NICC 6 and *R v Gribben* [2004] NICC 7.

[229] Criminal Appeal (NI) Act 1980, s 7.

[230] *Practice Statement (Crime: Life Sentences)* [2002] 3 All ER 412, adopted by the NICA in *R v McCandless* [2004] NICA 1, [2004] NI 69.

[231] For the applicability of the new system to persons held 'at the Secretary of State's pleasure' when the 2001 Order came into force, see *In re King's Application* [2002] NICA 47, [2003] NI 43.

[232] It was only in 2008 that Northern Ireland acquired a parole system. Before that there were Life Sentence Review Commissioners. See the Criminal Justice (NI) Order 1998, art 46. See now the Parole Commissioners' Rules (NI) 2009 (SR 82).

[233] Ibid art 46(2)(a).

[234] Life Sentences (NI) Order 2001, art 9(4). For a decision by Parole Commissioners overturned on judicial review, see *In re JR63's Application* [2011] NIQB 109, [2012] 1 BNIL 80.

[235] *Application by Martin Corey for Judicial Review* [2012] NIQB 56, applying the decision of the European Court of Human Rights in *A v UK* (2009) 49 EHRR 29.

report by the Criminal Justice Inspectorate (see para 7.97) in 2009 showed that, generally speaking, the arrangements for assessing and managing the risk presented by life sentence prisoners compared favourably with those operating in other jurisdictions.[236] A further report in 2012 noted that further improvements had been made to arrangements.[237]

Victims' rights

7.81　Under the Justice (NI) Act 2002[238] a scheme has been put in place whereby the victim of a crime (or a representative of the victim if the victim is dead) can apply to be kept informed by the Minister of Justice about the temporary release and discharge of the person imprisoned for the crime.[239] In certain circumstances, however, the Minister can refuse to provide the information and the scheme does not usually apply to the victims of offences committed by juveniles.

Independent Monitoring Boards

7.82　Each of the three prisons in Northern Ireland has an Independent Monitoring Board, which is appointed by the Secretary of State. Each Board has to meet at least once a month, sending copies of its minutes to the Secretary of State, and the prison must be visited by one member of the Board at least once a fortnight. Every Board member has free access at all times to all parts of the prison. He or she can hear any complaint or request which a prisoner may wish to make, if necessary out of the sight and hearing of prison officers. The Boards draw the attention of the prison governors to particular matters as well as publishing annual reports (available on the Prison Service's website). The Board's function is to satisfy itself on behalf of the general public as to the state of the prison premises, the administration of the prison and the treatment of the prisoners.

The Prisoner Ombudsman[240]

7.83　The role of the Prisoner Ombudsman for Northern Ireland (still a non-statutory post[241]) is to consider any eligible complaint referred by a

---

[236] *A Review of Transition to Community Arrangements for Life Sentence Prisoners in Northern Ireland.*
[237] *The Management of Life and Indeterminate Sentence Prisoners in Northern Ireland.*
[238] s 67.
[239] Prisoner Release Victim Information (NI) Scheme 2003 (SR 293).
[240] www.niprisonerombudsman.gov.uk.
[241] The current Prisoner Ombudsman very much wants the post to be made statutory. An opportunity to do this was not, however, taken when the Justice Act (NI) 2011 was enacted.

prisoner, or by a former prisoner (if no more than 21 days have elapsed since his or her release), regarding his or her treatment in prison. For the complaint to be eligible it must first have gone through the Prison Service's own three-stage complaints system and it cannot relate to a decision made by a Minister, a judge, the police or the Prosecution Service; nor can it relate to any ongoing criminal or civil court proceedings. The Ombudsman can, if he or she considers it fitting, make recommendations based on the complaint to the Secretary of State or to the Director General of the Prison Service, and the latter must respond within 21 days. An annual report has to be submitted to the Secretary of State. The Prisoner Ombudsman's website (under 'Publications') carries reports into individual deaths in custody. There are 23 such reports, covering deaths occurring between 2007 and 2013.

THE PROBATION SERVICE

7.84 The Probation Service in Northern Ireland is currently administered by the Probation Board[242] which, since the devolution of criminal justice in April 2010, has been an executive non-departmental public body within the Department of Justice, just like the Prison Service. In 2011–12 it cost nearly £19 million to run. The Board has a commitment to deal with persistent and/or violent offenders in a manner which reduces their offending and helps them to integrate into their communities. It must also protect the public and provide high quality information to the courts. There are about 20 probation offices throughout the province, all of which are listed in the telephone directory's yellow pages. Probation officers adhere to standards of practice issued by the Board with regard to the supervision of probation orders and community service orders.

7.85 The Service seeks to prevent re-offending by trying to reduce the number of custodial sentences imposed by the courts. Probation officers write pre-sentence reports (PSRs) on offenders found guilty in a court. These reports are expected to be called for when a court is considering whether to impose a community sanction such as a community service order or a supervision order (see para 8.51), but they are compulsory unless regarded as unnecessary in the circumstances (eg because the offence is so serious), before a court decides that a custodial sentence is appropriate. The reports attempt to give an objective assessment of the offender to the judge or magistrate, set out the courses of action available to the court and make recommendations as to which would be most appropriate in the particular case.

7.86 A court can place an offender on probation for a period between six months and three years. The order is not intended as a punishment but

---

[242] www.pbni.org.uk.

rather as an offer of rehabilitation. The officer will befriend, give guidance to and supervise the offender. Supervision within the community is not only better for the offender, it is also vastly cheaper than containment in prison, and the recidivism rate for those placed on probation (ie the proportion of offenders who re-offend) is much lower than for those who are given a custodial sentence. Probation officers also help to run the community service order scheme, whereby offenders aged 17 or over can be required to perform a set number of hours of community service. In 2010 the Criminal Justice Inspectorate (see para 7.97) reported that the community service schemes were well managed and made a positive contribution to the community. Reconviction rates for those given these orders were low when compared with other punishments.[243] On 31 March 2012 there were no fewer than 4,441 people under the supervision of probation officers in Northern Ireland.[244] The Service has recently been tasked with implementing 'supervised activity orders', which are community sentences imposed on people who default on the payments of fines.

7.87   In addition, the Probation Service provides welfare services for prisoners, prisoners' families and people recently released from prison. Whenever life sentence prisoners are taking part in the 'working out' scheme during the months before their release on licence, probation officers help to counsel them. They also maintain contact thereafter.[245] The Board also runs a Victim Information Scheme, which was assessed by the Criminal Justice Inspectorate in 2011;[246] as recommended in the CJI's report, during 2012–13 PBNI is co-ordinating efforts to amalgamate all post-conviction information schemes in Northern Ireland. The Board has a statutory responsibility to fund some voluntary projects operating in this field. The Northern Ireland Association for the Care and Resettlement of Offenders (NIACRO) and the Extern Organisation are the most prominent groups in the voluntary sector whose services overlap with those of the Probation Service and they receive substantial grants from the Board.

Rehabilitation of offenders

7.88   Under the Rehabilitation of Offenders (NI) Order 1978 an individual's sentence (whether or not it involves imprisonment) may in certain circumstances become 'spent', which means that from then on the person must be treated in most situations as someone who has not

---

[243] The report was entitled *An Inspection of the Probation Board for Northern Ireland Community Service Scheme.*
[244] *Annual Report and Accounts of the Probation Board of Northern Ireland 2011–12*, p 3.
[245] See Prison Act (NI) 1953, s 23.
[246] *The Care and Treatment of Victims and Witnesses in the Criminal Justice System in Northern Ireland.*

been convicted of, or even charged with, the offence in question. Such a rehabilitated person can even sue for libel or slander if someone later refers to the fact that he or she has been convicted of the offence, and the failure to disclose a spent conviction is not in law a proper ground for prejudicing a person as regards employment (except in relation to work with people aged under 18). The period which must elapse before a sentence becomes spent depends on the type and severity of the original sentence. For a prison sentence of up to six months, for instance, the rehabilitation period is seven years, while for sentences of between six and 30 months the period is 10 years. Prison sentences of more than 30 months are excluded altogether from the scheme. If a person is placed on probation the rehabilitation period runs simultaneously with the probation period, or for one year after the conviction, whichever is longer.

SERVICES FOR VICTIMS

Victim Support Northern Ireland

7.89 Victim Support Northern Ireland (VSNI) is the regional equivalent to the national charity for victims of crime in England and Wales. With the help of a grant from the Department of Justice, it assists victims and witnesses of all crimes free of charge by providing emotional support, information and practical help (see paras 8.46 and 8.71). First established in 1981, it now has offices in Ballymena, Belfast, Derry/Londonderry, Newry and Omagh and relies greatly on the work of more than 200 trained volunteers. Every year it assists more than 40,000 people, especially with tasks such as applying for criminal injuries compensation (see paras 9.82–9.88),[247] seeking help from other specialist organisations (eg in cases of domestic violence, murder or hate crime), and appearing as a witness in criminal court proceedings. Its service leaflet is available on the organisation's website.[248] In 2011 the Department of Justice also produced a useful code of practice for victims of crime.[249] This sets out more general information about the role of victims in the criminal justice system of Northern Ireland. An EU Directive on the rights of victims of crime has already been adopted by the European Parliament; if it is approved by the European Council it may require all jurisdictions in the UK to enhance the way in which it supports the victims of crime.

---

[247] In 2010–11, for example, VSNI helped more than 2,000 people to claim more than £4 million.

[248] www.victimsupportni.co.uk.

[249] www.dojni.gov.uk (under 'Publications', then 'C').

Impact statements

7.90   Victims can, if they wish, submit a victim impact statement to a court before it tries someone for the crime which has affected them. If the defendant is found guilty, the statement will help the sentencing judge to decide on the appropriate punishment to impose. The statement can also be a therapeutic exercise for the victim and an educative one for the convicted person. Instead, or in addition, the court can ask the Public Prosecution Service to obtain a victims impact report from a professional in the field. This will provide a specialist opinion on the trauma suffered by the victim and on his or her resulting needs. Neither of these procedures is currently backed by statutory provisions but in 2011 the Minister of Justice issued a consultation paper on the topic[250] and he proposes to include relevant provisions in the Faster, Fairer Justice Bill which will be introduced in the Assembly during 2013. Meanwhile, following a further consultation exercise in 2012[251] in the wake of a difficult case concerning child sex abuse,[252] the Minister has introduced *community* impact statements. These are designed to be used in high profile cases where an offence has had a significant impact on community confidence. The statements are to be written by a nominated representative of a group of people living within a particular locality who, indirectly, have been adversely affected by the crime or crimes in question.[253]

Victims of the troubles

7.91   As regards victims of the troubles in Northern Ireland, the Belfast (Good Friday) Agreement 1998 accepted that it was 'essential to acknowledge and address the suffering of the victims of violence as a necessary element of reconciliation'. In that regard the participants in the Agreement looked forward to the results of the work of the proposed Northern Ireland Victims Commission. In fact no such body was established for several years, although a myriad of voluntary victims' groups emerged in the interim.[254] The current Commission for Victims and Survivors was set up in 2008 as a non-departmental public body of the OFMDFM, its statutory basis being the Victims and Survivors (NI) Order 2006, as amended by the Commission for Victims and Survivors Act (NI) 2008. The latter Act was passed to

---

[250] *Provision of Victim Impact Statements and Victim Impact Reports* (2011).

[251] *Provision of Community Impact Assessments* (2012).

[252] The McDermott case, in Donagh, County Fermanagh. See www.thedetail.tv/issues/57/donagh--2/community-impact-statements-what-impact and *Chief Constable of the PSNI v McDermott and McDermott* [2012] NICC 23, [2012] 6 BNIL 17.

[253] See the Department of Justice's booklet, available online, on *Making a Community Impact Statement: What You Need to Know*.

[254] Eg Relatives for Justice, the Shankill Stress and Trauma Centre, and the WAVE Trauma Centre.

allow several people to be appointed as Commissioners, since there had been considerable controversy over the appointment of the single Interim Commissioner in 2005 (see para 2.51).[255] However, when the term of office of the people appointed under the 2008 Act came to an end in 2012, they were replaced by just one Commissioner. The Commissioner's duties include promoting an awareness of the interests of victims and survivors and of the need to safeguard those interests, keeping the adequacy and effectiveness of relevant law and practice and of the services provided for victims and survivors under review, and making arrangements for a Victims and Survivors Forum.[256]

7.92 Amazingly, it was not until 2012 that a comprehensive needs analysis was drawn up to identify the overall needs of victims and survivors of the conflict in Northern Ireland. A further report revealed that in just one year more than 57,000 people exposed to conflict-related trauma had presented with symptoms of clinical depression, while 18,000 people had displayed symptoms of post-traumatic stress disorder.[257] In 2012 a Victims and Survivors Service at last became operational, three years after the OFMDFM had published a consultation paper and a strategy on the subject. The new service (which operates separately from the Victims and Survivors Commission) provides support for all victims and survivors of the troubles, whether already belonging to a victims group or not, and promises to be responsive to the needs of victims and survivors based on their agreed need. It will better co-ordinate existing funding arrangements, ensure the sustainability of the help available, and conduct better evaluation of the services provided than has been the case to date. A Client Information Pack is accessible on the website of the Victims and Survivors Service.[258]

Dealing with the past

7.93 Ever since the Belfast (Good Friday) Agreement in 1998 there has been discussion about whether any formal process should be initiated to 'deal with the past' in Northern Ireland, such as occurred in South Africa with its

---

[255] A challenge was raised to the way in which the Northern Ireland Office (and the Secretary of State at the time, Peter Hain) went about appointing Mrs Bertha McDougall as the Interim Victims Commissioner in 2005, mainly based around the allegation that Mr Hain wanted to satisfy the wishes of the DUP in this regard. The Court of Appeal affirmed Girvan J's decision that the process had been unlawfully conducted, but not for all the reasons favoured by Girvan J: *An Application for Judicial Review by Brenda Downes* [2009] NICA 26. A later challenge to the appointment of four Commissioners failed in both the High Court and the Court of Appeal: *Re Williamson's Application for Judicial Review* [2010] NICA 8.
[256] Victims and Survivors (NI) Order 2006, art 6. The Forum comprises 25 members; the minutes of its latest meetings are available on the website of the Commission: www.cvsni.org
[257] *Troubled Consequences: A report on the mental health impact of the civil conflict in Northern Ireland* (2011).
[258] www.victimsservice.org.

Truth and Reconciliation Commission.[259] To date no official project has been agreed, but a number of separate initiatives can be considered as attempts to contribute towards a larger project. For example, several public inquiries have been conducted into high-profile killings (see para 7.43), the police have set up a Historical Enquiries Team to re-examine all deaths occurring as a result of the security situation between 1969 and 1997 (see para 7.50), the Coroners Service is working its way through a list of 'legacy inquests' (see para 6.35) and the Police Ombudsman has investigated allegations of police misconduct in several troubles-related cases (see para 7.62). A specialist reconciliation organisation, Healing Through Remembering, published an excellent survey of the options available in this area,[260] and this was followed by an assessment of community-based projects in the field commissioned by the Community Foundation of Northern Ireland.[261]

7.94   In 2006 the UK government set up its own commission to examine the options, the Consultative Group on the Past, which reported in 2009.[262] This proposed that an independent Legacy Commission should be established, combining processes of reconciliation, justice and information recovery, with a mandate to make recommendations to the UK government after five years. It would include a Review and Investigation Unit, backed by police powers, to take over the work of the Historical Enquiries Team and the Police Ombudsman on historical cases. The proposed Legacy Commission would consider how to mark the conflict through ceremonies and memorials. There would be no 'amnesty' for perpetrators of crimes but the nearest relative of any person who died as a result of the conflict in and about Northern Ireland (including people killed while committing crimes) should receive an ex-gratia 'recognition payment' of £12,000. Largely because of the controversy provoked by this last proposal, none of the ideas in the Consultative Group's report has yet been taken forward.[263] The last Labour Secretary of State, Owen Paterson, appeared to favour the creation of a centre comparable to that in Salamanca which documents the Spanish Civil War,[264] but again this proposal has not been developed. The OFMDFM, however, is in the process of converting the former prison site at Long Kesh / Maze into a Peace-building and Conflict Resolution Centre, funded by EU money.

[259] This sat from 1995 to 1998 and considered human rights abuses which occurred between 1960 and 1994.
[260] K McEvoy, *Making Peace With the Past: Options for Truth Recovery Regarding the Conflict In and About Northern Ireland* (Belfast, 2006).
[261] B Gormally and K McEvoy, *Dealing With the Past in Northern Ireland from Below: An Evaluation* (Belfast, 2009).
[262] This is sometimes referred to as the Eames-Bradley Report, after the co-chairs of the Consultative Group.
[263] They were also rejected by the Northern Ireland Affairs Committee of the House of Commons: see its 2nd Report of 2009–10, HC 171.
[264] www.bbc.co.uk/news/uk-northern-ireland-12087026.

OTHER CRIMINAL JUSTICE BODIES

7.95   A number of other bodies exist which have functions that help oil the wheels of the criminal justice system in Northern Ireland. Two which have recently been wound up, having performed valuable work since the Belfast (Good Friday) Agreement, are the Independent International Commission on Decommissioning[265] and the Independent Monitoring Commission.[266] Others, including the Public Prosecution Service, are considered in the next chapter.

The Forensic Science Agency

7.96   Forensic Science Northern Ireland (FSNI) is an executive agency sponsored by the Department of Justice in Northern Ireland and is situated in Carrickfergus.[267] It provides scientific advice and support to the police in the investigation of crime, to the office of the Police Ombudsman in its investigation of complaints against the police (see para 7.61), to the legal professions and the courts when they require scientific evidence, and to pathologists when they are investigating the causes of deaths. Its services are also available to those representing both defence and prosecution interests in criminal cases.

The Criminal Justice Inspectorate

7.97   The Justice (NI) Act 2002 provided for the creation of a Chief Inspector of Criminal Justice in Northern Ireland.[268] The Chief Inspector must inspect organisations such as the Police Service, the Forensic Science

---

[265] The IICD existed from 1992 to 2010 and was the outcome of an international treaty between the UK and Ireland. It was given power to operate a 'decommissioning scheme' under the Northern Ireland Arms Decommissioning Act 1997. The scheme identified an 'amnesty period' during which unlawfully held arms could be deposited or destroyed with impunity. No evidence of anything done, and no information obtained, in accordance with the decommissioning scheme was to be admissible in criminal proceedings. Most of the IRA's weapons were decommissioned by September 2005, the UVF's by June 2009, and the UDA's by February 2010. The IICD did not maintain a website, but some of its reports are available through the website of the Northern Ireland Office.

[266] www.independentmonitoringcommission.org. The IMC was established in 2004 through a treaty between the UK and Ireland and the Northern Ireland (Monitoring Commission etc.) Act 2003. It aimed to help establish a stable and inclusive devolved government in Northern Ireland by reporting on activities by paramilitary groups, on the normalisation of security measures, and on claims by Assembly parties that other parties, or individual Ministers, were not living up to the standards expected of them. By the time it ceased operating in 2011 it had issued 25 reports.

[267] www.fsni.gov.uk.

[268] s 45 and Sch. 7. See www.cjsni.gov.uk/index.cfm.

Agency, the State Pathologist's Department, the Public Prosecution Service, the Probation Board, the Prison Service,[269] the Youth Justice Agency, Health and Social Services Trusts,[270] and the Compensation Agency. However, in recognition that some existing bodies, such as HM's Inspectorate of Constabulary (see para 7.67), already carry out some inspections of these organisations, the Act goes on to say that the Chief Inspector must not carry out inspections if he or she is satisfied that the organisation is subject to adequate inspection by someone else.[271] It adds that before an inspection of the PSNI can take place the Chief Inspector must notify HM's Inspectorate of Constabulary which can, if it wishes, insist on being delegated the task of conducting the inspection.[272] Even if HM's Inspectorate does not so insist, the Chief Inspector of Criminal Justice must still obtain the approval of the Minister of Justice. HM Inspectorate acts as an advisory body to the Department of Justice in Northern Ireland regarding such matters as recruitment and equipment for the police.

7.98   The Chief Inspector must consult with the Minister of Justice and the Attorney General for Northern Ireland when preparing an inspection programme[273] and can also be required by the former to carry out an inspection or to review any matter relating to the criminal justice system in Northern Ireland.[274] But the Chief Inspector may not carry out inspections or reviews of individual cases.[275] The Chief Inspector must also prepare an annual report for the Minister of Justice.[276] The Inspectorate also now produces a periodic newsletter entitled *The Spec.*

7.99   The reports of the Inspectorate provide a wealth of information on the way the criminal justice system operates in Northern Ireland. A 2010 report analysed the problem of delay, which is much greater in Northern Ireland than in England and Wales.[277] The Inspectorate recommended that the quality and timeliness of the files the PSNI submits to the Public Prosecution Service (see para 8.34) should be of better quality and more timely, that the PPS and the Courts and Tribunals Service should have better case management systems, and that the Department of Justice should enhance its oversight in this field. The Chief Inspector also indicated that he

---

[269] In England and Wales there is a separate Inspectorate of Prisons. Its reports are very detailed and focus on whether the prisons are safe and healthy environments for prisoners and staff alike. The conditions in the prisons are measured against 'Expectations', which are based largely on international human rights standards.

[270] Only in so far as these Trusts provide secure accommodation for children who are the subject of custody care orders.

[271] Justice (NI) Act 2002, s 46(2).

[272] Ibid Sch 8, para 8.

[273] Ibid s 47(1).

[274] Ibid s 47(3) and (4).

[275] Ibid s 47(6).

[276] Ibid Sch 8, para 4.

[277] The report was entitled *Avoidable Delay.*

would report to the Minister of Justice on an annual basis on the progress being made by criminal justice agencies in reducing avoidable delay. In 2012 the Inspectorate produced influential reports on how the criminal justice system in Northern Ireland intervenes with young people at an early age and on how it deals with anti-social behaviour.[278]

The UK's National Preventive Mechanism

7.100   The Optional Protocol to the UN's Convention against Torture and other Cruel, Inhuman and Degrading Treatment or Punishment, which was adopted in 2002 and has been ratified by the UK, requires each ratifying State to put in place a National Preventive Mechanism to monitor the treatment of and conditions for detainees. In 2009 the UK Government announced that a total of 18 bodies would make up the UK's National Preventive Mechanism, the four in Northern Ireland being the Policing Board's Independent Custody Visiting Scheme (see para 7.60), the Independent Monitoring Boards (see para 7.82), the Criminal Justice Inspectorate (see para 7.97) and the Regulation and Quality Improvement Authority.[279] HM Inspectorate of Prisons in Great Britain coordinates the work of all the national mechanisms and communicates on their behalf to the Government.[280] In 2009 the Criminal Justice Inspectorate reported on the detention of persons in police custody in Northern Ireland as a contribution to the national mechanism.[281]

The Criminal Cases Review Commission[282]

7.101   The Criminal Cases Review Commission (CCRC) is a body established under the Criminal Appeal Act 1995, partly in response to a series of high-profile miscarriages of justice involving a number of people convicted by juries in England for crimes connected with the political affairs of Northern Ireland. The Commission is based in Birmingham and operates in relation to England, Wales and Northern Ireland. Scotland has its own separate Commission.[283]

---

[278] *Early Youth Interventions* and *Anti-Social Behaviour.*

[279] The RQIA was established in 2005 and part of its role is to inspect the provision of health and social care in places of detention, including prisons, secure accommodation centres for children, and centres where people are detained on the basis of their mental health or learning disability. It exercises functions previously exercised by (amongst others) the Mental Health Commission for Northern Ireland, which was abolished by the Health and Social Care (Reform) Act (NI) 2009, s 25.

[280] The first annual report was submitted in 2012 (covering the period 2010–11): Cm 8282.

[281] The report was entitled *Police Custody.*

[282] www.ccrc.gov.uk.

[283] www.sccrc.org.uk.

7.102   The CCRC's role is to conduct thorough reviews of convictions and sentences in suspected miscarriages of justice. If it considers that there is 'a real possibility' that a conviction or sentence would not be upheld by an appeal court (even though an unsuccessful appeal may have already taken place), it can refer the case to an appeal court. The Court of Appeal itself can also ask the CCRC to investigate and report to it on any matter and the Home Secretary can refer to the CCRC any matter concerning the possible exercise of the royal prerogative of mercy. For there to be a real possibility of an appeal against conviction succeeding there has to be an argument or evidence which was not raised during the trial or earlier appeal, or some other exceptional circumstances. The Commission usually elects to interview witnesses itself but it takes no further part in cases once they have been referred to an appeal court. A decision by the Commission not to refer a conviction to the Court of Appeal can be subjected to judicial review.[284]

7.103   The CCRC receives fewer applications, proportionately, from Northern Ireland than it does from England and Wales, but a greater proportion of those applications result in referrals to the Northern Ireland Court of Appeal. Figures show that more than 300 applications have been made to the CCRC by people in Northern Ireland since 1997 (just over 2 per cent of all those received), but that just over 7 per cent of these applications led to referrals to the Court of Appeal in Northern Ireland. About one in 14 of all the applications from Northern Ireland are referred, whereas the referral rate ratio for applications from England or Wales is one in 25.[285] One of the English cases involved Danny McNamee, convicted in 1987 of conspiracy to cause explosions relating to affairs in Northern Ireland, for which he received a 25-year prison sentence. His conviction was quashed in December 1997. In 2000 the conviction of Iain Hay Gordon for the 1952 murder in Northern Ireland of Patricia Curran, the daughter of a judge, was quashed after it had been referred to the Court of Appeal in Northern Ireland by the CCRC.[286] He had been found guilty but insane and had spent seven years in an asylum.

7.104   In recent years there has been a spate of cases referred by the CCRC to the Court of Appeal in Northern Ireland concerning convictions in the juryless Diplock courts in 1970s, 1980s, and 1990s. So far 29 of these have been determined by the Court of Appeal, and in as many as 26 the original convictions were quashed. In the most recent case, *R v Brown, Wright, McDonald and McCaul*,[287] the Court of Appeal quashed two of

---

[284] See eg *In re Torney's Application* [2003] NIQB 36.

[285] For more statistical details see the annual reports of the CCRC.

[286] See http://news.bbc.co.uk/1/hi/northern_ireland/1078576.stm. See too the cases of two juveniles convicted in 1980 of killing a police officer: *R v Gorman and McKinney* [2001] 8 BNIL 35.

[287] [2012] NICA 14. A further 28 applications to the CCRC were put on hold pending the outcome of this case: see *Annual Report of the CCRC for 2011–12*, p 13.

the convictions but upheld the other two. Appearing to depart from its previous practice, it ruled that, just because confessions had been made in circumstances that were not in conformity with the common law applicable at the time (because the juvenile suspects in question had not been given access to a solicitor or even to a parent), so long as they were in conformity with the statutory requirements as set out in the Northern Ireland (Emergency Provisions) Acts) the confessions would not be automatically treated as inadmissible evidence. If there was some other evidence to back up the confessions, they could be relied upon to convict the suspects.[288]

7.105 It must not be assumed, however, that every victim of a miscarriage of justice will receive compensation, even if he or she has spent years in prison as a result. A scheme was set up for the whole of the UK by the Criminal Justice Act 1988,[289] but compensation will not be paid if there has only been a new legal ruling on undisputed old facts rather than a finding that the judicial process has failed.[290] In a recent ruling the UK Supreme Court stated that '[a] new or newly discovered fact will show conclusively that a miscarriage of justice has occurred when it so undermines the evidence against the defendant that no conviction could possibly be based upon it'.[291] If there is an entitlement to compensation a specially appointed assessor will decide how much should be paid.[292]

7.106 In situations where the legal process is unable to resolve an apparent injustice, the Minister of Justice has a residual power under the royal prerogative of mercy. This is used, for example, when by mistake a prisoner has been released too early and it would be unjust to return him or her to custody, or where there is positive proof that a person could not possibly have been guilty of the crime in question and ought never to have been prosecuted for it. But it has not been applied in cases where, after the Belfast (Good Friday) Agreement 1998, people have been convicted of crimes committed prior to that date, because the Northern Ireland (Sentences) Act 1998 already provides that such people should serve a maximum of two years in prison.[293]

---

[288] For more information about such cases, see the Irish Centre for Wrongful Convictions: www.ic-wc.org.

[289] s 133.

[290] *In re Magee's Application* [2004] NIQB 57, which followed the quashing of the applicant's conviction: *R v Magee* [2001] 4 BNIL 15.

[291] *R (Adams) v Secretary of State for Justice* [2011] UKSC 18, [2012] 1 AC 48, at [55] (per Lord Phillips). Two appeals from the Court of Appeal in Northern Ireland were also considered in that case. See H Quirk and M Requa, 'The Supreme Court on compensation for miscarriages of justice: is it better that ten innocents are denied compensation than one guilty person receives it?' (2012) 75 *MLR* 387.

[292] See, eg, [2012] 10 BNIL 5.

[293] *McGeough v Secretary of State* [2012] NICA 28, [2012] 8 BNIL 41.

The Independent Commission for the Location of Victims' Remains[294]

7.107   In an attempt to deal with the vexed question of the 15 people who 'disappeared' during the troubles, the UK and Irish Governments created by statute an Independent Commission for the Location of Victims' Remains.[295] To encourage disclosures to the Commission, the legislation renders inadmissible in evidence in criminal proceedings any relevant information provided to the Commission and any information obtained directly or indirectly as a result of such information being so provided. To date, however, only eight bodies have been located. Republican paramilitaries have accepted responsibility for 11 of the 15 disappearances.

Access NI

7.108   In Northern Ireland an organisation called Access NI has been established to enable employers to make more informed recruitment decisions by providing them with information about the criminal history of people who are seeking work, whether paid or unpaid, with children or vulnerable adults.[296] The information is supplied through what is called the Disclosure and Barring Scheme.[297] In Great Britain the body responsible for monitoring that Scheme is now called the Disclosure and Barring Service,[298] an Agency of the Home Office based in Liverpool. There can be no disclosure of information without the consent of the person in question and he or she must be supplied with a copy of whatever is sent to the requesting body.[299] At the time of writing the Home Office is seeking to appeal to the Supreme Court against a decision of the Court of Appeal in England and Wales holding that certain aspects of the disclosure system is in violation of the right to a private life, guaranteed by Article 8 of the European Convention on Human Rights.[300]

---

[294] www.iclvr.ie/en/ICLVR/Pages/The%20Disappeared.
[295] Northern Ireland (Location of Victims' Remains) Act 1999 and, for Ireland, the Criminal Justice (Location of Victims' Remains) Act (Ir) 1999.
[296] www.accessni.gov.uk.
[297] See too S Mason, *Review of the Criminal Records Regime in Northern Ireland (Part One)* (2011) and *A Managed Approach (Part Two)* (2012).
[298] www.crb.gov.uk.
[299] Police Act 1997, Pt V (ss 112–127).
[300] *R (T) v Chief Constable of Greater Manchester* [2013] EWCA Civ 25.

8

Criminal Proceedings in Northern Ireland

INTRODUCTION

8.1 This chapter looks at the law relating to the way in which people who are suspected of involvement in crimes are processed through the criminal justice system in Northern Ireland.[1] It begins by explaining the crucial distinction between 'summary' offences and 'indictable' offences and continues by explaining how criminal proceedings are started in each case and, in particular, what rights are given to a person who has been arrested. It next describes the law on remand and bail before moving to consider the prosecution system, which again requires a distinction to be drawn between processes and outcomes in summary trials and those in trials on indictment (which are preceded by 'committal proceedings'). The chapter concludes with sections on the law relating to how children are dealt with by the criminal justice system and on the law of evidence in criminal cases.

SUMMARY AND INDICTABLE OFFENCES

8.2 Summary offences are relatively minor offences which have to be tried in a magistrates' court by a District Judge sitting without a jury. Proceedings usually have to be begun within six months of the offence having been committed.[2] A common example is careless and inconsiderate driving, which is an offence under article 12 of the Road Traffic (NI) Order 1995. Offences which must be tried on indictment are serious offences which have to be tried in the Crown Court by a judge and jury, although they are initially dealt with at committal proceedings in a magistrates' court. There is usually

---

[1] See too B Valentine, *Criminal Procedure in Northern Ireland* (Belfast, SLS Legal Publications, Belfast, 2nd edn, 2011); C White, *Northern Ireland Social Work Law* (Dublin, Tottel Publishing, 2004) ch 5.

[2] Magistrates' Courts (NI) Order 1981, art 18.

no time limit for the commencement of proceedings. Murder, manslaughter, rape and robbery are all offences in this category.

8.3   Owing to the terrorist threat in Northern Ireland, certain defendants can be tried on indictment in Crown Courts without a jury (see para 7.30). These trials occur whenever the Director of Public Prosecutions so certifies because one or more of a number of conditions has been satisfied, for example, that the offence in question was committed on behalf of a proscribed organisation.[3] This system is due to continue in place until at least the end of July 2013 but will probably be extended for a further two years.[4]

8.4   Some offences, called 'hybrid' offences, can be tried either summarily or on indictment. In Northern Ireland,[5] there is currently a choice of proceedings for three kinds of crime:

(1)   A handful of offences which are normally tried summarily can be tried on indictment if two conditions are satisfied:[6] (i) the offence must be one for which a person, if convicted, can be sent to prison for more than six months, and (ii) the defendant must have asked to be tried on indictment. An example of this type of hybrid offence is the improper importation of goods (ie smuggling), which is a crime under section 50(2) and (3) of the Customs and Excise Management Act 1979.

(2)   Some offences which are normally tried on indictment can be tried summarily if the District Judge (Magistrates' Court) who first hears the case at the committal stage considers that it is not a serious one and if the prosecution and defendant have no objections to a summary trial.[7] Examples of such offences are theft, indecent assault and assault occasioning actual bodily harm.[8] Also in this category are instances where a person under the age of 18 is charged with any indictable offence other than homicide.[9]

(3)   In many cases the statute which creates a crime expressly states that it can be tried summarily or on indictment. It is then up to the prosecution, bearing in mind the seriousness of the particular case, to decide which form of trial to use. An example of this kind of offence is dangerous driving, which is a crime under article 10 of the Road Traffic (NI) Order 1995.

---

[3] Justice and Security (NI) Act 2007, s 1(2)–(6).

[4] Justice and Security (NI) Act 2007 (Extension of duration of non-jury trial provisions) Order 2011 (SI 1720).

[5] The position in England and Wales is different.

[6] Magistrates' Courts (NI) Order 1981, art 28; see too the Magistrates' Courts Rules (NI) 1984 (SR 225), r 24.

[7] Ibid art 45 and r 45.

[8] These offences are listed in the Criminal Justice (NI) Order 1986, Sch 2, which replaced the Magistrates' Courts (NI) Order 1981, Sch 2.

[9] Criminal Justice (Children) (NI) Order 1998, art 17.

STARTING CRIMINAL PROCEEDINGS

8.5 Criminal proceedings are begun in one of three ways: by the issue of a summons, by the issue of a warrant of arrest, or by an arrest without a warrant. A sizeable proportion of persons appearing in court do so after having been originally arrested but then released and later summonsed. Being summonsed and being arrested are, however, quite distinct processes. Criminal proceedings cannot be started against a child under the age of 10.[10] This is the same age of criminal responsibility as in England and Wales. In Scotland and the Republic of Ireland it is 12.

8.6 If the police (or anyone else for that matter) believe that a person is guilty of a summary offence, or a not very serious indictable offence, they can give the details in a 'complaint' to a lay magistrate or to a clerk of petty sessions (see paras 4.23 and 4.27). If the lay magistrate or clerk of petty sessions is satisfied that there is sufficient evidence to suspect the person of having committed the offence, he or she will issue a summons by post giving details of the alleged offence and ordering the person to appear at a magistrates' court on a particular date to answer the complaint.[11]

8.7 In more serious cases, or where a District Judge is satisfied that a person suspected of a summary offence cannot for some reason be served with a summons, a warrant of arrest will be issued authorising the police to take a person into custody and then to a court to answer charges which may be brought.[12] Again, the District Judge must be satisfied that there is reasonable evidence to suspect a named person of a serious offence. The complaint to the District Judge must be in writing and substantiated on oath.[13] The details on the warrant must be completely accurate; if, for example, it gives the wrong home address for the person being arrested, it may be invalidated.[14] A clerk of petty sessions cannot issue a warrant.

8.8 A District Judge or higher judge also has the power to issue a warrant of arrest when a person who has been summonsed does not appear in court when ordered to do so.[15] This is known as a 'bench warrant'. If a warrant is issued in another part of the UK (eg Scotland) for the arrest of someone who is currently in Northern Ireland, the warrant can be 'executed' (ie the person can be arrested) in Northern Ireland only if it is 'backed' (ie endorsed) by a District Judge in Northern Ireland.[16]

---

[10] Ibid art 3: 'It shall be conclusively presumed that no child under the age of 10 can be guilty of an offence.'

[11] Magistrates' Courts (NI) Order 1981, art 20.

[12] Ibid art 20(5).

[13] Ibid art 20(7).

[14] *R v Leighton* [2002] NICC 10.

[15] Magistrates' Courts (NI) Order 1981, art 25(1).

[16] Petty Sessions (Ir) Act 1851, s 29.

Arrests without a warrant

8.9   The law on arrests is primarily set out in the Police and Criminal Evidence (NI) Order 1989 (the PACE Order), as amended by the Police and Criminal Evidence (Amendment) (NI) Order 2007. These make the law in Northern Ireland almost identical to that provided for England and Wales by the Police and Criminal Evidence Act 1984, as amended.[17] In both legal systems there are special arrest powers to deal with terrorist offences (see para 7.27). No person is under a legal obligation to accompany a police officer to a police station unless that person has been formally arrested (with or without a warrant). People who are simply 'helping the police with their inquiries' are present at the police station of their own free will and must be allowed to leave it if they want to.[18] By article 26 of the PACE Order a police officer may arrest without a warrant in the following circumstances:

- where a person is in the act of committing or is about to commit an offence;
- where the police officer has reasonable grounds for suspecting a person to be in the act of committing or to be about to commit an offence;
- where, provided that the police officer has reasonable grounds for suspecting that an offence has been committed, the officer has reasonable grounds for suspecting a person to be guilty of that offence; and
- where a person is guilty of having committed an offence which has actually been committed or is someone whom the police officer has reasonable grounds for suspecting to be guilty of that offence.

8.10   Prior to the PACE (Amendment) (NI) Order of 2007 these arrest powers could be used only in relation to 'arrestable offences', a category which comprised offences for which a person aged 21 or over could be sentenced to at least five years' imprisonment and some other specified offences. The position today is that the arrest powers 'are to have effect in relation to any offence whenever committed',[19] but the arresting police officer must have reasonable grounds for believing that it is necessary to arrest the person in question for any of the following reasons:

- to enable the name or address of the person to be ascertained;
- to prevent the person causing physical injury to him- or herself or any other person, suffering physical injury, causing loss of or damage to property, committing an offence against public decency, or causing an unlawful obstruction on a road;

---

[17] The law in Scotland is different.
[18] PACE (NI) Order 1989, art 31.
[19] PACE (NI) Order 1989, art 26A(3).

- to protect a child or other vulnerable person from the person;
- to allow the prompt and effective investigation of the offence or of the conduct of the person; or
- to prevent any prosecution for the offence from being hindered by the person's disappearance.[20]

8.11 There are two other types of situation in which a person can be arrested. One is when a police officer has reasonable grounds for believing that a breach of the peace is being committed or is about to be committed, with 'breach of the peace' meaning that harm is likely to be done to any person or a person's property in his or her presence. The other situation is where the police exercise one of their powers of arrest which are preserved by Schedule 2 to the PACE Order 1989. These include the power to arrest for illegal immigration, impersonation at a polling booth, escaping from custody or being absent without leave from a place of secure accommodation (see para 8.93).

8.12 The police may use reasonable force to effect an arrest.[21] The use of excessive force will make the arrest unlawful and, although not necessarily requiring the arrested person's immediate release, will justify a claim for compensation for assault (see para 9.78).

8.13 As far as the powers of private citizens to make arrests are concerned, article 26A of the PACE Order makes it clear that they are in two respects more limited than those of the police: (i) only if an offence has *in fact* been committed can a person arrest someone who is reasonably suspected of being guilty of that offence, and (ii) a person has no power to arrest someone who is reasonably suspected of being *about to* commit an offence. But before a private citizen can carry out an arrest he or she must have reasonable grounds for believing that it is not reasonably practicable for a police officer to make the arrest instead and that the arrest is necessary to prevent the person causing physical injury to him- or herself or any other person, suffering physical injury, causing loss of or damage to property, or making off before a police officer can assume responsibility for him or her.

Police powers to stop, question and search

8.14 In general the police have no power to stop anyone unless they arrest that person. Likewise, they can put questions to people but people do not have to answer those questions. And the police can search someone only if they have reasonable suspicion that the person is carrying a prohibited article. But

---

[20] Ibid art 26(4) and (5).
[21] Ibid art 88.

in Northern Ireland there is a special 'stop and question' power.[22] It permits a police officer to stop a person, even if in a vehicle, for so long as is necessary to question that person about his or her identity, movements, and what he or she knows about a recent explosion, about any other recent incident endangering life, or about a person who has been killed or injured in a recent explosion or incident. Failure to answer such questions to the best of one's knowledge and ability can give rise to a fine of up to £5,000. In the Terrorism Act 2000 there are also special search police powers throughout the UK to allow searches to be conducted of premises[23] (and in Northern Ireland there are additional powers to search for munitions and transmitters[24]). Moreover the 2000 Act allows a police officer to stop and search anyone whom he or she reasonably suspects to be a terrorist in order to discover whether they are in possession of anything which may constitute evidence that they are a terrorist, and any such thing that is found may be seized.[25]

8.15 Sections 44 to 47 of the Terrorism Act 2000 Act allowed the police in certain circumstances to stop and search persons even if there was no suspicion that they were in possession of prohibited articles. This power was used extensively in London and in Northern Ireland. When it was challenged in a case that went to the House of Lords, the judges unanimously upheld its compatibility with the European Convention on Human Rights,[26] but the European Court of Human Rights then ruled in the same case that the power to authorise and confirm the use of the powers, as well as the stop and search powers themselves, were neither sufficiently circumscribed nor subject to adequate legal safeguards against abuse. They were not, therefore, 'in accordance with the law' and so violated Article 8 of the European Convention.[27] In response the UK Government issued a 'remedial order' which temporarily replaced sections 44 to 47[28] until they could be permanently replaced by provisions in the Protection of Freedoms Act 2012.[29] The main change made by the Act, which applies throughout the UK, is that stops and searches can now be authorised only if a senior police officer reasonably suspects that an act of terrorism will take place and considers that the powers are necessary to prevent such an act. Another section of the Act limits the police's power to stop and search persons in

---

[22] Justice and Security (NI) Act 2007, s 21. A draft Code of Practice for this and other powers conferred by ss 21–28 of the 2007 Act has been circulated by the Northern Ireland Office for comment and should be in effect later in 2013.

[23] s 42.

[24] Justice and Security (NI) Act 2007, s 24. See too n 22 above. In *In re Canning's Application* [2012] NIQB 49, [2012] BNIL 59 Treacy J found that ss 21 and 24 of the 2007 Act were not per se incompatible with the European Convention on Human Rights.

[25] s 43.

[26] *R (Gillan) v Commissioner of Police for the Metropolis* [2006] UKHL 12, [2006] 2 AC 307.

[27] *Gillan and Quinton v UK* (2010) 50 EHRR 45, para 87.

[28] Terrorism Act 2000 (Remedial) Order 2011 (SI 631).

[29] ss 59–62.

Northern Ireland in order to search for munitions and transmitters to situations where the police have reasonable suspicions that they might find such items.[30] But it also allows a senior officer to authorise the use of these powers without reasonable suspicion if he or she reasonably suspects that the safety of any person might be endangered by the use of munitions or wireless apparatus.

THE RIGHTS OF ARRESTED PERSONS

8.16 Persons who have been arrested have the right to consult a range of statutory codes of practice. Codes have been issued to regulate their detention, treatment, questioning and identification.[31] There are separate codes for persons suspected of terrorist crimes and for the work of 'examining officers' (eg at ports) and 'authorised officers' (eg when investigating financial matters). Arrested persons must also be told at the time of their arrest why they are being arrested[32] and they must be released from custody as soon as it becomes apparent to the police that grounds for detaining them no longer exist.[33]

8.17 If it appears to the police that it may be necessary to keep an arrested person in police detention for more than six hours, the person must be taken to a 'designated' police station in Northern Ireland. Detention without charge is permissible for 24 hours but this can be extended to 36 hours if a police superintendent authorises it and if the offence in question is a serious one.[34] Detention beyond 36 hours is permissible only on the authority of a magistrates' court;[35] it can be extended by that court to 72 hours, and then again to 96 hours,[36] but that is the absolute maximum. If an ordinary citizen arrests someone the citizen can detain that person only if a breach of the peace would otherwise be likely. The person should be taken to a police station as soon as possible, otherwise the arresting citizen may be committing the tort of 'false imprisonment' and could be sued for compensation.

8.18 In Northern Ireland people arrested under the Terrorism Act are not detained in an ordinary police station but in a special 'serious crime suite' at Antrim police station, where there is space for ten detainees at any one time. They may be initially detained for 48 hours[37] (not just for 36 hours

---

[30] Ibid s 63 and Sch 6.
[31] Terrorism Act 2000, s 98.
[32] PACE (NI) Order 1989, art 30(3).
[33] Ibid art 35(2).
[34] Ibid arts 42–43. In cases where a person attends a court to answer existing charges, he or she can be remanded by the court so that the police can ask them questions about other offences, and then the 36-hour time limit does not apply: *Re Grindy and McCallum* [2011] NIQB 108, [2012] 1 BNIL 18 (Div Ct).
[35] Ibid art 44.
[36] Ibid art 45.
[37] Terrorism Act 2000, s 41(3).

as in other cases), but the police can apply to a court for permission to extend the detention by periods amounting to 12 days ('warrants of further detention'), making 14 days in all.[38] However the UK Government has drafted a Detention of Terrorist Suspects (Temporary Extension) Bill should the need for longer detentions recur, and it has retained the power to extend the maximum detention period up to 28 days if an emergency arises during a time between elections when Parliament is dissolved.[39] There is nothing in the European Convention on Human Rights to prevent such lengthy pre-charge detention periods, provided there are reasonable suspicions against the accused and the matter is being investigated expeditiously.[40]

The treatment of people who have been detained

8.19   Arrested persons must be allowed access to a solicitor, but in certain circumstances access can be delayed for up to 36 hours[41] (or 48 hours if the person is a suspected terrorist),[42] and no compensation is payable if the police wrongly deny access to a solicitor.[43] The grounds upon which access may be delayed are more numerous in terrorist cases too.[44] Arrested persons also have the right to have a friend or relative informed of their arrest.[45] The exercise of this right can also be delayed on the authority of a police superintendent and the same variations exist in relation to terrorist suspects as in cases of access to a solicitor.[46] In both terrorist and non-terrorist cases it is now accepted that arrested persons have the right to have their solicitor present whenever they are being questioned by the police.

8.20   The general rule is that no-one is legally obliged to volunteer information or to answer questions put by the police. But this right to silence is qualified in that prosecutors, judges and juries are permitted to draw inferences about guilt from an accused's silence in the face of questioning if the accused fails to mention a material fact which he or she later wishes to rely upon in his or her defence.[47] However, in all cases an accused cannot

---

[38] Ibid Sch 8, Pt III. The original maximum of 7 days' detention was doubled by an amendment made to the 2000 Act by the Criminal Justice Act 2003, s 306. It was increased again to 28 days by the Terrorism Act 2006 s 23(7) before being reduced to 14 days by the coalition Government in 2010. See now the Protection of Freedoms Act 2012, s 57.

[39] Protection of Freedoms Act 2012, s 58.

[40] B Dickson, 'Article 5 of the ECHR and 28-day pre-charge detention of terrorist suspects' (2009) 60 *NILQ* 231 and *In re Duffy (Colin) (No 2)* [2011] NIQB 16, [2011] 4 BNIL 10 (Div Ct).

[41] PACE (NI) Order 1989, art 58.

[42] Terrorism Act 2000, s 41(3) and Sch 8, paras 7 and 8. See, eg, *R v Chief Constable of the RUC, ex parte Begley and McWilliams* [1997] 1 WLR 1475.

[43] *Cullen v Chief Constable of the RUC* [2003] UKHL 39, [2003] 1 WLR 1763.

[44] Terrorism Act 2000, Sch 8, para 8(4).

[45] PACE (NI) Order 1989, art 57.

[46] Terrorism Act 2000, Sch 8, paras 6 and 8.

[47] Criminal Evidence (NI) Order 1988, art 3.

be committed for trial, be found to have a case to answer during a trial, or be convicted, solely on the basis of such inferences and inferences cannot be drawn at all if the accused has not first had the opportunity to be advised by a solicitor.[48] It should be noted as well that it is a criminal offence in Northern Ireland (but not in England and Wales) to fail to give information about an offence committed by some other person, although prosecutions for this offence are extremely rare.[49]

Cautions

8.21 Under a PACE Order Code[50] the police are required to caution a person being questioned in the following terms:

> You do not have to say anything, but I must caution you that if you do not mention when questioned something which you later rely on in court, it may harm your defence. If you do say anything it may be given in evidence.

A breach of a PACE Code does not of itself render a police officer liable to criminal or civil proceedings,[51] but if a complaint is lodged against the officer it may render him or her liable to disciplinary proceedings. Evidence obtained as a result of a breach of a Code will not automatically be declared inadmissible in later court proceedings brought against the detained person.[52]

Recording of interviews

8.22 Police interviews with PACE detainees are required to be audio-recorded.[53] There is no statutory requirement to video-record police interviews with PACE detainees but it does sometimes occur and a Code of Practice stipulates how video-recording should proceed if it does occur.[54] Police interviews with persons arrested in Northern Ireland under the anti-terrorist laws are always recorded in both ways and Codes of Practice on how the recordings are to take place have also been issued. Fingerprints can

---

[48] Criminal Evidence (NI) Order 1999, art 36. The equivalent provision in English law is the Youth Justice and Criminal Evidence Act 1999, s 58.

[49] Criminal Law Act (NI) 1967, s 5(1).

[50] Code C of the revised *Police and Criminal Evidence (NI) Order 1989 (Articles 60 and 65) Codes of Practice*, 2012, para 10.5.

[51] PACE (NI) Order 1989, art 66.

[52] See, eg, *R v Cross* [1997] 5 BNIL 18.

[53] Code E of the revised *Police and Criminal Evidence (NI) Order 1989 (Articles 60 and 65) Codes of Practice*, 2012 ('The tape-recording of interviews by police officers at police stations with suspected persons').

[54] Code F (2012). The latest versions of PACE Codes C, E, F and H are available on the Department of Justice's website.

be taken without the consent of the detained person if a police officer of at least the rank of superintendent gives written authorisation for them to be taken.[55] If the detained person ceases to be a suspect his or her fingerprints must be destroyed 'as soon as they have fulfilled the purpose for which they were taken'.[56] Following a decision by the European Court of Human Rights in *S and Marper v UK*[57] (see para 6.46), the Minister of Justice in Northern Ireland issued a consultation paper on how the law should be reformed[58] and provisions were later included in the Criminal Justice Act (NI) 2013.[59]

Searches and samples

8.23   The PACE Order regulates in detail the searching of detained persons and distinguishes between intimate and non-intimate body searches. Intimate searches are physical examinations of body orifices (except the mouth[60]). They can be carried out without consent only if there are grounds for believing that the person may have a concealed weapon or drug. The PACE Order, as amended,[61] also distinguishes between the taking of intimate and non-intimate body samples. The former can be taken only with the person's consent; they include blood and urine samples and dental impressions. Non-intimate samples, such as hairs from the head, saliva or footprints, do not require the person's consent. The police can also take an intimate sample (with consent) from a person who is *not* in police detention but from whom, in the course of an investigation, two or more non-intimate samples have been taken but have proved insufficient.[62] A non-intimate sample may likewise be taken from a person not in police detention without his or her consent if the person has already been convicted of, charged with, or informed that he or she will be reported for a recordable offence.[63] Special rules apply to persons suspected of road traffic offences.[64] As with fingerprints (see para 8.22), the Criminal Justice Act (NI) 2013 sets out new rules to govern the length of time DNA samples can be retained by the police.

---

[55] PACE (NI) Order 1989, art 61, as amended by the Criminal Justice (NI) Order 2004.

[56] Ibid art 61(3); but for a significant qualification to this rule see art 64(3AA), inserted by the Criminal Justice and Police Act 2001, s 83(4).

[57] (2009) 48 EHRR 50.

[58] *Consultation on Proposals for the Retention and Destruction of Fingerprints and DNA in Northern Ireland* (2011).

[59] S 9 and Sch 3. For the changes made to the law in England and Wales, see the Protection of Freedoms Act 2012, ss 1–25.

[60] Police (Amendment) (NI) Order 1995, art 5.

[61] By ibid art 8 and the Criminal Justice (NI) Order 2004.

[62] Ibid art 10.

[63] PACE (NI) Order 1989, art 63(3A), inserted by the Police (Amendment) (NI) Order 1995, art 11(2).

[64] Ibid art 62(11), as amended.

Overholding

8.24 A person who has been arrested unlawfully, or unlawfully treated while in detention, can bring a civil action for compensation against the police. The police will be liable for the civil wrongs (ie 'torts') of false imprisonment and/or assault (see para 9.78). The Court of Appeal in Northern Ireland has stated that the starting point for compensation in a straightforward case of false imprisonment is about £600 for the first hour of deprivation of liberty, while a period of 24 hours would normally attract an award of some £4,000 to £5,000.[65] However the wrongful police behaviour is not of itself a defence to a criminal charge brought against the victim of that behaviour: the person arrested can still be found guilty of an offence.

Charges

8.25 When the police officer in charge of the police station believes that there is enough evidence to show that the suspected person has committed an offence, the officer should either charge that person or tell him or her that he or she may later be prosecuted for that offence (eg by the issue of a summons). At that time the accused should again be cautioned in the following terms:

> You are charged with the offences(s) shown below. You do not have to say anything, but I must caution you that if you do not mention when questioned something which you later rely on in court, it may harm your defence. If you do say anything it may be given in evidence.[66]

Questions relating to an offence should not be put to a person after he or she has been charged with committing it, unless the questions are necessary to prevent harm to some other person or to clear up an ambiguity in a previous answer, or new information has come to light since the person was charged and it is in the interests of justice that he or she should be given an opportunity to comment upon it.[67] If the police decide not to charge a suspect he or she can instead be formally cautioned by a senior police officer and will not then have to appear in court. Such a caution will usually be administered only if the suspect has admitted guilt, and it is officially recorded. Cautioning is especially common in relation to juvenile offenders. If the police decide not to charge or formally caution the suspect, he or she should be released.

---

[65] *Dodds v Chief Constable of the RUC* [1998] NI 393.
[66] Code C of the revised *Police and Criminal Evidence (NI) Order 1989 (Articles 60 and 65) Code of Practice* (1996), para 16.3A.
[67] Ibid para 16.6.

BAIL AND REMAND[68]

8.26 Usually a person arrested with a warrant is held in custody pending a first appearance in court, but when issuing the warrant the District Judge may authorise the police to release the accused on bail once he or she has been arrested.[69] This means releasing the accused in exchange for a promise to return to the police station, or to attend at a magistrates' court, on a certain day. This promise, or the money which may have to be 'estreated' (ie forfeited) if the promise is broken, is called a 'recognisance'.[70] Since 2007, bail can also be granted by a District Judge in a terrorist case, except that, during the pre-charge detention period, which may last for up to 14 days (see para 7.33), no bail is possible. Police officers can also grant bail to persons following their arrest without the need to take them first to a police station (this is known as 'street bail').[71]

Police bail

8.27 Persons arrested with or without a warrant (except terrorist suspects) may also be released on what is called 'police bail', with or without a recognisance.[72] This can be granted subject to conditions, such as that the person bailed will allow the police to search his home without a warrant if they reasonably suspect that there are illegal drugs on the premises.[73] The custody officer at the station to which the arrested person is brought must release any person who has been charged unless, where the person is an adult, one of four conditions is met:

(1) his or her name or address cannot be ascertained;
(2) in the case of a person arrested for an imprisonable offence, there are reasonable grounds for believing that detention of the person is necessary to prevent him or her from committing an offence;
(3) there are reasonable grounds for believing that continued detention is necessary for the detainee's own protection or to prevent him or her from causing injury or damage to any person or property;

---

[68] In 2010 the Northern Ireland Law Commission (see para 3.67) issued a consultation paper on bail in criminal proceedings (NILC 7).

[69] Magistrates' Courts (NI) Order 1981, art 129, as amended by the PACE (NI) Order 1989, art 48(12).

[70] See the Magistrates' Courts (NI) Order 1981, arts 135–139, and the Magistrates' Court Rules (NI) 1984 (SR 225), rr 150–153. On this and other topics dealt with in this chapter, see M Allen and F McAleenan, *Sentencing Law and Practice in Northern Ireland* (Belfast, SLS Legal Publications, 3rd edn, 1998, with Supplement 2003). For a case on estreat of a recognisance, see *In re Maughan* [2010] NIQB 16, [2011] 6 BNIL 19.

[71] Criminal Justice (NI) Order 2004.

[72] PACE (NI) Order 1989, art 48.

[73] *In re McRandal's Application (Leave Stage)* [2012] NICA 22, [2012] 8 BNIL 12.

(4)   there are reasonable grounds for believing that the detainee will fail to appear in court or to answer bail, or will interfere with the administration of justice or with the investigation of any offence.[74]

Where a juvenile is concerned, continued detention can also be justified if the custody officer has reasonable grounds for believing that the juvenile ought to be detained in his or her own interests.

Remands

8.28   In summary proceedings, when a person who has been charged eventually appears in a magistrates' court, the prosecution or the defence may still not have fully prepared its case and the District Judge will then be asked to 'adjourn' (ie postpone) the hearing. In such circumstances the District Judge also has to decide whether to release or to 'remand' the accused, and, if the latter, whether to remand him or her in custody or on bail. In practice the views of the police are highly influential on these points. The factors which are meant to be taken into account include the character of the accused, the nature of the alleged offence and the strength of the evidence against the accused. Having considered such factors, the court should grant bail unless it is satisfied that the accused will not turn up again at court, will commit another offence or will try to obstruct the course of justice by, for instance, putting pressure on witnesses.[75]

8.29   Remands in custody cannot normally be for more than eight clear days, but they can be for 28 days in a case where the accused is already serving a prison sentence or is detained in a young offenders centre or juvenile justice centre.[76] Before the end of each period of remand the defendant must again be brought before a court; he or she can then reapply for bail but this will usually be refused unless there has been a significant change of circumstances.

8.30   If bail is refused in a magistrates' court, a further application can be made later, relying upon changed circumstances.[77] It is also possible for the defendant to exercise a common law right to apply to a judge of the High Court for bail, or for a variation to the condition on which bail has been granted,[78] but there will be great reluctance to overturn a District Judge's previous refusal. If the District Judge has awarded bail but at such a sum or on such conditions as to make it impossible for the defendant to accept

[74] Ibid art 39, as amended by the Police (Amendment) (NI) Order 1995, art 6.
[75] Magistrates' Courts (NI) Order 1981, art 133.
[76] Ibid art 47(2), as amended by the Criminal Justice (Children) (NI) Order 1998, Sch 5, para 18.
[77] See, eg, *Re Donaldson* [2002] NIQB 68.
[78] *In re McHugh's Application (Applicant for Bail)* [2011] NIQB 90, [2011] 9 BNIL 17.

release on those terms, the defendant can apply to the High Court to have the sum or conditions altered: excessive bail was made unlawful by the Bill of Rights 1688. In such circumstances the defendant can also apply for a writ of *habeas corpus*, which can lead to a declaration by the Divisional Court (a court within the High Court's Queen's Bench Division – see para 4.7) that the continued detention of the accused is unlawful.[79] Rather oddly, all applications to the High Court for bail or *habeas corpus* are considered to be civil, not criminal, proceedings. They therefore qualify for civil, not criminal, legal aid.[80] The prosecution also has the right to appeal to the High Court against the grant of bail by a magistrates' court.[81] In such instances the prosecution must give oral notice of the appeal at the conclusion of the magistrates' court proceedings and the court must then remand the person in custody until the appeal is determined.[82]

8.31   Where the accused is charged with an indictable offence, the Crown Court may admit to bail any person who has been committed for trial or who is in the custody of the Crown Court pending the disposal of his or her case.[83] There can be no appeal by either side against the decision of a Crown Court to grant or not grant bail. A person who has already been convicted can, however, apply for bail to the court which is hearing an appeal in the case.

8.32   The Criminal Justice (NI) Order 2003 empowers the Minister of Justice to set time limits for the completion of the preliminary stages of criminal proceedings or a maximum period during which an accused person may be held in custody while awaiting completion of those stages. Two reports by the Criminal Justice Inspectorate have been very critical of the delays in the current system.[84] In 2012 the Minister of Justice announced that before 2015 he would be introducing statutory time limits for courts dealing with crimes allegedly committed by young people. Statutory time limits are already in place in other parts of the UK.[85]

8.33   Once a person has been charged or summonsed for an offence the process of prosecution has begun. If at any stage it becomes clear that it is not going to be possible to prove the accused's guilt beyond reasonable doubt the charge should be dropped or ordered by a court to be withdrawn.

---

[79] See Rules of the Court of Judicature (NI) 1980 (SR 346), Order 54. '*Habeas corpus*' is Latin for 'have the body'.

[80] These legal aid schemes are explained in ch 11.

[81] Justice (NI) Act 2004, s 10.

[82] Magistrates' Courts (Amendment No 3) Rules (NI) 2004 (SR 433).

[83] Judicature (NI) Act 1978, s 51(4)–(8).

[84] *Avoidable Delay* (2010) and *Avoidable Delay – A Progress Report* (2012).

[85] In Scotland, for example, defendants generally have to be tried no later than 110 days after being committed for trial: see the Criminal Procedure (Scotland) Act 1995, s 65, as amended by the Criminal Procedure (Amendment)(Scotland) Act 2004, s 6. For the position in England and Wales, see the Criminal Procedure Rules 2012 (SI 1726).

THE PROSECUTION SYSTEM[86]

8.34   The Office of the Director of Public Prosecutions (DPP) was first created in Northern Ireland in 1972,[87] but it has recently been replaced by the Public Prosecution Service (PPS),[88] which was formally launched in 2005. The PPS is headed by the DPP, who is appointed by the Attorney General for Northern Ireland (after consultations with the Advocate General for Northern Ireland)[89] and must be a barrister or solicitor who has practised in Northern Ireland for at least 10 years.[90] The DPP must exercise his or her functions independently of any other person but may consult with the Attorney General and the Advocate General on any matter for which they are accountable to the Northern Ireland Assembly or the UK Parliament respectively (see paras 11.2–11.5).[91] The Attorney General may remove the DPP from office if a tribunal of inquiry reports that the DPP has misbehaved or is unable to perform the functions of the office.[92] An Annual Report is produced on the work of the PPS.[93] The latest annual report shows that in 2011–12 the PPS received 53,308 cases, with prosecutorial decisions being taken against 63,628 individuals. Complaints against the PPS can be reviewed by an Independent Assessor of Complaints.

8.35   In many instances, the consent of the DPP is required before prosecutions can officially be begun, and the Director can step in to take over any prosecutions that have not been instituted by the PPS.[94] In addition to actually conducting prosecutions, the DPP can require the police to investigate incidents which appear to involve an offence, or to further investigate matters already referred to the DPP.[95] If someone knows of evidence relating to an alleged crime, he or she is at liberty to make it known directly to the PPS rather than to the police. And if it appears to a coroner after an inquest that a criminal offence may have been committed, the coroner must submit a written report on the case for consideration by the DPP.[96]

---

[86] www.ppsni.gov.uk.

[87] By the Prosecution of Offences (NI) Order 1972.

[88] Justice (NI) Act 2002, s 29. The aim was to bring the office more into line with the Crown Prosecution Service in England and Wales, which was created by the Prosecution of Offences Act 1985. There is also HM Inspectorate of the Crown Prosecution Service in England and Wales, but this has no jurisdiction in Northern Ireland. Inspections of the PPS in Northern Ireland are conducted by the Criminal Justice Inspectorate (see para 7.97).

[89] Ibid ss 30(1) and 43(1).

[90] Ibid s 30(2).

[91] Ibid s 42(1), (3) and (4).

[92] Ibid s 43(2).

[93] Ibid s 38.

[94] Ibid s 31(1) and (4).

[95] This is not a power which the DPP has in England and Wales.

[96] Justice (NI) Act 2002, s 35(3), replacing the Prosecution of Offences (NI) Order 1972, art 6(2).

8.36   Once the police have completed their investigations, their file on the case will be passed to the PPS for a decision as to whether the accused should be prosecuted and, if so, for what. The PPS has staff working in four regions: Belfast, Eastern, Northern and Western, and Southern.[97] It employs its own barristers, who prosecute most of the cases in magistrates' courts and youth courts (including appeals in county courts), but for cases in the Crown Court, High Court and Court of Appeal it retains the services of senior self-employed barristers and then functions as their instructing solicitor. From time to time such barristers are invited to apply to be members of the senior or junior 'panel' of prosecuting advocates.

The Code for Prosecutors

8.37   The PPS has issued a Code for Prosecutors, laying down standards of conduct and guidance on general principles to be applied when determining whether criminal proceedings should be instituted.[98] The two tests to be applied are whether there is more than a 50–50 chance of proving the case beyond reasonable doubt and whether a prosecution would be in the public interest. If the PPS decides that no prosecution is justified, the charges must then be dropped, but if it decides that a prosecution is justified it will direct which charges are to be pressed and whether the trial is to be summary or on indictment (see paras 8.2–8.4). In cases involving possible intimidation of jurors the DPP will decide whether to 'certify' the case as one requiring trial by judge alone, without a jury (see para 7.30). Because of the need to ensure the independence of the PPS, decisions taken in relation to prosecutions are very rarely capable of being judicially reviewed.[99] But the PPS's Code states that in exceptional cases an expectation will arise 'that a reasonable explanation will be given for not prosecuting where death is, or may have been, occasioned by the conduct of agents of the State'.[100] The Code goes on to stress, however, that everything will turn on the particular facts and circumstances of each individual case, bearing in mind the need to protect the human rights of accused persons. In a report published in 2012 the Criminal Justice Inspectorate concluded that the PPS needed to make greater progress towards a more full and open engagement with all victims and urged it to develop further policies and procedures regarding the giving of reasons to victims for prosecution decisions.[101]

---

[97] It has six offices (or 'Chambers') in Ballymena, Belfast, Derry/Londonderry, Lisburn, Newry and Omagh.

[98] Justice (NI) Act 2002, s 37.

[99] *R v DPP, ex parte Adams* [2001] NI 1; *In re Thompson's Application* [2004] NIQB 62; *In re Boyle's Application* [2004] NIQB 63.

[100] Para 4.12.4 (2008).

[101] *Telling Them Why* (2012).

Disclosure requirements

8.38 During all criminal investigations, a disclosure officer examines material retained by the police and is responsible for revealing material to the prosecutor and disclosing material to the accused at the request of the prosecutor.[102] In order to ensure that the accused is treated fairly, the prosecutor must disclose to the accused (unless the court orders that it is not in the public interest to do so) any material, which in the prosecutor's opinion, might undermine the case for the prosecution.[103] The accused, if charged with an indictable offence, *must* give a defence statement to the court and the prosecutor. In summary proceedings, however, the accused is not required to give a defence statement, but may do so voluntarily..

Plea bargaining

8.39 In theory there is not meant to be any bargaining between the prosecution and the defence as to the offences, if any, to which the accused should plead guilty. In practice, however, it is acknowledged that such 'plea bargaining' does occur (as it does quite openly in the United States), but the rule is maintained that a trial judge must not indicate to the accused, or to a lawyer acting for the accused, the severity of the sentence which he or she intends to impose.[104] That said, a guilty plea will often lead to a sentence discount.[105]

8.40 During the troubles in Northern Ireland there were several attempts to try members of paramilitary organisations on the evidence of 'supergrasses', ie accomplices who, in return for lenient treatment from the state, provided evidence against their former colleagues.[106] This practice was eventually terminated because the Court of Appeal allowed many of the resulting appeals against conviction. Today it is possible to use accomplice evidence by treating the informer as an 'assisted offender' under the Serious Organised Crime and Police Act 2005.[107] This requires the informer to be tried, convicted and sentenced before the trial of anyone against whom he or she supplies evidence takes place. In the one instance where this has so

---

[102] *Criminal Procedure and Investigations Act 1996, s 23(1) Code of Practice*, Belfast, Northern Ireland Office, p 2.

[103] Criminal Procedure and Investigations Act 1996, s 3. For a case from Northern Ireland which was taken to the European Court of Human Rights on this point (unsuccessfully), see *McKeown v UK* App No 6684/05, judgment of 11 January 2011, [2011] BNIL 22. See too *R v Holden (Disclosure)* [2011] NICA 35, [2011] 7 BNIL 21.

[104] *Code of Conduct for the Bar of Northern Ireland*, ss 16.24 and 16.26.

[105] Criminal Justice (NI) Order 1996, art 33.

[106] See S Greer, *Supergrasses: A Study in Anti-Terrorist Law Enforcement in Northern Ireland* (Clarendon Press, Oxford, 1995).

[107] ss 71–75. See www.cps.gov.uk/legal/s_to_u/socpa_agreements_-_practical_note_for_defence _advocates.

far occurred in Northern Ireland, involving the trial of several alleged UVF paramilitaries based on the evidence of Robert and Ian Stewart, all but one of the defendants were acquitted of all the charges against them.[108] The judge did not, however, criticise the Public Prosecution Service for bringing the prosecution in the first place.

Private and agency prosecutions

8.41   In addition to 'public' prosecutions by the PPS, it is theoretically possible for any individual to bring a 'private' prosecution. But legal aid is not available for that procedure and it is believed that to date only one such prosecution has ever reached the Crown Court in Northern Ireland (where it failed). In Great Britain, however, there have been successful private prosecutions for manslaughter and rape. The DPP has the power to take over or abort a private prosecution if he or she thinks fit to do so at any stage of the proceedings, and any prosecution, whether public or private, can be brought to an end by the DPP entering what is called a *nolle prosequi* (a document of 'unwillingness to proceed'). This does not operate as a formal acquittal, so in theory the accused could be prosecuted later for the same offence.

8.42   Many official bodies employ staff to detect and investigate offences. When they think that they have sufficient evidence against a suspect they pass the case to the police or the PPS. This happens, for instance, in the so-called 'departmental' prosecutions, such as those instigated by the Social Security Agency in relation to false claims for social security benefits, the Driver and Vehicle Agency, TV Licensing, Land and Property Services, and Translink. It can be just as difficult to challenge the decision of one of these bodies not to prosecute someone as it can be to challenge such a decision by the Director of Public Prosecutions.[109]

SUMMARY TRIALS

8.43   Magistrates' courts deal with criminal cases in two different ways: they try persons accused of summary offences or indictable offences being dealt with summarily, and they undertake an initial examination of the case against persons accused of offences being tried on indictment. This latter

---

[108] *R v Haddock* [2012] NICC 5, [2012] 2 BNIL 33 (Gillen J). See too www.bbc.co.uk/news/uk-northern-ireland-17049262. On account of their willingness to testify against others, the Stewart brothers were given a tariff of just 3 years, rather than 22 years, for their part in murder.

[109] See, eg, *In re D's Application* [2003] NICA 14, where a man failed to get the Department for Regional Development to prosecute a Loyal Orange Lodge for allegedly erecting an Orange arch unlawfully.

sort of hearing is called a 'committal proceeding' because its object is to decide whether the defendant should be 'committed' (ie sent) for trial on indictment in the Crown Court (see para 8.62). The vast majority (around 98 per cent) of all criminal offences dealt with in Northern Ireland are tried summarily in magistrates' courts, more than half of the charges being motoring offences. Summary trial is quicker, less expensive and subject to less publicity. Furthermore, if the defendant pleads guilty or is convicted, the sentence which the magistrates' court will impose is likely to be much less severe than the sentence which would be imposed by the Crown Court.

8.44   In all criminal trials in Northern Ireland the proceedings are 'adversarial' in nature. This means that each side is engaged in a battle against the other, with the judge acting as a neutral umpire. The purpose is not necessarily to arrive at the truth but to win a game. In continental Europe a much more investigative (or 'inquisitorial') function is given to the judge.

8.45   A summary trial in a magistrates' court begins with the clerk of the court (the clerk of petty sessions) asking whether the defendant wishes to plead guilty or not guilty.[110] If the defendant has been summonsed for an offence which must be tried summarily (but in no other situation) a plea of guilty can be entered by post.[111] The defendant can then be tried without having to appear in court, and unless a custodial sentence is to be imposed he or she can even be sentenced while absent. In cases where there has been a 'plea' (ie an admission of guilt), the prosecutor will outline the facts of the case to the District Judge and will hand over a list of the defendant's previous convictions, if any. After listening to defence arguments for leniency ('a plea in mitigation'), the District Judge will pronounce a sentence.[112] The public are in favour of sentences being reduced to reflect the fact that the defendant pleaded guilty, but the Criminal Justice Inspectorate (see para 7.97) has reported that the system for processing guilty pleas in Northern Ireland does not work very efficiently.[113]

Contested cases

8.46   A plea of not guilty cannot, technically, be accepted through the post, but if no plea of guilty is received it will be assumed that the accused is not admitting the offence. If the accused does not turn up in court on the day in question, a warrant can be issued for his or her arrest or there can be a trial

---

[110] Magistrates' Courts (NI) Order 1981, art 22.

[111] Ibid art 24.

[112] For the order of proceedings in a summary trial, see the Magistrates' Courts Rules (NI) 1984 (SR 225), r 23.

[113] *The Use of Early Guilty Pleas in the Criminal Justice System in Northern Ireland* (2013).

in the defendant's absence. In contested cases the prosecutor will outline the facts and then call witnesses to give their evidence. The Northern Ireland Courts and Tribunals Service has produced an online leaflet containing useful information for those who are called as witnesses in a criminal court. An expenses allowance is usually payable to witnesses. The amount in question is changed every few years. It is generally less than the actual losses sustained but the court can award higher amounts if it thinks that the claim is reasonable.[114] A witness who is under the age of 17 at the time of the hearing will be eligible for assistance, which may include the screening of the witness from the accused, giving evidence by live link or in private, the removal of lawyers' wigs and gowns, video-recorded cross-examination, and examination through an intermediary.[115]

8.47   In limited circumstances evidence of the defendant's bad character can be presented (see para 8.103), but generally speaking any previous criminal record of the defendant cannot be revealed unless and until he or she has been found guilty of the latest offence – it then becomes relevant to the sentencing process.[116] The defendant or the defendant's lawyer can cross-examine any of the prosecution witnesses. At the end of the prosecution case the defendant can 'apply for a direction', that is, submit that he or she ought to be acquitted because the prosecution has failed to produce any evidence to establish an essential element of the offence. If the District Judge grants the direction, that is the end of the case and the defendant is free to go. If the application is rejected, the defence can either rest its case on that point or go on to call its own witnesses including, usually, the defendant.

8.48   The defendant used to have the right to make an unsworn statement from the dock, but this was taken away by the PACE (NI) Order 1989. A defendant must now indicate at the start of the defence's case whether he or she intends to give evidence, but he or she must be told that the court may draw such inferences as appear proper from a refusal to testify (see para 8.20).[117] The prosecution can cross-examine all the defence witnesses including the defendant (if he or she testified), but if it wants to introduce any new evidence to contradict something proved or said on behalf of the defence it must first ask the District Judge's permission to do so. When all the evidence has been given, the defence may make a final address to the District Judge outlining its arguments. The District Judge will then announce his or her decision and what punishment, if any, is to be imposed.

---

[114] See generally the Magistrates' Courts (Costs in Criminal Cases) (Amendment) Rules (NI) 1994 (SR 285).

[115] Criminal Evidence (NI) Order 1999, arts 4–21.

[116] In many European countries the defendant's previous criminal record can be admitted as evidence much earlier in the proceedings.

[117] Criminal Evidence (NI) Order 1988, art 4(1).

Sentences

8.49 Under the Criminal Justice (NI) Order 1996 the sentence imposed for an offence must be proportionate to the seriousness of the offence. The defendant may ask for other offences which he or she admits to having committed to be 'taken into consideration' (TICs).[118] Before coming to a view as to whether an offence is serious enough to merit a custodial sentence, a court must usually obtain and consider a pre-sentence report from the Probation Service (see para 7.85).[119] A magistrates' court may also (like the Crown Court) defer passing sentence for a period not longer than six months to allow the defendant's conduct *after conviction* to be taken into account when determining his or her sentence.[120] Under the Criminal Justice (No 2) (NI) Order 2004 a sentence can be increased if the offence in question was aggravated by hostility based on the victim's actual or presumed religion, race, disability or sexual orientation. This is the main way in which 'hate crime' is dealt with in Northern Ireland.[121]

8.50 Generally speaking, the most serious punishment which a District Judge has the power to impose is a fine of £5,000 or six months in prison, or both. If the offence is an indictable one being tried summarily the maximum prison sentence is 12 months, and this may extend to 18 months if consecutive terms of imprisonment are imposed for more than one indictable offence.[122] Prison sentences may also be 'suspended' for between one and three years[123] (between one and two years in England[124]), which means that they may be 'activated' if the convicted person commits another imprisonable offence within that period. Only about 5 per cent of defendants in magistrates' courts receive immediate custodial sentences, but the overall number sentenced in this way is still several times higher than the number sentenced to imprisonment by the Crown Court.

8.51 The Criminal Justice (NI) Order 1996 sought to emphasise the value of 'community sentences'. Probation orders, community service orders, supervision orders and attendance centre orders all fall within this category. So does a 'combination order',[125] which effectively combines the provisions of a probation order and a community service order. In a sense, disqualification from driving is a community sentence too because it serves to protect the

---

[118] Criminal Justice Act (NI) 1953, s 4.
[119] Criminal Justice (NI) Order 1996, art 21.
[120] Ibid art 6. See too Judge Smyth, 'Deferral of Sentence: Principles, Practice and Proposals' (2000) 51 *NILQ* 48.
[121] But it is also a specific offence to use threatening, abusive or insulting words or behaviour, with intent to stir up hatred or arouse fear or in circumstances where such hatred or fear is likely: Public Order (NI) Order 1987, art 9.
[122] Magistrates' Courts (NI) Order 1981, art 56.
[123] Treatment of Offenders (NI) Act 1968, s 18(1).
[124] Powers of Criminal Courts (Sentencing) Act 2000, s 118(2).
[125] art 15.

community against bad drivers. The 1996 Order also introduced the custody probation order – a sentence unique to Northern Ireland.[126] This is available where the court is of the opinion that a convicted person should serve a custodial sentence of 12 months or more. It requires the person to serve a shorter custodial sentence but then, on release from custody, to be supervised by a probation officer for between one and three years.

Compensation, forfeiture and restitution orders

8.52 Magistrates also have the power to make 'compensation orders' against a convicted person.[127] These require a person to pay compensation for any personal injury, loss or damage resulting from any offence for which the court has convicted that person. Losses arising from road traffic accidents are excluded from the scheme, unless the vehicle has been stolen or unless the offender is uninsured and compensation is not payable through the Motor Insurers' Bureau Uninsured Drivers Agreement. The maximum which can be ordered to be paid in respect of any one offence is £5,000, although compensation for bereavement can amount to £7,500.[128] Sums paid are deducted from any award of damages later obtained by the victim of the crime in civil proceedings but are additional to any sum ordered to be paid by the defendant to the state by way of a fine. The court must also give reasons if it does *not* grant a compensation order whenever it has the power to do so. Property used for the purposes of crime (including vehicles involved in the commission of any imprisonable offence under the Road Traffic (NI) Order 1981) can be ordered to be forfeited (ie given up)[129] and under the Theft Act (NI) 1969[130] any property which has been stolen, or its proceeds, can be ordered to be returned by the defendant to the victim of the theft by way of a restitution order.

Fines

8.53 The most common punishment in magistrates' courts is a fine. It is imposed in about one-half of all cases. Since 1984 there have been five scales for fines, the boundaries between the scales being set by secondary legislation from time to time. The current limits are £200 for Level 1; £500 for Level 2; £1,000 for Level 3; £2,500 for Level 4; and £5,000 for Level 5.[131] If legislation says that a person can be fined 'the prescribed sum' this

[126] art 24.
[127] Criminal Justice (NI) Order 1994, art 14.
[128] Fatal Accidents (NI) Order 1977, art 3A(3).
[129] Criminal Justice (NI) Order 1994, art 11.
[130] s 27, as amended by the Criminal Justice (NI) Order 1980, arts 6 and 12(2).
[131] Criminal Justice (NI) Order 1994, art 3(2).

means £5,000 unless a different amount is specified.[132] The maximum fine which a magistrates' court can impose on a child under the age of 14 is £200; for any other child, the maximum is £1,000.[133]

Enforcement of orders and fines

8.54 Compensation, forfeiture and restitution orders, as well as fines, are all ultimately enforceable by imprisonment. The length of the imprisonment will depend on the amount of money owed. A person fined by a magistrates' court can, for instance, be sent to prison for three months if the unpaid fine is between £2,500 and £5,000.[134] Apparently, 45 per cent of all fines are paid within the 28 days allowed for doing so in Northern Ireland, and a further 45 per cent are paid when steps are taken to enforce them. These are higher rates than elsewhere in the UK, but proportionately more people are imprisoned in Northern Ireland for non-payment of a fine. About 30 per cent of all admission to prisons in Northern Ireland are for fine default. In 2010 the Criminal Justice Inspectorate called for reforms to the enforcement system so that it would be less of a strain on police and prison resources,[135] and in a follow-up report in 2012 it announced that there had been some improvements to the system despite the fact that new committals to prison for fine default rose from 1,247 in 2009 to 2,179 in 2011.[136] The Courts and Tribunals Service put in place a reminder scheme to help prevent people from becoming fine defaulters and this resulted in 30 per cent fewer warrants being issued to arrest defaulters. 'Supervised activity orders', which are a community service based alternative to being sent to prison for non-payment of a fine, were piloted in Newry during 2012. The Minister of Justice intends to introduce radical reforms in this area through the Faster, Fairer Justice Bill which he will be bringing before the Assembly later in 2013.

Conditional and absolute discharges

8.55 Two further types of 'sentence' which a District Judge might impose are the 'conditional discharge' and 'absolute discharge' of the convicted person.[137] The former is like a suspended sentence in that the convicted person is released without punishment but may be sentenced at a later date

---

[132] Fines and Penalties (NI) Order 1984, art 4(8), as amended by the Criminal Justice (NI) Order 1994, art 3(1).
[133] Criminal Justice (Children) (NI) Order 1998, art 34.
[134] Criminal Justice (NI) Order 1994, art 4(1).
[135] The CJI's report was entitled *The Enforcement of Fines*.
[136] *The Enforcement of Fines* (2012).
[137] Criminal Justice (NI) Order 1996, art 4.

if he or she commits an offence during the period specified in the order (which cannot exceed three years). An absolute discharge means that no real punishment is being meted out (although disqualification from driving can still be imposed): it is not an acquittal, however, so technically the defendant still stands convicted of the offence.

Initial appeals

8.56 When a criminal case is tried summarily and the defendant is convicted, as the vast majority of them are, the defendant has the right to appeal within 14 days.[138] The defendant may wish to appeal against conviction, against sentence, or against both, although obviously there cannot be an appeal against conviction if the defendant pleaded guilty at the trial. He or she has a choice between two procedures: an appeal to a county court or an appeal by way of case stated to the Court of Appeal.

8.57 An appeal to a county court against conviction requires a complete rehearing of the case.[139] The county court judge (sitting without a jury) can reverse the conviction or confirm it – even on grounds different from those given by the District Judge. In these proceedings the judge can also increase or decrease the accused's sentence.[140] If the appeal is only against sentence, all that is required is a review of the accused's previous convictions, if any, and a reconsideration of his or her plea in mitigation.

8.58 An appeal by way of case stated to the Court of Appeal can be used only where there is a disputed point of law and no dispute about the facts.[141] Under this procedure the District Judge is asked by the side appealing (the appellant) to pose a question to the Court of Appeal for its opinion on what the law is on a particular point.[142] The Court of Appeal answers that question and then affirms, reverses or varies the decision appealed from.[143] It may not increase the defendant's sentence.[144] There are only a few appeals of this kind each year.

8.59 The prosecution has fewer rights of appeal. If the defendant is acquitted by a magistrates' court, or if a conviction is reversed by the county court, the prosecution cannot appeal against those decisions on the ground

---

[138] Magistrates' Courts (NI) Order 1981, art 144. The County Court (Amendment) Rules (NI) 1994 (SR 472), however, enable a county court, on application, to extend this time limit either before or after it expires.

[139] Ibid art 140 and Magistrates' Court Rules (NI) 1984 (SR 225), rr 154–177, as amended.

[140] County Courts (NI) Order 1980, art 28(3).

[141] Magistrates' Courts (NI) Order 1981, art 146 and Magistrates' Court Rules (NI) 1984 (SR 225), rr 158–160, as amended.

[142] Eg *Clinton v Bradley* [2000] NI 196.

[143] Magistrates' Courts (NI) Order 1981, art 147.

[144] Ibid art 153(1)(b).

that the facts were wrongly found by the District Judge or county court judge. The only avenue open to the prosecution is to appeal directly to the Court of Appeal on a point of law by way of case stated.[145] Even then the appeal can only be against an acquittal, not against too lenient a sentence.

Further appeals

8.60   If the accused has appealed to a county court the main way in which the case can be taken further is by either side stating a case from that court to the Court of Appeal.[146] All such decisions by the Court of Appeal are in turn appealable to the UK's Supreme Court.[147] Before this can happen, however, the permission either of the Court of Appeal or of the Supreme Court must be granted, and this will not occur unless the Court of Appeal first certifies that a point of law of general public importance is involved.[148] It is very rare for a case which has been tried summarily in Northern Ireland's magistrates' courts to travel as far as the highest court in the land, but one well-known example is *McEldowney v Forde*[149] (see para 3.47).

8.61   If appeal routes are exhausted but the accused person still feels that there has been a miscarriage of justice, he or she can refer the conviction or sentence to the Criminal Cases Review Commission in Birmingham (see para 7.101).[150]

COMMITTAL PROCEEDINGS

8.62   The other type of criminal case which a magistrates' court deals with is committal proceedings. These are held for persons charged with indictable offences which are not triable summarily or which, although triable summarily, the defendant or prosecution has elected to have tried on indictment. Their purpose is to decide if there is a *prima facie* case (ie a case 'on the face of it') for the accused to answer. A finding that there is such a case simply means that the defendant is then committed for trial to the Crown Court: it does not imply any assumption that the accused is guilty.

8.63   Today most committal proceedings take the form of a 'preliminary enquiry' (PE),[151] where copies of witnesses' written statements are simply

---

[145] Ibid art 146.
[146] County Courts (NI) Order 1980, art 61(1).
[147] Judicature (NI) Act 1978, s 41(1)(b) and Criminal Appeal (NI) Act 1980, s 31.
[148] Ibid s 41(2).
[149] [1971] AC 632.
[150] Criminal Appeal Act 1995, s 12.
[151] Magistrates' Courts (NI) Order 1981, arts 31–34 and Magistrates' Courts Rules (NI) 1984 (SR 225), rr 31–42.

presented to the court and, if either side so requests, read out aloud. In a 'preliminary investigation' (PI) evidence is given by word of mouth on oath; it is written down in court and is then called a 'deposition'. The witnesses are 'bound over' to attend and give evidence if required at the main trial.[152] In some cases, such as those involving child witnesses to violent offences,[153] the DPP can bypass committal proceedings altogether. In committal proceedings for 'certified' trials (ie those involving alleged terrorists, see para 7.30) the prosecution is entitled to insist on a PE rather than a PI, unless the court considers that in the interests of justice a PI should be conducted instead.[154] The PE process avoids a witness having to attend on two separate occasions to give evidence in court, once at the committal proceedings and again at the trial itself.

8.64   If the District Judge considers that there is not enough evidence to require the accused to answer the charge brought by the prosecution, he or she will not commit the accused for trial.[155] This is called 'discharging' the accused, and occurs very infrequently. The prosecution cannot appeal against a discharge but it can apply to a judge of the High Court or Crown Court for permission to present an indictment notwithstanding the absence of any committal by a magistrates' court.[156] This is known as a 'voluntary' bill of indictment and has also been used in cases where no committal proceedings at all have taken place (because, for example, the chief prosecution witness was an alleged accomplice of the defendant and the prosecution wish to protect him or her before the main trial).[157]

8.65   Committal proceedings in England and Wales were abolished by the Crime and Disorder Act 1998. In 2005 the Northern Ireland Office announced, after considering the responses to a consultation paper on the matter,[158] that its policy was to abolish the committal system in magistrates' courts in Northern Ireland and to replace it with one in which cases would be sent to the Crown Court without a committal hearing when they were deemed ready for a trial on indictment. The defence would then have the right to apply to the Crown Court for the charges to be dismissed if it felt the case was weak. In 2012 the Minister of Justice issued a consultation paper on reform of committal proceedings in Northern Ireland. This proposed that the taking of oral evidence and cross-examination of witnesses in committal proceedings should be ended but that the defendant would retain the right to

---

[152] Ibid art 38.
[153] Children's Evidence (NI) Order 1995, art 4.
[154] Justice and Security (NI) Act 2007, s 3.
[155] Magistrates' Courts (NI) Order 1981, art 37.
[156] Grand Jury (Abolition) Act (NI) 1969, s 2(2)(e).
[157] It occurred in *R v Crilly (Leave to Prefer Indictment)* [2010] NICC 19, [2012] NIJB 18, where Hart J granted leave for a voluntary bill of indictment to be granted against a man charged with the murder of a British soldier in 1977.
[158] *The Future of Committal Proceedings* (Northern Ireland Office, 2004).

make written representations on his or her behalf at the committal hearing. After considering responses to this paper,[159] the Minister indicated that he would be establishing a Procedural Reform Project Group to develop the details of the reform and that he would include them in the Faster, Fairer Justice Bill to be introduced in the Assembly in 2013.

TRIALS ON INDICTMENT

8.66 After the committal proceedings in a magistrates' court, the main trial in the Crown Court should start between eight days and 14 weeks later.[160] The PPS will prepare a 'form of indictment' containing details of the specific charges against the accused. Each particular offence charged in the indictment is known as a 'count'. In all cases there will be a jury of 12 persons, unless the trial has been 'certified' as involving terrorism (see para 7.30), in which event a judge will sit without a jury. Usually, trials take place at the Crown Court sitting for the place where the offence is alleged to have been committed, but a different venue can be arranged on account of special circumstances such as the convenience of witnesses, security factors or local sensitivities.[161]

Arraignment

8.67 Even before proceedings formally begin, the defence can ask the Crown Court judge to order a 'No Bill' in respect of any indictment presented to the court if he or she is satisfied that the documents do not disclose a case sufficient to justify putting the defendant on trial.[162] If this does not occur proceedings commence with the 'arraignment' of the accused, that is, with the court clerk asking the accused how he or she pleads to each count in the indictment. If the accused pleads guilty to all counts there will be no need for a jury to be sworn; the prosecution will outline the facts and the judge will pass sentence after considering the accused's previous convictions, if any, and any plea in mitigation by the accused's barrister. If the accused pleads not guilty to any count, and if the trial is not a certified one, a jury must be sworn from the panel already summoned to the court for that day.

---

[159] *Encouraging Earlier Guilty Pleas and Reform of Committal Proceedings: Report on Responses and Way Forward* (2012).

[160] Judicature (NI) Act 1978, s 48(5), Crown Court Rules 1979 (SR 90), r 44, and Crown Court Practice Direction of 12 October 1998 [1998] 8 BNIL 58. In England and Wales the maximum allowable delay is 8 weeks.

[161] s 48(1)–(4) of the Judicature (NI) Act 1978. Eg the trial of Hazel Stewart in 2011 took place in Belfast, even though the offences were committed in Castlerock, in the north-west of Northern Ireland.

[162] Grand Jury (Abolition) Act (NI) 1969, s 2(3). See, eg, *R v Crooks and others* [2012] NICC 25, [2012] 7 BNIL 11.

8.68   If the question of the defendant's mental fitness to be tried arises at the arraignment stage it is decided by the jury empanelled for the trial, but only after evidence has been presented by two medical practitioners. If the jury decides that the accused is fit to be tried, the trial itself must be heard by a different jury.[163] If the jury decides that the accused is not fit to be tried, another jury will then determine whether the accused did in fact do the act alleged. If it decides that the accused did do the act the court can make a hospital order, a guardianship order, a supervision and treatment order or an order for his or her absolute discharge.[164]

Juries

8.69   Jurors are selected by the Juries Officer of each county court division from lists drawn up annually from registers prepared by the Chief Electoral Officer for Northern Ireland.[165] Every registered elector aged between 18 and 70 is qualified for inclusion, although certain individuals (such as any person who in the last five years has been placed on probation) are disqualified from serving[166] and others, by reason of their jobs or because they are aged 65 or over, are either ineligible or excusable as of right.[167] In 2008 the Northern Ireland Office issued a consultation paper on reforming eligibility for jury service in Northern Ireland,[168] but nothing has yet come of that initiative. In 2011 the Minister of Justice consulted on what the upper age limit for jury service should be and he concluded that there should be no age limit but that the right to claim an excuse on age grounds should be available to persons aged 70 or over.[169] Jurors are paid allowances and can find out more about what is involved in being a juror by consulting the Tribunals and Courts Service's leaflet on the topic.[170] The Juries Officer selects a jury to serve not just for one particular trial but for all the hearings in a particular court or place over a prescribed period of time.

---

[163] Mental Health (NI) Order 1986, art 49, as amended by the Criminal Justice (NI) Order 1996, art 48.

[164] Ibid arts 49A and 50A, inserted by the Criminal Justice (NI) Order 1996, arts 49 and 51. In 2012 the Northern Ireland Law Commission issued a consultation paper on reform of the law in this area: *Unfitness to Plead* (NILC 13).

[165] Juries (NI) Order 1996.

[166] Ibid Sch 1, lists all those disqualified from jury service.

[167] Ibid Schs 2 and 3. In England and Wales many of the restrictions on eligibility for jury service were removed by the Criminal Justice Act 2003. Anyone wishing to be declared ineligible or excused from jury service in that jurisdiction now has to make a special application to that effect.

[168] *Widening the Jury Pool: Increasing Participation in the Criminal Justice System.* A summary of responses was issued in 2010.

[169] *The Upper Age Limit for Jury Service in Northern Ireland: Report of the Consultation* (2012).

[170] Available online.

8.70   When the members of a jury panel are being 'empanelled', that is, sworn in to serve a particular trial, a defendant can, without giving reasons, object to any 12 of them. This is called the right to a peremptory challenge and those members must then stand down.[171] Such challenges were abolished in England and Wales by the Criminal Justice Act 1988 but are still possible in Northern Ireland. After 12 peremptory challenges the defendant can challenge would-be jurors only if reasons are given, and the jurors will have to stand down only if the judge considers the reasons to be satisfactory. The prosecution has no right of peremptory challenge but can require any would-be juror to 'stand by', that is, to wait on one side until the rest of the jury group has been gone through to see if a full jury can be sworn.[172] If by then a full jury has not been sworn the prosecution can prevent a juror who has been stood by from serving only if it provides the judge with good reasons why this should be so. Even if the defence or the prosecution does not object to a particular juror, the judge may personally excuse jurors on the grounds of hardship or ill-health. It is a criminal offence to intimidate jurors (or witnesses).[173]

The giving of evidence

8.71   Once a jury has been empanelled for the case in hand examination, cross-examination and re-examination of witnesses will take place as in a summary trial, but will usually be conducted with the utmost attention to the law's many rules of the law on evidence (see paras 8.99–8.112). If the judge interferes by asking too many questions of the defendant rather than leaving this to the barristers involved, this may render the trial unfair.[174] All witnesses may remain in court during the hearing of evidence, unless a special application to exclude some of them is granted by the judge. This differs from the practice in England, where, more sensibly, witnesses remain outside the courtroom during the taking of other evidence.

Voir dire hearings

8.72   If at any stage of the trial either side wishes to produce evidence which may not, according to the strict rules of evidence, be admissible, the judge will ask the jury to withdraw while the judge hears the evidence alone and decides whether it is admissible. This is an example of what is called

---

[171] Juries (NI) Order 1996, art 15.
[172] See, eg, *R v Christie* (6 May 1997, Belfast Crown Court, unreported) and *R v King and Wilson* [1998] BNIL 15, which affirmed the Crown's right of stand by.
[173] Criminal Justice (NI) Order 1996, art 47.
[174] *R v Roulston* [2001] 3 BNIL 21.

a '*voir dire*' hearing, or a trial within a trial. If the judge decides that the evidence is admissible the jury will be recalled and the trial will proceed with the evidence being presented. If the judge decides that the evidence is not admissible the jury will be recalled and the trial will proceed with no mention being made of the inadmissible evidence. In this way the jury is protected from hearing evidence which, for one reason or another, the law considers to be improper. In 'certified' trials (see para 7.30) the judge who decides the *voir dire* issues will usually be the same judge as decides the issues of fact at the main trial. If the judge has held certain evidence to be inadmissible during the *voir dire* he or she is meant to forget all about that evidence when deciding the main issues, although the judge *can* instead direct that the main trial should be re-commenced before a different judge.

Verdicts

8.73   After all the evidence has been presented, the lawyers representing prosecution and defence make final speeches summarising their positions. The judge must then sum up the whole case for the jury by drawing its attention to the rival versions of the relevant facts and directing it on the relevant law to be applied to those facts. The judge might even give the jury a list of written questions to consider, in an effort to guide it through the complexities of the case. The jury, in turn, can pose further questions in writing for the judge.[175] The jury's final verdict should be unanimous, but need not be so if it has been deliberating for at least two hours and at least 10 of them agree on the verdict – this is called 'a majority verdict'.[176] If the jury finds it impossible to arrive even at a majority verdict the judge may discharge that jury and order a new trial before a different jury.

8.74   If the jury's verdict is 'not guilty' the accused must be acquitted and generally cannot be held in custody or tried again in connection with that offence. If charged again for the same offence the accused is said to have the defence of *autrefois acquit* ('formerly acquitted'); this is sometimes referred to as the principle of 'double jeopardy'. However, under the Criminal Justice Act 2003, if the Court of Appeal finds that there is 'new and compelling evidence',[177] a retrial can be ordered of someone who has previously been acquitted of a 'qualifying offence', a category which includes murder, rape, kidnapping and some sexual, drug and terrorist offences. If the verdict in a trial is 'guilty', the judge will pass sentence. Before doing so the judge may

---

[175] The questions sent to Sweeney J by the jury in the trial of Vicky Pryce in London in February 2013 betrayed 'fundamental deficits of understanding' of a jury's role. See www.bbc.co.uk/news/uk-21522521.
[176] Criminal Procedure (Majority Verdicts) Act (NI) 1971, s 1(1), as substituted by the Juries (NI) Order 1996, art 32(1).
[177] As defined in s 78 of the Act.

be addressed by the defence on points of mitigation as well as being assisted by reports from probation officers, welfare officers, doctors, etc.

Sentences

8.75 The sentencing powers of the Crown Court embrace all of those exercisable by magistrates' courts (see paras 8.49–8.55) but include as well powers conferred by the common law and legislation.[178] In England and Wales there is a Sentencing Guidelines Council,[179] chaired by the Lord Chief Justice. This indicates the factors which judges should bear in mind when calculating the appropriate sentence in a particular case. The Court of Appeal in Northern Ireland has said that sentences in Northern Ireland should apply the starting points recommended by that Council.[180] From time to time the Court of Appeal in Northern Ireland itself issues sentencing guidelines for the lower courts.[181] In July 2010 a Judicial Sentencing Working Group recommended that each year a list of priority areas in which sentencing guidance is required should be drawn up and that judges who are called upon in due course to hear cases in those areas should then prepare written judgments for the guidance of future courts.[182] The Lord Chief Justice set out a list of areas in which sentencing guidance was most required, which included domestic violence, serious sexual offences, people trafficking, attacks on public workers and vulnerable people, duty evasion and smuggling, and environmental crime. In 2012 the Lord Chief Justice's Sentencing Group issued a report which brings together all the sentencing guidelines so far complied by the Court of Appeal, the Crown Court and magistrates' courts.[183]

8.76 The most common Crown Court sentence is immediate imprisonment, the average sentence being about 30 months. A suspended sentence must not exceed seven years and the period of suspension must be between one and five years,[184] the sentence being liable to be activated if the offender commits

---

[178] For a survey of the 'ancillary orders' which judges have to consider when sentencing a convicted person, see the speech by Sir Declan Morgan LCJ to the Criminal Bar Association Annual Conference on 4 June 2011 (available on the website of the Northern Ireland Courts and Tribunals Service).

[179] www.sentencing-guidelines.gov.uk.

[180] *Attorney General's Reference (No 2 of 2004)* [2004] NICA 15.

[181] The website of the Judicial Studies Board for Northern Ireland contains copies of these guidelines: see *www.jsbni.com/Home/JSB_Header.htm*.

[182] The report is available through the website of the Courts and Tribunals Service.

[183] See www.courtsni.gov.uk/en-GB/Judicial%20Decisions/LCJ-sentence-group/Documents/ j_lcjsg_Dec12-report/Sentencing-Group-Report-Dec12.html. See too *Comparative Research into Sentencing Guidelines Mechanisms*, a paper produced by the Northern Ireland Assembly's Research and Information Service (2011).

[184] Treatment of Offenders Act (NI) 1968, s 18, as amended by the Treatment of Offenders (NI) Order 1989, art 9(1) and the Criminal Justice (NI) Order 1996, art 23.

another imprisonable offence during the period of suspension. The sentence which a convicted person receives will depend on a number of factors. Some of these relate to the nature of what the accused actually did at the time of or immediately after the crime (whether the crime was particularly brutal or dishonest, for instance) while others relate to the kind of person the defendant is – whether he or she is genuinely remorseful or easily influenced by others, etc. Each crime is subject to a maximum possible sentence, but not to any minimum. 'Proportionality' is the principal sentencing aim. It is notoriously difficult to compare sentences in different cases because the precise factors to be taken into account are unique to each case. If a dispute arises at the sentencing stage over the precise facts surrounding the offence in question, a further oral hearing (called a 'Newton hearing'[185]) may be required to settle the matter.

8.77 There are many offences for which the maximum punishment laid down by statute is life imprisonment, but the only offences for which that sentence *must* be imposed are murder[186] and genocide.[187] The death penalty was to all intents and purposes abolished in Northern Ireland in 1973, the last execution having taken place in 1964.[188] If a person is found not guilty by reason of mental illness, or if the court believes that a guilty defendant requires treatment in a mental hospital, he or she can be made the subject of a hospital order and sent to a mental hospital.[189]

Appeals

8.78 When a criminal case is tried on indictment, the accused person can appeal against conviction if the trial judge grants a certificate that the case is fit for appeal or if the permission of the Court of Appeal is obtained.[190] There is no case stated procedure for trials on indictment, nor is the judicial review procedure available. Pending the determination of an appeal, the Court of Appeal can permit the defendant to be released on bail, although this rarely occurs. If a defendant is convicted in a 'certified' trial (see para 7.30) the

---

[185] After *R v Newton* (1982) 77 Cr App R 13.

[186] Northern Ireland (Emergency Provisions) Act 1973, s 1.

[187] Genocide Act 1969, s 1.

[188] The last person sentenced to death in the UK was Liam Holden, who was convicted of killing a soldier in Northern Ireland in 1972. The sentence was commuted and he served 17 years in prison. In 2012 his conviction was quashed by the Court of Appeal because the prosecution could not prove that his confession to the crime had not been secured by subjecting him to torture in the form of waterboarding. See www.bbc.co.uk/news/uk-northern-ireland-18525630 and *R v Holden* [2012] NICA 26, [2012] 8 BNIL 22.

[189] Mental Health (NI) Order 1986, art 44. In 2005 the Shannon Clinic was opened at Knockbracken Healthcare Park in South Belfast. This can accommodate up to 34 patients, providing treatment and rehabilitation in a secure environment.

[190] Criminal Appeal (NI) Act 1980, s 1, as substituted by Criminal Appeal Act 1995, s 1(2). In this field see, generally, the Criminal Appeal (NI) Rules 1968 (SR 218), as amended.

judge must set out the reasons for the conviction,[191] and the defendant has a *right* to appeal to the Court of Appeal on any ground.[192]

8.79 In general the prosecution has no right of appeal against the acquittal of a defendant who has been tried on indictment. All that can be done at present is that the Director of Public Prosecutions can refer a point of law arising out of the acquittal to the Court of Appeal for its opinion.[193] This is only a reference and not an appeal, and even if the Court of Appeal considers that the trial judge made an error of law which resulted in an undeserved acquittal, the acquittal still stands. The Court of Appeal's opinion will simply guide the prosecution in future trials. The DPP has a separate power to refer a case to the Court of Appeal if he or she believes that the sentence imposed by the Crown Court is 'unduly lenient'.[194]

8.80 There are four possible outcomes to an appeal against conviction. The Court of Appeal may:

(1) allow the appeal and acquit the defendant if it thinks the conviction was unsafe;[195]
(2) allow the appeal but substitute a verdict of guilty of one or more other offences, in which event the Court of Appeal can also alter the defendant's sentence;[196]
(3) allow the appeal but order a retrial;[197] or
(4) dismiss the appeal.

In any appeal against sentence the Court of Appeal can also alter the sentence up or down.[198] In England and Wales, however, the Court of Appeal cannot increase a sentence on appeal.[199]

8.81 Decisions of the Court of Appeal relating to trials on indictment can be further appealed, by either the prosecution or the defence, to the UK's Supreme Court. But, as with appeals after summary trials, the leave of either the Court of Appeal or the Supreme Court is first required, and this is granted only if the Court of Appeal certifies that a point of law of general public importance is involved and if the Court of Appeal or the Supreme Court thinks that the point is one which ought to be considered by

---

[191] Justice and Security (NI) Act 2007, s 5(6). Juries, on the other hand, do not give reasons for their decisions.
[192] Ibid s 5(7).
[193] Criminal Appeal (NI) Act 1980, s 15.
[194] Criminal Justice Act 1988, s 36. See, eg, *Attorney General's Reference (No 6 of 2004)* [2004] NICA 33, where a 12-year minimum tariff for a brutal murder was increased to 15 years.
[195] Criminal Appeal (NI) Act 1980, s 2(2)
[196] Ibid ss 3 and 4. See too the Criminal Justice Act 2003, s 317.
[197] Ibid s 6.
[198] Ibid s 10(3).
[199] Criminal Appeal Act 1968, s 11(3).

the Supreme Court.[200] A 'reference' under the 1980 Act (see para 8.79) can also be further referred by the Court of Appeal to the Supreme Court, but the decision of the Supreme Court can still not reverse the original acquittal. Likewise, a decision by the Court of Appeal in relation to an 'unduly lenient' sentence (see para 8.79) may be referred to the Supreme Court if there is a point of law of general public importance at issue.

CHILDREN AND CRIMINAL JUSTICE

8.82   The operation of the criminal justice system in respect of children is the responsibility of a unit within the Department of Justice, and the Youth Justice Agency advises the Department on the provision of community based services, youth conferencing and secure custody.[201] The Justice (NI) Act 2002 states that the principal aim of the youth justice system is to protect the public by preventing offending by children.[202] It goes on to say that all persons operating the system must encourage children to recognise the effects of crime and to take responsibility for their actions but that they must also have regard to the welfare of children and to the furtherance of their personal, social and educational development. Efforts are made to keep the number of criminal proceedings against children to a minimum and 'restorative' justice schemes have been devised to help divert children from court and from detention.[203] If the police believe that a child may be in need of advice, guidance or assistance they are required to inform the local social services office, and if they suspect that a child has committed an offence they often prefer to rely on informal words of advice or official cautions rather than bringing the matter before a court.

8.83   There is a presumption in Northern Ireland's law that no child under the age of 10 can be guilty of an offence (this is commonly referred to as the 'age of criminal responsibility').[204] Any youth who has been arrested and charged should be released if he or she, or a parent or guardian, enters into a recognisance (see para 8.26), unless the charge is for a 'serious arrestable offence'[205] or the custody officer believes that the child should not be released for the protection of the public.[206] If the youth is not released, he or she must

---

[200] Ibid s 31(2).

[201] www.youthjusticeagencyni.gov.uk. The Agency publishes a quarterly magazine called *Youth Justice Connections*. Complaints against the Youth Justice Agency can be referred to an Independent Complaints Reviewer and from there to the Northern Ireland Ombudsman.

[202] s 53.

[203] Ibid ss 57–61.

[204] Criminal Justice (Children) (NI) Order 1998, art 3. The threshold in Northern Ireland is amongst the lowest in the world.

[205] For a definition, see Police and Criminal Evidence (NI) Order 1989, art 87, as amended. See too para 8.6.

[206] Criminal Justice (Children) (NI) Order 1998, art 6(3).

be detained by the police in Woodlands Juvenile Justice Centre in Bangor, County Down, before being brought before a magistrates' court.[207]

8.84   In 2011 the report of the Youth Justice Review, commissioned by the Minister of Justice the previous year, was published.[208] As well as describing and assessing the current system for dealing with young people caught up in the criminal justice system, it makes a number of recommendations for reform, many of them based on the language of human rights. It proposes a raising of the age of criminal responsibility to 12 (and thereafter, perhaps, to 14), the introduction of statutory time limits for cases involving young people, and an end to the practice of sending young people under the age of 18 to the Young Offenders Centre. Following further consultation on the Review, the last two of these reforms are in hand, but it looks as if securing cross-community support in the Northern Ireland Assembly for the first reform will be extremely difficult. The Review stopped short of recommending that the UN Convention on the Rights of the Child should be formally incorporated into the law of Northern Ireland, mainly because the Convention ranges far wider than criminal justice.

Youth courts

8.85   Criminal proceedings concerning young people under the age of 18 are dealt with by 'youth courts', which are essentially magistrates' courts by another name.[209] Two lay magistrates (see para 4.23), including at least one woman, will sit with the District Judge (Magistrates' Courts)[210] The judge has a casting vote if only one lay magistrate is present; otherwise decisions are reached by majority vote. Youth courts should sit at different times from other hearings in a magistrates' court so that there is little chance of children coming into contact with adult offenders,[211] and proceedings are held in private, with only court officials, the parties to the case, the parties' representatives, the parents or guardians of the child, representatives of the press and such other persons as the court may authorise, being present.[212] Children appearing in youth courts must be legally represented[213] and there are restrictions on what the press can report about the case.[214]

---

[207] Ibid art 8(3).
[208] Available on the website of the Department of Justice.
[209] Criminal Justice (Children) (NI) Order 1998 and the Justice (NI) Act 2002, s 63 and Sch 11. The procedures to be followed in youth courts are governed by the Magistrates' Courts (Criminal Justice (Children)) Rules (NI) 1999 (SR 7) and the Youth Conference Rules (NI) 2003 (SR 473).
[210] Children and Young Persons Act (NI) 1968, Schedule.
[211] Criminal Justice (Children) (NI) Order 1998, art 27(3).
[212] Ibid art 27(4).
[213] Ibid art 18.
[214] Ibid art 22(2).

8.86   Where a youth court remands or commits a child for trial, the child must be released on bail unless the court considers that a remand in custody is necessary to protect the public *and* the offence is a violent or sexual offence, is one for which an adult would be liable on conviction to be sent to prison for at least 14 years, or is an offence carrying a possible sentence of five years or more in prison and the child was either already on bail when he or she allegedly committed it or has been found guilty of such an offence within the last two years.[215] A remand in custody during the course of a hearing will be to Woodlands; remands to Hydebank Wood Young Offenders Centre are now only possible for young people aged 18 or over.[216] The PACE Order provisions concerning bail (see para 8.26), and the provisions concerning legal aid and advice (see paras 11.33–11.40 and 11.46–11.50) which apply to suspected adult offenders, apply similarly in cases involving children.

8.87   A youth court can try children summarily or can conduct preliminary enquiries or preliminary investigations into indictable offences (see para 8.62). It can also deal summarily with any indictable offence, apart from homicide, if it thinks that such a course is expedient and if both the prosecutor and the child (or, in the case of a child under the age of 14, the child's parent or guardian) consent.[217] In such a case the youth court, on making a finding of guilt, may issue any order which might have been made if the case had been tried by the Crown Court on indictment. It may therefore impose a much more serious sentence than an ordinary magistrates' court. If tried in a Crown Court a child may still be sent back to the youth court for sentencing.[218] Appeals against decisions by the youth courts go to the county court, where again two lay magistrates will sit as assessors alongside the county court judge. In 2012 there were 2479 young people dealt with by the youth courts, a drop of 26 per cent in two years.[219] The majority of the charges related to theft.

8.88   It is worth noting that the controversial Anti-social Behaviour (NI) Order 2004 allows magistrates' courts to issue anti-social behaviour orders (ASBOs) against children as well as adults if an application has been made by the police, a district council or the Northern Ireland Housing Executive. These are *civil law* orders but if they are breached the person in question can be convicted of a criminal offence. For that reason the law requires magistrates' courts to apply a high standard of proof before agreeing to

---

[215] As far as remands in custody are concerned, the requirement that custody is necessary to protect the public must be satisfied in *all* cases. The restrictions on imposing custodial sentences are less demanding, as they require only that custody be necessary to protect the public where the offence is violent or serious in nature (Criminal Justice (NI) Order 1996, art 19).

[216] Criminal Justice (Children) (NI) Order 1998, art 13(1)(b).

[217] Ibid art 17(1).

[218] Ibid art 32(1)(b).

[219] This figure has been compiled from the provisional statistics published on a quarterly basis by the Courts and Tribunals Service in its Magistrates' Courts Bulletins: see www.courtsni.gov.uk (under 'Services', 'Statistics and Research').

issue such an order.[220] In 2012 a report by the Criminal Justice Inspectorate (see para 7.97) noted that 40 per cent of all ASBOs in Northern Ireland are issued to people under the age of 18.[221] It recommended that in such cases a support package aimed at encouraging behavioural change by the young person should be an aspect of the conditions applied. It also suggested that ASBOs issued to children should be reviewed every six months and quashed or amended if that was appropriate.

The punishment of children

8.89   Although children can be punished for committing criminal offences, the words 'conviction' and 'sentence' must not be used in relation to children dealt with summarily; the expressions 'finding of guilt' and 'order made on a finding of guilt' must be used instead.[222] The guiding principle for the sentencing process, as with adults, is that the punishment must be commensurate with the seriousness of the offence.[223] As in care proceedings (see para 9.134), the youth court must consider all medical and welfare reports relating to the child before choosing from the wide selection of available 'disposals' (explained in paras 8.90–8.98 below). In cases where no custodial or community sentence is passed, or where the child is found not guilty, the court has the power to notify the social services of any matters it thinks fit, provided it considers that the welfare of the child requires this.[224]

Fines

8.90   While children can be fined for any offence other than murder, they are less likely to be fined than adults. A child under the age of 14 cannot personally be made to pay more than £200 (including costs) and any older child cannot be made to pay more than £1,000.[225] If the offender is under the age of 17, the amount payable in compensation to the victim of the offence is also limited to £1,000 (as opposed to the adult maximum of £5,000).[226] The child's parent or guardian will be ordered to pay the fine or compensation if the child is under the age of 16, and may be ordered to do so in any other case.[227]

---

[220] *R (McCann) v Crown Court at Manchester* [2002] UKHL 39, [2003] 1 AC 787.
[221] *Anti-Social Behaviour* (2012).
[222] Criminal Justice (Children) (NI) Order 1998, art 5.
[223] Of particular relevance are art 19 (restrictions on imposing custodial sentences) and art 37 (regarding the effect of previous convictions and of offending while on bail).
[224] Criminal Justice (Children) (NI) Order 1998, art 33.
[225] Ibid art 34 and Criminal Justice (NI) Order 1994, art 3(2).
[226] Criminal Justice (NI) Order 1994, art 14(11), as amended by Criminal Justice (Children) (NI) Order 1998, Sch 5, para 41(b).
[227] Criminal Justice (Children) (NI) Order 1998, art 35.

Youth conferencing

8.91   Youth conferencing is a process by which young people who admit their involvement in certain criminal behaviour, or are found guilty in a court, can be brought face-to-face with the victims of their crimes so that an action plan can be developed to prevent further offending and make amends to the victim. This approach to dealing with crime is often referred to as 'restorative justice'. When prosecutors refer young people to the Youth Conference Service,[228] rather than proceed with a prosecution, the resulting meetings are called 'diversionary youth conferences'. Otherwise references are by the youth court. In 2008 the Criminal Justice Inspectorate (see para 7.97) published a report evaluating the youth conferencing system and two years later it issued a follow-up report praising the progress that had been made in implementing the recommendations of the earlier report. A further report produced for England and Wales in 2010 heaped further praise on the Northern Irish youth conferencing system:

> We have been impressed by the restorative Youth Conferencing Service introduced in Northern Ireland five years ago and believe that its professionally co-ordinated approach provides a suitable model for England and Wales. Reconviction rates among young offenders involved in restorative justice processes are relatively low and youth conferencing in Northern Ireland has been accompanied by lower use of custody. Approval ratings among victims and all those involved are high. No one there suggests it is in any sense a 'soft' or easy option. Young offenders themselves acknowledge just how tough it has been to have to face up to the harm and misery they have caused their victims, their families and the community. Restorative justice is an approach whose time has come, and the results, when professionally managed, speak for themselves.[229]

It has also been suggested that youth conferencing may have had beneficial effects on post-conflict peace-building in Northern Ireland.[230]

Detention[231]

8.92   Detention in the Woodlands Juvenile Justice Centre in Bangor is available only for persons aged 16 or over[232] and can be imposed if the offence was so serious that only a custodial sentence can be justified or if the offence was of a violent or sexual nature and only a custodial sentence

---

[228] This is overseen by the Youth Justice Agency.
[229] *Time for a Fresh Start: The report of the independent Commission on youth crime and antisocial behaviour*, Chair's Introduction, 5.
[230] J Doak and D O'Mahony, 'In search of legitimacy: restorative youth conferencing in Northern Ireland' (2011) 31 *Legal Studies* 305.
[231] See further the Prisons and Young Offenders' Centre Rules (NI) 1995, as amended.
[232] See Treatment of Offenders Act (NI) 1968, s 5, as substituted by Treatment of Offenders (NI) Order 1989, art 7.

would protect the public from harm.[233] If the offence was one which could be punishable with 14 years' imprisonment in the case of an adult offender, the Minister of Justice can direct where the detention is to take place.[234] At any particular time there are usually 20 to 30 young people held at the Juvenile Justice Centre; in 2010–11 the average length of stay was 12 days, whereas in England and Wales it was six weeks. An inspection of the Centre was last conducted by the Criminal Justice Inspectorate in 2011.[235] While it praised much that was happening in the Centre, the report noted the adverse impact of the high numbers of children being sent to the Centre for less than 24 hours under the PACE Order. It also suggested that improvements should be made to the provision of education and health care at the Centre. The cost per occupant during 2010–11 was as high as £268,000.[236]

8.93   A young person can be ordered to be detained in the Juvenile Justice Centre at Woodlands in Bangor if he or she has been found guilty of an offence which, if an adult had committed it, would be punishable by a term of imprisonment.[237] The order requires the child to be detained for a set period followed by an equal period of supervision by a probation officer (or other person designated by the Minister of Justice). The normal duration of the order is six months (ie three months in detention and three under supervision), but the maximum permitted duration is two years.[238]

A probation order[239]

8.94   This type of order, which can only be imposed if the child consents,[240] places a child under the supervision of a probation officer (see para 7.84) for a period between six months and three years and can require the child to comply with any requirements which the court considers desirable in the interests of securing his or her rehabilitation, protecting the public from harm or preventing the child from committing further offences. If the probation order is breached, the child may then be dealt with as if found guilty of the original offence for which he or she was placed on probation.[241]

---

[233] Criminal Justice (NI) Order 1996, art 19.
[234] Criminal Justice (Children) (NI) Order 1998, art 45.
[235] *An Announced Inspection of Woodlands Juvenile Justice Centre* (2011).
[236] Ibid p 17.
[237] Criminal Justice (Children) (NI) Order 1998, art 39(1).
[238] Ibid art 39(2).
[239] Criminal Justice (NI) Order 1996, art 10 and Sch 1.
[240] Ibid art 10(3).
[241] Ibid Sch 2, para 3.

A custody care order

8.95   This order allows a child under the age of 14, instead of being given a custodial sentence, to be placed in secure accommodation for a set period of up to two years, followed by a period of supervision.[242] While being kept in secure accommodation the child must benefit from certain provisions of the Children (NI) Order 1995 (as if he or she were in care) but if a child runs away from such secure accommodation he or she can be arrested and the custody care order can be lengthened by up to 30 days; alternatively the child can be dealt with for the original offence as if he or she had just been found guilty of it. There are also penalties for breaching the supervision part of the custody care order.

An attendance centre order

8.96   This order requires the offender to attend a centre for a fixed number of hours.[243] A session of physical education is usually followed by a class (eg on first aid), employment in handicrafts, or other instruction. A child cannot be required to attend for a total of more than 24 hours, but a child aged 14 to 16 must attend for at least 12 hours.[244] In 2007 an independent report indicated that attendance centre orders were working well in Northern Ireland.[245]

Reparation and community orders

8.97   A reparation order requires the child to make reparation for the offence to a specified person (if that person agrees) or to the community at large, otherwise than by paying compensation.[246] Like a probation order, it needs the child's consent. It cannot be combined with a custodial sentence, a community service order or a community responsibility order (see para 8.98) and it cannot require more than 24 hours' activity by the offender. The reparation will usually be supervised by a probation officer or social worker and must be completed within six months of the order being made. If the reparation order is breached the child can be given an attendance centre order or can be dealt with for the original offence as if he or she had just been found guilty of it.

---

[242] Justice (NI) Act 2002, s 56, which inserts art 44A into the Criminal Justice (Children) (NI) Order 1998.
[243] Criminal Justice (Children) (NI) Order 1998, art 37.
[244] Ibid.
[245] H Dawson, S Dunn and V Morgan, *Evaluation of the Attendance Centre Order*, available on the Youth Justice Agency's website.
[246] Justice (NI) Act 2002, s 54 and Sch 10, inserting provisions into the Criminal Justice (Children) (NI) Order 1998.

8.98 A community service order is available only for persons aged 16 or over. It requires the young person to provide a specified service for a set number of hours between 40 and 240.[247] A community responsibility order requires the child to attend at a specified place for a number of hours of instruction in citizenship (no more than 40) and to undertake specified practical activities.[248] The instruction is to include information about the responsibilities which a person owes to the community and the impact of crime on victims and it must be received within six months of the order being made. The order cannot be combined with any other punishment and again requires the child's consent. If it is breached the child can be given an attendance centre order or a community service order or can be dealt with for the original offence as if he or she had just been found guilty of it. A report was published in 2006 evaluating the effectiveness of reparation orders and community responsibility orders.[249]

THE LAW OF EVIDENCE

8.99 There is a golden rule, as already emphasised (see para 7.8), that in a criminal case the burden of proof rests on the prosecution to show that the defendant is guilty beyond reasonable doubt. But the law of Northern Ireland, like the law of England and Wales, has a myriad of further rules and principles to specify the kind of information that qualifies as 'proof' in a court of law. There is little difference between the jurisdictions in these matters.[250] Courts in both jurisdictions are entitled to take 'judicial notice' of obvious facts, which means that formal evidence of the truth of those facts does not need to be put before the court. An example would be the fact that from Monday to Friday road traffic is much heavier at certain times of the day than at others. In Northern Ireland there is a special rule that judicial notice can be taken of the current law in England and Wales and in the Republic of Ireland;[251] law of other jurisdictions needs to be formally proved, usually by testimony from an expert witness.

8.100 The law recognises three types of evidence: testimonial evidence, circumstantial evidence, and real evidence. 'Testimonial evidence' is where someone goes into the witness box to give oral evidence in response to questions posed by the legal representatives acting for each side.

[247] Criminal Justice (NI) Order 1996, art 13.
[248] Justice (NI) Act 2002 s 55 and Sch 10, inserting new provisions into the Criminal Justice (Children) (NI) Order 1998.
[249] H Dawson, S Dunn, V Morgan, and C Donaghy, *An Assessment of the Reparation Order and Community Responsibility Order in Northern Ireland* (Belfast Northern Ireland Office, Research and Statistical Series, Report No 15).
[250] A good textbook is Raymond Emson, *Evidence* (London, Palgrave Macmillan, 5th edn, 2010).
[251] Judicature (NI) Act 1978, s 114(2).

'Circumstantial evidence' is a fact from which an inference can be drawn suggesting that another fact is true (eg X was the only other person in the room at the time when Y was killed in that room). In an appeal from Northern Ireland that reached the House of Lords, *McGreevy v DPP*,[252] it was held that, just because circumstantial evidence is inherently less reliable than testimonial evidence, this does not mean that a jury should always be directed to acquit the defendant if it is not convinced that the evidence is inconsistent with any other conclusion than that the defendant is guilty. 'Real evidence' is material which can be inspected by the court itself, such as the gun allegedly used in a shooting. If the real evidence is a document, the party relying upon it will usually have to produce the original version of that document, not a copy, and will have to show that it has not been forged.[253]

Competence to give evidence

8.101   An accused person cannot be compelled to give evidence, but may do so if he or she wishes. Only in limited circumstances can a judge or jury draw adverse inferences from the refusal of the accused to give evidence. The spouse or civil partner of the accused can be compelled to give evidence if called upon to do so by the accused, but can only be compelled to give evidence for the prosecution if the offence charged involves an assault on that spouse, civil partner or any person under the age of 17.[254] In criminal cases a person of any age or mental ability can give evidence provided he or she is able to understand the questions put to him or her and to give answers that can be understood.[255] A person can give *sworn* evidence only if he or she is at least 14 years of age and has 'a sufficient appreciation of the solemnity of the occasion and of the particular responsibility to tell the truth which is involved in taking an oath'.[256] It is the crime of perjury, punishable with up to seven years in prison, to wilfully give false sworn evidence;[257] to wilfully give false unsworn evidence is also a crime, punishable with up to six months in prison.[258]

8.102   If a person has witnessed a serious offence and has given a video-recorded account of the events when they were fresh in his or her memory, the video-recording may be submitted as evidence in court at a much later date.[259] Special measures can be taken to protect vulnerable and intimidated

---

[252] [1973] 1 WLR 276.
[253] Criminal Justice Act 2003, s 133.
[254] PACE (NI) Order 1989, art 79, as amended.
[255] Criminal Evidence (NI) Order 1999, art 31(1) and (3).
[256] Ibid art 33(2). The NIO has produced a helpful booklet entitled *Achieving Best Evidence in Criminal Proceedings (NI): Guidance for Vulnerable or Intimidated Witnesses, and Children*, available at www.nio.go.uk.
[257] Perjury (NI) Order 1979, art 3(1).
[258] Ibid art 35(2).
[259] Criminal Justice (Evidence) (NI) Order 2004, art 39(1).

witnesses, such as screening them from the accused when giving evidence in court.[260] It used to be compulsory for all children aged 16 or under to give evidence via a live link or through video-recorded evidence, but the law was changed in 2011 so as to make this procedure optional.[261] For some offences child complainants or witnesses cannot be directly cross-examined by the person accused of committing those offences.[262]

The criterion of relevance

8.103   Generally speaking, the main criterion for deciding whether evidence is admissible or not is its relevance. Information about a defendant's previous convictions is usually deemed to be irrelevant, as a person should be judged on what he or she has actually done, not on his or her propensity to act in a certain way in the past. But if a crime has been committed in a peculiar way, the fact that the defendant has used that particular *modus operandi* ('way of operating') on previous occasions may well make his or her convictions relevant (this is called 'similar fact evidence').[263] In certain situations, under the Criminal Justice (Evidence) (NI) Order 2004, the 'bad character' of the defendant can also be placed in evidence.[264] This is possible, for example, if the evidence is adduced to correct a false impression given by the defendant or if the defendant has made an attack on another person's character.[265] Just because evidence is relevant, however, does not mean that it has to be accorded much weight: its significance will depend on all the circumstances of the case.

Hearsay evidence

8.104   Hearsay evidence, which is evidence given by (A) about what (B) said, rather than direct evidence given by (B), is generally inadmissible because it tends to be inaccurate. But the Criminal Justice (Evidence) (NI) Order 2004 again affirms that there are several exceptions to that general rule. Hearsay evidence can therefore be admitted if a witness is unavailable to give direct testimonial evidence because he or she is dead, is physically or mentally ill, is living abroad, cannot be found, or is in fear.[266] *In R v Horncastle*[267] the UK

---

[260] Criminal Evidence (NI) Order 1999, arts 4–21.
[261] Justice Act (NI) 2011, s 8, amending the Criminal Evidence (NI) Order 1999, art 9. In England and Wales optionality was introduced by the Coroners and Justice Act 2009, s 100(4).
[262] Criminal Evidence (NI) Order 1999, art 23, as amended by the Justice Act (NI) 2011, s 13.
[263] See, eg, *R v M* [2011] NICA 18, [2011] 6 BNIL 44.
[264] See, eg, *R v Sloss* [2012] NICA 16, [2012] 6 BNIL 32.
[265] art 6(1).
[266] Ibid art 20(2).
[267] [2009] UKSC 14, [2010] 2 AC 373.

Supreme Court ruled that the current law on hearsay evidence in criminal cases is consistent with the requirements of the European Convention on Human Rights, and the Grand Chamber of the European Court of Human Rights later ruled that this is in fact so.[268] (In civil cases hearsay evidence is generally admissible, but there are safeguards in place to ensure that it is credible and given appropriate weight.[269])

Confessions

8.105   If a person makes a statement confessing to a crime, this is admissible as evidence in a court only if, when challenged to do so, the prosecution proves beyond reasonable doubt that the confession was not obtained by oppression or in consequence of anything said or done which was likely to render it unreliable.[270] But even if a confession is declared inadmissible under this rule, any facts discovered as a result of the confession *can* be admitted in evidence (contrary to what is termed 'the fruit of the poisoned tree' principle, which is commonly applied in the USA). Generally, though, a court in Northern Ireland will exclude a confession if the defendant made it without having been cautioned in accordance with the PACE Code.[271] There is no longer any special rule concerning the admissibility of confessions in terrorist cases in Northern Ireland.[272]

Privileged information

8.106   The law also recognises the so-called 'privilege against self-incrimination', which refers to the right we all have under common law not to produce any evidence which may expose us to a criminal charge. It is sometimes called the right to silence and Americans call it 'pleading the Fifth' because the privilege is guaranteed by the Fifth Amendment to the US Constitution. The law of evidence in Northern Ireland recognises one or two other privileges too. The legal advice which a client receives from his or her solicitor, and confidential communications which relate to contemplated legal proceedings, do not have to be disclosed to a court. This is because there is a public interest in a person being able to discuss his or her affairs completely privately with a legal adviser. But in a recent case

---

[268] *Al-Khawaja and Tahery v UK* (2012) 54 EHRR 23. A Chamber of the Court had found an incompatibility: (2009) 49 EHRR 1.

[269] See the Civil Evidence (NI) Order 1997, which largely mirrors the Civil Evidence Act 1995 for England and Wales.

[270] PACE (NI) Order 1989, art 74.

[271] *R v McKeown* [2000] NIJB 139; *R v Caraher and McGinn* [2001] 4 BNIL 42.

[272] PACE (NI) Order 1989, art 74 and the Terrorism Act 2000 (Cessation of Effect of Section 76) Order 2002 (SI 2141).

from Northern Ireland, *McE v Prison Service of Northern Ireland*,[273] the House of Lords confirmed that evidence of wrongdoing can still be obtained by covert surveillance so long as legal authorisation has been obtained for such action,[274] even if the surveillance takes place when a client is having a supposedly private conversation with his or her solicitor.

8.107 Any documents covered by legal professional privilege cannot be made the object of a search warrant unless this is authorised by a county court judge.[275] Information held by journalists is also privileged, up to a point. A journalist can be compelled to reveal his or her sources if this is necessary 'in the interests of justice or national security or for the prevention of disorder or crime',[276] and journalistic material can be made the subject of a search warrant if certain conditions are satisfied.[277] Whatever the rules within particular churches, the law of Northern Ireland does not recognise any evidential privilege in communications received by ministers of religion.

Illegally obtained evidence

8.108 Strange as it may seem, evidence obtained illegally, or without formal authorisation,[278] is not necessarily inadmissible. The House of Lords has affirmed that evidence obtained by torture cannot be admitted,[279] but it went on to rule (by a majority) that the burden rests on the defendant to show, even if only on the balance of probabilities, that the evidence was so obtained. It will often be very difficult, in practice, for the defendant to produce such proof, so the exclusionary rule is somewhat undermined. However, courts have a wide-ranging statutory discretion to exclude illegally obtained evidence:

> In any criminal proceedings the court may refuse to allow evidence on which the prosecution proposes to rely to be given if it appears to the court that, having regard to all the circumstances, including the circumstances in which the evidence was obtained, the admission of the evidence would have such an adverse effect on the fairness of the proceedings that the court ought not to admit it.[280]

This means that evidence can be excluded if the police have employed any sort of underhand tactics to obtain it. The House of Lords has also made it clear that victims' rights are important in this context, so if a person is

[273] [2009] UKHL 15, [2009] 1 AC 908.
[274] Under the Regulation of Investigatory Powers Act 2000, s 32.
[275] PACE (NI) Order 1989, art 11(1) and Sch 1.
[276] Contempt of Court Act 1981, s 10. But the PSNI's application to the county court in relation to journalist Suzanne Breen's contacts with the Real IRA failed: *BBC v PSNI* [2009] NICty 4, [2012] 1 BNIL 17.
[277] PACE (NI) Order 1989, art 11(1) and Sch 1.
[278] *Public Prosecution Service v Elliott and McKee* [2011] NICA 61, [2011] 8 BNIL 29.
[279] *A v Secretary of State for the Home Dept (No 2)* [2005] UKHL 71, [2006] 2 AC 221.
[280] PACE (NI) Order 1989, art 76(1).

convicted of a serious offence on the basis of evidence that was obtained by a more or less technical breach of the law the conviction may not be quashed on appeal.[281]

8.109 'Intercept evidence' (evidence obtained from covert surveillance of telephonic or electronic communications) is not admissible in a criminal trial.[282] This is often seen as an obstacle to the successful prosecution of terrorists, and even human rights organisations such as Liberty and the Committee on the Administration of Justice have called for intercept evidence to be made admissible in preference to the use of other anti-terrorist mechanisms such as control orders. But a high-level inquiry into the practicalities of this proposal concluded that it could not be done without giving away too much information about the sorts of surveillance techniques that are employed to gain the evidence in the first place.[283]

Opinion evidence

8.110 A witness must testify only about what he or she knows, not about what he or she thinks. 'Opinion evidence', as it is called, is admissible only if it is proffered by someone who is a recognised expert in the field in question – a psychiatrist, engineer, dentist, etc. It used to be the rule that expert witnesses were immune from being sued if they presented their evidence negligently, but in 2011 the UK Supreme Court swept away that immunity in *Jones v Kaney*.[284]

8.111 It was noted above that the prosecution is under a duty to disclose to the defence any information which may be of use to the defence (see para 8.38). The main exception to this rule is enshrined in 'the doctrine of public interest immunity' (PII). This allows certain details (such as the identity of a police informer) to be kept secret if there is a public interest at stake, such as the life of the informer, which outweighs the public interest in open justice. The House of Lords has ruled, in *R v H*,[285] that in appropriate cases the court should admit a summary of or extracts from the evidence, or documents in a redacted form. It even said that in exceptional cases the court might appoint 'special counsel' who can examine the evidence on the defendant's behalf and (without consulting with the defendant about what is contained in that

---

[281] *Attorney General's Reference (No 3 of 1999)* [2000] UKHL 67, [2001] 2 AC 91. For a case where the judge refused to exercise his discretion even though the confession in question had been made to a journalist who swore to keep it secret, see *R v McKeown* [2003] NICC 3.

[282] Regulation of Investigatory Powers Act 2000, s 17. See *Evidence for Change: Lifting the ban on intercept evidence in court* (University of Essex, Democratic Audit, 2007).

[283] Privy Counsellor Review Committee, *Anti-terrorism, Crime and Security Act 2001 Review*, HC 100, 2003–04.

[284] [2011] UKSC 13, [2011] 2 AC 398.

[285] [2004] UKHL 3, [2004] 2 AC 134.

evidence) make representations to the court on the defendant's behalf. PII certificates were used in many criminal trials in Northern Ireland during the troubles, but their use has become much less common. In 2005 the Attorney General for England and Wales issued *Guidelines on Disclosure*,[286] which are also applied in Northern Ireland.

Article 6 of the European Convention

8.112 Article 6 of the European Convention on Human Rights, which is part of the law throughout the UK by virtue of the Human Rights Act 1998, guarantees that when a person is being prosecuted for a criminal offence he or she is entitled to 'a fair and public hearing within a reasonable time by an independent and impartial tribunal established by law'. If a breach of this right to an unfair trial comes to light during the course of the trial itself the court has discretion to 'stay' (ie stop) the proceedings, but the House of Lords has said that this should occur only in exceptional circumstances.[287] The power to stay is an illustration of the courts' inherent jurisdiction, under the common law, to put an end to court proceedings if they constitute an 'abuse of process'. It might also be applied, for example, if during a person's trial it transpires that he or she has been the victim of 'entrapment' by the police (ie has been lured into committing an offence).[288] However the European Court of Human Rights has made it clear that it is largely for each State to decide upon its own rules of evidence and it will not usually declare that there has been an unfair trial merely because the outcome of the case appears on one view to be contrary to the weight of the evidence.

---

[286] Available at www.attorneygeneral.gov.uk.
[287] *Attorney General's Reference (No 2 of 2001)* [2003] UKHL 68, [2004] 2 AC 72. This was the first case in which the House of Lords sat as a bench of nine judges. The two Scottish judges dissented; in Scotland the rule had previously been that a stay should always be granted in cases of unfairness caused by delays.
[288] *R v Looseley* [2001] UKHL 53, [2001] 1 WLR 2060.

9

Private Law in Northern Ireland

BRANCHES OF PRIVATE LAW

9.1 The names of the various branches of private law are mostly self-explanatory. They include land law, contract law, company law, and family law. Each of these can in turn be subdivided, and some of the subdivisions overlap with other subdivisions or with other main branches of law; examples are landlord and tenant law, housing law, employment law, consumer law, banking law, partnership law, insolvency law,[1] divorce law, and child law. Of the less obviously named branches, the law of trusts mainly regulates the way certain forms of property are managed, while the law of torts is mostly concerned with the compensation of people who have been injured, or whose property has been damaged, as a result of someone else's carelessness or intentional misbehaviour. This chapter aims to give a brief overview of some of the more significant branches of private law. Readers are encouraged to follow up references in footnotes if they are looking for more detailed information.[2]

LAND LAW[3]

9.2 Land law is part of the larger branch of law known as 'property law', which refers to those parts of private law which set out our rights and duties in relation to the things we own or rent, or in which we have some other kind of interest. As the most important form of property is land, called, in law, 'real property', or, in the USA, 'realty' (an expression which in law embraces the buildings erected on land) the term property law is sometimes used as

[1] On this area see S and W Gowdy, *Individual Insolvency: The Law and Practice in Northern Ireland* (Belfast, SLS Legal Publications, 2012).
[2] See the wide-ranging online advice guide produced by the Northern Ireland Association of Citizens' Advice Bureaux, available at www.adviceguide.org.uk/nireland.htm. There is also useful legal information available at www.adviceni.net/advice/index.cfm
[3] New developments in the land law of Northern Ireland are best traced through the entries in nearly every issue of the Bulletin of Northern Ireland Law (see para 4.53). See too *Folio: Northern Ireland Conveyancing and Land Law Journal* (Belfast, SLS Legal Publications).

a synonym for land law. Strictly speaking, however, it should also refer to the law concerning property which is not land. There are innumerable forms of such property (collectively known as 'personalty'), ranging from the most tangible,[4] such as cars and antiques, to the most intangible,[5] such as shares in a company or premium bonds. Some of these types of intangible property, such as copyright, patents, trademarks and designs are referred to collectively as 'intellectual property'. Unfortunately there is no space in this book to address any of those specialised aspects of property law, but the relevant law in Northern Ireland is almost entirely the same as that which applies in England and Wales.

9.3   The law of Northern Ireland relating to interests in, and disposition of, land is however significantly different from that applying in England and Wales. In that jurisdiction the law was simplified by a group of Acts passed in the 1920s (the Birkenhead legislation), the most important of which was the Law of Property Act 1925. But Northern Ireland never followed that reform path. Instead the law of Northern Ireland is closer to that which applies in the Republic of Ireland, although new legislation enacted there in 2009 has created important differences between the two jurisdictions.[6] Reports by experts recommended significant reform of aspects of land law in Northern Ireland in 1967,[7] 1971[8] and 1990,[9] but only minor reforms were made in response to those reports,[10] with the result that today much of the law in force in Northern Ireland still dates back many centuries and is spread over a wide range of legislation. It was therefore no surprise that one of the first tasks which the new Northern Ireland Law Commission chose to undertake after it was created in 2007 (see para 3.67) was a further review of land law. Its final report on the matter, containing two draft reform Bills, was published in 2010.[11] Unfortunately the Bills have not yet been translated into Acts.

Estates and other rights relating to land

9.4   At present no-one fully 'owns' land in Northern Ireland: there is a fiction, deriving from feudal times, that all land belongs to the Crown and that the nearest an ordinary person can come to owning land outright is by

---

[4] A piece of tangible property is sometimes referred to as a *chose in possession*.

[5] A piece of intangible property is sometimes referred to as a *chose in action*.

[6] Land and Conveyancing Law Reform Act 2009 (Ir).

[7] *Report of the Committee on the Registration of Title to Land* (1967) (the Lowry Report).

[8] *Survey of the Land Law of Northern Ireland* (Belfast, HMSO).

[9] *Final Report of the Land Law Working Group* (HMSO, Belfast).

[10] See, eg, the Property (NI) Orders 1978 and 1997. Most of Part II of the latter Order (on the redemption of ground rents) was never brought into force before it was repealed by the Ground Rents Act (NI) 2001.

[11] *Land Law* (NILC 8). It stretches to 329 pages.

owning an 'estate' in land called a 'freehold estate' or a 'fee simple absolute'. Other, lesser, forms of ownership are 'fee tails', where land is held by one person until he or she dies and it passes automatically to that person's oldest child, and 'life estates', where land is held by one person (a 'life tenant') for as long as he or she lives but reverts to the fee simple owner when the life tenant dies. Then there is a 'leasehold estate', which is where someone rents, or 'leases', land from another person, usually for a fixed period, which may be renewable; the person paying rent is called a 'tenant' or 'lessee' and the person from whom the land is rented is called the 'landlord' or 'lessor'. In Northern Ireland some land is till held under a 'fee-farm grant', which is comparable to a fee simple absolute except.that an annual rent has to be paid to the freeholder, as if the land were held on leasehold.[12] All these forms of ownership are, at the moment, varieties of 'estates' in land recognised by the common law in Northern Ireland.

9.5   Land can also be co-owned. A 'tenancy in common' is where two or more people each own a stipulated fraction of the land (or, rather, of its value); this fraction can be bought and sold as if it were a wholly separate piece of property. A 'joint tenancy' is where two or more people each own the whole property together. While it is possible for one of the joint tenants to unilaterally 'sever' the tenancy, thereby transforming it into a tenancy in common, if this does not happen the proportion of the land owned by a joint tenant will be automatically transferred to the surviving joint tenant(s) when the former dies. Many husbands and wives, for example, are joint tenants of the matrimonial home and therefore enjoy this 'right of survivorship'. It means that a joint tenant cannot pass on his or her share of the tenancy in his or her will. The Northern Ireland Law Commission has recommended that, while joint tenants should continue to have the right to sever the tenancy, they should first of all be required to lodge a notice of their intention to do so in the appropriate registry (the Land Registry for registered land and the Registry of Deeds for unregistered land: for the difference see para 9.13 below).

9.6   Other, lesser, interests in land are recognized only through the system know as equity (see para 4.3), which means that they are not as well protected as legal estates or tenancies and can often be bought out if the legal estate in the same piece of land is transferred to someone who does not want the equitable interests to continue. Thus, even if a married couple are not co-owners of a matrimonial home, the spouse who is not the legal owner may be considered to have an equitable interest in the property by virtue of his or her occupation of, and contribution to the upkeep of, that home.[13] Equitable interests include those which are enjoyed by the beneficiaries of

[12] It has not been possible to create a new fee farm grant since 1997: Property (NI) Order 1997, art 28(1).

[13] See, eg, *Bank of Scotland plc v Brogan and Brogan* [2012] NICh 21, [2012] 10 BNIL 50.

a trust of land (see para 9.20). The courts have also developed an equitable doctrine known as 'proprietary estoppel'. This allows a person who has relied significantly upon a promise that land will be transferred to him or her to have that promise enforced in law even though no formal transfer of the land has taken place.[14]

9.7   There are various other rights which people may have in relation to land. An 'easement', for example, is a right to make use of another person's land for a certain purpose, such as a right of way or a right to fish. In Northern Ireland there are two traditional rights analogous to easements called 'agistment' and 'conacre'; the former is a right to graze livestock on someone else's land and the latter is the right to sow and harvest crops on someone else's land. A 'covenant' is a promise made in a deed to do or not do something in relation to land (eg a promise not to build on the land), and the person to whom this promise is originally made (the 'covenantee') can often enforce this promise against persons who later become owners of the land in succession to the covenantor. An 'option to buy' arises where, for example, a tenant takes a lease of property and insists on the inclusion in the lease of a clause which gives the tenant the freedom to buy the property outright after a certain period of time; this too is a right which can be enforced against the landlord and his or her successors in title. A person who is residing in a house as the spouse or civil partner of the owner of that house is also protected, to some extent at least, against the owner of the house designating it as security for a loan which he or she has accepted. Many of these rights over land need to be entered on the statutory charges register if they are to be fully enforceable (see para 9.13).

9.8   In its 2010 report, the Northern Ireland Law Commission recommended that the concept of estates in land should be abolished[15] and that instead the law of Northern Ireland should just recognise the rights of owners of land and the rights in respect of the same land of non-owners, such as tenants, mortgagees, easement-holders or people residing on the land. That reform would undoubtedly simplify the law.

Tenancies

9.9   A lot of land in Northern Ireland is held on very long leaseholds (eg 999 years) or under fee-farm grants (see para 9.4). This means that the lessee or grant-holder is in practice a freeholder but in law a tenant with a duty to pay rent – 'ground rent'. As a contribution to simplifying the land ownership system, the law of Northern Ireland now allows people to 'redeem' (ie buy out) the ground rent on their property, usually by paying

---

[14] See, eg, *Mulholland v Kane* [2009] NICh 9 (Deeny J).
[15] Ibid chs. 2 and 3.

a one-off lump sum equal to nine times the annual rent.[16] The Northern Ireland Law Commission has recommended that legislation should appoint a day on which annual ground rents of £10 or less should be automatically repealed on payment of £90.[17]

9.10 If a tenant wants to sell his or her tenancy, or sub-let it, he or she must first acquire the permission of the landlord.[18] The original lease will usually contain certain promises made by the landlord and tenant to each other (eg the landlord might promise to maintain the exterior of the property and to insure it, while the tenant might promise to keep the interior of the property in good repair and not to use the property for particular purposes). If either side then sells their interest in the property to someone else, or if the tenant sub-lets, these promises continue to be binding on their successors. The lease will also usually specify what the landlord can do if the rent is not paid; the default position in law is that once the rent is overdue by 12 months the landlord can apply to a court to have the tenant ejected.[19]

Business and private residential tenancies

9.11 Tenants who occupy business premises have more security of tenure than other tenants in that the landlord can refuse to continue the lease only if he or she is able to rely on one of the reasons specified in legislation (eg that the landlord wishes to use the property for his or her own purposes); the landlord cannot terminate the lease on a mere whim if the tenant wishes it to continue.[20] Moreover in Northern Ireland the law prohibits a business tenancy from allowing the tenant to contract out of his or her right to apply for a renewal of the tenancy.[21] Most business tenancies also contain rent review clauses, which determine when and how the amount of rent payable is to be reviewed. Disputes over whether a new tenancy should be agreed, and on what terms, including the amount of rent, can be dealt with by the Lands Tribunal (see para 9.18). Tenants of privately rented homes and flats also have additional protections accorded by legislation: they must, for example, be issued with a rent book which gives details of the lease and, unless the lease specifically provides otherwise, the landlord is under a duty

---

[16] Ground Rents Act (NI) 2001, s 5 and Sch 1, para 2; and the Ground Rents (Multiplier) Order (NI) 2002 (SR 228). In 2006 the Department of Finance and Personnel published a report on the way in which the redemption scheme was operating and it concluded that a multiplier of 9 was still appropriate.

[17] n 9 above, ch 13 and the report's draft Ground Rents (Amendment) Bill (NI).

[18] Landlord and Tenant Law (Amendment) (Ir) Act 1860, ss 10 and 18 (known as Deasy's Act).

[19] Ibid s 52.

[20] Business Tenancies (NI) Order 1996, art 12(1).

[21] In its report on business tenancies published in 2011 (NILC 9) the Commission recommended a partial relaxation of this prohibition.

to keep the property in good repair and to ensure that the electricity, gas, heating, water, and sanitation arrangements are in good working order.[22] The tenant, on the other hand, is under a duty to make good any damage that is done to the property and to keep the interior in reasonable decorative order.[23] Some private tenancies are controlled (see para 6.84) and every year or so the Department for Social Development issues an order increasing the rents that have to be paid for those tenancies.[24]

9.12   A lease needs to be distinguished from a 'licence', which is the kind of right held by a lodger. A licence gives rise to a mere contractual right, not to an interest in the land itself. In recent years the courts have developed criteria for distinguishing between the two concepts but at the same time they have begun to give licensees rights which are not much weaker than those which lessees enjoy. The chief difference between a licence and a lease is that the former does not ensure that the licensee has *exclusive possession* of the premises.[25] The Northern Ireland Law Commission is content to allow the law to be developed by the courts and has therefore not recommended any legislative reform in this area.[26]

Conveyances

9.13   The 'conveyancing' (ie transfer) of land is complicated in Northern Ireland by the fact that about half of all the land is registered, meaning that 'title' to it (ie ownership of it) is indicated at a central Land Registry,[27] while the rest of the land is unregistered, meaning that its ownership is indicated only through the 'deeds' (ie the legal contracts) by which that ownership was created and which are kept in a Registry of Deeds.[28] The registered land in Northern Ireland is mostly in rural areas or on the edges of towns where relatively new housing estates have been built. The ultimate goal is to have all land registered, but that will take several more years to achieve even though the whole of Northern Ireland has been a compulsory registration area since 2002.[29] This means that when unregistered land is transferred, a title is created for it in the Land Registry. There is, in addition, a statutory charges register in Northern Ireland. This was created in 1951 to allow

[22] Private Tenancies (NI) Order 2006, arts 5 and 7.
[23] Ibid art 8.
[24] See, eg, the Registered Rents (Increase) Order (NI) 2010 (SR 285). In 2009 the Department issued a consultation paper on reforms to the private rented sector (*Building Sound Foundations*).
[25] *Street v Mountford* [1985] AC 809.
[26] n 9 above, paras 4.12 and 4.13.
[27] Land Registration Act (NI) 1970 and Registration (Lands and Deeds) (NI) Order 1992. See A and E Moir, *Moir on Land Registration: A Guide to Land Registration Law and Practice in Northern Ireland* (Belfast, SLS Legal Publications, 2012).
[28] Registration of Deeds Act (NI) 1970 and Registration (Lands and Deeds) (NI) Order 1992.
[29] See the Compulsory Registration of Title (No 2) Order (NI) 2002 (SR 401).

certain interests in land to be publicly notified so that future purchasers of that land will more easily be made aware of them.[30]

9.14   A contract for the sale of land has to be in writing and signed by the party against whom it is being enforced.[31] A contract for the lease of land lasting for longer than one year also has to be in writing, and signed by the landlord.[32] The actual conveyance of land has to be achieved by a deed, which is a contract under seal, although today the 'seal' can merely be a symbol to that effect. The Northern Ireland Law Commission has not made recommendations in this area because it is conscious that in the near future the transfer of land will probably occur through electronic means and it does not want to pre-empt what legal measures may then need to be put in place.[33] Currently, if a contract for the sale of land has been significantly performed, despite all the requisite formalities not having been fully complied with, the common law will sometimes still treat it as valid under what is known as 'the doctrine of part performance'.[34]

Mortgages[35]

9.15   When a person buys a house using a mortgage, the legal situation, if the land in question is registered, is usually that the lender of the money acquires a statutory charge over the house until the purchaser fully pays off the mortgage. If the land is unregistered the borrower will grant a lease, or a sub-lease, of the land to the lender.[36] A purchaser who enters into a loan to buy a house, and who puts up the house as security for the loan, is called a 'mortgagor' and the lender is called a 'mortgagee'. The mortgagor has the right to pay off the mortgage, a right referred to as 'the equity of redemption', and any clause in the mortgage which operates to make it very difficult for the mortgagor to pay it off may be invalidated by the courts as 'a clog on the equity of redemption'. When another person goes to buy a house which is still mortgaged the mortgage will show up in the statutory charges register. Usually a mortgage relating to a private home makes the home security only for the money lent to purchase that house. An 'all monies mortgage', by contrast, is one where the house in question becomes security

---

[30] See now Land Registration Act (NI) 1970, ss 86–92.

[31] Statute of Frauds (Ireland) 1695, s 2.

[32] Landlord and Tenant Law (Amendment) (Ir) Act 1860, s 4.

[33] A consultation paper on electronic registration was issued by Land and Property Services in 2009 (see www.lpsni.gov.uk). It has resulted in the Land Registration (Electronic Communications) Order (NI) 2011 (SR 158).

[34] See, eg, *Hamilton v Judge* [2009] NICh 4 (Deeny J).

[35] See, generally, C O'Neill, *The Law of Mortgages in Northern Ireland* (Belfast, SLS Legal Publications, 2008).

[36] The Northern Ireland Law Commission has recommended that the creation of mortgages by way of a charge should be extended to unregistered land: n 9 above, para 8.8.

for all the money owed by the mortgagor to the mortgagee, even if it is a debt completely unrelated to the purchase of the house (eg an overdraft or a credit card debt). The only significant changes recommended by the Northern Ireland Law Commission to the law of mortgages are that the powers of lenders should be exercisable only for the purposes of protecting the property or realising the security and that, in the case of mortgages of private homes, the lender should not be able to take possession of the house without first obtaining a court order, unless the borrower gives up possession voluntarily.[37]

Adverse possession

9.16 Land can also be acquired under the doctrine of 'adverse possession', colloquially known as 'squatting'. This arises whenever someone occupies another person's land for at least 12 years,[38] provided that the squatter is able to show that he or she intended to be in possession of the land to the exclusion of all others during that period and that the occupation was indeed 'adverse' to the previous owner's possession (ie it was not consented to by that owner).[39] The rationale for the doctrine is that land is too precious an asset to remain unclaimed for longer than 12 years: 'use it or lose it' is the relevant catchphrase. The way in which the doctrine operates in respect of registered land in England and Wales was altered by legislation some years ago,[40] but no such reform has occurred in Northern Ireland and in its 2010 report the Northern Ireland Law Commission said it was not in favour of materially altering the law in this area at that time.[41]

Compulsory purchase

9.17 Land can also be compulsorily purchased if it has been made the object of a 'vesting order', issued by the Department for Social Development or a local authority in Northern Ireland. The vesting order automatically transfers the land to the Department or local council without the need for any conveyance, free of all estates and claims which previously existed in relation to it.[42] But of course the Department or council must pay compensation to those who previously had rights over the land, otherwise

---

[37] n 9 above, ch 8.
[38] Land Registration (NI) 1970, s 53, for registered land; Limitation (NI) Order 1989, art 21, for unregistered land.
[39] For a case where the claim was unsuccessful see *Gallagher v Northern Ireland Housing Executive* [2009] NICA 50.
[40] Land Registration Act 2002.
[41] n 9 above, ch 12.
[42] Planning (NI) Order 1991, art 87; Local Government Act (NI) 1972, Sch 6, para 6(1).

the transfer would be a breach of the right to property guaranteed by the Human Rights Act 1998.[43]

The Lands Tribunal

9.18 The Lands Tribunal for Northern Ireland was set up by the Lands Tribunal and Compensation Act (NI) 1964.[44] It is technically not a tribunal at all but a proper court, although it is not always presided over by a judge. There are at present only two members, one of whom is a High Court Judge who serves as the part-time President of the Tribunal, and the other of whom is a chartered surveyor. The Lands Tribunal has its own courtroom and offices in the Royal Courts of Justice in Belfast, but it will also sit in a courthouse convenient to the location of the land concerned whenever the parties prefer such a venue for a hearing.

9.19 The functions of the Lands Tribunal are varied. One of its most important is to resolve disputes over the amount of compensation to be paid for the compulsory acquisition of land or for the damage caused to land by, for instance, the making of roads.[45] Another important function is the hearing of appeals and references concerning the valuation of land for rate relief purposes.[46] The Tribunal must also deal with the renewal of business tenancies[47] and the modification of legal obligations which are allegedly impeding the enjoyment of land, such as rights of way.[48] Moreover, parties can agree to ask the Lands Tribunal to sit in private as an arbitrating body to settle disputes concerning the value, use or development of land (eg in the context of a rent review dispute). In all cases there is no limit to the value of the land which may be at issue, in contrast with the jurisdiction of the county court in land matters. Decisions of the Lands Tribunal are final as regards the determination of facts, but they can be appealed to the Court of Appeal on a point of law. Summaries of the decisions appeared in the now discontinued *Bulletin of Northern Ireland Law* (see para 4.53)[49] and a Table of Cases from 1990 (plus a few earlier ones) is on the Tribunal's

---

[43] This is because the Act makes Article 1 of Protocol 1 to the European Convention on Human Rights part of the law of the UK. See paras 6.22–6.27.

[44] www.landstribunalni.org.

[45] Eg under the Land Commission (NI) Order 1982. See too N Dawson, 'Modification and Extinguishment of Land Obligations under the Property (NI) Order 1978' (1978) 29 *NILQ* 223 and *Ward v Northern Ireland Housing Executive* [2004] 2 BNIL 65.

[46] Under the Rates (NI) Order 1977, which provides for appeals against decisions of the Commissioner of Valuation to be taken to the Lands Tribunal.

[47] Under the Business Tenancies (NI) Order 1996. See N Dawson, *Business Tenancies in Northern Ireland* (Belfast, SLS Legal Publications, 1994).

[48] See generally S Witchell, *Residential Property Law in Northern Ireland* (Belfast, SLS Legal Publications, 2000).

[49] For examples of two Lands Tribunal decisions on compulsory acquisition of land, see [2012] BNIL 45 and 46.

website. All recent decisions are also available on the *Lexis* database (see para 4.48).

TRUST LAW

9.20   To discourage too much property becoming vested in one person, the law of England and Ireland has devised methods for splitting up the interests which might be held in some property. A person who owns a house, for instance, might lease it to someone or give an interest in it to a building society in return for a mortgage. The most important device which common law legal systems have developed for splitting up people's interests in property is the 'trust'. If a fund of money or an asset is held on trust, the purse-strings are controlled by persons called 'trustees' and the people who actually receive payments out of the fund are called the 'beneficiaries' of the trust. Because this device was developed in the old courts of equity, as opposed to the King's courts, the trustees are said to have the legal title to the property or money whereas the beneficiaries are said to have an equitable interest in it. The trust property never becomes the trustee's 'own' property, so if a trustee goes bankrupt the trust money cannot be used to pay off his or her personal creditors. Most trusts are created deliberately, through a trust deed, but the law of Northern Ireland also recognises a category of 'constructive trusts', which are trusts that are deemed to exist in law whenever one person receives property, the benefit of which, in good conscience, should be enjoyed by someone else. An example is where a person acting as an agent (eg an estate agent) is given a bribe by someone in order to ensure that the agent's principal (eg the owner of a house for sale) enters into a contract of sale with the person paying the bribe. In such circumstances, on one view at least, the agent who receives the bribe is deemed in law to be a constructive trustee of that bribe for the principal.[50]

9.21   Today the context in which people most usually come into contact with a trust is through their pension arrangements. Money paid into occupational pension schemes, whether by employers or employees, is usually held in a trust fund which is managed by trustees who have the power to invest the money on the stock market to try to enhance the amount ultimately payable by way of pensions to the beneficiaries of the trust, the retired employees. Another important context in which trusts operate is that of taxation: many very rich people use trusts to reduce their liability to income tax, capital gains tax or inheritance tax. Indeed much of today's law concerning the rights and obligations of trustees and beneficiaries derives from decisions taken by courts in the nineteenth and twentieth centuries involving such people. Governments are increasingly trying to close the loopholes in taxation law,

---

[50] *Attorney General for Hong Kong v Reid* [1994] 1 AC 324 (Privy Council).

so tax avoidance through manipulation of the trust device is becoming ever more difficult. However tax avoidance is not illegal. A failure to pay tax that is due is called tax evasion, and the criminal penalties for that can be severe. Even failing to submit a tax return to HM Revenue and Customs by the notified deadline can incur an automatic fine of £100.

9.22   When acting as a trustee a person must exercise 'such care and skill as is reasonable in the circumstances'.[51] In addition the trustee must act prudently, loyally and in good faith. He or she has the power to make any kind of investment that could be made if he or she were absolutely entitled to the assets of the trust, but the trustee cannot invest in land other than through loans that are secured on land.[52] If a trustee breaches the duties or powers conferred by the law or by the express terms of the trust document itself, beneficiaries of the trust can sue the trustees for compensation for 'breach of trust'.

Charities

9.23   The trust mechanism is also used by many charitable organisations, although a lot of the larger charities now function as companies limited by guarantee (see para 9.68). Charitable trusts are treated differently in law from other trusts in that they do not need to specify particular beneficiaries, the capital in the trust fund can be prevented from being transferred to anyone else, they are mostly exempt from various taxes such as income tax,[53] corporation tax, capital gains tax, stamp duty and rates, and if the charitable trust 'fails', in the sense that the purpose for which it has been established can no longer be fulfilled, the assets remaining in the trust fund can be distributed in a way which meets other purposes that are as close as possible to those which were originally intended (this is called 'the *cy-près* doctrine'). The Charities Act (NI) 2008 defines 'charitable purpose' quite broadly. It embraces the advancement of education, religion, health, citizenship, community development, the arts, culture, heritage, science, amateur sport, human rights, conflict resolution, religious or racial harmony, equality, diversity, environmental protection, animal welfare, and the relief of those who are in need by reason of poverty, youth, age, ill-health, disability, or other disadvantage.[54] In addition, the purpose must be 'for the public benefit', a term clarified by the Charities Act (NI) 2013.[55] The 2008 Act also created for the first time a Charity Commission

---

[51] Trustee Act (NI) 2001, s 1(1).

[52] s 3(1) and (3).

[53] And charities can claim from the State the income tax which would otherwise be payable on the donations made by taxpayers. On this area in general see K O'Halloran and R Cormacain, *Charity Law in Northern Ireland* (Dublin, Round Hall Sweet & Maxwell, 2001).

[54] s 2(2).

[55] Ibid s 2(1)(b). The 2013 Act (in s 2) also restores a previous provision concerning gifts for mixed purposes, which had been repealed by the 2008 Act.

for Northern Ireland, the objectives of which include increasing public confidence in charities, promoting compliance by charity trustees with their legal obligations, and enhancing the accountability of charities to donors, beneficiaries and the general public.[56] The Commission must also maintain a register of charities[57] and it can institute inquiries regarding charities, either generally or for particular purposes.[58] If an organisation wishes to challenge a decision by the Commission that it cannot be registered, it can take its complaint to the Charity Tribunal for Northern Ireland, with an appeal possible to the High Court.[59]

SUCCESSION LAW[60]

9.24   The rules of succession law lay down what must happen to a person's property when he or she dies. Anyone over the age of 17 is entitled to dispose of their property after death by leaving a will: the person who makes a will is called a 'testator' (or sometimes 'testatrix' if female). Anyone who dies without leaving a will is said to die 'intestate'. The law of succession in Northern Ireland applies to people who die at a time when they are domiciled in Northern Ireland. 'Domiciled' does not necessarily mean that they were living in Northern Ireland when they died; it means that Northern Ireland was the place where they had a current intention to permanently reside, even if they were temporarily residing elsewhere. If a person has been missing for seven years, an interested person can apply to the High Court for a declaration that the person can be presumed to be dead.[61] On the back of that presumption the court can determine the domicile of the missing person and the rights of others to the missing person's property.

Making a will

9.25   To make a legally valid will a testator usually has to comply with the requirements of the Wills and Administration Proceedings (NI) Order 1994.[62] This means that the will has to be in writing and signed either directly by the testator or by someone else in the presence of the testator and

---

[56] Ibid s 7(2). See www.charitycommissionni.org.uk.
[57] Ibid s 16.
[58] Ibid s 22
[59] Ibid ss 12, 14 and 180(1).
[60] For an accessible insight into this area of law see S Grattan, *Wills and Intestacy: A Short Guide* (Belfast, SLS Legal Publications, 3rd edn, 2007). See too her much more detailed *Succession Law in Northern Ireland* (Belfast, SLS Legal Publications, 1996).
[61] Presumption of Death Act (NI) 2009; *Application for a Declaration of the Presumed Death of O'Flaherty* [2012] NICh 2, [2012] 2 BNIL 107. See also para 3.21 and Appendix 2.
[62] art 5.

at the direction of the testator. The signature must be added in the presence of at least two witnesses and each of those witnesses must, in the presence of the testator, also sign the will and acknowledge both signatures. The will must also be worded in such a way as to indicate that the testator intended by his or her signature to give effect to the will. The only people who can make a valid will without complying with the formalities just mentioned are soldiers or airmen in actual military service and sailors 'at sea'. In a moving case from Northern Ireland, *Re Jones*,[63] a soldier who was shot while serving there during the troubles made it clear while being taken to hospital that if he did not survive he wanted his 'stuff' to go to 'Anne' (his fiancée). In a later dispute this was held to be a valid will which replaced an earlier one the soldier had made.

9.26   Under the common law, the testator must have the proper mental capacity to make a will. This means that he or she must understand not only that the purpose of the document is to give away property to one or more people for whom he or she has regard but also that other people excluded from the will may have had some expectations in relation to it. If someone later challenges the testator's mental capacity the person who wishes to argue that the will is nevertheless valid must seek to prove that the testator did indeed have the requisite understanding when the will was made. If the testator is a mental patient as defined in the Mental Health (NI) Order 1986, that is, someone who is incapable, by reason of mental disorder, of managing and administering his or her property and affairs,[64] the High Court can make a will for that patient.[65] Such a 'statutory will' must still be witnessed by at least two witnesses but it must also be signed by the person who is authorised by the Court to sign on the testator's behalf and be sealed with the official seal of the High Court's Office of Care and Protection (see para 11.7).[66]

9.27   It is not uncommon for wills to be challenged on the ground that the testator was unduly under the influence of someone who happens to be a significant beneficiary of the will. Anyone who alleges this has to prove it, and this is not an easy process. There has to be real coercion; if a person merely stands by and allows the testator to be generous towards him or her just because the testator feels grateful to that person this is not enough to invalidate the will.

9.28   Anyone with sight can be a witness to a will, even if they do not know the testator or are under 18 years of age, but, crucially, no witness to a will (nor their spouse) can benefit from a will. The signature of a witness who is named as a beneficiary in the will still makes the will valid, but the

[63] [1981] 1 All ER 1.
[64] Mental Health (NI) Order 1986, art 97(1).
[65] Ibid art 99(1)(e).
[66] Ibid art 100(1).

gift in the will to that witness is void.[67] The only exception to this rule is when there are two other signatures to the will from people who are not beneficiaries.[68] Alterations to a will should be made in the same way as the will itself,[69] although it is sufficient if the testator and witnesses add their signatures 'opposite or near to' the alteration.[70] It is safer to produce a separate document, called a 'codicil', or even a whole new will.

Revoking a will

9.29   A will remains valid until revoked. It is revoked automatically if the testator gets married or enters into a civil partnership, but otherwise revocation requires another validly drafted will containing a clause which expressly revokes the earlier will or a clear act which destroys the earlier will. Implied revocation by a later will is possible, but the earlier will remains valid to the extent that it is still consistent with the later will. An act of destruction, according to the legislation, has to be something as serious as burning or tearing;[71] merely writing 'revoked' across it in large letters would not be enough if the document itself still survives.

The content of a will

9.30   Unlike in some European countries, including Ireland, a testator in Northern Ireland (and in England and Wales) has almost complete freedom to dispose of his or her property by will as he or she pleases. However, a testator does not have the freedom to leave by will property which he or she holds as a joint tenant (see para 9.5): the testator's share of the property will pass automatically on his or her death to the other joint tenant(s). A testator can indicate in his or her will that the successor to his or her pension entitlement should be person X, but the trustees of the pension fund do not necessarily have to abide by that instruction since technically the successor's right to the pension fund is not the testator's to pass on. A further significant exception to the principle of testamentary freedom is that, under the Inheritance (Provision for Family and Dependants) (NI) Order 1979, people who were in fact financially dependant on the testator, including cohabitees,[72] are entitled to make an application to court to argue that the will has not made 'reasonable financial provision' for them. As with the doctrine of undue influence (see para 9.27), this kind of claim can be hard

---

[67] Wills and Administration Proceedings (NI) Order 1994, art 8.
[68] Ibid art 8(3).
[69] Ibid art 11.
[70] Wills Act 1837, s 21.
[71] Wills and Administration Proceedings (NI) Order 1994, art 14(1)(d).
[72] Succession (NI) Order 1996, art 4.

to substantiate, and it must usually be made within six months of probate being granted for the will (see para 9.34), but in the right circumstances it can be applied to thwart the express wishes of a vindictive testator when these are challenged by an impoverished child.[73]

9.31   If a beneficiary of a will has died before the testator, the legacy in question will become part of the residue of the testator's estate unless the testator has made specific provision in the will for what is to happen in this eventuality. An exception to this rule relates to legacies given to children: if they die before the testator dies then their own children will take the legacy instead, divided between them in equal shares (*'per stirpes'*).[74] If the beneficiary of a will was a spouse or registered civil partner of the testator when the will was made but the marriage or partnership has in the meantime been dissolved, the gift to that spouse or partner fails and becomes part of the residuary estate. But the rest of the will remains valid, unless the testator has remarried.[75] A testator can also hide the identity of the eventual beneficiary of a will by leaving property to person X and then secretly agreeing with X that when the testator dies X will actually pass on the property to another named person. But for such a 'secret trust' to be effective it has to be backed up by solid proof of the separate agreement.

Intestacies

9.32   The property of people in Northern Ireland who die intestate (ie without making a will), is distributed in accordance with rules laid down in the Administration of Estates Act (NI) 1955. In the typical situation where a person dies leaving a spouse or a registered civil partner and at least one child, his or her personal property (ie not any land) and up to £250,000 will automatically go to the surviving spouse or partner and that spouse or partner will also get one-half of what is left while the other half goes to the child. The distribution is the same if the survivors are the spouse or partner and the deceased's parents (the deceased not having had children), except that the surviving spouse or partner then gets up to £450,000 of any money belonging to the deceased.[76] Former spouses or civil partners cannot take any of the intestate's property under these rules.

9.33   It is only if a person dies intestate leaving no spouse or children that the law has to look at who are the 'next-of-kin' of that person. In that case it is the parents who have first call on the deceased's property; if the parents

---

[73] See, eg, *Ilot v Mitson* [2011] EWCA Civ 346.
[74] Wills and Administration Proceedings (NI) Order 1994, art 22.
[75] Ibid art 13(1)(b).
[76] The amounts mentioned in this paragraph were set by the Administration of Estates (Rights of Surviving Spouse or Civil Partner) Order (NI) 2007 (SR 452).

are no longer alive the property will go (equally) to the deceased's brothers and sisters (including half-brothers and half-sisters). If there are no such siblings it is the surviving grand-parents who take, and if they are dead it is the deceased's uncles and aunts (or their children). Children born when their parents were not married are treated in the same way as children born when their parents were married. Step-children and step-brothers or step-sisters are not treated as children or siblings of the deceased, so they cannot benefit from his or her intestacy. But adopted children are treated as natural children of the intestate and they lose their right to inherit on the intestacy of their natural parents.[77] If no next-of-kin of the deceased can be traced, an intestate's property will ultimately pass to the Crown as what are called '*bona vacantia*' (literally 'vacant goods').[78]

Probate and letters of administration

9.34   When a person dies, his or her estate has to be administered.[79] The persons who are responsible for this are called, in law, the personal representatives. If these people are identified in a will they are known as 'executors'. Usually two people will be so identified, although according to the law of Northern Ireland any number (even just one) can be appointed. An executor *can* also be a beneficiary of the will (it is only witnesses who cannot be), and he or she can also be paid for being an executor out of the testator's assets if this is provided for in the will. When they begin to administer a will, executors are said to be 'taking out probate'. If a person dies intestate the personal representatives, who are then termed 'administrators', 'take out letters of administration'. The persons entitled to act in this capacity in intestacies include (in this order) the deceased's spouse or civil partner, the children of the deceased, the parents of the deceased, and the brothers and sisters of the deceased. If letters of administration are wrongly granted, a person with prior entitlement (such as a child of the deceased who comes to light), can have the grant revoked.[80] Before probate or letters of administration are issued (from the Probate Office in Belfast or Derry), proof will have to be supplied that inheritance tax has already been paid on the estate. If a will has been made it then becomes a publicly available document and can be inspected in the local Probate Office. Some national newspapers announce, in the cases of large estates, the value of what has been disposed of by certain wills.

---

[77] Adoption (NI) Order 1987, art 40(1) and (2).
[78] Administration of Estates Act (NI) 1955, s 16.
[79] The website of the Northern Ireland Courts and Tribunals Service has a useful booklet entitled *Dealing with a Deceased Person's Estate* (2009).
[80] As in *In re Donnelly (deceased)* [2009] NICh 1 (McCloskey J).

9.35   Probate and letters of administration are not necessary when the estate in question comprises only cash and a few personal possessions. In those situations several banks and other financial institutions are authorised to pay out up to £10,000 to the person who appears to be entitled to probate or letters of administration or to be the actual beneficiary of the testacy or intestacy.[81]

CONTRACT LAW

9.36   The content of the law of contract in Northern Ireland is virtually identical to that in England and Wales, but the sources of the law (ie the legislation and the relevant cases) are often different. In both jurisdictions there is comparatively little legislation in the field of contract law: most of the law has been made by judges. There is no book which deals exclusively with Northern Ireland's contract law.[82] English books therefore need to be used,[83] with references to Northern Irish legal sources being substituted where appropriate.

Forming a valid contract

9.37   Contracts are born, live and then die. They are born when parties reach an agreement to exchange something, though sometimes the agreement is implied rather than express (as when you put money into a slot machine to buy a bar of chocolate). In general, contracts do not have to be in any special form – they can be created entirely silently, or orally, or by writing. However contracts for the sale of land, for a loan of money in exchange for a security interest in goods, for the transfer of shares in a public company, and most consumer credit agreements, must all be in writing. These rules are set out in Acts of Parliament, including the very old Statute of Frauds (Ireland) Act 1695 (see too para 9.14).

9.38   When judging whether there is an agreement between parties a court will usually analyse the lead-up to the alleged agreement by looking for an offer from one of the parties and an acceptance of that offer by the other party. The agreement is clinched (ie the contract comes into existence) when the acceptance is communicated to the person who made the offer, and if the

---

[81] Administration of Estates (Small Payments) (Increase of Limit) (NI) Order 2004 (SR 48), art 2.

[82] But there is a 60–page booklet: B Dickson, *A Short Guide to Contract Law in Northern Ireland* (Belfast, SLS Legal Publications, 3rd edn, 2005). See too L Tracey, *An Introduction to Business Law* (Dublin, Chartered Accountants Ireland, 2010), chs 3 and 4.

[83] An insightful yet easy-to-read English law textbook is E McKendrick, *Contract Law* (London, Palgrave Macmillan, 9th edn, 2011).

acceptance is made by a letter this is deemed in law to be communicated at the moment it is placed in the post (even if it is then delayed in the post or gets lost). The law also requires the terms of the agreement to be sufficiently certain: any vagueness about the core exchange element to the agreement will make it void and therefore of no effect. Partly for that reason the law also frowns on 'agreements to agree'. In *Lonergan v McCartney*,[84] for example, there was a clause in a lease which gave the tenant the chance to buy the premises at a price 'to be mutually agreed' with the landlord's representative. This was held to be too uncertain a provision to create an agreement because the price of something, especially land, is a crucial part of the contract.

9.39   The things being exchanged must also have a real value (promising to transfer something to someone in exchange for that person's promise to pray for the promisor would not satisfy this requirement, for example[85]) and promising to pay for something after it has already been received will not constitute a contractual promise. In general terms, as well, a person (A) cannot sue someone else (B) for breaking a promise unless (A), as opposed to some third person (C), has promised to pass something of real value to (B). And a person cannot create a contract by promising to do something he or she is already legally required to do, so if a debtor promises to pay off part of an existing debt this will not prevent the creditor from later suing the debtor for the remainder of the amount which was originally owing, even if he or she has expressly promised not to do so. This might seem harsh, but the law generally prefers to make people keep to their original promises unless a wholly new contract is substituted for those promises. If a debtor pays part of the original debt and adds something extra (two tickets for the theatre, say) then the creditor's acceptance of the theatre tickets will be enough to prevent him or her from suing for the remainder of the original amount owing. This exchange element in a contract is called, in law, 'consideration'. Some reformers would like to see the requirement for consideration abolished, adopting instead a rule that a promise should be enforceable in law if it was seriously intended, but such a change does not seem imminent in Northern Ireland. The furthest the courts have so far been prepared to go by way of exception to the requirement for consideration is to rule that if someone makes a promise which is intended to be binding, and another person relies upon that promise to his or her detriment, the promise may be enforceable in law; this is known as 'the doctrine of promissory estoppel'.

9.40   Only people aged over 17 years of age can make totally valid contracts. In general a contract made by a person who is under 18 years of age, or who suffers from mental incapacity, is enforceable *by* that person (if the other person knew about the age factor or the mental incapacity) but not *against* that person.

---

[84] [1983] NI 129.
[85] See *O'Neill v Murphy* [1936] NI 16.

9.41 Another general rule is that a contract between two parties cannot confer rights or impose duties on a third person. This is known as the principle of 'privity of contract'. But there are a number of statutory and common law exceptions to it. The most far-reaching statutory exception is the Contracts (Rights of Third Parties) Act 1999, which applies in England, Wales and Northern Ireland. It allows a third party to enforce a contract between two other people if the contract expressly states that he or she can do so or if the contract purports to confer a benefit on the third party and it does not appear on a proper construction of the contract that the parties did not intend the contract to be enforceable by the third party. Under the Third Parties (Rights Against Insurers) Act (NI) 1930, a third person can sue the insurer of one of the contracting parties if suing that party would otherwise be futile because of his or her insolvency. Under the common law, contractual rights can be 'assigned' (ie sold) to a third person and contracts can be made through agents (such as estate agents or travel agents).

Contractual terms

9.42 A contract's terms are either 'express' or 'implied', but the law implies terms only if legislation requires this or it is otherwise necessary to give business efficacy to the contract. Legislation implies several important terms into consumer and employment contracts (see paras 9.49, 9.94 and 9.105), and they can also be incorporated by custom and practice.[86] There are fairly strict legal limits on terms which try to exempt a party's liability for breaching the contract, but if the exemption clause is explicit and clear, and especially if it is in a contract made between two businesses, the courts will still uphold it.[87] The Unfair Contract Terms Act 1977 provides that in most cases an exemption clause will be valid only if, in all the circumstances, it is reasonable.[88]

9.43 A contract will not be valid if it was entered into as result of one party making a misrepresentation to the other, or applying duress or undue influence, or permitting the other to labour under a fundamental mistake. On the other hand, the essence of commerce is that one party tries to strike as good a deal as possible with the other, so the law is reluctant to label hard bargaining as illegal or to say that people should not bear responsibilities for their own mistakes. In *Flynn v Reid* a Belfast jeweller mistakenly charged

---

[86] *MacDonnell v Northern Area Health and Social Services Board* [2009] NICty 2 (Judge Smyth), where a term was implied allowing performance related pay.

[87] As in *Photo Productions Ltd v Securicor* [1980] AC 827, where Securicor were able to rely upon an exemption clause when, far from protecting a factory as they were meant to do, one of their employees deliberately burnt it down.

[88] For an example of a case where the clause passed the reasonableness test see *Lisburn City Centre Management Ltd v Keag* [2010] NIQB 134 (Weatherup J).

a customer £1,225 for a diamond ring rather than £2,225; in later court proceedings the judge held that the jeweller could not recover the additional £1,000.[89] Unless a mistaken party can show that they did not actually intend to contract with the person they appeared to contract with (because of some subterfuge on the part of the latter individual), the law will say there *is* a valid contract.[90] In exceptional circumstances it will hold a contract to be invalid on the basis of one party's 'economic duress'. In most of these situations the party who suffers as a result of the misrepresentation, duress or mistake cannot claim compensation from the offending party; this can occur only if the offending party has been fraudulent or negligent. Indeed the victim of a negligent misrepresentation can claim damages either under the Misrepresentation Act (NI) 1967 or under the common law.[91]

9.44   For reasons of public policy the law refuses to recognise some contracts as enforceable. These include contracts to commit a crime or to have sex. In England and Wales the Gaming Act 2005 made gambling contracts enforceable for the first time,[92] although it permits the Gambling Commission to make a bet with a licensed bookmaker void if it is satisfied that the bet was 'substantially unfair'.[93] But that Act does not apply in Northern Ireland, so technically bets are still legally unenforceable there. Contracts which restrain a person's ability to trade (eg by restricting a firm's freedom to supply goods to whomever it wishes) are also unenforceable unless they are deemed to be reasonable. In the Northern Irish case of *Vendo plc v Adams* the judge struck down a clause restraining a franchisee of a truck cleaning business from setting up a rival business for 18 months after leaving the claimant's business, but the same judge upheld another clause restraining the franchisee from enticing away the claimant's customers during that 18 month period.[94]

Terminating a contract

9.45   Contracts are brought to an end by the mutual agreement of the parties or once the contract has been fully performed. If one party prevents the other from fully performing he or she must still pay the other a reasonable sum for what has already been done (this sum is called a *'quantum meruit'*, meaning 'the amount it is worth'). If something happens to 'frustrate' the performance of the contract and it is not the fault of either party (eg a

---

[89] [2002] 8 BNIL 12.
[90] This was confirmed by the House of Lords in *Shogun Finance Ltd v Hudson* [2003] UKHL 62, [2004] 1 AC 919.
[91] *Hedley Byrne & Co Ltd v Heller & Partners Ltd* [1964] AC 465.
[92] s 335.
[93] s 336.
[94] [2002] NI 95.

singer's illness means that a concert has to be cancelled), the Frustrated Contracts Act (NI) 1947 allows the losses suffered by the two parties to be fairly shared. In all other situations, however, if a contract is not performed despite one party's promise that it would be performed, that party is liable to pay damages to the other party for breach of contract. In that sense liability for breach of contract is 'strict' – virtually no excuse is available. In situations where the breach is of an important term of the contract (called a 'condition'), the innocent party can treat the contract as at an end as well as claiming damages. If one party notifies the other that he or she is not going to be able to perform a condition as promised, the innocent party can either terminate the contract and claim damages straightaway or wait until the time comes when performance was due and claim damages then (this is known as 'the doctrine of anticipatory breach').

9.46   The parties can include a clause in their contract which stipulates how much should be paid by way of compensation if there is a breach of the contract, but this clause will not be enforceable in a court if it in facts imposes a 'penalty' by requiring an amount of compensation to be paid which is totally out of proportion to the loss actually suffered. A contracting party who claims damages will recover only for those types of loss which, at the time the contract was made, the defendant ought to have contemplated as being liable to occur if the contract was breached. If (A) promises to repair a broken window in (B)'s house in return for payment, but then fails to turn up to do so, (B) can claim the extra costs incurred in arranging for someone else to do the work, or perhaps the costs that flow from extra rain damage caused to (B's) possessions, but (B) cannot claim for losses incurred because a thief burgles the house by climbing in through the broken window. Drawing the line between losses that could have been reasonably contemplated and those that could not have been (and are therefore too 'remote') is often very difficult. Once the type of loss recoverable has been identified, the precise amount of money payable will be calculated by assessing how much it will cost to put the claimant into the position he or she would have been in if the original contract had been performed as promised. Often this means including in the damages the lost profit which the claimant had hoped to make on the deal (eg by re-selling the goods being bought from the defendant). In contracts where the whole point was to give pleasure (eg a contract to go on holiday), the damages can include an amount representing lost enjoyment.

9.47   Occasionally other remedies besides damages can be claimed by the victim of a breach of contract. These include injunctions and decrees of specific performance (which order the offending party to perform the contract). But specific performance will not normally be ordered in the context of personal services, because it is against public policy to force one person to perform services for another against his or her will.

9.48   Generally speaking a person wanting to sue for breach of contract must do so within six years of the breach occurring, but in cases where the contract is in the form of a deed (as in contracts for the transfer of land) the limitation period is 12 years.[95]

CONSUMER LAW

9.49   Consumer law is largely a sub-branch of contract law, although consumers are also protected by tort law and criminal law. There is virtually no difference between the substance of the law on consumer protection in Northern Ireland and the law in England and Wales. The Sale of Goods Act 1979 applies in both jurisdictions, as do the Unfair Contract Terms Act 1977, the Unfair Terms in Consumer Contracts Regulations 1999[96] and the Consumer Protection from Unfair Trading Regulations 2008.[97] The last two sets of Regulations derive from EU Directives.

Consumer rights

9.50   The main rights which consumers have against sellers in Northern Ireland are the following:

- They are entitled to claim their money back if they buy goods which are not of satisfactory quality, ie the goods do not meet the standard that a reasonable person would regard as satisfactory, taking account of the description of the goods, their price, and all the other relevant circumstances.[98]
- They are entitled to claim their money back if they buy goods which are not reasonably fit for the purpose for which they were bought.
- Any 'exemption clause' which the seller might try to rely upon in relation to a consumer, who is asserting the above rights, is of no value in the eyes of the law.[99] Indeed it is a criminal offence to display such a notice at any place where consumer transactions take place.[100]

9.51   To benefit from these protections the buyer must have bought the goods from someone selling in the course of a business (ie not a private seller) and must not have been aware of the defect in question when the goods were bought. Moreover the goods bought must be of a type that are

---

[95] Limitation (NI) Order 1989, arts 4 and 15.
[96] SI 2083.
[97] SI 1277.
[98] Sale of Goods Act 1979, s 14(2A).
[99] Unfair Contract Terms Act 1997, s 6.
[100] Consumer Transactions (Restrictions on Statements) Order 1976 (SI 1813), art 3(a).

ordinarily supplied for private use and consumption (not, for example, large manufacturing equipment). A person who buys goods at an auction is also not a consumer.

9.52 Consumers have further rights against the manufacturers of goods, even if they have not bought the goods from that source. For a start, if the manufacturer provides a consumer with a guarantee in relation to goods, this guarantee does not reduce the buyer's existing statutory rights.[101] Manufacturers also owe a duty of care to the ultimate consumer of their goods, as the famous case of *Donoghue v Stevenson* makes clear.[102] If this duty is breached, a person who suffers loss or injury as a result can sue the manufacturer for the tort of negligence (see para 9.76). Under the Consumer Protection (NI) Order 1987 the manufacturer's liability is made more strict in that there will be liability if a defect in the product causes the injury or loss, whether or not the claimant can show that there was a breach of a duty of care. The manufacturer has a defence if he or she can show that the product was not defective when it left their hands or that it was defective because of the design of a larger product of which it formed a part.[103] It is also a criminal offence to supply to any consumer, in the course of a business, goods which are not reasonably safe.

9.53 People who buy goods on hire-purchase enjoy largely the same rights regarding the quality of the goods as do people who buy them outright. Likewise, people who enter into 'regulated agreements' for credit benefit from the protection afforded by the Consumer Credit Act 1974, which applies throughout the UK. They have, for example, a 'cooling-off period' of five days during which they can change their mind if they sign a credit agreement away from the business premises of the creditor. If a person uses a credit card to buy goods, and the supplier of those goods breaks the contract with the buyer, the buyer can then sue the credit card company as well as the supplier (so if the supplier goes into liquidation, the buyer can still recoup his or her losses from the credit card company). The same benefit does not accrue from using a debit card.

9.54 People who enter into contracts for the supply of work and materials (eg they engage a firm to paint their house) are protected against breaches of that contract in the same way as consumers who buy faulty goods.[104] The same Act protects people who contract for services only (eg they engage a firm to advise them on how to invest their money). Where a person supplies services in the course of a business, the law implies a term into the contract

[101] Unfair Contract Terms Act 1977, s 5.
[102] [1932] AC 562. The House of Lords held in this case that if it was proved that a bottle of ginger beer did in fact contain the remains of a decomposed snail, the manufacturer of the drink would be liable to the person who drank the beer, even if he or she had not bought it but was given it by someone else.
[103] Consumer Protection (NI) Order 1987, art 7.
[104] Supply of Goods and Services Act 1982.

requiring the service to be carried out with reasonable care and skill.[105] If the price is not specified the law will also imply a term that the price to be paid should be a reasonable one.[106] Moreover, anyone contracting with a consumer must not try to perform the contract in a substantially different way from that which would be reasonably expected by the consumer.[107] Thus, if a person books a holiday to Spain through a travel agency, the agency cannot later try to fob him or her off with a holiday to Turkey. People who enter into timeshare and property exchange contracts are also protected, thanks to regulations issued pursuant to EU law.[108]

Exemption clauses

9.55   If a consumer is faced with an exemption clause in a contract the other party to the contract can rely upon it only if the clause has been incorporated into the contract in accordance with the law. The law requires that it be contained in a document signed by the consumer or that reasonable notice of the clause has been given to the consumer before the contract is entered into. If you buy something and are only informed thereafter that there is an exemption clause in the contract, the clause is ineffective. Moreover, even if the clause has been properly incorporated it can be relied upon only if it clearly covers what has in fact happened. If, for example, it expressly exempts a supplier of goods for a breach of the contract this will not be enough to exempt the supplier for the tort of negligence.[109] In addition, the law pays no regard whatsoever to a clause which tries to exempt anyone from liability for injuries or death caused to a consumer.[110]

9.56   In many situations, even if an exemption clause has been incorporated and clearly covers what has since transpired, it can be relied upon only if it is reasonable, and legislation sets out what factors will be borne in mind by a court when it is deciding if that test has been satisfied.[111] The factors include the relative strength of the bargaining positions of each party and whether the claimant knew or ought to have known of the existence and extent of the term. If a clause is held to be reasonable, however, it may still fail to satisfy yet another requirement, namely that it must not be unfair, as prescribed by the Unfair Terms in Consumer Contracts Regulations 1999. Those regulations require an exemption clause not to be contrary to 'good faith' and not to cause a 'significant imbalance' in the rights and duties of

[105] Ibid s 13.
[106] Ibid s 15.
[107] Unfair Contract Terms Act 1977, s 3(2)(b).
[108] Timeshare, Holiday Products, Resale and Exchange Contracts Regs 2010 (SI 2960), implementing Directive 2008/122 EC.
[109] *White v John Warwick & Co Ltd* [1953] 1 WLR 1285.
[110] Unfair Contract Terms Act 1977, s 2(1).
[111] Ibid Sch. 2.

the contracting parties to the detriment of the claimant. They also permit bodies representing consumers to complain to the Office of Fair Trading about the use of unfair terms (see para 9.59).

9.57 The law prohibits people from, in the course of a business, applying a false trade description to goods.[112] To break that law is a criminal offence, but one of the available defences is that the defendant made a reasonable mistake, or reasonably relied upon false information supplied by another person.[113] A separate law makes it an offence for a person, in the course of his or her business, to give a misleading indication to consumers as to the price at which goods or services are available.[114] A Code of Practice has been issued by the Department of Enterprise, Trade and Investment in Northern Ireland to give traders some practical guidance on how to indicate prices.[115]

9.58 In Northern Ireland the responsibility for supervising and enforcing trading standards (including trade descriptions) rests with what is now the Trading Standards Service,[116] while the control of food hygiene is part of the duties of the local district councils. There is in addition a branch of the UK's Food Standards Agency in Belfast.[117] These are the bodies which instigate prosecutions under the relevant legislation. Local government is also responsible for the establishment of consumer advice centres. In Northern Ireland there is at present only one such centre, in Belfast.[118] Its work is supplemented by that of the Citizens' Advice Bureaux.

The Office of Fair Trading[119]

9.59 The Office of Fair Trading (OFT) was re-launched for the whole of the UK under the Enterprise Act 2002, which considerably strengthened the law relating to consumer education and protection, codes of practice and market investigations. The OFT collects evidence relating to business practices which may adversely affect the economic, health, safety or other interests of consumers. It is the licensing body for organisations wishing to give credit to consumers.[120] It can also consider 'super-complaints'[121] referred to it by designated consumer protection bodies. The General Consumer

---

[112] Trade Descriptions Act 1968.
[113] Ibid s 24(1).
[114] Consumer Protection (NI) Order 1987, art 13.
[115] Consumer Protection (Code of Practice for Traders on Price Indications) Approval Order (NI) 2006 (SR 371).
[116] www.tssni.gov.uk. There are offices in Belfast and in Armagh, Ballymena, Derry/Londonderry and Enniskillen.
[117] www.food.gov.uk/northernireland.
[118] In Wellington Place (tel: 028 9032 8260).
[119] www.oft.gov.uk.
[120] Consumer Credit Act 1974, ss 21–42.
[121] Defined in the Enterprise Act 2002, s 11(1).

Council for Northern Ireland (see para 9.60), for example, referred a super-complaint about the market for personal banking services in Northern Ireland. The OFT does not deal directly with complaints received from individual members of the public, except in so far as these suggest a course of conduct detrimental to consumers as a whole, which the OFT can then try to have altered, if necessary through court proceedings.

The General Consumer Council[122]

9.60   This is a statutory body[123] which is independent of government even though its members are appointed by the Department of Enterprise, Trade and Investment and it is funded by that Department. It watches over consumer interests and speaks on consumers' behalf to the government, nationalised and private industries, and commercial enterprises of all sorts. It has powers to carry out research, provide information and investigate matters of consumer concern, and has particular responsibilities in the realms of food, transport, gas, coal and electricity. Unfortunately the Council does not possess the power to compel other bodies to act on its views. It seeks to influence rather than to enforce.

Regulatory bodies

9.61   Many private bodies exist to help consumers in relation to particular industries or professions. Trade associations, such as those for manufacturers of electrical appliances, often run their own complaints machinery. The insurance industry has an Insurance Ombudsman Bureau. The Press Complaints Commission[124] can deal with complaints about newspaper articles, including those printed by local and provincial newspapers in Northern Ireland, although someone who complains to it must give a written undertaking that he or she will not begin a legal action against the newspaper at some later date, and the Commission is powerless to award any effective remedy to the complainant. Complaints about advertisements in newspapers, on television or at the cinema can be made to the Advertising Standards Authority,[125] while the Office of Communications (OFCOM) handles complaints about the content of television and radio programmes and regulates most aspects of the telecommunications industry throughout the UK.[126] There is a Northern Ireland Authority for Utility Regulation

---

122 www.gccni.org.uk.
123 See the General Consumer Council (NI) Order 1984.
124 www.pcc.org.uk.
125 www.asa.org.uk.
126 www.ofcom.org.uk. OFCOM was created by the Office of Communications Act 2002 and given additional functions by the Communications Act 2003, ss 1–31.

which oversees the electricity, gas, water and sewerage industries in Northern Ireland.[127] Again, however, none of these bodies can grant remedies to complainants beyond condemning what has been done.

COMMERCIAL LAW

9.62   Commercial law is basically that part of contract law which contains rules governing non-consumer contracts. It is about the contracts that businesses make with each other, and it includes sub-fields such as banking law, competition law, insurance law and international trade law. In all of these areas the law of Northern Ireland is identical to that in England and Wales.[128] The institutions involved, explained below, are UK-wide bodies too.

The Competition Commission[129]

9.63   The Competition Commission replaced the former Monopolies and Mergers Commission in 1999.[130] Its main function is to investigate and report on matters referred to it by the Government or, more commonly, by the Office of Fair Trading (see para 9.59). The matters referred to the Commission will relate to mergers, monopolies, anti-competitive practices, the regulation of utilities, the costs and general efficiency of nationalised industries and the performance of public sector bodies. The aim of its investigations may simply be to examine the facts, or to assess whether the action in question will operate against the public interest. In the latter event the Commission will have to take into account, amongst other things, the interests of consumers, the need to reduce costs and the importance of developing new manufacturing techniques. The Commission holds formal confidential hearings at which witnesses are examined and interested parties are represented by barristers. Its reports are laid before Parliament and published but the government is not obliged to heed the recommendations. Appeals against some of the Commission's determinations are heard by the Competition Appeal Tribunal.[131]

---

[127] www.uregni.gov.uk. The name was conferred by the Water and Sewerage Services (NI) Order 2006, art 3(1), but the Utility Regulator also has functions under the Energy (NI) Order 2003.

[128] The best general book is E McKendrick, *Goode on Commercial Law* (London, Penguin Books, 4th edn, 2010).

[129] www.competition-commission.gov.uk.

[130] See the Competition Act 1998, ss 45–49, and the Enterprise Act 2002, ss 185–187.

[131] www.catribunal.org.uk. This was created on 1 April 2003 by the Enterprise Act 2002, s 12 and Sch 2.

The Financial Services Authority[132]

9.64 The Financial Services Authority (FSA) is an independent statutory body given powers by the Financial Services and Markets Act 2000. It is financed by the financial services industry but its Board is appointed by the Government. The FSA has a wide range of rule-making, investigatory and enforcement powers and now regulates the whole of the financial services industry in the UK, including banking, insurance and investments. It does not, however, deal with personal loans or credit cards (these are still the concern of the Office of Fair Trading: see para 9.59) nor with pensions (which are the concern of the Pensions Regulator). The 2000 Act requires the FSA to maintain confidence in the industry, to ensure that consumers are properly protected and to reduce financial crime. Its inspectors visit registered financial bodies of all types and scrutinise their annual reports. Recommendations can be made to government departments on what reforms are required. Complaints about matters falling within the remit of the FSA can now be taken to the Financial Services and Markets Tribunal,[133] which can direct what action the FSA should take on a particular issue. In 2009 the FSA's chairman, Lord Turner, published a review which identified the changes that needed to be made to the regulation of the UK's banking industry in order to ensure that the global banking crisis of 2008 could not recur.[134]

Ombudsman's offices in the commercial sector

9.65   The Financial Services Ombudsman (FSO) acts as the industry's own dispute resolving mechanism (as an alternative to the courts)[135] and has been set up under statute.[136] It covers the fields of insurance, banking, mortgage lending, credit unions, friendly societies, investments and stock broking, but it does not look at private money lending, at complaints about the way particular investments have performed or at the commercial judgement of companies. A complaint made against one of the companies covered by the FSO which is not dealt with satisfactorily by the company's own complaints procedure can be referred to the FSO within six months of the final decision by the company concerned. Even charities, trusts and small businesses can lodge complaints. If a firm fails to comply with the FSO's request for relevant information this is tantamount to contempt of court.[137]

---

[132] www.fsa.gov.uk.
[133] Financial Services and Markets Act 2000, s 152.
[134] *The Turner Review*, available on the FSA's website.
[135] www.financial-ombudsman.org.uk. There is no one person acting as the Financial Services Ombudsman, but rather a panel of ombudsmen.
[136] Financial Services and Markets Act 2000, s 225 and Sch 17.
[137] Ibid ss 231–232.

If a settlement cannot be arrived at, a formal adjudication will be made by the Ombudsman and his or her decision is binding on the firm in question, up to the amount of £100,000. There can be no recourse against any of the Ombudsman's decisions to the courts, but legal rights are otherwise unaffected by the scheme. The service is free and confidential

9.66 There also exists an Independent Housing Ombudsman Service,[138] an Ombudsman for Estate Agents[139] and a Pensions Ombudsman.[140] The last of these deals with complaints about the way pension schemes are run, while complaints about the marketing of such schemes are dealt with by the FSO. For complaints about HM Revenue and Customs there is an official called an Adjudicator,[141] based in London. He or she looks into allegations of excessive delay, mistakes, discourtesy and the use of discretion, but does not examine issues of law or tax liability.

COMPANY LAW

9.67 Company law merits consideration here because of its practical importance. A lot of company law applicable in the UK now derives from the EU, which has issued many Directives in the field. Again the law in Northern Ireland is virtually identical to that in England and Wales. Companies are now UK companies, not just Great Britain or Northern Ireland companies as used to be the case,[142] and the same legislation applies to all of them. But companies can still be registered in Northern Ireland and the register can be consulted at Companies House in Belfast. It currently contains some 38,000 'live' companies. The website of Companies House has a number of forms and guidance booklets for those who want to form companies or limited liability partnerships (LLPs).[143]

Types of companies[144]

9.68 Companies can be classified in different ways. Some are established by Royal Charter, like the BBC; others are created by legislation, such as

---

[138] www.ihos.org.uk.

[139] www.oea.co.uk.

[140] www.pensions-ombudsman.org.uk. Decisions of the Pensions Ombudsman can be appealed to the Court of Appeal. For a Northern Ireland example, see *Ewing v Trustees of Stockham Valve Ltd Staff Retirement Benefits Scheme* [2000] 9 BNIL 50.

[141] www.adjudicatorsoffice.gov.uk.

[142] Companies Act 2006, which came into force in 2009. This is an extremely long Act comprising 47 Parts, 1300 sections and 16 Schedules. It applies to Northern Ireland as well as to England and Wales.

[143] www.companieshouse.gov.uk.

[144] For more details see L Tracey, *An Introduction to Business Law in Northern Ireland* (Dublin, Chartered Accountants Ireland, 2010), ch 11.

the Northern Ireland Housing Executive;[145] the rest are established by registration. Companies can also be either limited or unlimited; if they are limited the liability of their members is capped either in accordance with the amount that is still unpaid on the shares they own (a company limited by shares) or in accordance with the amount the members have undertaken to contribute to the assets of the company if it is wound up (a company limited by guarantee).[146] Companies limited by guarantee are often clubs, societies, non-governmental organisations or charities. It is no longer possible to form a company limited by guarantee with a share capital.[147] Limited companies can also be 'community interest companies', which were provided for by legislation passed in 2005.[148] In addition, companies can be public or private. Public companies are companies that are registered as public companies with a minimum share capital of £50,000 and a limited liability;[149] their names must end with the words 'public limited company' or 'plc'. Private limited companies cannot offer any securities of the company to the general public,[150] which basically means that they cannot advertise for funds from the public. Limited companies have to use the word 'limited' ('Ltd') in their title unless they are exempt from doing so, as charities are.[151] A subsidiary company is one in which another company (the 'parent company') has a controlling interest,[152] but a subsidiary company cannot itself be a member of its holding company.[153] Multinational companies are those which operate in more than one country: they may set up subsidiary companies in some states or simply operate there as a foreign company. Under the EU's rules, companies established anywhere in the EU have a right to establish themselves anywhere else in the EU.

A company is a separate legal person

9.69   Once a company is formed (ie 'incorporated') through the submission of documents called a 'memorandum of association' and 'articles of association', it becomes, in law, a person.[154] A government Minister can, however, order the company to change its name if it is too like the name of an existing company[155] and the Attorney General has a common law power to institute court proceedings to cancel the registration of a company if

---

[145] Created by the Housing Executive Act (NI) 1971.
[146] Companies Act 2006, s 3.
[147] Ibid s 5.
[148] Companies (Audit, Investigations and Community Enterprise) (NI) Order 2005.
[149] Companies Act 2006, ss 761 and 763.
[150] Ibid s 755.
[151] Ibid s 60.
[152] Ibid s 1159 and Sch 6.
[153] Ibid s 136.
[154] *Salomon v Salomon & Co Ltd* [1897] AC 22.
[155] Companies Act 2006, s 67.

he or she thinks it has been formed for an illegal purpose.[156] The fact that the company is a separate legal person from the people who own it means that only the company itself (through its directors) can sue if a wrong is done to the company (this is known as the rule in *Foss v Harbottle*[157]) and only the company itself can insure its property (this was established in a case that went to the House of Lords from Northern Ireland in the 1920s[158]). But the rule in *Foss v Harbottle* has been seriously qualified by legislation, which allows any member of a company to apply to a court for an order that the company's affairs are being conducted in a manner that is unfairly prejudicial to the interests of members generally or to some part of its members.[159] Such an order might be granted where the company has acted in a way which conflicts with promises made to the member in question, even if that promise was not enshrined in a formal contract.[160] A company can now be found guilty of criminal offences, including even manslaughter.[161] The so-called 'corporate veil' can also be lifted in a variety of other situations, such as when the people running a company do so in a fraudulent manner: they then become personally liable for the company's debts[162] and can be found guilty of a criminal offence.[163]

9.70   Under the common law a company can only carry out those objects which are listed in its memorandum of association,[164] but under legislation, except for companies that are charities,[165] 'the validity of an act done by a company shall not be called into question on the ground of lack of capacity by reason of anything in the company's constitution'.[166] The company's articles of association set out the rights and duties of the company's members, and these are enforceable under the law unless the alleged breach is a mere technicality. If the articles of association do not specifically restrict the company's objects, they are deemed to be unrestricted in law.[167]

---

[156] *R v Registrar of Companies, ex parte Attorney General* [1991] BCLC 476, where a company was set up to run a prostitution business.

[157] (1843) 67 ER 189.

[158] *Macaura v Northern Insurance Co* [1925] AC 619.

[159] Companies Act 2006, s 994(1).

[160] *O'Neill v Phillips* [1991] 1 WLR 1092.

[161] Corporate Manslaughter and Corporate Homicide Act 2007. 'Homicide' here refers to Scottish law.

[162] Insolvency (NI) Order 1989, art 177. Art 178 treats 'wrongful trading' in a similar way.

[163] Companies Act 2006, s 993.

[164] *Ashbury Carriage Co v Riche* (1875) LR 7 HL 653.

[165] Companies Act 2006, s 42.

[166] Ibid s 39(1).

[167] Ibid s 31(1).

The management of a company[168]

9.71   A company is managed by its directors, and people dealing with the company are entitled to assume that the directors have the power to do what they are doing.[169] The overall control of the company rests with the members, who must meet at least once a year. Every company must also have a secretary, who is its chief administrative officer, and that person can also be a director (but not a sole director). The law contains a myriad of rules governing the rights and responsibilities of company directors,[170] accounts and reports,[171] audit,[172] and share capital.[173] An 'annual return' must be made to the Companies Registry providing information about matters such as the principal business activities of the company, its directors, its share capital and its shareholders.[174] Annual accounts do not have to be lodged in the Companies Registry but they do have to be sent to every member of the company and to be available for inspection by the company's officers at all times. The accounts have to be audited by qualified, registered, auditors,[175] unless the company is exempt from this requirement by virtue of being a 'small' company with a turnover of less than £6.5 million per year and less than 50 employees.[176] Only public companies have to hold annual general meetings, preceded by at least 21 days' notice,[177] and usually the company's annual reports and accounts will be considered at those meetings. There are strict rules concerning resolutions and voting arrangements.

9.72   The Companies Act 2006 codifies the duties of company directors for the first time. Apart from needing to be aged 16 or over, there are no qualifications needed to be a director, but each director owes what is called a 'fiduciary duty' to the company and must, for example, exercise reasonable care, skill and diligence and avoid conflicts of interest.[178] If a director seriously defaults on his or her duties, the Government can apply to a court to have that person disqualified from serving as a director for a specified period.[179]

---

[168] See L Tracey, *An Introduction to Business Law in Northern Ireland* (Dublin, Chartered Accountants Ireland, 2010), chs 12 and 13.

[169] Companies Act 2006, s 40(1).

[170] Ibid Pt 10 (ss 154–259).

[171] Ibid Pt 15 (ss 380–474).

[172] Ibid Pt 16 (ss 475–539).

[173] Ibid Pt 17 (ss 540–657).

[174] Ibid ss 854–857, as amended by the Companies Act 2006 (Annual Return and Service Addresses) Regs 2008 (SI 3000).

[175] Ibid s 475.

[176] Ibid s 477. Dormant companies are also exempt: s 480.

[177] Ibid s 307(A2)(2)(a), inserted by the Companies (Shareholders' Rights) Regs 2009 (SI 1632), and s 336.

[178] Ibid ss 174 and 175.

[179] Company Directors Disqualification (NI) Order 2002, as amended in 2005.

The liquidation of a company

9.73 If a company cannot pay its debts it is said to be insolvent, and the law of Northern Ireland provides detailed rules on what steps then need to be taken to protect the company's creditors.[180] An attempt to rescue the company can be made by 'putting it into administration', which requires a court order. The person appointed as the administrator, who takes office initially for no longer than 12 months, will take control of the company and re-organise it in a way which might enable some or all of its debts to be paid and allow the company to survive in some shape or form. If the administration is successful the administrator will then apply to the High Court to have the administration 'discharged' (ie terminated). If the administration is not successful an application will usually be made to have the company wound up, or 'liquidated'. The more common type of liquidation is voluntary liquidation, which is triggered by members or creditors of the company. A compulsory liquidation occurs when the High Court issues an order to that effect in response to an application from one or more of the creditors of the company. The High Court will appoint a person known as the Official Receiver to manage the liquidation of the company if someone has not already been appointed as the liquidator. When an individual cannot pay his or her debts he or she can be made the subject of a bankruptcy order. The law in Northern Ireland on both company insolvencies and personal bankruptcies is very similar to that which applies in England and Wales.

TORT LAW[181]

9.74 In Northern Ireland tort law is, again, virtually identical to that in England and Wales. On some matters there are separate pieces of legislation for the two jurisdictions, but these are usually worded in ways that are indistinguishable. Thus, Northern Ireland has its own legislation on occupiers' liability,[182] on employers' liability[183] and on defences such as contributory negligence.[184] As far as case law is concerned there are no significant variations. Indeed tort cases from Northern Ireland have occasionally gone as far as the House of Lords and are still cited in English courts as binding precedents.

9.75 During World War II, as an economy measure, the size of juries in civil cases in Northern Ireland was reduced from 12 to seven, and it was

---

[180] Insolvency (NI) Orders 1989 and 2005. See too n 1 above.
[181] See L Tracey, *An Introduction to Business Law in Northern Ireland* (Dublin, Chartered Accountants Ireland, 2010), ch 2.
[182] Occupiers' Liability Act (NI) 1957 and Occupiers' Liability (NI) Order 1987.
[183] Employers' Liability (Defective Equipment and Compulsory Insurance) (NI) Order 1972.
[184] Law Reform (Miscellaneous Provisions) Act (NI) 1948, s 2.

never increased again after the war. Juries were still used in tort cases much more frequently than in England right up until the 1970s. Today, as in England, they are mostly confined to cases of defamation. The use of juries in civil cases was apparently one reason why awards of compensation in tort cases often tended to be higher than in comparable cases in England and Wales and also why insurance premiums tended to be higher in Northern Ireland. Today the norms in both jurisdictions are much more similar, as is indicated by a comparison between the two booklets issued for each jurisdiction by the respective Judicial Studies Boards, *Guidelines for the Assessment of General Damages in Personal Injury Cases*.[185] As in England and Wales, an appeal court in Northern Ireland will be prepared to alter a lower court's conclusion on the appropriate amount of damages to be awarded to a claimant only if it is based on a wrong principle in law or on a misapprehension of the facts.[186]

The tort of negligence

9.76 As in other common law jurisdictions the law of torts in Northern Ireland recognises a set number of types of claim. The commonest by far is the tort of negligence, which is where someone breaches what the law calls a duty of care and as a result causes foreseeable injury to someone. The duty of care exists whenever, as in England and Wales, there was 'a relationship of proximity' between the claimant and the defendant and in all the circumstances it would be 'just, fair and reasonable' to impose a duty of care.[187] In novel situations it can be difficult for a court to decide if a duty of care is owed. In a case in 2010, for example, a judge in Northern Ireland held that a duty of care was not owed to children born as a result of *in vitro* fertilisation procedures if they were born with a darker skin than their parents due to a mix-up during the insemination process.[188] The standard of care required in any case where a duty exists is that which can reasonably be expected, but it is not necessarily enough for the defendant to say that he or she followed traditional practices in a particular profession or industry. A professional person can also be held liable in the tort of negligence if he or she has given careless advice, as in *Devine v McAteer*,[189] where bad advice was given on whether an investment of money would bring a tax saving.

---

[185] In Northern Ireland the latest edition of this is the third, published in 2008.
[186] *Wilson v Gilroy* [2008] NICA 23, [2009] NI 46, [5] (per Kerr LCJ).
[187] This is the language used by the House of Lords in *Caparo Industries plc v Dickman* [1990] 2 AC 605.
[188] *A (A minor) and B (A minor) v A Health and Social Services Trust* [2010] NIQB 108 (Gillen J). In June 2011 the Court of Appeal of Northern Ireland rejected an appeal in this case.
[189] [2008] NIQB 150 (Deeny J).

Vicarious liability

9.77 For economic reasons the law accepts that ordinary employees are unlikely to be able to afford to pay damages to someone who is injured by their negligence, so it requires employers to carry the liability instead, provided the employee was acting in the course of his or her employment at the time. This is called 'vicarious liability'. In *Century Insurance Co Ltd v Northern Ireland Road Transport Board*[190] a tanker driver struck a match to light a cigarette while he was transferring petrol to an underground storage tank; this caused a serious fire for which his employers were held liable because he was held to be acting in the course of his employment. But in *Hunter v Department for Regional Development* an employee who caused an injury to someone by pulling a chair from under her at an office party was held not to be acting in the course of his employment.[191]

Other torts

9.78 People who are injured through intentional as opposed to negligent violence can sue for the tort known as trespass to the person (which is the civil law version of the crime of assault). The victims of the bomb in Omagh in 1998, for example, sued four men who were allegedly implicated in that incident.[192] If a person improperly detains another person, that can be the tort of false imprisonment (see para 8.24). As well, a person can sometimes take advantage of legislation which imposes a duty on someone to do something: if the duty is not complied with and a person is injured as a result, he or she can sue for the tort of breach of statutory duty if the court thinks that part of the purpose behind the legislation was to allow such claims. A common example of this is the duty imposed on the Roads Service of Northern Ireland to maintain the roads.[193] In *Adamson v Department for Regional Development*,[194] for example, a disabled man recovered damages on this basis when he was injured after his foot slipped on a loose flagstone. Sometimes the law creates what are, in effect, statutory torts, such as when it allows people to claim compensation if they are discriminated against on the grounds of, say, gender or race. The Protection from Harassment (NI) Order 1997 allows the victim of harassment to obtain a court injunction

---

[190] [1942] AC 509.
[191] [2008] NIQB 88 (Stephens J).
[192] *Breslin v McKenna* [2009] NIQB 50, [2009] 6 BNIL 133. The High Court held the four men liable. Two of them successfully appealed ([2011] NICA 33), but the case against them was ordered to be re-tried and they were again held liable ([2013] NIQB 35). For a case where the driver of an IRA getaway car successfully sued the British government when he was shot, see *McKeever v Ministry of Defence* [2011] NIQB 87, [2011] 10 BNIL 105.
[193] Roads (NI) Order 1993, art 8(1).
[194] [2010] NIQB 136 (Morgan LCJ).

ordering the harasser to stop his or her behaviour.[195] The Human Rights Act 1998 permits claims to be made against public authorities for beaches of rights guaranteed by the European Convention on Human Rights (see paras 6.22–6.27). There is also a tort known as misfeasance in public office, which is intended to ensure that public officials do not cause losses to the very people they are employed to help.[196]

9.79   The law of Northern Ireland also allows compensation to be claimed if someone's interest in land is interfered with by a 'nuisance'.[197] And of course there is a remedy available if someone's reputation is damaged through untrue statements made orally ('slander') or in a written or recorded form ('libel').[198] In Northern Ireland these defamation claims are sometimes heard by a judge sitting with a jury of seven people; a jury will often be good judges of whether a person's reputation has in fact been damaged or not. But a judge can dispense with a jury if he or she feels that the issues in dispute are complex.[199] Judges in Northern Ireland, like those in England and Wales, are still in the throes of developing the tort of breach of privacy[200] and they have even issued so-called 'super-injunctions', which prohibit the reporting of the very existence of a court order preventing the publication of private information.[201]

Defences

9.80   Two common defences to claims in negligence or breach of statutory duty are that the claimant voluntarily accepted the risk involved in the incident[202] and that the claimant was him- or herself negligent in a way which contributed to the incident. In *Proctor v Young and Coleraine Borough Council* a woman who was injured when her horse stumbled over a hole on a beach where she was riding was held to have accepted that risk because she had ridden there for many months,[203] and in *KW (A Minor) v Bolton* a claimant's damages were reduced by 25 per cent when it was shown that he

---

[195] See, eg, *McComb v Rogan and Allen* [2008] NIQB 144 (McCloskey J).

[196] Eg *McQuillan Envirocare Ltd v Antrim Borough Council* [2010] NIQB 130, where a claim in relation to the refusal of a waste disposal licence failed.

[197] Eg *McGauley, Campbell and Shannon v Multi-Development UK Ltd* [2010] NIQB 82 (Weatherup J).

[198] See Sir John Gillen, 'Practice and Procedure in Defamation Proceedings in Northern Ireland' (2012) 63 *NILQ* 137.

[199] For an example of a successful defamation action (in which the jury was dismissed by agreement between the parties after four days) see *O'Rawe v William Trimble Ltd* [2010] NIQB 135.

[200] See, eg, *Lee v News Group Newspapers Ltd* [2010] NIQB 106.

[201] Four super-injunctions were issued between 2007 and 2011: www.bbc.co.uk/news/uk-northern-ireland-13668622.

[202] This is called the defence of *volenti non fit iniuria* (meaning 'an injury cannot be done to a willing person').

[203] [2009] NIQB 56, [2009] 3 BNIL 165 (Gillen J).

had contributed to the injuries of his eight-year-old son by not ensuring that he was wearing a seat-belt when travelling in the back of the car.[204]

9.81   Generally speaking, tort claims must be brought within six years of the incident in question, but claims for personal injuries must be brought within *three* years while claims for defamation or for breach of European Convention rights have to be brought within *one* year.[205] Claims that are made too late are said to be 'statute barred'. There is a lot of law on how exactly compensation should be assessed in tort cases, especially negligence claims. If someone has died, his or her dependants can make claims under the Fatal Accidents Acts (NI) 1959–1977 and the method for calculating damages payable to a deceased's executor or administrator under this legislation is still governed to some extent by what was said by the House of Lords in the Northern Ireland appeal of *Mallett v McMonagle*.[206] Special legislative provision has been made by the Northern Ireland Assembly for victims of asbestosis in the Damages (Asbestos-Related Conditions) Act (NI) 2011. Victims of crimes can also sometimes claim compensation from the State, as explained in the following section.

COMPENSATION FOR CRIMINAL OFFENCES

9.82   As already pointed out (see para 7.5), the law of Northern Ireland makes a basic distinction between civil wrongs and crimes. The former are acts for which private individuals can seek redress, whereas crimes are acts by which the state is offended. Even though one and the same act can constitute both a civil wrong and a crime, the two forms of misbehaviour are processed quite differently by the legal system. The victim of a civil wrong *sues* the perpetrator of the act for *damages*; the state *prosecutes* and *punishes* him or her for the crime. But for a number of reasons things may not work out so neatly, certainly from the point of view of the victim. First, the perpetrator of the act may never be caught; second, even if caught, the perpetrator may not be convicted; and third, even if caught and convicted, the perpetrator may not be able to afford to compensate the victim. For a long time, therefore, the State has operated compensation schemes to which the victims of some crimes can have recourse. In Northern Ireland there are in fact three such schemes. One deals with crimes that cause injuries, another with crimes that cause damage to property, and a third with losses suffered as a result of activities by the security forces in their fight against terrorism.

---

[204] [2009] NIQB 89 (McCloskey J).
[205] Limitation (NI) Order 1989, arts 6 and 7; Human Rights Act 1998, s 7(5).
[206] [1970] AC 166.

Criminal injuries compensation

9.83   Following a review of the law published in 1999[207] the Northern
Ireland Office made significant changes to the law by the Criminal Injuries
Compensation (NI) Order 2002 (despite the fact that not one MLA or MP
from Northern Ireland voted in favour of such a change when the Order
was debated in the Northern Ireland Assembly and at Westminster).[208] The
amount of compensation received is now governed by the Northern Ireland
Criminal Injuries Compensation Scheme 2009.[209] The Scheme is administered
by the Compensation Agency, which is located within the Department of
Justice,[210] and a copy is available on its website.[211] There is no longer any
right to claim legal aid when making a claim for compensation, but help
under the legal advice and assistance scheme is available for claimants who
meet the tight financial eligibility requirements (see para 11.33).

9.84   To be eligible for consideration for compensation an applicant must
be a person who was physically or mentally injured as a result of a crime
of violence (including arson or poisoning). Traffic offences, however, are
excluded and where the violence has occurred within a household (eg child
abuse) certain further conditions must be satisfied before compensation
can be claimed. Moreover, the applicant must have been injured seriously
enough to qualify for at least the minimum award available under the Scheme
(currently £1,000), or be a dependant or relative of a victim of a crime of
violence who has since died, and the injury must have been sustained within
the previous two years (unless in the particular circumstances of the case it
is reasonable and in the interests of justice to consider older cases).[212] This
two-year time limit is one year less than the period allowed for personal
injury claims brought directly against the person who caused the injury (see
para 9.81),[213] but a lot longer than the previous tight time limit for criminal
injury claims of just three months.

9.85   A number of other important factors are identified in the Scheme as
having an impact on an applicant's success in making an application.[214] These
include whether or not the police were informed of the crime at the earliest
possible opportunity, whether the applicant was prepared to help the police
in their efforts to prosecute the offender, and whether the applicant him- or
herself has a criminal record. An award may be reduced if the conduct of the

---

[207] *Report of the Review of Criminal Injuries Compensation in Northern Ireland* (1999).

[208] The topic was not yet a devolved responsibility.

[209] Made under art 3 of the 2002 Order. Earlier Schemes still apply to injuries sustained prior
to the introduction of the 2009 Scheme.

[210] A favourable inspection report on the Agency was published by the Criminal Justice
Inspectorate in 2006 (see para 7.97).

[211] www.dojni.gov.uk/index/compensation-tariff-scheme-legislation-2009_.pdf.

[212] See para 19 of the 2009 Scheme.

[213] Limitation (NI) Order 1989, art 7.

[214] Paras 14(1)(a)–(e).

applicant before, during or after the incident in question makes a full award inappropriate, and 'conduct' includes excessive consumption of alcohol or use of illicit drugs.[215]

Calculating criminal injuries compensation

9.86 The Scheme sets out a 'tariff' for compensation, dependent on the nature of the injury sustained. There are 25 tariff levels, ranging in monetary terms from £1,000 to £250,000. In a standard case a perforated ear drum will attract compensation of £1,750 (level 4), a broken lower arm £3,300 (level 7), and loss of the sight of one eye £22,000 (level 17). Additional sums can be paid in respect of loss of earnings and other special expenses, and in cases of fatal injury a bereavement support payment can be made. In place of making legal aid available for such claims, the 2002 Order required the Secretary of State to designate a body able to provide advice, assistance and support to claimants. The body so designated is Victim Support (NI).

9.87 If compensation is paid but the Compensation Agency then discovers that the claimant did not make full and true disclosure, the Secretary of State can apply to a county court for reimbursement from the recipient. Likewise, if someone is later convicted of the criminal offence which caused the criminal injury, the Compensation Agency can apply to a county court for an order that this person must pay to the Agency the whole or a part of the compensation already paid to the victim.

Challenging a decision on compensation

9.88 The 2009 Scheme allows for decisions on compensation to be reviewed and goes on to provide for appeals against reviewed decisions to be submitted within 90 days to adjudicators on an appeals panel appointed for that purpose by the Secretary of State. The existence of the appeals panel relieves the county court of its role in hearing such appeals but that court still has jurisdiction to hear claims by the Secretary of State for the recovery of money from the person who committed the crime in question or (in cases where the victim has been doubly compensated as a result of other court proceedings) from the victim him- or herself.[216] Decisions taken by the Criminal Injuries Compensation Appeals Panel can be subjected to judicial review (see para 6.5),[217] but otherwise they cannot be challenged on

---

[215] Para 15(1).
[216] Criminal Injuries Compensation (NI) Order 2002, arts 14 and 15. The county court continues to hear appeals in cases of compensation under the Justice and Security (NI) Act 2007 (see para 9.92).
[217] See, eg, *In re Skelly's Application* [2004] NIQB 53.

their merits. However, if an injured person's condition deteriorates after an award of compensation has been made, he or she may ask the Compensation Agency to review its earlier decision.

Criminal damage compensation

9.89   The scheme for compensating people who have suffered criminal damage is a little more technical than the criminal injuries scheme. The legislation now applicable is the Criminal Damage (Compensation) (NI) Order 1977. Except in relation to agricultural buildings and property, compensation for damage is available only if it has been caused by three or more persons who have 'unlawfully, riotously or tumultuously assembled together', or by an act committed maliciously by a person acting for an organisation engaged in terrorism. Compensation for unlawful removal of property (ie looting) is restricted to situations where the removal takes place in the course of a riot causing more than £200 worth of damage to the building where the property was located.

9.90   To qualify for compensation a person must serve on the Compensation Agency and on the police, within 10 days of the damage being caused, a notice of intention to apply for compensation. This notice must fully and truthfully disclose certain facts. Within a further four months the application itself must be made. The Compensation Agency decides what amount of compensation, if any, should be paid having regard to all such circumstances as are relevant and in particular to the conduct of the applicant and whether all reasonable precautions were taken to reduce or avoid the loss. No compensation at all is provided for the first £200 of any loss, and it cannot be paid for lost money or jewellery or for any loss for which the applicant has already received adequate compensation under a statute or at common law (as in a civil action for damages).

9.91   Anyone who at any time has been a terrorist or a member of an organisation engaged in terrorism is barred from recovering compensation, with the exception that the Secretary of State may in any particular case make an *ex gratia* (ie voluntary) payment in the public interest. Appeals against the Compensation Agency's decisions on criminal damage claims still go to the county court, not to an Appeals Panel, and have to be lodged within six weeks.

Compensation under the anti-terrorism legislation

9.92   If any property is taken, occupied, damaged or interfered with by security forces acting under the Justice and Security (NI) Act 2007, compensation must be paid by the Secretary of State, again acting through the Compensation Agency.[218] The only exception is that no person who has been convicted of a terrorist offence has a right to compensation in respect of acts done in connection with that offence. Applications for compensation have usually to be submitted within 28 days of the act which is the subject of the complaint. Failing acceptance of the amount offered as compensation, the claimant can appeal to a county court. In its report on the work of the Compensation Agency published in 2004,[219] the Northern Ireland Affairs Committee of the House of Commons (see para 2.18) stated that there had been 'blatant exploitation and abuse' of the compensation provisions in the anti-terrorism legislation, especially in the two years following the coming into force of the Terrorism Act 2000. The Committee estimated that £5 million had been lost through such fraud. The Criminal Justice Inspectorate (see 7.91) conducted an inspection of the Compensation Agency in 2006 and did a follow-up review in 2007.[220] In 2011–12 the Compensation Agency dealt with about 5,000 claims for criminal injuries, awarding nearly £12 million in compensation; it handled nearly 750 claims for criminal damage, for which nearly £6 million was awarded.[221]

EMPLOYMENT LAW[222]

9.93 There are no really fundamental differences between employment law in Northern Ireland and employment law in Great Britain, but the legislation which applies is to be found in different documents. For example, instead of the Health and Safety at Work etc Act 1974 and the Employment Rights Act 1996, Northern Ireland has the Health and Safety at Work (NI) Order 1978 and the Employment Rights (NI) Order 1996. A lot of the employment law in the UK now derives from Directives of the EU. These have been issued because if a single European market is to work properly it is important that the rights of workers throughout the EU are more or less the same.

The definition of an employee

9.94 Whether someone is in an employment relationship with someone else is often a tricky issue. This is demonstrated by the recent case of *McDonnell*

---

[218] Justice and Security (NI) Act 2007, s 38 and Sch 4
[219] *The Compensation Agency*, 3rd Report of 2003–04 (HC 271).
[220] *Inspection of the Compensation Agency Northern Ireland* (2006); *Compensation Agency* (2007).
[221] *The Compensation Agency 2012–15 Business Plan*, pp 6–7.
[222] For useful information on employment rights that (with very small exceptions) applies as much to Northern Ireland as it does to England and Wales, see www.direct.gov.uk/en/ Employment/index.htm.

v Henry,[223] where the Lord Chief Justice of Northern Ireland agreed that no single test has been devised to resolve the often vexed question of whether a worker is to be deemed an employee:

> The decision can only be taken on the basis of the particular facts of each specific case taking into account the nature of the relationship between the parties, the type of work to be carried on, the level of control exercised by the party engaging the worker and all other relevant factors, of which there may be many.[224]

Employment is still seen as basically a contractual relationship, but there are now so many rights and duties written into the relationship by legislation that some view employment as being more akin to a 'status'. In any event, an employee has no entitlement to a written contract as such, but does have an entitlement to be supplied with written standard terms and conditions.[225] These must indicate matters such as the hours of work, the rate of pay, the number of holidays, and the notice which must be given by the employer or the employee if either of them wishes to bring the employment to an end. People who work part-time, or on a fixed-term contract, have much the same rights as full-time permanent workers and can usually claim compensation if they are treated differently.[226]

Employees' rights

9.95   While in work, employees have the right to an itemised pay statement every time they are paid,[227] and they must be paid at least the national minimum wage.[228] Deductions cannot be made from wages unless they have been agreed in advance or are allowed by legislation. People who work in shops, for example, can have their pay deducted if the takings at the till do not match the value of items sold.[229]

9.96   There are also strict regulations on how long a person can be required to work without a break, especially at night time, and every employee must be offered at least four weeks' paid leave every year.[230] There are some exceptions, such as for domestic servants or people who work in transport or the fishing industry.

---

[223] [2005] NICA 17, [2006] NI 53.
[224] Ibid [30].
[225] Employment Rights (NI) Order 1996, Pt III (arts 45–59).
[226] Part-Time Workers (Prevention of Less Favourable Treatment) Regs (NI) 2000 (SR 319); Fixed-Term Employees (Prevention of Less Favourable Treatment) Regs (NI) 2002 (SR 298).
[227] Industrial Relations (No 2) (NI) Order 1976.
[228] National Minimum Wage Act 1998.
[229] Wages (NI) Order 1988, art 4.
[230] Working Time Regs (NI) 1989 (SR 386). For two disputes that went to the Court of Appeal of Northern Ireland on working time in a hospital environment see *Blakley v South Eastern Health and Social Services Trust* [2009] NICA 62 and *Martin v Southern Health and Social Care Trust* [2010] NICA 31.

9.97 Under the so-called TUPE Regulations,[231] when an employer's firm is taken over by another firm the employees of the original firm have the right to be employed by the new employer on the same terms and conditions. The new employer cannot dismiss an employee because of the transfer unless there is an economic, technical or organisational reason requiring a reduction in the workforce, in which case the law on redundancy rights will apply (see para 9.104).[232] If employees feel that any of their employment rights have been denied to them, they can take a complaint to an industrial tribunal (see paras 9.106–9.108).[233]

Discrimination claims

9.98 Employees benefit from the protections accorded by equality law (see para 6.47), so they can complain if they suffer a disadvantage based on their gender, race, disability, age or sexual orientation.[234] They can also complain if they have been victimised for making a complaint, even one that proved unfounded.[235] Northern Ireland has also had laws against discrimination based on religious belief or political opinion in the employment context since 1976,[236] and even though people in Great Britain acquired similar protection in 2003[237] the law in Northern Ireland is still more sophisticated, as is explained in an earlier section of this book (see para 6.50). It also protects people against discrimination in public appointments.[238] Employees are protected too if they 'blow the whistle' on some wrongdoing within their place of employment.[239]

9.99 Women employees who become pregnant cannot be dismissed for that reason,[240] and they are entitled to six months of maternity leave, no matter how long they have worked for their current employer. If they have already worked for that employer for six months (by the 15th week before the baby is due) they are entitled to an additional six months of maternity leave, making a year in all. They must not be discriminated against during their

---

[231] Transfer of Undertakings (Protection of Employment) Regs 2006 (SI 246), implementing Council Directive 2001/23/EC.

[232] For a case on unfair dismissal in a TUPE situation, see *Miller v Glendinning and Cunningham* [2012] 2 BNIL 20.

[233] Police officers are not employees and so cannot access industrial tribunals, but they can sometimes apply for an application for judicial review: see, eg, *In re Pollock's Application* [2012] NIQB 67, [2012] 10 BNIL 65.

[234] For a comparison of two disability discrimination cases see [2012] BNIL 19.

[235] *Stirrup v Ufuoma Obahor* [2011] 9 BNIL 18.

[236] Fair Employment (NI) Act 1976, later supplemented by the Fair Employment (NI) Act 1989 and the Fair Employment and Treatment (NI) Order 1998.

[237] Employment Equality (Religion or Belief) Regs 2003 (SI 1660).

[238] See, eg, *Lennon v Department for Rural Development* [2012] 7 BNIL 14.

[239] Public Interest Disclosure (NI) Order 1998.

[240] If they are, they can claim compensation for automatically unfair dismissal.

maternity leave (as regards, say, pension rights or holiday entitlements[241]), with the exception that they are not entitled to be paid their full wages during that time. Their precise entitlement regarding pay will depend on their contract of employment, but most employees qualify for statutory maternity pay, which for six weeks is 90 per cent of the employee's gross weekly earnings and for the next 33 weeks is capped at a specified sum. Women who do not qualify for statutory maternity pay may be eligible for maternity allowance (capped for the full 39 weeks) or for employment and support allowance, which is paid to people who cannot work due to illness or disability. Fathers are entitled to up to two weeks' statutory paternity leave and two weeks' statutory paternity pay. An EU Directive of 2010 proposes extensions to the right of parents to claim unpaid parental leave.[242]

Sickness and dependants

9.100   Employees who are sick for more than four days in a row can claim statutory sick pay from their employer if their employer does not already have a more generous scheme in operation.[243] The payments can be made for up to 28 consecutive weeks. Employees must also be allowed time off, with pay, to carry out certain duties as an official of a trade union or (if under official threat of being made redundant) to look for alternative work. They must get time off *without* pay if they need to look after a dependant or if they are engaged in trade union activities. If they have a child below the age of six (or below the age of 18 if the child is disabled) employees can apply for 'flexible working', which means that the employer must seek to re-arrange the employee's working arrangements in order to fit with his or her caring duties.[244] But if agreement cannot be reached the employee cannot insist on being allowed to work flexibly.

Strikes

9.101   There is a right for employees to strike, but only if they first comply with certain conditions regarding ballots and notice.[245] 'No strike clauses' in employment contracts are generally unenforceable in law.[246] Striking

---

[241] Holidays can be added to the start or end of the maternity leave, provided the leave does not extend over two holiday year periods.
[242] Directive 2010/18/EU.
[243] Statutory Sick Pay (NI) Order 1994.
[244] Employment (NI) Order 2002.
[245] Industrial Relations (NI) Order 1992, art 20.
[246] Ibid art 26. The police cannot strike because it is an offence, punishable with up to two years in prison, to cause, or to do any act calculated to cause, disaffection among members of the police force: Police (NI) Act 1998, s 68.

employees are not entitled to be paid while on strike, and they can be dismissed if their absence from work is deemed to constitute misconduct. Trade unions, and their officials and members, have been granted immunity from being sued for various 'economic torts' (such as interfering with contracts, or intimidation), provided the action they have taken was in contemplation or furtherance of a trade dispute.[247] Thus picketing is usually not unlawful. But these immunities do not apply in relation to many forms of 'secondary industrial action', where, for example, a striking worker threatens to interfere with contracts of employment with another employer.[248] Pickets can be found guilty of obstructing the highway or of breaching the requirements regarding lawful meetings.[249] The official Code of Practice on Picketing[250] recommends that there should be no more than six pickets at an entrance to a workplace.

Dismissals and redundancies

9.102   Probably the most important right employees have (but they only have it if they have worked for their employer for at least a year) is the right not to be unfairly dismissed and to seek compensation if they are unfairly dismissed.[251] The dismissal will be unfair if no reasonable employer could have taken the decision to dismiss,[252] and there is a duty on the employer to show that the dismissal was for a substantial reason such as the employee's incompetence or misconduct. In some instances (such as dismissal on the grounds of pregnancy, trade union membership, whistle-blowing or asserting certain rights), the dismissal will be treated as automatically unfair in the eyes of the law. If an employee feels that he or she has no option but to resign from the job in view of the employer's behaviour, this can count as 'constructive dismissal' and can still give rise to a claim for compensation. But constructive dismissal can be difficult to prove,[253] and the amount of compensation awarded to an unfairly dismissed employee can be reduced if the fault of the employee has contributed to the dismissal.[254] Compensation will comprise a basic award, calculated in accordance with the age and length of service of the employee, as well as a compensatory award,

---

[247] Ibid art 15.

[248] Ibid art 17.

[249] Set out in the Public Order (NI) Order 1987.

[250] Issued by the Department for Employment and Learning (but dating from 1998).

[251] Industrial Relations (NI) Order 1996, art 126. In England, Wales and Scotland the qualifying period is two years.

[252] See, eg, *Ulsterbus v Henderson* [1989] IRLR 251 (CA). For notes on six recent cases see [2009] 1 BNIL 29.

[253] See, eg, *Cochrane v Roadside Motors Coleraine Ltd* [2012] 9 BNIL 25. For a contrast, see *Praxis Care Group v Hope* [2012] NICA 8, [2012] 4 BNIL 24.

[254] For notes on how these concepts of contributory fault and constructive dismissal are applied in practice, see [2011] 1 BNIL 31 and 32, and [2010] 3 BNIL 28.

calculated on the basis of actual and projected lost earnings.[255] An unfairly dismissed person will sometimes win an order of reinstatement, but this is rare because it is normally against public policy to require someone to enter into an employment relationship with a particular person. If an employee is unfairly dismissed because the proper procedures have not been adhered to, but would have been dismissed anyway if they had been adhered to, the employee's compensation can be reduced to reflect this.[256]

9.103   Under the Employment (NI) Order 2003 the law of Northern Ireland required employers and employees to abide by statutory dispute resolution procedures. If they did not do so, the amount of money awarded by way of compensation could be reduced or increased accordingly.[257] The Employment Act (NI) 2011 has changed this so that matters are now governed by a new code of practice issued by the Labour Relations Agency (see para 9.112). This means that the focus is no longer on the technical requirements of a statutory process but on the substance of the issues in dispute. If the code of practice is not adhered to, this can be taken into account if the dispute later comes before an industrial tribunal.

9.104   Employees do not have the right not to be made redundant, but they have the right not to be unfairly selected for redundancy and the right to be compensated if they are made redundant. In many situations the employer has to follow stipulated procedures if the redundancy is not to be deemed unfair.[258] The amount of compensation payable for redundancy will depend on the employee's age, length of service, and current salary level, and there is a cap on what the total can be.

Trade unions

9.105   Trade unions can seek to be officially recognised so that they can negotiate with employers on behalf of their members.[259] In any such negotiations employers are under a statutory duty to disclose relevant information about their firm to the trade union representatives. Any 'collective agreement' resulting from such bargaining will be presumed not to be legally enforceable unless it contains a clause expressly saying the contrary,[260] but its provisions may nevertheless be impliedly incorporated

---

[255] The maximum basic and compensatory awards are usually increased each year: see the Employment Rights (Increase of Limits) Order (NI) 2013 (SR 23).

[256] This is the rule derived from *Polkey v A E Dayton Services Ltd* [1988] AC 344; its application in Northern Ireland is discussed at [2011] 8 BNIL 24.

[257] For examples of how these penalties operate see the three cases noted at [2010] 1 BNIL 31.

[258] See the Employment Rights (NI) Order 1996, Pt XIII (arts 216–226). For notes on five recent decisions see [2009] 4 BNIL 54.

[259] Trade Union and Labour Relations (NI) Order 1995.

[260] Industrial Relations (NI) Order 1992, art 26.

into individual employment contracts.[261] Unions must keep a register of their members' names and addresses and inform them about the union's financial affairs. Funds must not be used for political purposes unless this has been approved by a secret ballot of the members. A person in Northern Ireland called the Certification Officer has the job of dealing with complaints that trade unions (or indeed employers' organisations) are not complying with their statutory requirements (see para 9.111). An appeal can be lodged against a decision by the Certification Officer to the Court of Appeal in Northern Ireland.[262]

Industrial tribunals

9.106 The aspect of employment law which most obviously distinguishes it from most other branches of law is that disputes which cannot be resolved within the workplace are initially dealt with by specialist bodies. In England and Wales these are called 'employment tribunals', with appeals going to the Employment Appeals Tribunal and then to the Court of Appeal. In Northern Ireland they are called 'industrial tribunals',[263] with appeals going straight to the Court of Appeal in Northern Ireland. There is also a specialist tribunal which deals with cases of alleged religious or political discrimination in the workplace – the Fair Employment Tribunal (see paras 6.55 and 9.109).

9.107 Industrial tribunals are staffed by a President, a Vice-President, a small group of chairpersons, and approximately 270 lay members. The lay members are appointed by the Department for Employment and Learning, while the more senior members are appointed by the Northern Ireland Judicial Appointments Commission (see para 4.32). All are expected to act completely independently. When hearing individual cases the tribunal sits as a bench of three (one chairperson and two lay members), in six different venues in Northern Ireland. The commonest cases are those concerning redundancy, unfair dismissal, discrimination, or activities on behalf of a trade union. Proceedings for a tribunal hearing are begun by the applicant sending an application to the Office of Industrial Tribunals and the Fair Employment Tribunal (OITFET).[264] They are meant to be informal, and no legal aid is currently available for them, with each of the two sides usually bearing its own costs.

9.108 There are quite strict time limits for bringing a complaint to an industrial tribunal. In cases of alleged unfair dismissal the time limit is three

---

[261] As in *Murdock v South Eastern Education and Library Board* [2010] NICh 18 (Deeny J).
[262] See, eg, *Bell v Communication Workers Union* [2011] NICA 7, [2011] 7 BNIL 26.
[263] See the Industrial Tribunals (NI) Order 1996, as amended, and the Industrial Tribunals (Constitution and Rules of Procedure) Regs (NI) 2004 (SR 165). And www.employmenttribunalsni.co.uk.
[264] www.industrialfairemploymenttribunalsni.gov.uk.

months. In cases of alleged discrimination it is six months. If the tribunal decides that the applicant is in the right, the particular remedy granted will depend on the nature of the application. If the claim is in respect of redundancy or maternity pay the tribunal may assess the amount of payments due; if it is a claim in relation to unfair dismissal the tribunal may order the reinstatement of the employee, or compensation, or both; if the complaint relates to discrimination an order can be issued requiring the discrimination to be stopped and compensation to be paid. A register of all decisions is open for public inspection at the OITFET and copies of some decisions are available online.[265] Awards of money can be enforced, if necessary, through the Enforcement of Judgments Office (see para 10.36). Decisions can be challenged through judicial review proceedings (see para 6.5) or, more commonly, through stating a case on a point of law for the Court of Appeal in Northern Ireland (as with magistrates' courts and county courts: see para 10.22).[266]

The Fair Employment Tribunal

9.109   This tribunal (the FET) was set up by the Fair Employment (NI) Act 1989 to adjudicate upon individual complaints of discrimination on grounds of religious belief or political opinion and to enforce against employers affirmative action plans now directed by the Equality Commission. Its workings are explained in more detail elsewhere in this book (see para 6.55).[267]

The Industrial Court

9.110   The Industrial Court for Northern Ireland,[268] which is the counterpart of the Central Arbitration Committee in Great Britain, deals with challenges to collective agreements, pay structures or wages orders which are alleged to be discriminatory. It also has functions relating to trade union recognition.[269] Certain of the Court's decisions, while not in themselves enforceable in ordinary courts, can lead to the incorporation of new terms into individual contracts of employment. As in the case of tribunals, a sitting of the Court comprises one independent chairman (the President of the Court) plus two lay members selected from panels representing both sides of industry.

[265] www.bailii.org/recent-accessions-nie.html#nie/cases/NIIT.
[266] As in *Perceval-Price v Department of Economic Development* [2000] NI 141. In *SCA Packaging Ltd v Boyle* [2009] UKHL 37, a case stated from Northern Ireland which eventually reached the House of Lords, the Law Lords were very critical of the use of the case stated procedure whenever a tribunal has reached a fully reasoned decision; they thought the Court of Appeal should decide which issues in the case, if any, are worthy of attention.
[267] Fair Employment Tribunal (Rules of Procedure) Regs (NI) 2004 (SR 164).
[268] Industrial Courts Act 1919. The Court was not actually established until 1964. See now the Industrial Relations (NI) Order 1992, arts 91, 91A, 92 and 92A.
[269] Employment Relations (NI) Order 1999.

The Northern Ireland Certification Office

9.111 The role of the Northern Ireland Certification Office[270] is to supervise the activities of trade unions and employers' associations.[271] He or she receives the annual financial returns of these organisations and deals with complaints from trade union members about political funds, amalgamations and elections. The Office reimburses unions for certain costs incurred in conducting secret ballots. Decisions of the Certification Office can be appealed to the High Court and from there to the Court of Appeal.

The Labour Relations Agency[272]

9.112 The Labour Relations Agency (LRA),[273] like its equivalent in England and Wales, the Advisory, Conciliation and Arbitration Service (ACAS),[274] is a body independent of government and operating under the direction of a Board comprising representatives of employers, employees and others, all appointed by the Department for Employment and Learning.

9.113 The LRA's mission is to contribute to economic prosperity and organisational effectiveness in Northern Ireland through promoting best practice in the workplace, fostering good employment relations, providing accurate advice and information, and preventing and resolving disputes. To help avoid industrial relations problems, it provides confidential, free, expert advice on all aspects of employment relationships. It runs workshops and seminars and deals with thousands of inquiries each year from individuals asking about their employment rights. The LRA's website carries useful summaries of, and links to, all the employment legislation currently applying in Northern Ireland, and it publishes various Advisory Guides (eg on bullying at work). In addition the LRA issues codes of practice on matters such as disclosure of information to trade unions, disciplinary and grievance procedures, and redundancy procedures.[275] The Codes have no binding legal force but they are taken into account by industrial tribunals when deciding disputes. There are also government-backed codes on picketing[276] and on ballots for industrial action.[277]

---

[270] www.nicertoffice.com. The website carries the Office's annual reports, its hearing procedures and its decisions and orders.

[271] See the Employment Relations (NI) Order 1999, art 28 and Sch 6, amending the Industrial Relations (NI) Order 1992.

[272] www.lra.org.uk.

[273] See the Industrial Relations (NI) Orders 1976 and 1992.

[274] www.acas.org.uk.

[275] These can all be downloaded from the Agency's website.

[276] Issued under the Industrial Relations (NI) Order 1992, art 95.

[277] www.delni.gov.uk. The latest version of this code was produced in 2010.

9.114   If there is a dispute involving an individual's employment rights the matter will be automatically referred to the LRA by the OITFET (see para 9.107), unless it relates to a claim for redundancy payment or for written particulars of a contract of employment. A conciliation officer in the Agency will then try to arrive at a mutually agreed settlement, a service which is again free and confidential. If its conciliation process is unattractive or unsuccessful, the LRA can try to resolve industrial disputes by referring them to independent arbitration.[278] A further, but rarely used, alternative is for the LRA to hold a formal inquiry into the issues raised by an individual dispute, this being an effective way of proceeding where there may be considerable public interest or concern in the dispute. It also maintains a list of experts who can examine claims for equal pay for work of equal value. And if there is a dispute between an employer and a group of employees the LRA can attempt collective conciliation.

Health and safety

9.115   The Health and Safety at Work (NI) Order 1978 placed new basic duties regarding safety at work on employers, the self-employed, employees, and those manufacturing and supplying articles and substances for use at work. An employer, for instance, must, as far as is reasonably practicable, provide equipment and systems of work which are without risks to health, and must also provide such training as is necessary to ensure safety at work.[279] Failure to comply with the Act can be a criminal offence. There is also a common law duty on employers to take reasonable care for the safety of their employees,[280] and if this duty is broken a person who suffers an injury can sue the employer in the ordinary courts for compensation. There are further specific duties imposed by legislation such as the Factories Act (NI) 1965: these too, if broken, can give rise to claims in the ordinary courts for the tort of breach of statutory duty (see para 9.60). Generally speaking, though, failure to comply with the Health and Safety at Work (NI) Order 1978 does not give rise to a possible claim for damages,[281] but a failure to comply with regulations made by government departments under powers conferred by that Order can often leave an employer open to being sued.[282] Employers must also undertake risk assessments[283] and consult with safety representatives appointed by trade unions.[284] If standards are not met the

[278] See the Labour Relations Agency Arbitration Scheme Order (NI) 2012 (SR 301).
[279] art 4 of the 1978 Order.
[280] *Wilsons & Clyde Coal Co Ltd v English* [1937] 3 All ER 628.
[281] art 43(1) of the 1978 Order.
[282] Ibid art 43(2). See, eg, the Provision and Use of Work Equipment Regs (NI) 1999 (SR 305) and *Hyndman v Brown and Colin Bradley Ltd* [2012] NICA 3, [2012] 5 BNIL 95.
[283] Management of Health and Safety at Work Regs (NI) 2000 (SR 388), reg 3.
[284] Safety Representatives and Safety Committee Regs (NI) 1979 (SR 437).

employer can be fined. As an example, when an assistant on a bin lorry was accidentally killed at a dumping site in Belfast, the City Council was fined £40,000.[285]

9.116 Responsibility for implementing the 1978 Order now rests with the Health and Safety Executive for Northern Ireland (HSE),[286] which has a board of nine people appointed by the Minister for Enterprise, Trade and Investment. The HSE inspects places of work, investigates accidents, makes recommendations to government departments, and arranges for research, training and the provision of information, such as guides to relevant new legislation. The HSE does not itself issue regulations, but it does publish codes of practice, which have a semi-legal status in that a breach of them is evidence of dubious practices but no offence in itself. Health and safety in shops, and in offices in the private sector, remains a matter for environmental health officers of district councils in Northern Ireland.[287]

FAMILY LAW

9.117 Family law deals with all the legal issues that can arise when people cohabit, get married, enter a civil partnership, get divorced or have children. On most of these matters the law in Northern Ireland is identical to that in England,[288] but again the actual legislation involved may not be the same. For instance, England and Wales have the Matrimonial Causes Act 1973 and the Children Act 1989, but Northern Ireland has the Matrimonial Causes (NI) Order 1978 and the Children (NI) Order 1995.

Cohabitees

9.118 Increasingly, people who live together without being married to each other or in a civil partnership with each other are treated under the law as if they are in fact married or in a civil partnership. For the purposes of claiming some welfare benefits, for example, they are regarded as husband and wife. They can also claim protection under the legislation on domestic violence (see para 9.122) and if one of the cohabitees dies the other can make a claim for maintenance if he or she was a close family relative or a dependant of the deceased (see para 9.30).[289] As yet cohabitees have no specific property

---

[285] *R v Belfast City Council* [2009] NICC 3 (Hart J).
[286] www.hseni.gov.uk.
[287] The precise division of labour between the HSE and district councils is set out in the Health and Safety (Enforcing Authority) Regs (NI) 1999 (SR 90).
[288] For an account of the 'law of relationship breakdown' see C White, *Northern Ireland Social Work Law* (Dublin, Tottel Publishing, 2004), ch 9.
[289] Inheritance (Provision for Family and Dependants) (NI) Order 1979, art 3(1).

or succession rights in relation to each other, but a cohabitant who has lived in the same house as a deceased person for two years immediately preceding that person's death can apply for some payments to be made to him or her out of the deceased's estate, without first having to prove that they were dependant on the deceased at the time of the death (see para 9.30).[290]

Engagements

9.119 The law barely recognizes the concept of an engagement any longer. If one side breaks off the engagement the other cannot sue for breach of promise to marry, as used to be the case.[291] Gifts given in anticipation of the marriage taking place can be recovered, but there is a legal presumption that the gift of an engagement ring is absolute, come what may.

Marriage

9.120 In Northern Ireland's law, marriage is 'the voluntary union for life of one man and one woman to the exclusion of all others'.[292] Each party must be aged 16 or over and not closely related to each other. But cousins can marry each other and a step-parent may marry his or her step-child and a father- or mother-in-law may marry their daughter or son-in-law.[293] It used to be the law that even if a person had a gender reassignment operation they could not then marry someone of the gender they used to have, but the Gender Recognition Act 2004 has allowed people throughout the UK to officially change their gender for virtually all purposes, including marriage. There has also been reform in relation to the formalities that have to be gone through for a valid marriage; the ceremony can take place in any place that is licensed. The Forced Marriage (Civil Protection) Act 2007 applies in Northern Ireland as well as in England and Wales, and protection orders have occasionally been issued to protect young girls from being compelled to marry someone they would rather not.[294] It seems unlikely that in the near future there will be sufficient cross-community support in the Northern Ireland Assembly for a Bill authorising same-sex marriages to take place in Northern Ireland.

9.121 Once married, spouses have a duty to live together. It used to be the case that there was always implied consent to sexual intercourse

---

[290] Ibid art 3(1A) and (1B).

[291] The right was abolished by the Family Law (Miscellaneous Provisions) (NI) Order 1984, art 15.

[292] *Hyde v Hyde* (1866) LR 1 P & D 130, at 133 (per Lord Penzance).

[293] Family Law (NI) Order 1993. The restrictions on marriages between fathers-in-law and daughters-in-law, and between mothers-in-law and sons-in-law, were removed by the Law Reform (Miscellaneous Provisions) Order 2006, art 3.

[294] *In the Matter of G and D (Minors)* [2011] NICA 55, [2011] 9 BNIL 37.

and that therefore a husband could never be convicted of the rape of his wife, but that position was changed by a decision of the House of Lords in a case in 1991.[295] If a person has already made a will by the time he or she gets married, the marriage automatically revokes it. If no later will is made then the surviving spouse has guaranteed inheritance rights to the deceased's property (see para 9.32). But if a later will *is* made the person making it can distribute his or her property in whatever way he or she prefers – there is no obligation to leave property to a surviving wife or husband. A surviving spouse can, however, make an application to a court for some financial relief out of the deceased's estate (see para 9.30)[296] and in making its award the court may take into account what the surviving spouse might have received had the marriage ended in divorce rather than death (the so-called 'notional divorce' factor). Moreover, married couples do not have a duty to share property – they are free to make their own arrangements in that regard. If disputes arise concerning who owns what, an application can be made to a county court or the High Court to get this resolved.[297] If one member of the couple is tried for a criminal offence, the prosecution can compel the other spouse to give evidence against the defendant only if the offence is question is one involving violence or sex (see para 8.99).

Domestic violence

9.122 Anyone who is cohabiting with another person, whether married or not, and whether in a straight or a gay relationship,[298] can seek protection from a magistrates' court if they are subjected to domestic violence.[299] A non-molestation order restrains a violent party from threatening, pestering or harassing the other person or from acting in a particular way such as making abusive telephone calls. It can last for any period of time. An occupation order requires the respondent not to enter specified premises or places near where the applicant lives (but it cannot be made applicable to premises outside Northern Ireland). It can remain in force for up to 12 months but can be extended if necessary. Either kind of order can be granted very quickly if an emergency arises. It is a criminal offence to disobey them and the person who does so can be arrested without a warrant.[300]

---

[295] *R v R* [1992] 1 AC 599.
[296] Inheritance (Provision for Family and Dependants) (NI) Order 1979.
[297] Married Women's Property Act 1882, s 17.
[298] Law Reform (Miscellaneous Provisions) (NI) Order 2005, art 12.
[299] Family Homes and Domestic Violence (NI) Order 1998.
[300] Ibid art 26, and the PACE (NI) Order 1989, art 26(2)(g).

Maintenance

9.123   If disputes over financial matters arise during a marriage (eg the husband has deserted his wife and is no longer contributing anything from his salary to help pay for her household expenses) an application can be made to a magistrates' court for a 'financial provision order', sometimes called 'maintenance'.[301] The applicant must show that the other spouse has failed to provide reasonable maintenance for the applicant or for a child of the family, that he or she has committed adultery, that he or she has deserted the applicant, or that he or she has behaved in such a way that the applicant cannot reasonably be expected to live with that spouse. The court order can require the respondent spouse to make a weekly or monthly payment to the other, or a lump sum payment. The order can remain in place indefinitely, until the applicant dies or remarries, or unless the spouses live together again for six months. If circumstances change, either spouse can go back to the court to ask for the financial provision order to be varied. In cases where the claim for maintenance is large, the matter will be dealt with by the High Court and not a magistrates' court.[302]

Terminating a marriage

9.124   If, after at least two years of marriage, a spouse no longer wants to live with the other spouse but does not want to get a divorce, he or she can apply to the High Court (or to a county court if the application is undefended) for a decree of judicial separation. The applicant has to show that the other spouse has committed adultery, has deserted the applicant, has lived apart for at least two years, or has otherwise behaved in such a way that the applicant cannot reasonably be expected to live with him or her. When making such an order the court can also issue orders concerning financial provision, and once an order for judicial separation has been made each spouse loses their inheritance rights if the other spouse dies without making a will.

9.125   To get a divorce a spouse has to prove one of the grounds mentioned in the previous paragraph or have lived apart from the other spouse for five years, and the marriage must be shown to have 'broken down irretrievably'.[303] But again the marriage must have lasted for at least two years. Even in cases where the other spouse is not opposing the divorce petition, the petitioner must still give oral evidence in court,[304] so the whole process cannot be conducted by post, as it can in England and Wales. A defended divorce petition has to be dealt with by the High Court. If the

---

[301] Matrimonial and Family Proceedings (NI) Order 1989.
[302] Matrimonial Causes (NI) Order 1978, art 29.
[303] Ibid art 3(1).
[304] Ibid art 3(3).

court agrees to grant a divorce it first issues a conditional document, called a *decree nisi*, which is made absolute after a further six weeks have elapsed. Only then is either of the parties free to remarry. If either of them does so before that time they are committing the crime of bigamy. But a divorce, unlike a marriage, does not automatically revoke a spouse's existing will.

9.126   Instead of seeking a divorce a small minority of married couples prefer to seek a decree of nullity, which declares that a marriage cannot be considered valid in the first place. This is the case, for example, if the marriage has not been sexually consummated due to the impotence or wilful refusal of one of the parties.

9.127   The most difficult issues in many divorces concern the division of assets. When it issues the *decree nisi* the court will usually order 'ancillary relief'. This can take the form of periodical payments, lump sum payments, or property adjustment orders. Usually the main asset in dispute is the former matrimonial home, but one of the parties' future pension rights might need to be re-distributed too. The general rule is that the court must try to achieve 'a clean break', which means making an order that will put an end to the parties' mutual financial obligations as soon as is just and equitable after the grant of the divorce decree.[305] In general the courts of Northern Ireland follow the lead given by the highest courts in England and Wales on these issues.[306] If a respondent does not comply with a court order in such a case, he or she can be fined or even sent to prison.[307] In 2012 the UK Supreme Court gave guidance on how to distribute property that was jointly owned by cohabiting couples before they split up: the court is entitled to impute an intention to each of the parties that they should take a share of the property which the court considers fair having regard to the whole course of dealing between the parties in relation to the property.[308]

CHILD LAW[309]

9.128   Most of the current law concerning the care and welfare of children derives from the Children (NI) Order 1995. This Order brought the law in Northern Ireland largely into line with that in England and Wales under the Children Act 1989.[310] It also, to some extent, incorporated principles laid

---

[305] Ibid art 27A.
[306] Typical examples are *D v D* [2010] NIMaster 5 and *S v S* [2010] NIMaster 7 (Master Redpath), [2010] 9 BNIL 24, 25.
[307] *In the Matter of C and C* [2010] NIFam 17, [2011] 4 BNIL 31.
[308] *Jones v Kernott* [2011] UKSC 53, [2012] 1 AC 776.
[309] See C White, *Northern Ireland Social Work Law* (Dublin, Tottel Publishing, 2004), chs 6, 7 and 8.
[310] See generally M Long and G Loughran, *The Law of Children in Northern Ireland: The Annotated Legislation* (Belfast, SLS Legal Publications, 2004) and K O'Halloran, *Child Care and Protection: The Law and Practice in Northern Ireland* (Dublin, Round Hall, 2003).

down in the United Nations' Convention on the Rights of the Child 1989, the most widely ratified of all the world's human rights treaties. Article 3 of the Order stipulates that:

- in any court proceedings the welfare of the child is to be the paramount consideration;
- courts should ensure that delay is avoided; and
- courts should issue a court order only if to do so is better for the child than making no order at all.

9.129   There is a Children Order Advisory Committee, chaired by a High Court judge, which advises the Lord Chancellor and the Minister of Justice on how best to address the difficulties facing children in the civil court system of Northern Ireland, especially delay. The Committee is supported by three Family Court Business Committees, each chaired by a family care centre judge. In 2010 the Advisory Committee published a new edition of its very useful *Best Practice Guidance* for Children Order cases.

9.130   In Northern Ireland there is also a strong network of voluntary and community organisations working with and for children to help ensure that their rights are protected. In 1997 a Children's Law Centre was established and it has since developed a range of advisory services for children, parents and carers. Other prominent non-governmental organisations active in the field are Save the Children, Barnardos, the NSPCC and Include Youth. 'Children in Northern Ireland' is an umbrella group which tries to ensure that there is co-ordination of activities in this area. In 2003 a statute-based Northern Ireland Commissioner for Children and Young People was appointed (see para 6.62). The Safeguarding Board Act (NI) 2011 provided for the creation of a Safeguarding Board for Northern Ireland, the main function of which is to ensure the effectiveness of what is done by other bodies to promote the welfare of children.[311] It has a duty to set up Safeguarding Panels dealing with different aspects of children's lives. The Board has replaced the former Regional and Area Child Protection Committees.

Children in need or at risk

9.131   Parents have a legal duty to care for their children. If the parents are living apart the one who is caring for the children can apply to the Child Support Agency for an order requiring the absent parent to make payments to help support the child. In some cases the magistrates' courts also have jurisdiction to make maintenance orders in favour of children (see para 9.123), and if an absent parent continues to ignore an order from the Child

---

[311] In 2012 the Department of Health, Social Services and Public Safety issued guidance for the new Board. It is available on the Department's website: www.dhsspsni.gov.uk.

Support Agency the Agency can apply to a magistrates' court for a warrant committing the absent parent to prison. A court order is also required if the parentage of a child is disputed and tests need to be carried out to determine the truth.

9.132   In 2011 the Office of the First Minister and Deputy First Minister published a Child Poverty Strategy for Northern Ireland, as it was obliged to do by statute.[312] The Northern Ireland Executive's progress in implementing the strategy will be monitored by the Social Mobility and Child Poverty Commission, which is an advisory non-departmental public body established under the Welfare Reform Act 2012. The Commission is also tasked with challenging non-governmental institutions, such as universities and businesses, to improve their performance on social mobility, that is, on ensuring that children who begin life in disadvantaged circumstances can escape from them and acquire a better standard of living for themselves.

9.133   A court can order that children who are at risk must be removed from potentially dangerous situations and placed in care.[313] According to the NSPCC there were 2,511 'looked after' children in Northern Ireland at the end of March 2011. These were children who had been abused or who were considered to be at risk of abuse, whether physical, sexual or emotional. If a Health and Social Services Trust decides to place a child's name on the Register the child's parents can appeal to an appeals panel and they can then seek judicial review of the appeals panel's decision if they disagree with it.[314]

Family proceedings courts and family care centres

9.134   When dealing with the care of children a magistrates' court is known as a family proceedings court,[315] and at county court level, family care centres have been established to hear appeals from family proceedings courts. There is a further right of appeal to the High Court.[316] Family proceedings courts (like youth courts: see para 8.83) normally consist of a bench of three members, one of whom will be a District Judge acting as the chairperson. The others will be lay magistrates, including at least one woman (see para 4.23–4.24).[317] Family care centres are presided over by a county court judge who will have received training in Children Order work. Although they are distinct courts in their own right, family care centres

---

[312] Child Poverty Act 2010, ss 12 and 13. The document is entitled *Improving Children's Life Chances*.
[313] Children (NI) Order 1995, arts 50 and 63.
[314] See, eg, *A and B v Hospitals Trust* [2004] NIQB 22.
[315] Children (NI) Order 1995, art 164(4).
[316] Ibid art 166.
[317] Children and Young Persons Act (NI) 1968, Sch.

generally sit in the same building as the designated county court (where child-friendly waiting facilities now exist).[318] A family proceedings court or family care centre may hear a case in total privacy if it considers it expedient to do so in the interests of the child and, unless the court directs otherwise, no report or picture in any newspaper or broadcast can reveal the identity of any child involved.[319]

9.135 A contrast can be drawn between public law and private law applications to these courts. Public law proceedings occur when the state intervenes through, for example, one of the Health and Social Services Trusts. A Trust has a duty to investigate when there is reasonable cause to suspect that a child in its area is suffering significant harm.[320] It will then submit to the court a report on the home surroundings, school record, physical and mental health and the character of the child. In reaching its decision in any case, the court must take such reports into consideration, have regard to the welfare of the child and, if appropriate, take steps to remove the child from undesirable surroundings and to secure that proper provision is made for his or her education and training. Private law applications are those made in the course of domestic proceedings in magistrates' courts or matrimonial cases in the county court or High Court.[321] They constitute a significant majority of all the applications dealt with.

Guardians ad litem

9.136 In public law cases involving children (when they are in care or are being considered for adoption, for example), the law provides that their interests should be protected by a 'guardian *ad litem*',[322] and the Northern Ireland Guardian *Ad Litem* Agency has been created to oversee the work of these professionals.[323] Guardians *ad litem* are experienced social workers whose function in Children Order cases is to make sure that the applications put forward by the Health and Social Services Trusts actually meet the needs of the children in question. They appoint a solicitor to act for the child (unless one has already been appointed) and to provide a report to the court advising on the child's interests.[324]

---

[318] The Children (Allocation of Proceedings) Order (NI) 1996 (SR 300), as amended, provides for the commencement and transfer of proceedings between the various competent courts.
[319] Children (NI) Order 1995, art 170(2).
[320] Ibid art 66.
[321] Definitions of 'public law' and 'private law' are extracted from *The Children Order Advisory Committee First Annual Report* (1998), 7.
[322] Children (NI) Order 1995, arts 60 and 61. '*Ad litem*' is Latin for 'for the case'.
[323] In accordance with art 60(7) of the Children (NI) Order 1995 and the Guardians *Ad Litem* (Panels) Regs (NI) 1996 (SR 128).
[324] Magistrates' Courts (Children (NI) Order 1995) Rules (NI) 1996 (SR 323), r 12, and Family Proceedings Rules (NI) 1996 (SR 322), rr 4.12.

Court orders

9.137 It is important to note that the Family Division of the High Court or *any* magistrates' or county court can make any of the orders available under the Children (NI) Order 1995 if the need to do so arises in the course of other business, such as divorce proceedings. In this way, the three court levels have 'concurrent jurisdiction'. The Children Order provides for a wide range of court orders, the most common of which are the following:

(1) *Residence order.*[325] This order sets out the arrangements to be made concerning the person with whom a child is to live. If a residence order is made in favour of the father of a child and the father does not already have parental responsibility,[326] the court must also make an order giving him that responsibility – see point (5) below.

(2) *Contact order.*[327] This is an order requiring the person with whom a child lives to allow the child to visit, stay or otherwise have contact with the person named in the order.

(3) *Care order.*[328] These make up the bulk of public law applications. They aim to have a child placed in the care of a designated authority. A court may make such an order only if it is satisfied that the child is suffering, or is likely to suffer, significant harm, and that that harm stems either from the care currently being given to the child or from a contention that the child is beyond parental control. Often an *interim* care order is granted while a fuller assessment is made of the child's position. The Children (Leaving Care) Act (NI) 2002, one of the few Acts passed by the Northern Ireland Assembly when it sat between 2000 and 2002, gives further rights to children in care.

(4) *Emergency protection order.*[329] In cases where a child or young person is considered to be the victim of abuse, he or she can be removed to a place of safety and made the subject of an emergency protection order. This can last for a maximum of eight days and may be extended, once only, for a further seven days.[330] If the situation is not deemed urgent enough for the emergency protection procedure, a child can be made the subject of a child assessment order,[331] which allows an investigation to be conducted into the child's safety and well-being.

(5) *Parental responsibility order.*[332] This order applies only where the child's father and mother were not married to each other at the time of his or her birth or where an unmarried father has not jointly registered

[325] Children (NI) Order 1996, art 8.
[326] Ibid art 12.
[327] Ibid art 8.
[328] Ibid art 50.
[329] Ibid art 63. For a case dealing with a human rights aspect of these orders, see para 3.29.
[330] Ibid arts 64(2), (3), (4) and (5).
[331] Ibid art 62.
[332] Ibid art 7.

the child's birth with the child's mother.[333] In such circumstances the mother has parental responsibility for the child but a court may, on an application made by the father, order that he has parental responsibility for the child, or the father and mother may by agreement provide for the father to undertake responsibility. A child of sufficient understanding may, with the leave of the court, apply him- or herself to have a parental responsibility order brought to an end by an order of the court.

(6)   *Prohibited steps order.*[334] This is an order that no step which could be taken by a parent in meeting his or her parental responsibility for a child, and which is of a kind specified in the order, shall be taken by any person without the consent of the court. It could stop a parent from taking a child out of the jurisdiction, for instance.

(7)   *Supervision order.*[335] This kind of order requires someone with parental responsibility for a child or someone with whom the child is living to take all reasonable steps to ensure that the child complies with certain specified directions. Such orders normally lapse after one year, but can be extended for a maximum period of three years.[336] Moreover an Education and Library Board can apply for an education supervision order.[337] This requires the Board to 'advise, assist and befriend the supervised child and his or her parents in such a way as will, in the opinion of the supervisor, secure that he or she is properly educated'.[338]

(8)   *Secure accommodation order.*[339] Health and Social Services Trusts can place a child in secure accommodation (defined as 'accommodation provided for the purpose of restricting liberty') but must seek the permission of a court if it wishes to extend any placement beyond a period of 72 hours. Under the Children (Secure Accommodation) Regulations (NI) 1996, secure accommodation must be provided by *statutory* children's homes, of which there is only one in Northern Ireland – Shamrock House Secure Unit located at the Lakewood Centre in Bangor.

Adoption

9.138   A child can be formally adopted in Northern Ireland only if a county court or the High Court issues an order to that effect. It used to be the case,

---

[333] For the latter of these two situations see the Family Law Act (NI) 2001, s 1, amending the Children (NI) Order 1995, art 7.
[334] Children (NI) Order 1995, art 8.
[335] Ibid art 54.
[336] Ibid Sch 3, para 6.
[337] Ibid art 55(1)
[338] Ibid Sch 4, para 2(1)(a).
[339] Ibid art 44.

unlike in the rest of the UK, that unmarried couples (whether heterosexual or homosexual) could not jointly adopt a child in Northern Ireland, but a ruling by the House of Lords ruled that that was a violation of the Human Rights Act 1998 because it discriminated against unmarried people.[340] When the Northern Ireland Executive refused to change the legislation to reflect this decision the Northern Ireland Human Rights Commission brought a successful application for judicial review,[341] but at the time of writing this ruling is being appealed to the Court of Appeal by the Minister of Health. A court can make an adoption order even though the child's natural parent or parents do not agree to this, provided the court is satisfied that parental consent is being withheld unreasonably.[342] Voluntary adoption agencies are now regulated by law.[343]

Abortion

9.139 The Abortion Act 1967, which applies throughout England, Scotland and Wales, has never been extended to Northern Ireland, where the law remains governed by the Offences Against the Person Act 1861, as interpreted by the courts.[344] Today an abortion is possible only if the life of the mother is at immediate risk or if her physical or mental health is at risk over a long term.[345] In *Family Planning Association of Northern Ireland v Minister for Health, Social Services and Public Safety*[346] the Family Planning Association succeeded in persuading the Court of Appeal that the law in Northern Ireland was too uncertain, and the Department of Health, Social Services and Public Safety was accordingly ordered to produce clearer guidance for use by doctors. When such guidance was eventually produced in 2009[347] it was soon ordered to be withdrawn following a legal challenge by an anti-abortion group.[348] Following a further application for judicial review brought by the Family Planning Association in early 2013 new guidance was at last produced.[349] Apparently over a thousand women

[340] *In re G (Adoption: Unmarried Couple)* [2008] UKHL 38, [2009] 1 AC 173. See also para 3.29.
[341] *Application by the Northern Ireland Human Rights Commission* [2012] NIQB 77. See too para 6.30.
[342] Adoption (NI) Order 1987, art 16(2). See, eg, *In re TM and RM (Freeing Order)* [2010] NIFam 23 (Morgan LCJ).
[343] Voluntary Adoption Agencies Regs (NI) 2010 (SR 289).
[344] ss 58 and 59.
[345] *R v Bourne* [1939] 1 KB 687.
[346] [2004] NICA 39.
[347] *Guidance on the Termination of Pregnancy: The Law and Clinical Practice in Northern Ireland*.
[348] Girvan J held that aspects of the guidance dealing with counselling and conscientious objection did not give fully clear and accurate guidance: *Application by the Society for the Protection of Unborn Children for Judicial Review* [2009] NIQB 92.
[349] See the press release from the FPA dated 27 February 2013, available on www.fpa.org.uk.

travel from Northern Ireland to England each year to have an abortion, at their own expense.[350] In 2012 the Minister of Health announced that in 2011–12 there had been just 35 terminations of pregnancy in Northern Ireland, compared with 43 in 2010–11 and 36 in 2009–10.[351] In 2012 a Marie Stopes clinic opened in Belfast to provide lawful abortions, but in March 2013 some MLAs sought to get the provision of abortions other than through the National Health Service prohibited by law.[352] On that occasion they were not successful.

[350] In 2008, 1,173 women made the trip: www.fpa.org.uk/pressarea/pressreleases/2009/25november2009.
[351] See www.dhsspsni.gov.uk/termination-statement (22 August 2012).
[352] Through an amendment to the Criminal Justice Bill then going through the Assembly.

10

Civil Proceedings in Northern Ireland

THE NATURE OF CIVIL PROCEEDINGS

10.1   The purpose of civil proceedings is to allow individuals and companies to make claims for the protection of their rights under the law. They differ from criminal proceedings in that they do not seek to punish someone through imprisonment, a fine or a community sentence. Instead civil proceedings seek to require a person to pay compensation to the other party to the dispute, or to take some other action that benefits that party. The dispute belongs to the parties (who are called the plaintiff[1] and the defendant), so they can at any time (even after the court has started to hear the case, or when an appeal is taking place) agree between themselves to settle the matter without waiting for a court order. The civil court must be officially notified of any settlement (so that 'judgment by consent' can be decreed) and it must grant its approval before a civil action involving a person under the age of 18 can be settled. The question of who is to bear the costs of a settled action is usually made part and parcel of the settlement agreement, but failing this the court can order the costs to be 'taxed' (ie assessed by a court official). In this chapter an outline is provided of how the nature of civil proceedings differs in Northern Ireland depending on the court where the proceedings take place.[2] We will look in turn at proceedings in magistrates' courts, small claims courts, county courts and the High Court. We conclude with a few words about how civil judgments are enforced.

CIVIL PROCEEDINGS IN A MAGISTRATES' COURT

10.2   The main types of civil cases which a magistrates' court can deal with are 'domestic' cases, claims to recover small debts, claims to deprive

---

[1] In England and Wales the courts now use the word 'claimant' instead of 'plaintiff'. In this book both terms are used interchangeably.
[2] See too C White, *Northern Ireland Social Work Law* (Dublin, Tottel Publishing, 2004), ch 3.

someone of the occupation of land and applications for licences. A few words will be said about each of these.[3]

Domestic cases

10.3   Domestic cases are those involving family matters. Remedies for domestic violence or for disputes over the care of children are available to cohabitees as well as to people who are married, but at present only someone who is married can claim financial assistance from his or her partner. In emergencies a non-molestation or occupation order can be made without first hearing from the person who is the subject of the order; this is called an *ex parte* application. The person who is the subject of the order will be given the opportunity to present his or her side of the story at a later stage. If the parties are already involved in family proceedings in a different court (eg a divorce hearing in a county court), an application for a non-molestation or occupation order can be dealt with there. When sitting to hear domestic cases the magistrates' court acts as a 'family proceedings court'. If necessary, the proceedings can be transferred to a 'family care centre' within a county court, or even to the Family Division of the High Court (see paras 9.134 and 9.137). In all courts domestic cases are heard at different times from other cases and *in camera* (ie with the general public excluded).

Small debts

10.4   Claims to recover small debts are a second common type of civil case in a magistrates' court. Examples of such cases are claims for arrears of income tax, national insurance contributions, VAT, rates and rent. Generally speaking, the debt in question must be for less than £100, but larger sums are also recoverable if legislation so provides (as the Rent (NI) Order 1978 does in the case of rent). Claims for debts can usually be issued at any time within six years after the debt falls due. They can also be dealt with by 'small claims courts', which are really a branch of the county courts (see para 10.8).[4] Numerically the recovery of small debts is the largest part of the civil jurisdiction of magistrates, but legally they are not the most difficult of cases to resolve.

---

[3] For further details see the Magistrates' Courts (NI) Order 1981 and the Magistrates' Courts Rules (NI) 1984, both of which have been frequently amended.
[4] The *Review of the Civil Justice System in Northern Ireland* (2000), para 21, recommended that this duality should continue.

Land cases

10.5 Claims to deprive someone of the occupation of land are in this context known as 'ejectment proceedings'. They can be brought by landlords to get rid of tenants who are no longer entitled to stay on the premises. But unless a statute provides otherwise, a magistrates' court has jurisdiction in such matters only when premises have been let at a rent which is less than £110 per year. Most commercial and residential tenancies would therefore not be affected by this procedure were it not for the fact that the Housing (NI) Order 1981 confers special recovery rights upon housing associations and the Northern Ireland Housing Executive.

Licences

10.6 A magistrates' court can issue a bookmaker's licence, but only a county court can issue a bookmaking office licence.[5] Similarly, a magistrates' court can renew licences authorising the sale of alcohol and certificates registering a club, but only a county court can issue the initial licence or certificate.[6] Magistrates deal with appeals against certain decisions taken by bodies such as education authorities too. For instance, if an Education and Library Board refuses to issue a licence to someone under the age of 16 to allow the child to participate in public performances on the stage, an appeal can be heard by a magistrates' court. District councils, not magistrates' courts, issue licences for places of entertainment and for sex establishments;[7] appeals against a refusal of such licences go to a county court.

Appeals from a magistrates' court

10.7 As in criminal cases (see para 8.55), if either side is dissatisfied with the decision of a magistrates' court in a civil matter it may appeal against that decision in one of two ways:

- by way of ordinary appeal to a county court, where there will be a complete rehearing of the factual *and* legal issues, or

---

[5] See the Betting, Gaming, Lotteries and Amusements (NI) Order 2005, arts 8(1) and 12(1).
[6] The relevant legislation includes the Betting, Gaming, Lotteries and Amusements (NI) Order 2005, the Licensing (NI) Order 1996 and the Registration of Clubs (NI) Order 1996. The Department for Social Development publishes guides to the law on these matters and also on Sunday trading. Licences to sell alcohol or to run a club must be renewed every five years. In 2011 the Department for Social Development issued a consultation paper entitled *Future Regulation of Gambling in Northern Ireland*, mainly to take account of the rise in internet and interactive television gambling.
[7] Local Government (Miscellaneous Provisions) (NI) Order 1985, arts 3 and 4, Schs 1 and 2.

- by way of a 'case stated' to the Court of Appeal, where only points of law will be considered.

If the first course is taken, there is then a further right of appeal for either side on a point of law (by way of case stated) to the Court of Appeal. In appeals from magistrates' courts or county courts the decision of the Court of Appeal is usually final. The only occasion the case can be taken to the Supreme Court of the UK is when it concerns the validity of a piece of legislation passed by the Northern Ireland Parliament or Assembly.[8]

SMALL CLAIMS COURTS

10.8   The small claims court is a special kind of county court provided for by the County Court Rules.[9] The court is presided over by a district judge, whose chief task is to deal with claims which are for less than £3,000.[10] The procedure used for dealing with these claims is known, misleadingly, as 'arbitration'.

10.9   However some types of dispute which may involve less than £3,000 cannot be resolved in a small claims court at all and must be taken to a county court in the normal way. These 'excepted proceedings' include disputes involving personal injuries,[11] road accidents,[12] libel or slander, a gift under a will, the ownership of land, and the property rights of married couples. Also, no claim can be made for an 'injunction' to stop someone doing something. All other cases involving £3,000 or less *must* now be brought under the small claims procedure.

Procedure

10.10   To make a claim in a small claims court the applicant sets out the details on an application form and sends it with two copies to a county court office, together with the court fee.[13] A copy of the application form and a notice as to when and where the hearing is to take place will be returned to the applicant. Another copy is sent to the person against whom

---

[8] Judicature (NI) Act 1978, s 42(6).
[9] County Court Rules (NI) 1981, Order 26. See too the County Courts (NI) Order 1980, art 30(3).
[10] County Courts (Financial Limits) Order (NI) 2011 (SR 65).
[11] In England and Wales personal injury claims of up to £1,000 *can* be dealt with by the small claims court.
[12] As to what constitutes a road accident, see *Pedlow v Dept for Regional Development* [2003] 3 BNIL 108.
[13] The fee is between £30 and £100 depending on the size of the claim. The Northern Ireland Courts and Tribunals Service publishes a helpful leaflet explaining the procedure used in small claims courts; it is also available online.

the claim is being made (the respondent) to find out if he or she intends to dispute the claim and to submit a counterclaim. The hearing should take place within three months of the application being submitted and over one-half of all applicants tend to win their case at the hearing. The vast majority of small claims are undefended; most of the cases, however, are claims brought by shops and companies *against* consumers, not the other way round.

10.11   The procedure at the hearing is intended for use by individual applicants without the need for legal or lay representation. In practice, however, solicitors are present in many of the cases, and advice workers occasionally represent claimants. Legal aid is *not* available, although some claimants may be entitled to advice under the green form scheme (see para 11.33). Compared with proceedings in a proper court, the hearing will be informal and the normal rules of evidence will not apply; it will sometimes take place in a small room of the courthouse.[14] If the parties agree, the district judge may even decide the claim on the basis of written evidence only. If a witness is reluctant to attend, the party wishing to call the witness can oblige him or her to attend by applying to the district judge for a witness summons.

10.12   The district judge's decision will usually be announced as soon as the hearing is over. If the losing party does not comply with whatever order is made, the winner can take the case to the Enforcement of Judgments Office (see para 10.36). If one party wishes to appeal against the decision of a district judge, he or she can only ask for a case to be stated on a point of law, not fact, to the Court of Appeal. Rights of appeal are deliberately restricted so as to prevent undue consideration of what are, relatively speaking, minor disputes.

10.13   Neither of the parties can (except rarely) recover his or her costs from the other party in a small claims arbitration (except the fee payable with the application form), so any travel expenses incurred by witnesses and the charge of any lawyers who are engaged for the case will have to be borne by the party calling the witness or employing the lawyer. This applies also to the cost of engaging an expert (eg a building contractor) to report on some matter, but the district judge may ask for a report from an independent expert to clarify a technical point and the cost of this will then be borne by the court office and not by the parties. The only occasion on which a district judge may award costs to one party is where the other party's conduct has been unreasonable.

---

[14] Though the European Court of Human Rights has stressed that small claims proceedings should invariably be open to the public: *Scarth v UK* (1998) 28 EHRR CD47.

European small claims procedure

10.14   Further to an EU Regulation issued in 2007, there is now a European small claims procedure which allows speedy cross-border civil or commercial litigation to take place anywhere in the EU (except Denmark) if the claim is for less than 2000 euros (about £1,850).[15] It has been available in all EU Member States since 2009 and is an alternative to existing national procedures. The procedure also facilitates the mutual recognition and enforcement of such judgments within EU States. The County Court Rules in Northern Ireland have been amended to take account of the EU Regulation.[16]

CIVIL PROCEEDINGS IN A COUNTY COURT

10.15   With the establishment of the Crown Court in 1979 county courts in Northern Ireland became almost exclusively civil courts, although they still hear appeals from criminal cases dealt with by magistrates' courts (see para 8.56). The civil work of county courts is much more varied than that of magistrates' courts, but it is still subject to restrictions as regards both type and size of claim. The main types of case dealt with in a county court are as follows:[17]

- actions in tort, or for breach of contract, where the amount claimed is less than £30,000[18] (£3,000 in libel or slander claims); a county court can deal with any debt claim for a sum greater than £30,000, provided that the parties themselves agree to this; claims in contract or tort for less than £10,000 (if not dealt with by the small claims court: see para 10.8) will be heard by a district judge, not a county court judge;

- actions for the recovery of land or involving disputed claims to the ownership of land where, generally speaking, the land does not have an annual rateable value of more than £500[19] (or £4,060 if the land is wholly or partly uninhabited);

- Chancery work, such as the management of funds held in trust, the enforcement of mortgages, the ending of partnerships and the supervision of contracts for the sale of land, provided that in all these cases the sum

[15] Regulation (EC) No 861/2007.
[16] County Court (Amendment No 2) Rules (NI) 2009 (SR 176).
[17] For further details see County Courts (NI) Order 1980 and County Court Rules (NI) 1981 (SR 225), both as amended. See too B Valentine, *Civil Proceedings: The County Court* (Belfast, SLS Legal Publications, 1999).
[18] Following a period of consultation by the Minister of Justice, this sum was raised from £15,000 on 25 February 2013: County Courts (Financial Limits) Order (NI) 2013 (SR 18).
[19] In some cases (eg under 'Deasy's Act' 1861), the figure is £1,000. The figure for commercial property was amended to £4,060 by the Revaluation (Consequential Provisions) Order (NI) 2003 (SR 73).

of money or value of property involved is less than £45,000 or the annual rateable value of any land involved is less than £500 (in the county courts, Chancery work is referred to as 'Equity' business: see para 4.3);

- disputes as to the validity of a will and as to who is to act as the executor of a will, or administrator of the estate of someone who dies without making a will (see para 9.34), provided that in such cases the estate does not exceed a value of £45,000 after payments of all taxes, etc; this heading includes disputes over a legacy if the property in question has a value of less than £15,000;
- undefended petitions for divorce, and certain applications for a share in matrimonial property (regardless of the value of the property);
- applications concerning the care and welfare of children;
- applications to adopt children;
- applications in cases involving domestic violence;
- discrimination cases where the claim relates to the provision of goods or services (if it relates to employment it will be dealt with by an industrial tribunal or the fair employment tribunal: see paras 9.106–9.109);
- applications brought under the Consumer Credit Act 1974, for instance, to re-open a credit agreement of less than £15,000 on the ground that its terms are extortionate;
- applications for licences to sell alcohol or to open bookmaking premises, and applications for certificates to register a club, together with appeals against the refusal of some licences by others (see para 10.6);
- actions to recover rates under the Rates (NI) Order 1977 and applications to determine the proper rent for a protected tenancy under the Rent (NI) Order 1978.

Civil bills

10.16   County court cases are usually begun by the claimant, or the claimant's solicitor, issuing a document called a 'civil bill', which will be delivered by hand or posted to the defendant. The civil bill is a way of proceeding which is peculiar to the island of Ireland and dates back to mediaeval times. It does not require any carefully worded pleadings as in High Court proceedings (see para 10.23) and is dealt with by a judge sitting without a jury.

10.17   If the defendant wishes to contest the civil bill, he or she has a period of three weeks within which to notify this to the claimant and the court by submitting a document called a 'notice of intention to defend'. The claimant has a further six months in which to inform the court and the defendant that the case is ready for hearing (in which case a 'certificate of readiness' is issued), otherwise the matter will be referred to a judge who can set a date for a hearing, 'stay' (ie stop) the proceedings, or dismiss the case. In debt cases, if the defendant decides not to defend the civil bill or fails to serve the appropriate notice, the claimant can apply to the court for a judgment against the defendant without the need for a hearing.[20]

10.18   In cases where the amount of compensation claimed in the civil bill is uncertain (ie it is a claim for 'unliquidated damages'), the claimant can apply for an 'interlocutory' (ie provisional) judgment for an amount to be assessed afterwards by a district judge. If this is granted, the plaintiff must send any supporting evidence to the chief clerk of the court, who then issues a summons which is served on the defendant at least seven days before the assessment of the damages is due to take place. If the defendant wishes to give evidence at the assessment, both the plaintiff and the court must be notified of this in writing. A district judge gives a 'decree' (or final judgment) for the amount assessed.

10.19   Generally speaking, as you would expect, the proceedings in county courts are more formal than in magistrates' courts but less formal than in the High Court. If the case is not settled by the parties the county court judge will usually deliver a judgment as soon as the parties have completed the submission of their arguments. In only a few cases will judgment be 'reserved' to a later date.

Undefended divorce cases

10.20   County court cases concerning family matters are begun either by issuing a summons or by lodging a 'petition'. Since 1981 county courts in Northern Ireland have been able to grant divorces, but only in undefended cases. The petitioner must still attend to give evidence – a divorce cannot be obtained entirely 'by post', as in England and Wales. Legal aid is available to cover divorce cases, whether defended or undefended (see para 11.39). The High Court also has jurisdiction to grant divorces (see para 9.125). A consultation paper on reform of divorce law was issued by the Office of Law Reform as far back as 1999,[21] but no new legislation has yet resulted.

Appeals to and from a county court

10.21   County courts hear appeals from civil as well as criminal cases heard in magistrates' courts, although the criminal workload is by far the more demanding. As in criminal cases (see para 8.56) there will be a complete

---

[20] See County Court Rules (NI) 1981 (SR 225), Order 12.
[21] *Divorce in Northern Ireland – A Better Way Forward.*

rehearing in the county court when it is dealing with a civil appeal and the court can uphold, vary or reverse the decision of the magistrates' court. A person who is aggrieved by a decision of a county court in the exercise of its 'original' (ie non-appellate) civil jurisdiction may appeal either by way of a full rehearing to the High Court or by way of case stated on a point of law to the Court of Appeal. The High Court can itself then state a case on a point of law for the opinion of the Court of Appeal. Whichever path is followed, the decision of the Court of Appeal is final unless the validity of a piece of legislation passed by the Northern Ireland Parliament or Assembly is at issue.[22]

PROCEEDINGS IN THE HIGH COURT

10.23   Unlike that of the inferior courts (magistrates' courts and county courts), the jurisdiction of the High Court of Northern Ireland is limited neither geographically nor by the value of the claim. It also has an inherent jurisdiction over and above what is specifically allocated to it by legislation.[23] It is exclusively a civil court (although it sometimes deals indirectly with criminal matters when considering applications for judicial review or bail applications). For reasons of administrative convenience its business is distributed between its three divisions as follows:

- *Queen's Bench Division*: claims for compensation for personal injury or for damage caused to a person's property or reputation (ie 'tort' claims); claims for breach of contract; claims concerning ships ('admiralty actions'); applications for judicial review of the actions or decisions of public authorities (these are treated in some detail at paras 6.5–6.11); all business not specifically assigned to another division, including various appeals.
- *Chancery Division*: disputes concerning the distribution of a dead person's property; difficulties arising out of the management of trust funds, including a charity's funds; the enforcement of mortgages and other securities; problems concerning partnerships and companies; bankruptcies; copyright; the supervision of contracts for the sale of land; the correction of deeds.
- *Family Division*: petitions for divorce or nullity; property claims between married couples; disputes over a person's marital status or legitimacy; applications concerning the wardship, guardianship, adoption, or care and welfare of children; applications for the right to be the executor of a person's will or to manage the property of someone who dies without having made a will; matters affecting persons who have a mental illness.

[22] Judicature (NI) Act 1978, s 42(6).
[23] This is mainly applied in situations where vulnerable people are in need of legal protection.

10.24   The High Court in England and Wales is currently comprised of the same three divisions, but there are in addition some informally organised sub-divisions. In Northern Ireland there are only two of these, namely the Companies Court within the Chancery Division and the Commercial Court within the Queen's Bench Division.[24] It is also necessary to note the existence of what are called Divisional Courts, not to be confused with the courts of the three separate divisions (see also para 4.7). A Divisional Court is a court *within* a division and usually comprises two, or three, judges. It hears special appeals or particular types of cases as a court of first instance. In England there are Divisional Courts within all three divisions but in Northern Ireland there is just one, the Divisional Court of the Queen's Bench Division.[25]

10.25   Proceedings in the High Court can be begun in a variety of ways, depending on the type of claim being made.[26] In all Divisions the proceedings can be rather formal and ponderous.

Pleadings in a Queen's Bench action

10.26   In the Queen's Bench Division the most typical claim is one made following an accident on the roads or at work. The claimant sets the ball rolling by issuing a 'writ of summons', which warns the defendant that a claim is being made and states the general nature of that claim. The writ will be delivered by hand or special delivery post. If the defendant wishes to have a chance to contest the claim he or she should, within 14 days, 'enter an appearance' with the court by handing in or posting the appropriate document. If the defendant does not do this the claimant can obtain a judgment without further argument, provided it is proved that the writ of summons was properly delivered. This is called 'a judgment in default of appearance'.

10.27   Even after an appearance has been entered, the claimant may be so confident of the defendant's lack of defence to the claim (except perhaps as to the *amount* of compensation being claimed) that he or she will apply for what is called a 'summary judgment', that is, judgment without a full-scale hearing. Another way in which cases can be brought to a conclusion without a full hearing taking place is if the defendant pays a sum of money into the relevant court office (ie makes a 'lodgment') and the claimant, within three

---

[24] On the latter, see C Dunford, *Litigation in the Commercial List in Northern Ireland* (Belfast, SLS Legal Publications, 2012).
[25] In England the Divisional Court of the Queen's Bench Division hears appeals from magistrates' courts in criminal cases. In Northern Ireland these are heard by county courts.
[26] For further details see B Valentine, *Civil Proceedings: The Supreme Court* (Belfast, SLS Legal Publications, 1997) and the Rules of the Court of Judicature (NI) 1980. A version of these Rules, updated to 31 August 2012, is available on the website of the Northern Ireland Courts and Tribunals Service.

weeks, decides to accept this amount in settlement of the claim. This 'stays' (ie stops) the proceedings. If a payment into court has been made but not accepted, the judge and jury must not be told about this in case it prejudices their decision on whether and to what extent the defendant is liable.

10.28 If the defendant enters an appearance and the claimant does not apply for summary judgment, the claimant should, within six weeks, send the defendant a document called a 'statement of claim', which specifies the precise facts and law on which the claim is based and asks for particular remedies. The defendant should respond to this, within three weeks, by sending to the plaintiff a 'defence'. This document will deny most of the allegations made in the statement of claim and may well be accompanied by a counterclaim which makes allegations against the claimant. Within a further three weeks the claimant should produce a 'reply to the defence' and, if necessary, a 'defence to the counterclaim'. All these documents are called 'pleadings', and the general rule is that points not raised in the written pleadings cannot later be argued orally in court. For a Northern Ireland case where the failure of the claimant's lawyers to plead certain points ultimately led to rejection of the case in the House of Lords, see *Farrell v Secretary of State for Defence*.[27]

10.29 At this juncture the pleadings are normally closed, although further documents can be served with the special permission of the court. Pleadings are meant to serve the purpose of making each side aware, before the case comes to trial, of what exactly the other side is arguing. In practice, however, the lawyers drafting these documents prefer to hedge their bets, so that when the case does come to court they will not be prevented from arguing a certain point just because it was not mentioned in the pleadings. But in recent years the judges have issued several Practice Directions to try to ensure that pleadings are more specific. The time limits for serving the various pleadings are, as well, often ignored in practice, by agreement of both sides.

Interlocutory proceedings

10.30 Once the pleadings in a Queen's Bench action have been closed, the plaintiff can apply within six weeks to have the case set down for trial at some future date. But further pre-trial procedures can still be taken to ensure that when the case does reach the trial stage it will be dealt with as efficiently as possible. These further proceedings are called 'interlocutory proceedings'. Examples are applications for the 'discovery' (ie disclosure) of documents or for the serving of 'interrogatories' (ie important preliminary

[27] [1980] 1 WLR 172.

questions). There is also a right to apply for disclosure of documents held by persons not involved in the court case.[28]   The process known as 'an application for a summons for directions', where a party seeks a ruling from a judge on a preliminary point, is commonly used in England but is not known in Northern Ireland.

The decision-making process

10.31   If the case eventually comes to trial, which will be many months or even years after the issue of the writ, it will usually be held in the presence of a judge sitting alone. Until 1987 it was quite common in Northern Ireland for cases to be heard by a judge sitting with a jury (of seven persons), but the province then adopted the English rule whereby trials without a jury are the norm unless special circumstances warrant otherwise. Only actions such as claims for libel will now be heard by a jury.[29] When a judge *does* sit with a jury it is the judge's task to make sure that the jury understands what law must be applied to the facts. The jury decides which version of the facts to believe, whom to hold liable and what amount of compensation (if any) is to be paid. This power to decide what remedy to give distinguishes the role of the civil jury from that of the criminal jury (see para 8.68) and the coroner's jury (see para 6.34). If there is no jury and the judge deems it necessary for a detailed assessment to be made of the compensation due, that issue will be referred to a High Court Master (see para 4.25).

10.32   In most cases the judge will award compensation by referring to the Judicial Studies Board of Northern Ireland's 'Green Book', which sets out guidelines for the assessment of damages in personal injury cases. These are based on what are believed to be the rates currently used in the negotiation and settlement of claims.[30] There is general agreement that compensation awards are on average slightly higher in Northern Ireland than in comparable cases in England and Wales, a factor contributing to higher insurance premiums in Northern Ireland.

Actions in the Chancery and Family Divisions

10.33   High Court proceedings in the Chancery and Family Divisions may be just as cumbersome as those in the Queen's Bench Division, but because

---

[28] See *O'Sullivan v Herdmans Ltd* [1987] 1 WLR 1047.

[29] The Courts and Tribunals Service has produced an explanatory information booklet, available online, for people who are called to serve on a High Court jury. When jurors first arrive at court they are also shown a video explaining their role.

[30] *Guidelines for the Assessment of General Damages in Personal Injury Cases in Northern Ireland* (3rd edn, 2008).

in such cases there is often little argument about the relevant facts giving rise to the action (the dispute being really about whether some legal rule applies) the legal procedures are sometimes speedier and more informal. Again, many such actions are settled out of court. Chancery actions are usually started by a document called 'an originating summons', which does not then lead to an exchange of pleadings. The matter is heard in the absence of a jury by a Master (see para 4.25) or by a High Court judge sitting in 'chambers' (ie the judge's own private office). Witnesses usually do not have to be present at the hearing because the evidence is presented in the form of written statements, called 'affidavits', rather than as oral testimony. Affidavits are documents sworn by the maker to be true in the presence of a Commissioner for Oaths – all solicitors in Northern Ireland are also Commissioners for Oaths.

10.34 An action in the Family Division, such as a request for a divorce, is usually begun by the petitioner lodging a petition with the court and serving a copy of it on the respondent. The petitioner is no longer *required* to appear in open court to give an oral account of the grounds for the petition, but this does usually still occur. There will of course be no jury involved. Many family actions are undefended, which obviously allows them to be processed more quickly and cheaply. What might delay the proceedings is the necessity for the judge to be satisfied that, when the parties to the action have children, the welfare of these children is being protected. There may also be complications over the division of the family property, a matter which is usually dealt with by a Master or a judge in chambers. Applications by a married person for an award of money against his or her partner are made by originating summons and not by petition.

Appeals from the High Court

10.35 For cases begun in the High Court, appeals lie directly to the Court of Appeal. The appeal takes the form of a full rehearing, with usually a word-for-word transcript of the evidence being placed before the judges but no re-examination of witnesses. The Court of Appeal can overturn the decision on whether or not the defendant is liable, but it cannot recalculate the damages to be awarded; that issue has to be sent back to the High Court for retrial. There is a further avenue of appeal to the UK's Supreme Court, provided either the Court of Appeal or the Supreme Court gives permission. Usually only two or three such appeals arise in Northern Ireland each year. An even rarer procedure is that provided for by the Administration of Justice Act 1969, whereby there can be a direct appeal straight from the High Court in Northern Ireland to the Supreme Court. This 'leapfrog' procedure is possible only if all the parties to the case agree to it and if the proposed appeal raises a question of law of general public importance involving either the interpretation of a piece of legislation or an issue on which the High Court must follow a precedent laid down by a higher court. It seems, however, that no leapfrog appeal has yet been made from the High Court of Northern Ireland.

ENFORCING CIVIL JUDGMENTS[31]

10.36   The fact that a court order has been issued in favour of the winner of litigation does not necessarily mean that he or she will receive the money (or whatever else is awarded) from the other side. Sometimes the loser is not willing to pay and has to be forced to do so. Ensuring that the loser of litigation complies with a court order can often be as difficult as obtaining that order in the first place. Since 1971, however, the task has been simplified in Northern Ireland through the creation of the Enforcement of Judgments Office (the EJO), which is part of the Northern Ireland Courts and Tribunals Service. It handles virtually all types of money judgments in civil cases, the principal exception being those issued against a spouse requiring maintenance payments to be made to the other spouse or to a child. The EJO enforces civil judgments of magistrates' courts and county courts (including small claims courts) as well as of the High Court, whereas in England and Wales the judgments of each of these courts are enforced in different ways.

10.37   The EJO keeps a register of judgments, which can be searched, on payment of a small fee, by anyone who needs to know whether there is an unpaid judgment against the name of a particular person or company. The person ordered by a court to pay money to another is called a 'judgment debtor'. If the person who is owed the money (the 'judgment creditor') thinks that more than a reasonable time has elapsed since the judgment was issued, he or she may get the EJO to send the debtor 'a notice of intent to enforce'. This orders the debtor to pay the money within 10 days. If the debtor still refuses to pay after that period has elapsed, the creditor may apply to the EJO for actual enforcement of the judgment. This can cost quite a bit of money (eg £261 in respect of a £1,600 judgment),[32] so before good money is thrown after bad the creditor should make sure that the debtor does in fact have assets out of which the value of the judgment can be realised. Money spent on enforcing a judgment is added to the amount owed by the judgment debtor. Interest on the judgment debt is also payable.

---

[31] See generally D Capper, *The Enforcement of Judgments in Northern Ireland* (Belfast, SLS Legal Publications, 2004) and the Judgments Enforcement (NI) Order 1981 and the Judgments Enforcement Rules (NI) 1981 (SR 147), as amended.
[32] See the Judgments Enforcement Fees Order (NI) 1996 (SR 101), as amended.

10.38   In response to an enforcement application the EJO will interview the debtor to assess his or her means and will proceed to enforce the award in whichever of a number of ways it thinks fit. It may, for instance, make an order that property belonging to the debtor should be seized and sold, an order that goods on premises occupied by the debtor should be deemed to be in the custody and possession of the EJO, or an order that the debtor's earnings should be 'attached' so that the debtor's employer must make periodical deductions from the debtor's wages or salary and pay them directly to the EJO on the creditor's behalf.

10.39   The EJO may postpone enforcement if it thinks that the debtor's property ought to be administered for the benefit of all the creditors and not just those who have applied for enforcement.[33] Or if the EJO thinks that enforcement within a reasonable time is impossible, it must issue a notice to that effect and, after hearing the parties, grant 'a certificate of unenforceability'. In these circumstances, or if the EJO otherwise fails to extract any money from the debtor, the creditor is not allowed to resort to self-help and must come to terms with the fact that the judgment in his or her favour is worthless.

10.40   Against some of the EJO's orders, such as an order for the transfer of possession of land or attachment of earnings, an aggrieved party may appeal to the High Court; against the rest an appeal may be made, on a question of law only, to the Court of Appeal. In both instances the decision of the court in which the appeal is heard is final.

---

[33] The EJO also maintains a case-tracking system, available on the website of the Northern Ireland Courts and Tribunals Service.

11

Lawyers in Northern Ireland

INTRODUCTION

11.1   As in England and Wales, Scotland, and the Republic of Ireland, but unlike many other common law countries such as the United States and Canada, Northern Ireland has a split legal profession. Solicitors deal with clients who contact them directly for professional legal help, usually when buying a house, making a will, or seeking a divorce. Barristers do not usually deal with clients directly but are briefed by solicitors when clients want to take matters to court. Some solicitors do court work as well, but in cases coming to the High Court or Crown Court in Northern Ireland it is very rare for a solicitor to speak on his or her client's behalf rather than a barrister doing so. For many years Northern Ireland has had more solicitors and barristers per head of population than have other parts of the UK or Ireland. The problem is a constant headache for the Council of Legal Education for Northern Ireland, which is the body with responsibility for deciding policies and setting standards concerning admission to the legal professions. This chapter begins by looking at the role of the 'law officers' (principally the Attorney General) and then proceeds to explain the work of solicitors and barristers in Northern Ireland, how they are regulated, and how people become members of those professions. The chapter concludes by describing the various state-funded schemes for helping people pay for their legal help and explains the basis on which lawyers charge for their services.

LAW OFFICERS

The Attorney General and the Advocate General

11.2   The Attorney General of England and Wales is the chief law officer of the UK Government,[1] with responsibility for advising government

---

[1] The Attorney General heads the Treasury Solicitor's Department: www.treasury-solicitor. gov.uk.

departments and representing the Government's interests in important legal disputes. He or she is a political appointee (although not a full member of the Cabinet) and answers questions on legal matters in Parliament. By tradition the Attorney General is meant to be non-political when giving legal advice (eg on whether the invasion of Iraq in 2003 was permitted under international law[2]) or when acting in his or her capacity as head of the barristers' profession (the Bar).

11.3 Before the abolition of the Stormont Parliament in 1972 there was a separate Attorney General for Northern Ireland. During the period of direct rule, and before responsibility for policing and criminal justice was devolved to the Northern Ireland Assembly in 2010, the English Attorney General acted for Northern Ireland as well,[3] although a senior and junior barrister were appointed to be the Attorney General's counsel in most cases requiring his or her involvement in Northern Ireland. Such counsel would, for instance, act for the Government in cases brought against it under the European Convention on Human Rights. Now that policing and criminal justice have been devolved, a separate Attorney General has been appointed for Northern Ireland by the First and Deputy First Ministers acting jointly, but not as a political appointee.[4] The Attorney General for England and Wales continues to have responsibilities concerning the remaining 'reserved' and 'excepted' matters, and when acting in that capacity he or she is known as the Advocate General for Northern Ireland.[5] In England and Wales the Attorney General has a deputy called the Solicitor General, although he or she too is also a barrister and a political appointee. No such office exists in Northern Ireland, but there is a 'Solicitor to the Attorney General' who is responsible, under the direction of the Attorney General, for the conduct of litigation undertaken by the Attorney or in those cases in which the Attorney is not instructed by the Northern Ireland Executive's Departmental Solicitor's Office.

11.4 Prior to the devolution of justice to the Northern Ireland Assembly in April 2010, the Attorney General for England and Wales (acting as the Attorney General for Northern Ireland) had the power to exercise some important discretions relating to criminal prosecutions in Northern Ireland. He or she could, for instance, stop prosecutions by submitting a document called a *nolle prosequi* ('unwilling to prosecute') or refer supposedly lenient sentences to the Court of Appeal (see paras 8.58 and 8.68). But the effect of the

---

[2] After extracts from the Attorney General's initial advice on this were leaked to the press, the government eventually put the whole document into the public domain on 28 April 2005. In this document he hedged his bets as to whether an invasion would be illegal, but 10 days later his advice was clear that it would be legal.

[3] Northern Ireland Constitution Act 1973, s 11.

[4] Justice (NI) Act 2002, s 22(2). Under s 26 the Attorney General must submit an annual report to the First Minister and Deputy First Minister.

[5] Ibid s 27 and Sch 7.

devolution process has been to transfer those powers to the Director of Public Prosecutions and deny them to the new locally-based Attorney General.[6] This situation is currently under consideration by the Minister of Justice because without oversight by the Attorney General the Public Prosecution Service may not be as accountable as it needs to be. The Attorney General does take the lead in prosecuting people (including newspapers and other media organisations) for the crime of contempt of court, and also in seeking injunctions to prevent such contempt from occurring in the first place (eg if it comes to light that a company is about to broadcast a television or radio programme that may be in breach of the contempt laws).[7] In addition, under section 8 of the Justice (NI) Act 2004, the Attorney is required to produce guidance for criminal justice organisations on the exercise of their functions in a manner consistent with international human rights standards. Before producing such guidance the Attorney has to consult with the Advocate General for Northern Ireland. Although this work was commenced prior to the devolution of criminal justice to the Northern Ireland Assembly in 2010, it is still a work in progress.

11.5 In matters concerned with private law the Attorney General's approval is needed for actions taken by citizens to protect the public interest. These are called 'relator actions',[8] and they are usually taken to seek injunctions to stop certain actions from occurring. Exceptionally they can be initiated by the Attorney General in person. Sometimes the Attorney General, or a representative, is asked to attend court as *amicus curiae*, that is, 'a friend of the court', to give general legal advice on points at issue in a case. The Attorney can also apply to intervene in court cases to make submissions about matters of significant public interest.[9] The Attorney General can even participate in proceedings of the Northern Ireland Assembly (to the extent permitted by its Standing Orders) but cannot vote there,[10] and has the power to challenge in court legislation of the Northern Ireland Assembly if he or she believes that the Assembly has no power to make it (see para 2.31).[11] The Attorney General can also direct the holding of an inquest even if a coroner has decided that an inquest is not necessary.[12]

---

[6] Justice (NI) Act 2002, s 41. But under s 30(1) it is the Attorney General who appoints the DPP: see para 8.34.

[7] See, eg, *Re Attorney General for Northern Ireland's Application* [2004] NIJB 97.

[8] For further details see T Ingman, *The English Legal Process* (Oxford, Oxford UP, 13th edn, 2010), 370.

[9] *Northern Ireland Road Transport Board v Benson* [1940] NI 133. Eg the current Attorney General intervened in *In re McCaughey* [2011] UKSC 20, [2012] 1 AC 725.

[10] Justice (NI) Act 2002, s 25(1).

[11] Northern Ireland Act 1998, s 11(1) (referring Assembly Bills to the UK Supreme Court) and s 71(2) (bringing proceedings concerning any legislation on human rights grounds).

[12] Coroners Act (NI) 1959, s 14; for a case where this happened, see *In re Hemsworth's Application* [2003] NIQB 5.

The Crown Solicitor

11.6   The Advocate General (not the Attorney General) appoints the Crown Solicitor for Northern Ireland,[13] whose office is part of the Northern Ireland Office and whose services are available to any UK government department or Northern Ireland executive authority, including the Police Service, the Policing Board and the Chief Electoral Office. Most of the Crown Solicitor's work has to do with civil rather than criminal court actions, because the latter are usually handled by the Director of Public Prosecutions (see para 8.34). A lot of the work is in the area of debt recovery, but the office also handles civil litigation, conveyancing and probate (ie the administration of someone's property after he or she dies) as well as judicial review applications (see para 6.5).

The Official Solicitor

11.7   The Official Solicitor, who has an office in the Royal Courts of Justice, represents the interests of litigants in cases where they would not otherwise be adequately protected, such as cases involving children or people who suffer from a mental disability (known as 'patients'). He or she must conduct such investigations and render such assistance as is required by the direction of a court. The Official Solicitor acts as the 'Controller' of property for a large number of children and sometimes deals with conveyancing and the administration of the estates of deceased patients. He or she may also be invited by a court to represent children in wardship, adoption or child care cases, including cases where consent to medical treatment is required. The unit within the High Court which deals with the administration of the affairs of mental patients is called the Office of Care and Protection, about which more information can be found on the website of the Northern Ireland Courts and Tribunals Service.[14]

SOLICITORS

11.8   Solicitors became a distinct self-governing profession in Ireland with the creation of the Law Society of Ireland in 1830. In 1922 a Royal Charter was granted to the profession in Northern Ireland to permit the setting up of the Incorporated Law Society of Northern Ireland.[15] Under a statute passed

---

[13] Justice (NI) Act 2002, Sch 7, para 14, amending the Northern Ireland Constitution Act 1973, s 35.

[14] Under 'Services'. The office is equivalent to the Office of the Public Guardian in England and Wales.

[15] www.lawsoc-ni.org. The website carries a copy of the 1922 Royal Charter. For an account of the Society since its foundation, see A Hewitt, *The Law Society of Northern Ireland: A History* (Belfast, 2010).

in 1938 (superseded by an Order in Council in 1976,[16] itself amended in 1989) the Law Society obtained the power to issue regulations governing the education, the accounts and the professional conduct of solicitors. Copies of the latest version of all of these are available on the Law Society's website. All solicitors in Northern Ireland must register with the Law Society every year (although they need not necessarily become members) and an annual practising certificate will be granted only if the Law Society is sure, amongst other things, that the solicitor is properly insured against loss wrongfully caused to clients. Information relevant to the solicitors' profession in Northern Ireland is included in the Law Society's monthly magazine called *The Writ*, also available online via the Law Society's website. Every practising solicitor must now also undertake 'continuing professional development' (CPD) in the form of training courses.[17]

11.9   Solicitors are of course listed in the telephone directory and there are directories on the websites of the Law Society of Northern Ireland and the Northern Ireland Legal Services Commission (NILSC) (see para 11.47).[18] Solicitors are restricted in how they can advertise themselves. They cannot try to attract business through, for example, price-cutting or sharing offices with non-solicitors. Nor can they form themselves into limited companies, only partnerships. These rules exist to protect the interests of clients and to maintain the integrity of the profession as a whole.

11.10   In March 2013 there were well over 2,000 solicitors in Northern Ireland, spread over approximately 400 firms.[19] The firms vary in size from the small one person office to the large firm which may have several partners and employ several assistants. The firm will also employ secretarial staff and perhaps one or two apprentice solicitors. Unlike many English firms, solicitors in Northern Ireland do not employ assistants called legal executives. Some large English forms of solicitors have recently opened branches in Belfast but these mainly carry out work supplied by other branches of those firms abroad.

The work of a solicitor

11.11   The daily work of a solicitor can be very varied. Most of it is office work, although solicitors do have what is called 'the right of audience' in magistrates' courts and county courts (and occasionally in the Crown Court), which means that they can speak on behalf of their clients in those

---

[16] Solicitors (NI) Order 1976.
[17] See the Solicitors Training (Continuing Professional Development) Regs (NI) 2004 (not issued as a Statutory Rule but available on the Law Society's website).
[18] www.nilsc.org.uk.
[19] Not everyone with a practising certificate will be in private practice, but the vast majority will be.

courts. Traditionally that is the role of barristers, and in the higher courts it is nearly always a barrister who represents a litigant. But solicitors can take a course for a 'certificate in advocacy', which gives them the right of audience in the higher courts.[20] Solicitor-advocates can even be appointed as Queen's Counsel (see para 11.21). The largest single category of solicitors' work is conveyancing (ie the legal transfer of land: see paras 9.13–9.14). Other important categories are matrimonial work, succession work (ie dealing with the consequences of a death), criminal work and accident compensation claims. If the firm is large enough it will probably have a litigation department to deal with cases which may involve court actions. The vast majority of such actions are eventually settled out of court and it is an essential part of a solicitor's function to try to arrange such settlements. In order to reduce the pressure on courts, and to keep down costs, some solicitors offer an 'alternative dispute resolution' (ADR) scheme for people involved in commercial disputes.[21] Under this scheme, the parties share the costs.

11.12   If a solicitor's work does not involve a dispute with another party, it is called non-contentious work. The charges for this type of work are calculated on a different basis from that used for contentious work (see para 11.51). All solicitors can also function as Commissioners for Oaths, and a small number act as notaries public (they are listed on the Law Society's website). The former are required as witnesses for certain official documents, although they cannot witness documents prepared by themselves or by their opponents in a case. Notaries public are lawyers who can witness documents for use abroad.

11.13   For two types of work solicitors in Northern Ireland currently have a virtual monopoly: the drawing up of a conveyance on the sale of land (see para 9.13) and the taking out of probate or letters of administration when someone dies (see para 9.34). It is a criminal offence, with some minor exceptions, for anyone who is not a solicitor to undertake either of these tasks if payment is demanded for the work. In England the first of these monopolies was removed when the Administration of Justice Act 1985 provided for the licensing of non-solicitor conveyancers, but as yet this freedom has not been extended to Northern Ireland.

Complaints against solicitors

11.14   If you wish to complain about a solicitor you should first of all discuss the matter thoroughly with the solicitor involved. Every firm of solicitors must now have in place a formal complaints handling process for

[20] This right was extended by the Justice Act (NI) 2011, ss 88–90.
[21] See n 15 above; there is a downloadable leaflet about the scheme.

their clients. You should bear in mind, however, that, because solicitors are 'officers of the court', their primary duty is not to their clients but to the courts. They certainly must act for you to the best of their ability but this does not allow them to conceal evidence or to ignore established procedures. If you are not satisfied with your solicitor's explanation in relation to your complaint you can write to the Law Society about the matter. All complaints are dealt with in the first instance by Society staff and the more serious cases are considered by the Society's Professional Conduct Committee, which comprises non-lawyers as well as lawyers.[22] Where it finds the complaint merited, the Committee may reprimand the solicitor and/or direct him or her to take certain steps. If the complaint is about the solicitor's charges, the Committee can also determine the appropriate amount of money to be paid, provided the complaint was lodged within six months' of the solicitor's bill being sent to the client. The Committee cannot, however, award any compensation to the complainant.

11.15 The most serious cases can be referred by the Committee to the Solicitors Disciplinary Tribunal, which is independent of the Law Society and again contains lay representatives. The Tribunal has the power, amongst other things, to strike a solicitor off the Solicitors' Roll, to impose a fine of up to £3,000 and to order the solicitor to pay back all or part of the legal fees for the work in question. An appeal against a decision of the Disciplinary Tribunal can be taken by any person affected by it to a judge of the High Court.

The Lay Observer

11.16 Since 1977 Northern Ireland has had an official called the Lay Observer,[23] a non-lawyer whose job it is to report on the nature of complaints made to the Law Society about the conduct of solicitors and the manner in which those complaints have been dealt with by the Society.[24] The commonest complaint tends to be about undue delay.

11.17 In order to alleviate public anxiety at the lack of scrutiny of solicitors' and other legal services, the Government declared its intention as far back as the early 1990s to appoint a Legal Services Ombudsman for Northern Ireland,[25] a post now in existence for England and Wales. Such an Ombudsman, as befits his or her title, would have much greater investigative powers than those of the Lay Observer, including the power to recommend

---

[22] In England and Wales a separate Office for the Supervision of Solicitors has been established.
[23] Solicitors (NI) Order 1976, art 42, as amended by the Solicitors (Amendment) (NI) Order 1989, art 17.
[24] See www.layobserverni.com.
[25] See *Legal Services in Northern Ireland: The Government's Proposals*, Northern Ireland Courts Service, 1991.

the payment of compensation to victims of solicitor misconduct. As yet, however, no further steps have been taken to implement this proposal in Northern Ireland.

BARRISTERS

11.18   In a small proportion of the cases handled by solicitors it will be necessary for the services of a barrister to be used. Barristers, or 'counsel' as they are sometimes called, are experts in advocacy (ie oral argument). They began to organise themselves in Ireland as a professional body (the Bar) as long ago as the thirteenth century and in 1541 their headquarters became the King's Inns in Dublin. Following the partition of Ireland in 1921, judges and practising barristers in Northern Ireland formed their own Inn of Court of Northern Ireland in 1926. The governing bodies of the profession are the Inn of Court's 'benchers', who include all the High Court and Court of Appeal judges, and (more importantly) the Executive Council of the Inn of Court. The Bar Council, elected by practising barristers, oversees standards within the profession and in effect acts as the profession's 'trade union'.

11.19   In contrast to solicitors, who mostly work in formal partnerships, barristers are self-employed and are not permitted to form partnerships. In England they share premises known as chambers and are referred to as having tenancies in those chambers. In Northern Ireland (as in Scotland and the Republic of Ireland) the tradition is for all barristers to work out of a Bar Library, which is situated beside the Royal Courts of Justice in Belfast.[26] There are no barristers' clerks in Northern Ireland, the officials who effectively act as business managers in barristers' chambers in England and Wales and who take a commission on the fees earned by the barristers. In Northern Ireland the fees are negotiated directly between barrister and solicitor. As it is technically the solicitor who engages the barrister, even though the client may have asked for a particular barrister to be used, the barrister cannot sue the client for fees if they are not paid; indeed by legal custom the barrister cannot sue the solicitor either. Like solicitors, barristers must complete some hours of 'continuing professional development' each year. Also, since 2004 newly called barristers have to complete within one year a Northern Ireland Bar Advocacy Training Course and a Northern Ireland Bar Ethics Course.

11.20   A solicitor will need to consult a barrister whenever an expert's opinion is required as to the chances of successfully arguing a particular point in court. The client cannot usually approach the barrister directly, but the Bar Council does operate a scheme which licences some professional organisations to have direct access to barristers. A written opinion by

---

[26] www.barlibrary.com.

the barrister will often satisfy the client's needs, and even if the case does eventually come to court the client will probably meet the barrister there for the first time. For cases being heard in the High Court it is the barrister who drafts the pleadings. Once a barrister is involved in a case he or she will advise the client whether or not to accept an offer of settlement.

Queen's Counsel

11.21 Every few years experienced barristers in Northern Ireland are invited to apply to the Lord Chief Justice to 'take silk', that is, to become a Queen's Counsel (QC).[27] This is an indicator of the barrister's seniority and expertise. The recruitment process is audited by the Judicial Appointments Commission (see para 4.32). After appointment as a QC a barrister will not generally appear in court without a 'junior', as all other barristers are called, and will charge higher fees. Most judicial appointments are open to practising barristers of a number of years' standing, so needless to say many of the judges are former QCs. The first ever female QC in Northern Ireland was appointed only in 1989.

11.22 In March 2013 there were 680 barristers in private practice in Northern Ireland, of whom 86 were QCs. There are many more non-practising barristers whose membership of the Bar Library has lapsed. The Bar Library publishes an annual Directory listing the contact details and interests of all barristers in Northern Ireland.[28]

Complaints against barristers

11.23 Barristers are meant to comply with the Bar's Code of Conduct and with its Fitness to Practise Rules.[29] Complaints that they have not done so should be directed to the Professional Conduct Committee of the Bar Council of Northern Ireland, which may arrange a hearing on the matter. There are two lay persons on this Committee. If a complaint is serious the Committee may refer it to a Disciplinary Committee of the Executive Council of the Inn of Court of Northern Ireland. Any decision to suspend or disbar a barrister can be taken only by the benchers of the Inn of Court. It was only in 2000 that it became possible to sue barristers for their negligent performance as advocates in court.[30]

[27] The expression 'taking silk' derives from the fact that the gown worn by a QC is partly made of silk.
[28] Available at www.barlibrary.com.
[29] Ibid.
[30] *Arthur J S Hall (a firm) v Simons* [2002] 1 AC 615.

Pro bono and public interest work

11.24   There is not a strong tradition of lawyers doing pro bono work in Northern Ireland, that is, work for which no payment is demanded. In London and elsewhere many lawyers will represent people at little or no charge because they are already earning a lot from other work they do and they want to give something back to society. The Bar Council and the Law Society of Northern Ireland have, however, set up the Northern Ireland Lawyers Pro Bono Group,[31] within which a number of lawyers have undertaken to provide their services free of charge for up to three days or 20 hours every year.

11.25   In 2009 a further initiative was taken when the Public Interest Litigation Support Project was set up in Belfast with the help of charitable funding.[32] As with other public interest projects around the world, this one promotes litigation as a means of bringing about social change. Lawyers employed by the project will focus on using human rights and equality laws to take cases to court on behalf of groups who are disadvantaged.

LEGAL EDUCATION

11.26   There is practically no instruction given about the law to school-children in Northern Ireland. The province's Council for the Curriculum, Examinations and Assessment does not have a syllabus in law at either GCSE or 'A' Level. Any examinable courses which are followed will therefore usually be organised from England and will deal with English law. At the further and higher education levels it is possible to study law at a number of colleges and at the Schools of Law in Queen's University Belfast and the University of Ulster (Jordanstown and Magee campuses). Both universities offer a variety of undergraduate and postgraduate degree programmes, some of which can be taken through part-time study. An undergraduate degree in law is called an 'LLB', short for 'Bachelor of Laws'. The Open University offers modules in law too, although only in English law.

11.27   To become a solicitor or barrister in Northern Ireland a person has to complete successfully the vocational courses organised either by the Institute of Professional Legal Studies,[33] which is currently part of Queen's University Belfast, or by the Graduate School of Professional Legal Education, which is part of the University of Ulster at Magee. You can apply for these courses if you have a recognised law degree (of at least second class honours standard if you want to be a barrister) or if, having obtained another

---

[31] www.barlibrary.com/about-us/ni-lawyers-pro-bono-group.
[32] www.pilsni.org.
[33] www.qub.ac.uk/ipls, where much more detail about applying to the Institute is contained.

kind of degree, you have first completed a Masters in Legal Science degree at Queen's University (this takes two years full-time or three years part-time). All applicants for the Institute or Graduate School must, however, sit an admissions test specifically designed to assess their aptitude for practising law. In 2013 there are 120 places available on the Institute's course for trainee solicitors and 30 places for prospective barristers (the latter number is to fall to 20 in 2014); there are also 28 places for trainee solicitors at the Graduate School at Magee. Every year there is very stiff competition for training places at the Institute and Graduate School: usually the ratio is three or four applicants for every place.

Trainee solicitors

11.28 For intending solicitors the Institute and Graduate School courses are a component part of a two year 'apprenticeship'. The first four months of the two-year apprenticeship (September to December) are spent in a solicitor's office, the student having had to find a so-called 'master' before gaining admission to the Institute or Graduate School (this is often a major stumbling-block for applicants, even those who do very well in the admissions test). The next 12 months (except for University vacations, when the students are expected to be back in their offices) consist of lectures and vocational exercises at the Institute or Graduate School, at the end of which the student sits examinations for a Certificate in Professional Legal Studies (at the Institute) or a Postgraduate Diploma in Legal Practice (at the Graduate School). The service in a solicitor's office is then continued for a further eight months[34] and at that point the student is qualified to hold a 'restricted' practising certificate.[35] This means that for the next two years the solicitor cannot practise on his or her own account or in partnership, but only as an assistant solicitor in a firm or under a solicitor in a public body or government department. A solicitor in practice must also pay an annual fee to the Law Society for a practising certificate.

Pupil barristers

11.29 For intending barristers the Institute course runs for nine months, from October to June. They then obtain their Certificate in Professional Legal Studies and are 'called to the Bar' in the following September. For

---

[34] When accompanying their masters, pupil solicitors *are* permitted to attend interviews between criminal suspects and the police: *In re Campbell's Application* [2010] NIQB 40.

[35] Restrictions can be opposed for other reasons too. Appeals against these lie first to the Council of the Law Society and then to the Lord Chief Justice. See, eg, *In the matter of a Solicitor* [2001] NIJB 179.

a further 12 months they must serve a 'pupillage', acting as 'pupils' to an experienced 'master' (who will be a practising barrister of at least eight years' standing). During the first three months of this year the pupils accompany their master to court and learn how things are done in practice; during the next three months they can take some minor cases by themselves, but only after the first half of the year can they accept other types of fee-earning work. It may be some months before they actually begin to receive an income from the briefs they have handled for solicitors. Barristers, too, must pay for an annual practising certificate as well as a fee for using the Bar Library.

11.30   In exceptional cases the arrangements just described for admission to the legal professions may be altered. This is particularly so for applicants who have already worked as a law clerk in a solicitor's office for seven years, who are university lecturers in law, or who are professionally qualified in other jurisdictions. People who fully qualify as solicitors in England and Wales have the right to transfer their practising certificate to Northern Ireland, as do solicitors qualified in the Republic of Ireland, provided that in all cases they have practised for at least three years before transferring. Solicitors qualified in Scotland have first to do courses in wills and conveyancing at the Institute of Professional Legal Studies in Belfast. Barristers qualified in England and Wales can transfer to Northern Ireland provided that they have completed a 12-month pupillage under the supervision of a practising barrister in England and Wales. Barristers qualified in the Republic of Ireland can transfer only if they are of at least three year's standing at the Bar in that jurisdiction. There are no reciprocal arrangements concerning the transfer of barristers qualified in Scotland. The European Communities (Services of Lawyers) Order 1978 allows lawyers qualified in other EU states, under strict conditions, to provide services in the UK which could otherwise be provided only by barristers or solicitors.

STATE HELP WITH LEGAL COSTS

11.31   There are, in effect, four separate schemes under which the State provides financial assistance in legal matters. They are:

(1)   legal advice and assistance
(2)   assistance by way of representation
(3)   civil legal aid
(4)   criminal legal aid.

Each of these schemes operates under the Legal Aid, Advice and Assistance (NI) Order 1981, as amended and supplemented by numerous sets of regulations. In 2011–12 about 102,000 people obtained some form of state help with their legal costs in Northern Ireland.[36] The annual cost of legal aid per head of population was £46.69, compared with figures of £37.88 for Scotland and £29.58 for England and Wales.[37]

11.32   By and large the schemes operate regardless of the nature of the legal problem involved, but a few special problems are not covered, such as libel and slander[38] or queries about the law outside Northern Ireland. Some matters are catered for by separate specially designed schemes, like the assistance which the Equality Commission for Northern Ireland, the Northern Ireland Human Rights Commission and the Northern Ireland Commissioner for Children and Young People are empowered to give in some cases of alleged discrimination or breach of human rights. Individuals may also receive financial assistance from private sources; an employer or a trade union may give help, as may a professional association or a club, such as the Automobile Association. It is also possible to take out insurance against the incurring of legal expenses (this is usually an option when insuring a car).

LEGAL ADVICE AND ASSISTANCE

11.33   This scheme is popularly referred to as 'the green form scheme', because of the colour of the application form which solicitors have to submit to the Northern Ireland Legal Services Commission (NILSC: see para 11.47). It is available for anyone aged 16 or over, provided that the financial eligibility criteria are also met. Solicitors can claim £43.25 an hour for their work, and £3.35 for each letter they write or telephone call they make, but unless they get special permission the maximum they can claim in any one case is £88 per case, a figure which has not changed for several years.

11.34   The eligibility test is a purely financial one: the 'merits' of the legal position are irrelevant. At present an applicant with no dependants does not qualify if his or her 'disposable capital' (ie savings) exceeds £1,000. Even if the applicant's disposable capital is less than £1,000 he or she will qualify for advice and assistance only if they are in receipt of a so-called 'passport benefit' such as income support, jobseekers' allowance or pensions credit (working families tax credit is not a passport benefit), or if their 'disposable income' is less than £234 per week.[39] 'Disposable income' basically means

[36] Committee for Justice of the Northern Ireland Assembly, 20 May 2010, evidence from Mr David Lavery, Director of the Northern Ireland Courts and Tribunals Service.
[37] *The Times*, 21 April 2011, p 27.
[38] Libel is the permanent (eg written) form of defamation; slander is the impermanent (eg spoken) form.
[39] Legal Advice and Assistance (Financial Conditions) Regs (NI) 2009 (SR 103). This limit has remain unchanged since 2009. The financial test is not applied when someone is seeking help with a case before the Mental Health Review Tribunal and no contributions have to be made by such a person: Legal Advice and Assistance (Amendment) Regs (NI) 2012 (SR 419).

the applicant's take-home pay, less the cost of regular living expenses (eg for rent and food).

11.35   Normally the capital and weekly income of the applicant's spouse or partner (whether same-sex or not) will be included in the calculations of capital and income. But certain sums will not be counted as disposable if there are children in the family.[40] The applicant will be required to make a contribution to the advice and assistance granted if his or her disposable income exceeds £100 per week, the size of the contribution depending on the size of the excess.[41] In England and Wales the contributory part of the green form scheme was abolished in 1993, so only persons in receipt of passport benefits, or having less than £234 weekly disposable income, are now eligible for assistance there, albeit free of charge.

11.36   Since the introduction of the Police and Criminal Evidence (NI) Order 1989 (the PACE Order), a person detained in a police station is entitled to have access to a solicitor (see para 8.19). To provide for such access the legal advice and assistance scheme has been amended to allow solicitors who attend such detainees (often, of course, at unsocial hours and at very little notice) to receive up to £200 without the need to apply for special authority from the Law Society.

11.37   The difference between the value of the work done for a client under the advice and assistance scheme and the amount of contributions which the client may have to pay is recoverable by the solicitor out of (in order of priority):

(1)   the costs which the other side agrees, or is ordered by the court, to pay to the assisted person

(2)   the property which is recovered or preserved for the assisted person in the case, unless it is exempted property such as a house or maintenance payments

(3)   the fund for civil legal services which is maintained by the NILSC (see para 11.47).

In short, under the green form scheme, if the applicant wins the case he or she will normally end up paying little or nothing towards the overall costs involved; any contribution already paid will be recouped by the award of costs made in the applicant's favour by the judge. If the applicant loses the case, the cost to him or her should normally not exceed the amount of the contribution payable under the scheme. If a person who is assisted by representation is ordered by the court to pay the costs of the proceedings, he or she does not have to pay more than what the court thinks is reasonable

---

[40] Legal Aid (Assessment of Resources) Regs (NI) 1981 (SR 189), as amended.
[41] Legal Advice and Assistance (Financial Conditions) Regs (NI) 2009 (SR 193) and Legal Advice and Assistance (Amendment) Regs (NI) 2009 (SR 102).

having regard to all the circumstances. The other side may recover the balance of the costs from the NILSC (see para 11.47).

11.38 In 2011–12 legal advice and assistance was granted in approximately 43,000 cases. The amount paid out was £4.7 million (£500,000 more than in the previous year), which was about 5 per cent of the total sum spent on legal aid in 2011–12.[42]

ASSISTANCE BY WAY OF REPRESENTATION

11.39 The only situations in which solicitors can personally represent an assisted person in court or at a tribunal under the legal advice and assistance scheme is when they have been given express permission to do so under the ABWOR scheme ('assistance by way of representation'). This is possible, for example, in certain civil proceedings in magistrates' courts (domestic cases, debt or land cases and some welfare cases). Since the coming into force of the Children (NI) Order 1995 this has been a particularly important type of assistance. However the NILSC will grant its approval for such representation only if it is shown that there are reasonable grounds for taking, defending, or being a party to the proceedings. This 'merits' test distinguishes the ABWOR scheme from the ordinary legal advice and assistance scheme. ABWOR is also available for proceedings at the Mental Health Review Tribunal (see para 4.31) and for some hearings involving prisoners or detainees. In cases of ABWOR the disposable capital limit for eligibility is the same as for civil legal aid (£3,000). But the rule still applies that only £88 worth of assistance is obtainable unless the Law Society grants an extension.

11.40 In 2011–12 ABWOR was granted in some 12,300 cases, at a total cost of £11.8 million (£1.4 million more than in the previous year). This accounted for 12 per cent of all the money spent on legal aid in Northern Ireland during 2011–12.[43]

CIVIL LEGAL AID

11.41 Legal aid for court proceedings in civil cases was not introduced in Northern Ireland until 1965, 16 years after its introduction in England and Wales. Even then it was difficult to access, as was made clear when people who complained about the discriminatory allocation of public housing in Northern Ireland in the mid-1960s were denied any state help with their legal claims. Today the decision on whether to grant civil legal aid in any

---

[42] *Annual Report and Financial Statements of NILSC 2011–12*, p 16.
[43] Ibid.

particular case is taken by officials at the NILSC, to whom the application forms are submitted by solicitors. Persons living outside Northern Ireland can apply for legal aid for civil proceedings which are to take place within Northern Ireland, but persons living in Northern Ireland who want legal aid for proceedings taking place elsewhere must apply to the authorities in that jurisdiction.

11.42   In 2011–12 civil legal aid was granted in about 9,400 cases, at a cost of £37.7 million (£12 million more than in the previous year). This represented 38 per cent of all legal aid expenditure in 2011–12.[44]

The financial and merits tests

11.43   An important difference between the civil legal aid scheme and the legal advice and assistance scheme (apart from ABWOR) is that for the former there is not only a financial eligibility test but also a merits test. As regards the financial limits, in March 2013 civil legal aid was available for those whose disposable capital was not more than £6,750 and whose disposable income did not exceed £9,937 per annum. For cases involving personal injury claims these limits are increased to £8,560 and £10,955 respectively.[45] An applicant for civil legal aid will have to make contributions towards the cost of the aid if his or her disposable capital is more than £3,000 or their disposable income is more than £3,355.[46] Any part of the excess capital can be requested as a contribution, but only one quarter of the excess income can be requested. Disposable capital and income are calculated in similar ways to those already described for legal advice and assistance, except that the calculation is performed by the Legal Aid Assessment Office of the Social Security Agency.

11.44   Once the financial eligibility test has been satisfied, the NILSC must still be persuaded that the applicant has reasonable grounds for being a party to the proceedings and that it would not be unreasonable for legal aid to be granted in the particular circumstances of the case. So if the action is a trivial one, or if the cost to the NILSC would be disproportionate to the advantage that might be gained from the litigation, legal aid may still be refused even if the applicant is financially eligible. It will also be refused if the application is in connection with a matter in which numerous persons have the same interest and it would be reasonable and proper for those other persons to bear the costs.[47] As it can take several weeks for both the

---

[44] Ibid.

[45] Legal Aid (Financial Conditions) Regs (NI) 2009 (SR 104). The limits have not changed since 2009.

[46] Legal Aid (Financial Conditions) Regs (NI) 2005 (SR 66).

[47] Legal Aid (General) Regs (NI) 1965 (SR 217), reg 5(11)(b). This was applied in *Re Hartley's Application* [2001] 3 BNIL 54, where a Sinn Féin councillor applied for legal aid

financial and merits tests to be considered, there is a procedure for applying for an 'emergency certificate', which can be granted at once. Approximately one-third of all applications are emergency applications.

11.45 If a civil or emergency certificate is refused on the ground that the merits test has not been satisfied, the applicant may appeal to a committee of the NILSC but not to a court. At many appeals applicants or their solicitors appear in person to argue their points. The applicant may also seek judicial review of the Committee's refusal to grant legal aid if he or she has reasons for suggesting that no reasonable committee could have reached that decision,[48] and the NILSC will even consider an application for legal aid to take such proceedings!

CRIMINAL LEGAL AID

11.46 The two distinguishing features of the criminal legal aid scheme in Northern Ireland[49] are that the decision whether or not to grant legal aid is taken by the court itself (not by a solicitor or by the NILSC) and that, if it is granted, the aid is *free*. Unlike the scheme in England, no contributions are required from the aided person. For aid to be granted it must simply appear to the court that the applicant's means are insufficient to obtain legal help in preparing and conducting a defence. The scheme allows for a criminal legal aid certificate to be granted to persons who have been charged with a criminal offence or who have been brought before a criminal court on a summons. It operates in the youth courts too, where parents or guardians can apply for aid on behalf of children or young persons.

11.47 Applications are best made through a solicitor. They can be made by letter addressed to the clerk of the petty sessions for the relevant district, but if unsuccessful at that stage a later application can be made at the hearing itself. In practice most applications are made orally at the hearing. The applicant will usually be asked to fill out a form stating his or her means,[50] although there is no rigid financial eligibility test as there is for legal advice

in respect of judicial review proceedings relating to alleged discrimination against a group of Sinn Féin councillors on Belfast City Council. By way of contrast see *In re Green's (Brigid) Application* [2012] NIQB 48, [2012] 6 BNIL 48, where the applicant won her appeal against the refusal of legal aid to allow her to bring an application for judicial review challenging the Police Ombudsman's report on the police investigation of the attack on the Heights Bar in Loughinisland in1994.

[48] *In re Jordan's Application* [2003] NICA 30; for an example of an unsuccessful application in this context, see *In re Murphy's Application* [2003] NIQB 55.
[49] *Use of Legal Services by the Criminal Justice System*, a report by Criminal Justice Inspection Northern Ireland (2011), 6.
[50] See the Schedule to the Legal Aid in Criminal Cases (Statement of Means) Rules (NI) 1999 (SR 223).

and assistance or civil legal aid. Having received an application the court may ask the Social Security Agency to inquire into the applicant's means and report back to the court. If it transpires that the statement of means provided to the court by the applicant is incorrect, the court may take action to recover some or all of the costs from the applicant. Under the Justice Act (NI) 2011,[51] rules have been made to require legally-aided defendants who have been convicted in the Crown Court to pay back such part of their legal aid as is reasonable in all the circumstances of the case, bearing in mind the defendant's own financial resources. They require the defendant to disclose information about his or her means and allow the judge to order the freezing of the defendant's assets pending the supply of such information.[52]

The merits test

11.48   Under the merits test it must also appear to the court that it is desirable in the interests of justice that the applicant should have free legal aid. The sorts of factors which the court will take into account in applying this merits test (the so-called 'Widgery criteria' because they were put forward by a Committee chaired by the Lord Chief Justice of England of that name[53]) are the gravity of the criminal charge, the ability of the applicant to present his or her own case and the nature of the defence. If a court has any doubts whether the applicant qualifies for aid, these must be resolved in favour of granting it, even when the applicant intends to plead guilty to the criminal charges. In cases where the charge is murder, or in situations where a court intends to sentence the defendant to imprisonment or detention in a young offenders centre, criminal legal aid *must* be offered. The aid comes in the form of a criminal legal aid certificate. A solicitor and, where necessary, a barrister are assigned to the case by the court after it has taken into account any representations which the applicant may want to make on this matter.

11.49   In appeals from the Crown Court to the Court of Appeal (or, further, to the Supreme Court) legal aid is obtainable under provisions in the Criminal Appeal (NI) Act 1980; in these cases the legal aid is administered separately by the Northern Ireland Courts and Tribunals Service and the fees payable are assessed by the Taxing Master (see para 4.26).[54]

11.50   In 2011–12 criminal legal aid was granted in about 38,000 cases in Northern Ireland. The cost was £45 million (a reduction of £7.2 million

---

[51] Section 81(2) inserts a new art 33A into the Legal Aid, Advice and Assistance (NI) Order 1981.
[52] Criminal Legal Aid (Recovery of Defence Costs Orders) Rules (NI) 2012 (SR 268).
[53] Cm 2934; 1966.
[54] For a dispute over legal aid for an appeal to the Court of Appeal, see *John J Rice & Co v Lord Chancellor (Criminal Appeal Costs, R v Latimer)* [2012] NIQB 28, [2012] 5 BNIL 48.

on the previous year's amount), which was 45 per cent of the year's total expenditure on legal aid.[55] By 2014–15 the cost is forecast to reduce to £35 million.

THE NORTHERN IRELAND LEGAL SERVICES COMMISSION[56]

11.51   After the coming into force of the Legal Aid, Advice and Assistance (NI) Order 1981 ministerial responsibility for legal aid, advice and assistance in Northern Ireland rested with the Lord Chancellor rather than the Secretary of State for Northern Ireland, but the Law Society of Northern Ireland retained responsibility for administering civil legal aid and administered criminal legal aid on behalf of the Courts Service. The Lord Chancellor's Department, however, retained control over the financial eligibility tests for the schemes, and over the level of fees payable to lawyers in criminal cases.

11.52   Following concerns over the ballooning costs of providing legal aid in Northern Ireland, a consultation paper was issued in 1999[57] and a White Paper in 2000.[58] These eventually led to the Access to Justice (NI) Order 2003, which transferred responsibility for the civil and criminal legal aid schemes to the new NILSC,[59] partly mirroring a similar body in England and Wales.[60] Panels of lawyers have been co-opted as sub-committee members of the Commission to deal with appeals against funding decisions. The NILSC has an internal system for dealing with complaints but it is also subject to oversight by the Parliamentary Commissioner for Administration (the Ombudsman) (see para 6.12).

11.53   The Commission has drawn up a 'funding code',[61] which sets out the criteria according to which decisions are taken on whether applications are meritorious. It also commissioned research into the state of legal need in Northern Ireland.[62] The Commission has still to develop a code of conduct

---

[55] *Annual Report and Financial Statements of NILSC 2011–12*, 16.

[56] D Capper, 'The Legal Services Commission – Brave New World for Legal Aid' (2003) 54 *NILQ* 447.

[57] *Public Benefit and Public Purse: The Future of Legal Aid in Northern Ireland* (1999).

[58] *The Way Ahead: Legal Aid Reform in Northern Ireland*, Cm 4849. See too the report of the Northern Ireland Affairs Committee of the House of Commons: *Legal Aid in Northern Ireland*, 4th Report of 2000–01, HC 496.

[59] See L Allamby, 'Legal Aid Reform: A View from the Voluntary Sector' (2002) 53 *NILQ* 167.

[60] Also called the Legal Services Commission, set up by the Access to Justice Act 1999. The body in England and Wales, however, was much more developed, running both a Community Legal Service and a Criminal Defence Service: see www.legalservices.gov.uk. It is to be abolished under the Legal Aid, Sentencing and Punishment of Offenders Act 2012, whereby an executive agency within the Ministry of Justice will administer the delivery of legal aid services in England and Wales. Art 5 of the Access to Justice (NI) Order 2003 authorises the Secretary of State to replace the NILSC with two separate bodies at some future date.

[61] In accordance with the Access to Justice (NI) Order 2003, art 15.

[62] T Dignan, *Legal Need in Northern Ireland: Literature Review* (2004) (available on the NILSC's website).

for those providing criminal defence services in Northern Ireland[63] and it plans to develop a wider range of standard fees for legally aided work. It has power to set up its own salaried lawyer structure and to enter into contracts with legal service providers, including those in the voluntary sector, for specialist or new services. In that eventuality all such providers will have to register with the Commission and comply with codes of practice to ensure quality control. One of the key questions for the NILSC is the extent to which legal aid should continue to be made available for personal injury litigation.[64] The Access to Justice (NI) Order 2003 makes provision for conditional fee agreements to be permitted, whereby lawyers get paid only if they win.[65]

11.54   The Minister of Justice, since taking up office in 2010, has been very concerned at the rising costs of legal aid in Northern Ireland. He has succeeded in turning the tide regarding criminal legal aid by introducing more fixed fees for certain types of work and reducing the rates at which longer running cases are funded. He has recently turned his attention to civil legal aid, particularly in family law cases. Every year since its foundation in 2003 the annual accounts of the NILSC have been 'qualified' (ie not fully approved) by the Northern Ireland Audit Office because of insufficient evidence being available as to the level of potential fraud in applications for legal aid and uncertainties as to the amount of legal aid liabilities.[66]

LEGAL COSTS

11.55   The cost of employing a professional lawyer can be very high. In cases of genuine hardship some form of legal aid may be available, as the previous sections have explained, but if a person does not qualify for legal advice and assistance, or for legal aid, the choice is stark: he or she must either try to conduct their legal affairs in person or else engage a solicitor and run the risk of incurring significant expenditure. Generally speaking it is very risky for someone who is untrained in the law to attempt to conduct his or her own legal affairs: 'litigants in person' are few and far between.[67] In non-criminal cases a litigant can have a friend in court to help with the

---

[63] Access to Justice (NI) Order 2003, art 22. See Judge D Smyth, 'An Excellent Service and a Catalyst for Change: The Future Provision of Criminal Defence Services in Northern Ireland' (2002) 53 *NILQ* 179.

[64] See D Capper, 'Personal Injury Litigation – The Case for Legal Aid' (2002) 53 *NILQ* 137, where a Contingency Legal Aid Fund is canvassed.

[65] A Morris, 'Conditional Fee Agreements in Northern Ireland: Gimmick or Godsend?' (2005) 56 *NILQ* 38.

[66] See *Report of the NIAO on the Northern Ireland Legal Services Commission Account for the year ended 31 March 2012*.

[67] In 2012 the Northern Ireland Courts and Tribunals Service published a very useful 42-page booklet, available on its website, entitled *A Guide to Proceedings in the High Court for People Without a Legal Representative*.

case (such people are called 'McKenzie friends' after the name of the case in which their appearance was first approved[68]), but this person is not usually permitted to speak on the defendant's behalf.[69] The alternative of engaging a solicitor will not, however, always be unattractive. If the legal matter is one which involves a dispute with another person, rather than a non-contentious matter like drafting a will, the litigant may well recover from the other party to the dispute most of what he or she has had to pay to their solicitor (provided he or she wins the dispute). A solicitor's bill, when it is finally received, should itemise all the work carried out and the corresponding charge made for each item.

Non-contentious work

11.56   A bill for a solicitor's non-contentious work will be made up as follows:

- a charge for 'disbursements', or 'outlays', such as the stamp duty on the value of a house or the fee for obtaining probate of a will;
- a professional fee;
- VAT, at 20 per cent, on those items liable to it (which include the professional fee).

11.57   The size of the professional fee will depend on such factors as the time involved in handling the affair, the complexity of the affair, and the value of the property concerned. In some matters, though not often, the fee is determined in accordance with guidelines laid down either by the Law Society or a local solicitors' association. Solicitors acting in house conveyances must now provide a written statement of their proposed fees at the outset. Their charge for managing a deceased's estate may be a percentage of the value of that estate.

11.58   If a client is dissatisfied with a bill provided by a solicitor for non-contentious work, two things can be done. He or she can require the solicitor, within a month, to obtain what is called a Remuneration Certificate from the Law Society. This will state the charge which would be a fair and reasonable one for the work done in the case and the client will then have to pay that amount. Alternatively, or in addition, the client can apply within three months to have the costs officially assessed (ie 'taxed') by the Taxing Master (see para 4.26). There is a small initial fee for applying to the Taxing Master, although after the Taxing Master has dealt with the case the person who loses

[68] *McKenzie v McKenzie* [1970] 3 All ER 1034 (CA).
[69] 'McKenzie friends' may also be excluded from certain proceedings: see, eg, *Re D's Application* [2000] NIJB 248. In 2012 the Lord Chief Justice issued a Practice Note on *McKenzie Friends* in civil and family courts in Northern Ireland (available on the website of the Northern Ireland Courts and Tribunals Service).

the argument over the bill must pay an additional 15 per cent of the amount in dispute by way of a fee to the Taxing Master's office. These so-called 'solicitor and client' applications to the Taxing Master are quite unusual.

COSTS IN CRIMINAL PROCEEDINGS

11.59 A solicitor's contentious work consists of all the business which eventually leads to appearances in court. If judicial proceedings are begun, but are settled before the date fixed for the trial, all the work done up to then is usually classified as non-contentious. In considering how much a client will have to pay for contentious work it is essential to distinguish between criminal proceedings and civil proceedings. In both it is also essential to bear in mind the implications of the legal aid schemes.

Legally aided criminal work

11.60 The NILSC will pay the following fees for work done under the green form scheme, whether in criminal or civil cases: £54.50 an hour for advocacy, £43.25 an hour for preparation and attendances at meetings, £24.25 an hour for waiting and travelling, £11.75 for each telephone call when advice is given on the Police and Criminal Evidence legislation, and £3.35 for all letters (other than acknowledgements or fixing appointments) and for telephone calls (whether in or out). A one-third uplift is payable for unsociable hours on travel, waiting and attendance times. These rates have not been upgraded for a number of years.

11.61 The costs payable to lawyers involved in cases where a criminal legal aid certificate has been issued are mostly regulated by the Legal Aid in Criminal Proceedings (Costs) Rules (NI) 1992,[70] as amended. These specify how much is to be paid in respect of work done in magistrates' courts, appeals to the county court and bail applications in the High Court. Different fees are listed for different types of work and usually on the basis of prescribed hourly rates. Costs in respect of work done for youth conferences are paid in accordance with a regime set out in the Legal Aid for Youth Conferences (Costs) Rules (NI) 2003[71] and costs in respect of legally aided work in the Crown Court are governed by the Legal Aid for Crown Court Proceedings (Costs) Rules (NI) 2005.[72] This last set of rules was amended in 2011 so as to revoke the provisions made for increased levels of fees in exceptional cases and for special hourly rates in very high cost cases; the

[70] SR 314.
[71] SR 512.
[72] SR 112.

range of standard fees was extended to cover all criminal trials lasting up to 80 days and the standard fees were reduced for cases where there have been guilty pleas.[73] These changes met with stiff opposition from both barristers and solicitors, despite the fact that published figures showed that in the financial year 2009–2010 the 100 top-earning barristers had collectively earned almost £30 million in criminal legal aid payments.

Work in criminal cases that is not legally aided

11.62   If a criminal legal aid certificate is not granted the defendant can conduct his or her own defence, but in serious cases this is not at all wise. If the defendant loses the case, as mentioned above, it is now possible in Crown Court cases for an order to be made requiring the defendant to pay back some of the legal aid he or she has received to date (see para 11.47). On the other hand, if the defendant wins the case and is acquitted it is also very rare in Northern Ireland for the prosecution to be ordered to pay the defendant's costs. It is only when the prosecution, or the defence, has been outrageously unsubstantiated that the costs will be ordered 'to follow the event', that is, paid by the losing side.

11.63   If an order as to costs is made by a magistrates' court, the precise amount due will be calculated in accordance with the Magistrates' Courts (Costs in Criminal Cases) Rules (NI) 1988,[74] as amended. These allow for up to £75 per lawyer per day, although the court can order payment of a greater sum if the proceedings are exceptionally long, difficult or complex. The recipient of the costs award will also be reimbursed the court fees which have had to be paid during the proceedings, these too being fixed by regulations. Costs in respect of legally aided work in the Crown Court are now governed by the Legal Aid for Crown Court Proceedings (Costs) Rules (NI) 2005, referred to above (see para 11.61). The Rules set out in some detail the method for determining the costs due in a 'standard' case. A basic trial fee is supplemented by a refresher fee (paid on a daily basis), special additional fees (eg for late sittings) and a travel allowance, with the amounts in question differing depending on which of nine categories the offence being tried falls into. A trial for burglary, for example, will attract a basic trial fee of £1,900 for a solicitor, £2,275 for a junior counsel acting without a QC, and £3,500 for a QC, with the respective daily refresher fees being £500, £325 and £500. In non-standard cases the exact amount payable will be determined by the Taxing Master (see para 4.26).

---

[73] Legal Aid for Crown Court Proceedings (Costs) (Amendment) (Rules (NI) 2011 (SR 152).
[74] SR 136.

11.64   In criminal appeals, whether in a county court or the Court of Appeal, the precise amount payable by way of costs, in the absence of agreement between the parties, will usually be assessed by the Taxing Master (see para 4.26), who is obliged by statute to allow such sums as are reasonably sufficient to compensate the party for the expenses properly incurred.

COSTS IN CIVIL PROCEEDINGS

Legally aided civil work

11.65   A civil legal aid certificate will cover legal services by a solicitor or barrister both before and during a court hearing. Practically every type of hearing is within the civil legal aid scheme, with the exception of most tribunals (other than the Lands Tribunal and Immigration Tribunals[75]), arbitrations (which include proceedings in a small claims court) and coroners' courts. Particular types of claims are also excluded, such as libel and slander claims,[76] admitted debts, and claims relating to elections.

11.66   The solicitor will be paid for the work, as will any barrister involved in the case, out of the NILSC's fund for civil legal services. In proceedings at or above High Court level the work will generally be paid for at 95 per cent of the normal rate for work not legally aided. In county court proceedings the full rate will be paid if the costs are 'taxed' by a Master (see para 4.26). If the costs are not taxed, as in all magistrates' court proceedings, the sums paid will be in accordance with scales of remuneration laid down in regulations,[77] although in exceptional cases a judge can order that these scales should be disregarded.

11.67   Once the case is over, any costs recovered by the assisted person by virtue of a court order or agreement must be paid to the NILSC. If these exceed the sums paid out by that Commission on the assisted person's behalf the excess is retained by the Commission; if they are less, the balance is recouped from the assisted person's contributions (with any unused portion of the contributions then being returned). Even if the contributions are not enough to satisfy the debt owed to the NILSC, a 'charge' (ie a legal claim) may be imposed on any property recovered by the proceedings. But certain forms of property, such as maintenance payments, are exempt from this

---

[75] Legal Aid (Asylum and Immigration Appeals) Regs (NI) 2007 (SI 1318).

[76] This has been held not to breach the European Convention on Human Rights: *In re Lynch's Application* [2002] 5 BNIL 44.

[77] The Legal Aid (Remuneration of Solicitors and Counsel in County Court Proceedings) (Amendment) Order (NI) 2003 (SR 43) increased the maximum amounts allowable to lawyers acting for legally aided persons in the county court to accord with the scale costs prescribed by the County Court (Amendment No 2) Rules (NI) 2002 (SR 412).

charge. If an assisted person happens to be insured against the legal expenses incurred, the insurance money received must be paid to the NILSC. If the Commission is still owed money after all this, the loss must be borne out of the public purse. If an unassisted party wins a case against an assisted party the court may order the former's costs to be paid by the NILSC, provided that this is just and equitable in all the circumstances and that (except in appeals) the unassisted party would otherwise suffer financial hardship.[78]

Work in civil cases that is not legally aided

11.68 It is official policy that the full costs of running the civil justice system in the UK should be paid for by court fees. In a magistrates' court, a small claims court or a county court the fees for issuing proceedings and for the various pieces of work which a solicitor or barrister might do are laid down in regulations.[79] Parties are usually left to bear their own fees and lawyers' costs even if they win the case, but in a case involving family disputes it is more normal in Northern Ireland for the court to award costs against the loser of the case. In a small claims court the claimant will recover the initial application fee from the other party if the claim is upheld. In a county court, by way of example, a solicitor's costs for work done in a case where £4,500 is claimed will be approximately £1,200 and a barrister's costs will be about £260.

11.69 To encourage settlements out of court, the scales of costs in county court cases are greatly reduced if a defendant agrees to satisfy a claim within 14 days of the service of the plaintiff's civil bill or if he or she fails to defend the action. A defendant can also safeguard the position on costs by 'paying into court' so much of the plaintiff's claim as the defendant is prepared to concede. If the plaintiff does not accept this payment but then does not succeed in getting a higher award from the court, he or she will have to pay virtually all the costs, both his or her own as well as the defendant's. The costs allowed to a successful claimant may also be reduced if the sum won in the case is less than the minimum which that level of court is designed to deal with, as the case should really have been brought in a lower (and therefore cheaper) court. If the court's order for costs is not enough to reimburse the winner completely for his or her outlay, he or she must bear the balance.

---

[78] Access to Justice (NI) Order 2003, art 19.
[79] The Magistrates' Courts Fees Order (NI) 1996 (SR 102), as amended, and the County Court Fees Order (NI) 1996 (SR 103), as amended. A full list of the fees payable is on the website of the Northern Ireland Courts and Tribunals Service.

Proceedings in the High Court and above

11.70　Here too the court fees are set out in regulations, but lawyers' costs are not specified to the same extent as in proceedings in lower courts. There are fixed costs only for cases where, in effect, the defendant does not submit a defence to the claim.[80] Naturally, both fees and costs are higher than in county courts.[81] Queen's Counsel are more likely to be involved; their charges are high, and the junior counsel who assist them usually get two-thirds of the fee paid to the senior.[82] The practice regarding payments into court and low successes is the same as in the county court (see para 11.69).

11.71　The decision as to which side is to bear the costs in these higher court proceedings is in the discretion of the court, but in the vast majority of cases the loser will be ordered to pay most, if not all, of the winner's costs. The actual amounts to be paid will be agreed between the parties or, in the absence of any agreement, assessed by the Taxing Master (see para 4.26). The Master will allow costs only for work which was essential, or proper. This is called assessment of costs on a 'party and party' basis. A litigant in person in the High Court can be allowed up to two-thirds of what the costs would have been if he or she had engaged a solicitor.

Proceedings in a tribunal

11.72　Tribunals do not normally have the power to order one side to pay the other side's costs. As legal aid is generally not available for tribunal proceedings, the parties usually end up paying their own costs. In some situations, however, the tribunal can make payments to cover travel expenses and loss of earnings. Exceptionally (eg if the respondent's arguments are considered frivolous or vexatious), a tribunal may order the respondent to pay the applicant's costs. This occurred in *Johnston v Chief Constable of the RUC*,[83] a well-known case where female police reservists successfully complained of sexual discrimination (see para 5.26).

---

[80] See Appendix 3 to Order 62 of the Rules of the Court of Judicature (NI) 1980 (SR 346), as amended.

[81] For further details on the level of fees in the High Court, see the Supreme Court Fees Order (NI) 1996 (SR 100), as amended, and the Supreme Court Taxing Office Practice Direction 2004 No 1 [2004] 4 BNIL 111.

[82] When junior counsel at the Bloody Sunday Inquiry were offered just 50 per cent of QCs' rates (which is closer to the practice in England and Wales) they brought judicial review proceedings against the Tribunal: see *In re Kennedy and others' Application* [2001] 1 BNIL 52.

[83] [1987] QB 129.

Proceedings to enforce a judgment

11.73   If the losing side refuses at first to comply with a judgment, the cost of enforcing the judgment can be quite substantial in relation to the size of the judgment. The fees payable to the Enforcement of Judgments Office are laid down by the Judgments Enforcement Fees Order (NI) 1996, as amended, and to these must be added the solicitor's fee for acting on the winner's behalf. The fee for lodging notice of intent to apply for enforcement of a judgment is just £20, but the fee for an actual application for enforcement grows with the size of the judgment in question. For instance, enforcement of a judgment for £1,000 incurs a fee of £181, but this rises to £645 if the judgment is for £10,000.[84] If the losing side can afford to pay the judgment debt, the enforcement costs are added to it; otherwise the enforcement costs must be written off by the 'winning side' as part of the bad debt.

[84] Full details are available on the website of the Northern Ireland Courts and Tribunals Service: www.courtsni.gov.uk.

Appendices

Appendix 1

Civil Aviation Act 2012

CHAPTER 19

Explanatory Notes have been produced to assist in the
understanding of this Act and are available separately

Civil Aviation Act 2012

CHAPTER 19

CONTENTS

CHAPTER 2

COMPETITION

CHAPTER 3

GENERAL PROVISION

Interpretation

Other general provision

Appendix 2

Presumption of Death Act (Northern Ireland) 2009

2009 CHAPTER 6

An Act to make provision in relation to the presumed deaths of missing persons; and for connected purposes. [2nd July 2009]

BE IT ENACTED by being passed by the Northern Ireland Assembly and assented to by Her Majesty as follows:

Declarations of presumed death

Declarations of presumed death

1.—(1) Where a person who is missing–

(a) is thought to have died; or

(b) has not been known to be alive for a period of at least 7 years, any person may apply to the High Court for a declaration that the person (in this Act referred to as the "missing person") is presumed to be dead.

(2) The High Court has jurisdiction to entertain proceedings for a declaration

under subsection (1) if (and only if)–

(a) the missing person was domiciled in Northern Ireland on the date on which he or she was last known to be alive or had been habitually resident there throughout the period of one year ending with that date;

(b) the applicant–

(i) is the spouse or civil partner of the missing person; and

(ii) is domiciled in Northern Ireland on the date when the proceedings are begun or has been habitually resident in Northern Ireland throughout the period of one year ending with that date; or

(c) the applicant is a close relative of the missing person where the missing person is a victim of violence (within the meaning of section 1(4) of the Northern Ireland (Location of Victims' Remains) Act 1999 (c. 7)).

(3) Where an application under subsection (1) is made by a person other than–

(a) the spouse or civil partner of; or

(b) a close relative of,

the missing person to whom the application relates, the High Court must refuse to hear the application if it considers that the applicant does not have a sufficient interest in the determination of that application.

(4) In subsections (2)(c) and (3)(b), "close relative", in relation to a missing person, means–

(a) the parent or child of that person; or

(b) the sibling (whether of the full blood or the half blood) of that person.

Making of declaration of presumed death

2.—(1) Where on an application for a declaration under section 1 the truth of the proposition to be declared is proved to its satisfaction, the High Court must make that declaration and–

(a) where the Court is satisfied that the missing person has died, the Court must include in the declaration a finding as to the date and time of death and, where it is uncertain when, within any period of time, the missing person died, the Court must find that he or she died at the end of that period;

(b) where the Court is satisfied that the missing person has not been known to be alive for a period of at least 7 years, the Court must include in the declaration a finding that the missing person died at the end of the day occurring 7 years after the date on which he or she was last known to be alive.

(2) The High Court, on the dismissal of an application for a declaration under section 1, may not make any declaration for which an application has not been made.

(3) No declaration which may be applied for under section 1 may be made otherwise than under section 1 by any court or tribunal.

(4) Where, for the purpose of deciding any issue before it, a court or tribunal has to determine any incidental question relating to the death of a person, the court or tribunal may determine that question (but only for the purpose of deciding that issue), and in the determination of that question, the court or tribunal must apply the criteria set out in subsection (1).

Effect of declaration of presumed death

3. Subject to sections 5 and 6 where–

(a) no appeal is brought against a declaration under section 1 within the time allowed for appeal; or

(b) an appeal against such a declaration is brought and the appeal is dismissed or withdrawn,

the declaration shall be conclusive of the matters contained in it and shall, without any special form of words, be effective against any person and for all purposes including the ending of a marriage or civil partnership to which the missing person is a party and the acquisition of rights to or in property belonging to any person.

Powers of the High Court

4. (1) The High Court, when making a declaration under section 1, may–

(a) determine any question relating to the interest of any person in the property of the missing person;

(b) make such order in relation to any rights to or in any property acquired as a result of the making of the declaration as it considers reasonable in the circumstances of the case; or

(c) determine the domicile of the missing person at the time of his or her presumed death.

(2) An order under subsection (1)(b) may, subject to any conditions specified therein, direct that the value of any rights to or in any property acquired as a result of the declaration shall not be recoverable by virtue of an order made under section 6(2).

Variation orders

5. (1) A declaration under section 1 may, on an application made at any time by any person, be varied or revoked by an order of the High Court.

(2) The Court must refuse to hear an application under subsection (1) if it considers that the applicant does not have a sufficient interest in the determination of that application.

(3) An order made under subsection (1) is referred to in this Act as a "variation order".

(4) A variation order may make any determination referred to in section 4(1)(a) or (c).

(5) Notice of the making of a variation order shall be served by the Court on–

(a) the Registrar General;

(b) any person who applied for the declaration under section 1 to which the application under subsection (1) relates.

Appendix 3

Statutory Instruments
2007 No. 911 (N.I. 5)
Northern Ireland

The Northern Ireland Policing Board (Northern Ireland)
Order 2007

Made - - - - 21st March 2007

Coming into operation - 26th March 2007

At the Court at Buckingham Palace, the 21st day of March 2007

Present,
The Queen's Most Excellent Majesty in Council

Whereas a draft of this Order in Council has been approved by resolution of each House of Parliament: Now therefore, Her Majesty, in exercise of the powers conferred by paragraph 1(1) of the Schedule to the Northern Ireland Act 2000 (c.1), and of all other powers enabling Her in that behalf, is pleased, by and with the advice of Her Privy Council, to order and it is hereby ordered, as follows:—

Citation, commencement and interpretation

1.—(1) This Order may be cited as the Northern Ireland Policing Board (Northern Ireland) Order 2007.

(2) This Order shall come into operation on 26th March 2007.

(3) The Interpretation Act (Northern Ireland) 1954 (c.33) applies to this Order as it applies to an Act of the Assembly.

Modification of Schedule 1 to the Police (Northern Ireland) Act 2000

2. After paragraph 2 of Schedule 1 to the Police (Northern Ireland) Act 2000 (c.32) (membership of the Northern Ireland Policing Board: application of Parts II and III of the Schedule) insert—
"Restoration of devolved government under Northern Ireland (St Andrews Agreement) Act 2006

2A.—(1) This paragraph applies if, by virtue of section 2(2) of the Northern Ireland (St Andrews Agreement) Act 2006 (c.53), the Secretary of State makes a restoration order under section 2(2) of the Northern Ireland Act 2000 providing for section 1 of that Act to cease to have effect on 26 March 2007.

(2) Where this paragraph applies, the effect of paragraph 2(1) and (2) is modified as follows.

(3) On 26 and 27 March 2007 Part II below shall continue to have effect in relation to the Board (and accordingly Part III below shall not have effect).

(4) On 28 March 2007—

   (a) if the Secretary of State has made an order by virtue of section 2(3) of the Northern Ireland (St Andrews Agreement) Act 2006 revoking the restoration order with effect from that date, Part II below shall continue to have effect in relation to the Board;

   (b) if he has not made such an order, Part III below shall come into effect on that date in relation to the Board (and accordingly Part II below shall cease to have effect)."

Independent members of the Policing Board

3.—(1) In paragraph 6(2) of that Schedule (which defines expressions for the purposes of Part III of that Schedule) insert at the end—
""transitional period" means the period for which independent members of the Board are appointed in accordance with paragraph 8(4A)."

(2) In paragraph 8 of that Schedule (independent members of the Northern Ireland Policing Board) after sub-paragraph (4) insert—

"(4A) In relation to the first appointment of members of the Board following the coming into effect of this Part in accordance with paragraph 2A(4)(b), the Secretary of State may, notwithstanding anything in sub-paragraph (1), so exercise his powers of appointment under paragraph 6(1)(b) as to secure that—

(a) he appoints independent members of the Board only from among persons holding office as members of the Board immediately before the making of the restoration order mentioned in paragraph 2A(1), and

(b) all appointments made in accordance with paragraph (a) are for the same term of office (the "transitional period"), which must not exceed four months.

(4B) Where a vacancy in the membership of the Board arises as a result of—

(a) a person holding office as a member of the Board immediately before the making of the restoration order mentioned in paragraph 2A(1) being unavailable to take up office under sub-paragraph (4A), or

(b) an independent member of the Board appointed in accordance with sub-paragraph (4A) ceasing to hold office before the end of the transitional period, no appointment shall be made to fill the vacancy, and paragraph 6(1)(b) shall have effect subject to this sub-paragraph."

Chairman and vice-chairman of the Policing Board

4. In paragraph 11 of that Schedule (chairman and vice-chairman of the Northern Ireland Policing Board) after sub-paragraph (8) insert—

"(9) Any appointment of a chairman or vice-chairman during the transitional period shall be for a term expiring at the end of the transitional period."

Christine Cook
Deputy Clerk of the Privy Council

EXPLANATORY NOTE

(This note is not part of the Order)

This Order amends the Police (Northern Ireland) Act 2000 with respect to the membership of the Northern Ireland Policing Board.

Appendix 4

Statutory Rules Of
Northern Ireland

2010 No. 148
DANGEROUS DRUGS

The Misuse of Drugs (Amendment) Regulations
(Northern Ireland) 2010

Made - - - - - - - - - - - - - - - - - *12th April 2010*

Coming into operation - - - - - - *16th April 2010*

The Department of Health, Social Services and Public Safety makes the following Regulations in exercise of the powers conferred by sections 7, 10, 22 and 31 of the Misuse of Drugs Act 1971(a) as adapted by sections 7(9), 31(4) and 38 of that Act and now vested in it(b).

In accordance with section 31(3) of that Act, it has consulted with the Advisory Council on the Misuse of Drugs.

Citation and commencement

1. These Regulations may be cited as the Misuse of Drugs (Amendment) Regulations (Northern Ireland) 2010 and shall come into operation on 16th April 2010.

(a) 1971 c.38. Section 22 of that Act was amended by section 177(1) of, and paragraph 12 of Schedule 4 to, the Customs and Excise Management Act 1979(c.2)

(b) S.R. & O.(N.I) 1973 No. 504, Article 5(a) and S.I.1999/283 (N.I. 1), Article 3(6)

Interpretation

2.—(1) In these Regulations, "the 2002 Regulations" means the Misuse of Drugs Regulations (Northern Ireland) 2002(**c**).

(2) The Interpretation Act (Northern Ireland) 1954(**d**) shall apply to these Regulations as it applies to an Act of the Assembly.
Amendments to the 2002 Regulations

3. The 2002 Regulations shall be amended as follows.

4. In Schedule 1 (which specifies controlled drugs subject to the requirements of regulations 14, 15, 16, 18, 19, 20, 23, 26 and 27)—

(a) in paragraph 1(a), after "Methcathinone", insert—

"4–Methylmethcathinone";

(b) after paragraph 1(1), insert—

"(m) Any compound (not being bupropion, diethylpropion, pyrovalerone or a compound for the time being specified in sub-paragraph (a) above) structurally derived from 2-amino-1–phenyl-1–propanone by modification in any of the following ways, that is to say—

(i) by substitution in the phenyl ring to any extent with alkyl, alkoxy, alkylenedioxy, haloalkyl or halide substituents, whether or not further substituted in the phenyl ring by one or more other univalent substituents;

(ii) by substitution at the 3-position with an alkyl substituent;

(iii) by substitution at the nitrogen atom with alkyl or dialkyl groups, or by inclusion of the nitrogen atom in a cyclic structure".

Sealed with the Official Seal of the Department of Health, Social Services and Public Safety on 12th April 2010
(L.S.)

Norman Morrow
A senior officer of the Department of Health, Social Services and Public Safety

---

(**c**) S.R. 2002 No. 1. Relevant amending Regulations are S.R. 2003 Nos 314, 324 and 420, S.R. 2005 Nos 119, 360 and 564, S.R. 2006 Nos 44, 214, 264 and 334, S.R. 2007 No. 348 , S.R. 2009 Nos 389 and 390
(**d**) 1954 c.33 (N.I)

EXPLANATORY NOTE

(This note is not part of the Regulations)

These Regulations insert 4–Methylmethcathinone (commonly referred to as Mephedrone) and other cathinone derivatives into Schedule 1 to the Misuse of Drugs Regulations (Northern Ireland) 2002 ("the 2002 Regulations"). The schedule in which a controlled drug is placed primarily affects the extent to which the drug can be lawfully imported, exported, produced, supplied or possessed and dictates the record keeping, labelling and destruction requirements in relation to that drug.

Appendix 5

Robinson (Iris) v Sunday Newspapers Ltd (2011)

Neutral Citation: [2011] NICA 13

| *Ref:* | MOR8183 |

Judgment: approved by the Court for handing down

(subject to editorial corrections) *

| *Delivered:* | 24/5/11 |

IN HER MAJESTY'S COURT OF APPEAL IN NORTHERN IRELAND

BETWEEN:

IRIS ROBINSON
Plaintiff/Appellant;

-and-

SUNDAY NEWSPAPERS LIMITED
Defendant/Respondent.

Before: Morgan LCJ, Higgins LJ, and Girvan LJ

MORGAN LCJ

[1]   This is an appeal from an interlocutory decision made by Treacy J on 22 April 2010 in relation to an application for an injunction made on 16 April 2010. Mr Macdonald QC and Mr MacMahon appeared on behalf of the appellant and Mr Hanna QC and Mr Millar for the respondent. We are grateful to all counsel for their helpful oral and written submissions.

Background

[2]   The appellant is a former MLA. She suffered an episode of severe mental ill health in the form of depression following revelations about her private life in January 2010. The revelations led to considerable media coverage. [Text removed].

[3]   On 4 and 11 April 2010 the Sunday World published a series of articles with headlines which included "We Find Iris", "The Scarlet Woman Goes for a Stroll" and "Give us a Ring Iris". They were accompanied by photographs of the plaintiff taken in London by or on behalf of the newspaper. The appellant issued a writ seeking damages for breach of confidence/ misuse of private information, harassment and breach of her rights under Arts 2 and 8 ECHR, and for an injunction preventing future surveillance and photographing of the plaintiff and publication of information about her mental health including the location of her treatment.

[4]   The learned trial judge made interlocutory orders on 16 April 2010 in the terms sought on consent of the parties and fixed the hearing of any application to vary or discharge that Order for 21 April 2010. At the hearing on 16 April the appellant sought an Order that the hearing to which the application related should be heard in private. Although the respondent at that stage did not oppose the making of such an Order Treacy J indicated that he would have to be persuaded that such a course was appropriate.

[5]   In support of the application for the injunction the appellant's solicitor filed an affidavit in which he stated that the pictures published by the respondent newspaper were taken while the appellant was out for a walk as part of her ongoing rehabilitation and treatment. [Text removed].

[6]   Dr [text removed] swore two affidavits for the hearing on 21 April. In his first affidavit he said that any further press surveillance or media coverage relating to her mental health or ongoing medical treatment and rehabilitation, including the taking of photographs, would increase the risk of her self-harming or taking her own life and would be likely to prolong her current episode of mental ill health. In his second affidavit he said that intrusive media coverage would continue to pose risks to the plaintiff while she was receiving in-patient treatment and during subsequent outpatient treatment for her illness.

[7]   At the hearing on 21 April the appellant's first application was that the hearing of the injunction application should be in private. It is common case that this application proceeded in open court and it appears that at least one member of the public was present. It was possible to deal

with the application without reference to the affidavits. The basis of the application was that the substantive application could not be presented without referring to sensitive and intensely private material which would, if disclosed in open court, defeat the object of the application itself and generate further publicity.

[8]   Treacy J reminded himself of the well established jurisprudence on the importance of the principle of open justice not being eroded (*Scott v Scott* [1913] AC 417 and *AG v Leveller Magazine* [1979] AC 440) which were discussed by Kelly LJ in *R v Murphy and anor* [1990] NI 306. He noted later cases which restated the need to be vigilant against the erosion of the principle. He set out the reasons for this. Open justice deters inappropriate behaviour on the part of the court, maintains public confidence in the administration of justice, increases the opportunity for more relevant evidence to emerge and makes uninformed and inaccurate comment about the proceedings less likely (*Ex p. Kaim* [1999] QB 966, per Lord Woolf at 967). Most recently, the Supreme Court in *Al-Ghabra* [2010] UKSC 1 found that in an extreme case, where identification or publication of an individual's name could put their life or that of their family in danger, freedom of expression should yield to the right to life and the court could make an anonymity order.

[9]   The learned trial judge noted that on 19 April the respondent's solicitors had written to the appellant's solicitors asking how the appellant came to have sight of the articles dated 4 and 11 April, who brought the articles to the appellant's attention and for what reason they were brought to her attention. No answer to that correspondence was made by the time of the hearing before him.

[10]   Treacy J found that there was no evidence that the hearing of the case in public, if accompanied by restrictions on publication, would increase the risk of suicide. The risk to her was caused by intrusive media surveillance and reporting. This risk could be mitigated or removed by a reporting restriction. A secret hearing would not address the mischief. In any event, if the appellant succeeded on the substantive action, the coercive orders which would necessarily follow would prevent repetition of the impugned actions.

Fresh evidence

[11]   On the hearing of the appeal the appellant sought leave to introduce two further affidavits. The first was a further affidavit from Dr [text removed] sworn on 27 April. He explained that as a result of the media intrusion the appellant's treatment programme had to change. [Text removed]. He [text removed] was of the view that media attention would damage her mental

health, increase the risk of self harm or suicide, impede her treatment and delay her recovery. He also stated that if as a result of a public hearing her medical condition and ongoing treatment were to become widely known or she had a reasonable apprehension that these matters were liable to become more widely known her mental health would deteriorate, there would be a materially increased risk of suicide or self harm, her treatment would be prejudiced and her recovery impeded.

[12]   The second affidavit was sworn on 17 May by the appellant's solicitor. He explained that Dr [text removed] did not undertake medico-legal work and had declined, therefore, to swear an affidavit. Dr [text removed] had not been able to examine the appellant until just before his third affidavit. This was prompted by a comment in the judgment that there was no affidavit from the treating psychiatrist. The second issue addressed was a press statement issued on behalf of the Robinson family on 6 April after the first article. This statement noted that the appellant had been diagnosed as being acutely mentally ill and had been on suicide watch. [Text removed]. The third issue concerned the delay in issuing proceedings. The appellant's family were reluctant to encourage legal proceedings. They hoped that the press statement would discourage further coverage. The contents of the Sunday World published on 11 April indicated that the respondents were not likely to desist unless restrained. The fourth issue concerned the failure of the appellant herself to make an affidavit. It was not considered necessary or desirable to do so when she was undergoing inpatient psychiatric treatment.

[13]   Where there has been a trial or hearing on the merits fresh evidence is generally only admitted if the conditions set out in *Ladd v Marshall* [1954] 1 WLR 1489 are satisfied. These are that the evidence could not with reasonable diligence have been obtained for the trial, that it will probably have an important influence on the result and that it appears credible. These tests can be relaxed if the trial was on affidavit (see *McKernan v HM Prison Governor* [1983] NI 83) or on an appeal in interlocutory proceedings (see *Forward v West Sussex CC* [1995] 4 All ER 207). The court is bound to decide the facts of the case as they exist at the date of the appeal. Since this was a trial on affidavit in an interlocutory matter and the material was relevant to issues noted by the learned trial judge in his judgment we, therefore, concluded that we should admit the fresh evidence taking into account that there was no prejudice to the respondent in doing so.

The submissions of the parties

[14]   The appellant submitted that ordering a hearing in private would be a precautionary step which could be reversed by publication of the judgment

or transcript after the hearing if it was found to be appropriate to do so. It would, by contrast, be impossible to repair the damage done by a refusal to make such an order if it turned out that such an order was necessary. The appellant referred to the State's positive duty to protect her rights under Articles 2, 3 and 8 ECHR. Mr Macdonald relied on recent case law on how the balance should be struck between the appellant's right to privacy and the media's right to freedom of expression (*Murray v Big Pictures (UK) Ltd* [2008] EWCA Civ 446 at paras 35-40, per Sir Anthony Clarke MR, *Mosley v News Group* [2008] EWHC 1777 (QB) at paras 8-10, per Eady J). There was a need for an intense focus on the comparative importance of the specific rights being claimed in the individual case (*S (a child)* [2004] UKHL 47 at para 17, per Lord Steyn). Proportionality was central to the balancing test (*Douglas v Hello! Ltd* [2001] QB 967 at [137], per Sedley LJ). While arguing that it was not uncommon for well-known persons to obtain such an order on the basis of their privacy rights alone, the applicant said that cases based on the right to life were rarer. Where that right was engaged a step which mitigated the risks to the appellant's Article 2 rights constituted insufficient protection.

[15]   The appellant further submitted that the learned trial judge did not take into account the full range of media in which damaging information could leak out if the hearing was in open court. He was wrong to think that a reporting restriction was sufficient. He had failed to consider both the old-fashioned method of word of mouth in a small jurisdiction and the new media of social-networking sites and Twitter. The appellant argued that users of both of these latter forms of communication were likely to be less respectful of a reporting restriction and harder to enforce against than the traditional media. It was also argued that internet publication could take place outside the jurisdiction and that the local court could not control such publication.

[16]   Finally the appellant submitted that it was impossible for the case to be properly argued without opening the evidence of Dr [text removed]. His evidence was not already in the public domain. The effect of the judgment was to require her to put this information into the public domain without proper consideration of her rights under Arts 2, 3 and 8 ECHR.

[17]   The respondent relied on the case law set out by the learned trial judge stressing the importance of open justice and the need to ensure that the courts did not create myriad exceptions to it. Mr Hanna relied on the remarks of Tugendhat J on the importance of this principle in *LNS v Persons Unknown* [2010] EWHC 119. That judgment also noted correctly that the burden of proof in displacing the principle lies on the appellant.

[18]   Dr [text removed]'s fresh evidence could have been provided at an earlier date. That evidence did not suggest that an open hearing, as opposed to future media reporting of the case, would cause further detriment to the appellant's mental health or increase her risk of suicide. [Text removed].

Consideration

[19]   In this case there is a significant degree of agreement between the parties about the legal principles which are applicable. The appellant agrees that the principle of open justice is an important safeguard against judicial arbitrariness or idiosyncrasy and maintains public confidence in the administration of justice (see Lord Diplock in *AG v Leveller Magazine* [1979] AC 440 at 449). Lord Steyn made it clear in *Re S (a child)* [2005] 1 AC 593 at 604 that given the number of statutory exceptions a court has no power to create by a process of analogy, except in the most compelling circumstances, further exceptions to the principle of open justice.

[20]   In support of its submissions on the importance of open justice the respondent relied on the remarks of Tugendhat J in *LNS v Persons Unknown* [2010] EWHC 119. That was a very different case to this where the persons subject to the proposed order were not represented and unlikely ever to see some at least of the material on which the judge was asked to act. It is of significance, however, that at paragraph 22 of that judgment Tugendhat J recognised that it was not uncommon in cases where an injunction was sought in relation to the publication of private information to hold a private hearing since without such an order the application would be self defeating. That is a reflection of the fact that the necessity test which Treacy J derived from *AG v Leveller Magazine* was satisfied in those cases. *Al-Ghabra* [2010] UKSC 1 is authority for the unsurprising proposition that the test may also be satisfied in a case involving a threat to life because of the state's obligation to take positive steps to protect the citizen's rights under Article 2 of the ECHR where there is a real and immediate risk to life. These cases and many others are authority for the proposition that the principle of open justice may have to give way to the need to protect convention rights.

[21]   The respondent for its part recognises that this is a case where some restriction on the information which should be made available to the public may be necessary. The extent of that restriction will only, of course, be apparent after the hearing of the injunction application. The respondent submits that if a restriction is necessary it can be achieved by reporting restrictions which will prevent public reporting of the hearing. It is submitted that it is the public reporting of the hearing that is the potential cause of the risk to life or the risk of harm in this case and that measures short of a private hearing can deal satisfactorily with that risk. Similarly if

the appellant satisfies the court that there is an interference with private life through publication contrary to Article 8 ECHR this again can be controlled by reporting restrictions.

[22]   In each case in which a departure from the principle of open justice is sought it is necessary to examine closely the particular circumstances to see whether the high threshold required for such a departure is justified. This is a case in which there is evidence that the appellant has undergone two periods of inpatient treatment for mental health difficulties where on each occasion there was a substantial risk of her causing herself serious physical harm as a result of her illness. The medical evidence indicates that there would be a materially increased risk of suicide or self harm if as a result of a public hearing matters relating to her current medical condition and ongoing treatment were to become more widely known.

[23]   We have no reason to doubt that if there was a reporting restriction that it would be meticulously honoured by the respondent and any other reputable publisher. It is also clear, however, from the manner in which the respondent reported its coverage of this issue on 4 and 11 April that the progress of the medical treatment of the appellant is an issue about which there appears to be a high degree of interest in at least some elements of the media. It is, therefore, appropriate to infer similar interest among some elements of the public.

[24]   We are satisfied that we should take judicial notice of the fact that social networking sites, Twitter and the internet generally now provides an alternative means of publication to traditional daily or Sunday newspapers. Although the numbers of persons to whom the publication is made may be considerably less than the circulation of a popular Sunday newspaper publication on the internet is difficult to control and in particular the source of the publication may be outside the jurisdiction of the court. Publication can also occur on a more limited basis by word of mouth. The hearing of the application will inevitably involve the discussion of aspects of the appellant's treatment and condition. In view of the interest to which we have referred in the appellant's medical treatment in the preceding paragraph we consider that there is a real danger that if these proceedings were open to the public the information disclosed in the hearing would be disseminated on the internet even if a reporting restriction was imposed.

[25]   It is also necessary to keep in mind that what is sought to be protected in these proceedings is information in relation to the medical treatment of the appellant. The application does not seek to prevent publication in respect of any other matters concerning the appellant so the scope of what it is sought to protect is limited. On the other hand the nature of the matter

which it is sought to protect is the sort of private information which Article 8 ECHR may well prevent being made public so it is necessary to recognise that this information may well be entitled to protection long after any issue about the risk to the appellant's health has abated.

[26]   A private hearing does not necessarily exclude public access to the material indefinitely. If the respondent succeeds in preventing the continuation of the injunction there may then be publication of the matters raised at the hearing. In any event the trial judge will have to make a decision as to what if any material should be disclosed in a judgment. If so satisfied after the hearing the trial judge can direct the availability of a transcript. Although it is true that a private hearing inevitably prevents the scrutiny of the proceedings that attendance of the public ensures, the obligation on the judge to publish as much as possible after the hearing operates as a balance to that loss.

[27]   In light of the risk of publication identified in paragraph 24 above and the potential consequences of such publication by way of harm to the appellant we consider on the material before us that the positive obligation under Articles 2 and 3 ECHR requires us to direct a private hearing of the application for the continuation of the injunction. Although the appellant advanced grounds on Article 8 ECHR also that argument was not extensively developed and it is not necessary for us to deal with it. Accordingly we allow the appeal.

[28]   At the start of the hearing of this appeal the appellant submitted that we should deal with it in private since in order to advance the case it would be necessary to rely on much of the medical information with which the case was concerned. In cases of this type such a course is often followed as is clear from paragraph 22 of *LNS v Persons Unknown*. We have no doubt that this was the correct course in this case. This judgment sets out some of the history of the medical treatment of the appellant and should not, therefore, be disclosed at this time. The case will be put into the list of the senior Queen's Bench judge who will determine how to proceed with the interlocutory application and the action generally. The judge will take into account any new materials or circumstances drawn to his attention. Any application for disclosure of this judgment should be made in the first instance to the judge dealing with the injunction application and the action.

[29]   We should make it clear that the appellant has not sought anonymity in these proceedings nor sought to conceal from the public the fact that she is bringing these proceedings. The interlocutory order made by Treacy J does not prohibit publication of the fact that the plaintiff has been suffering from ill-health in the form of depression, that she has been under suicide watch and that she has received treatment for same.

Index

(paragraphs in bold type are where the matter in question is discussed in some detail)